Identity
and the Sacred

HANS MOL

Identity and the Sacred

A sketch for a new social-scientific theory of religion

THE FREE PRESS

A Division of Macmillan Publishing Co., Inc.

NEW YORK

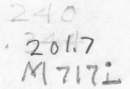

The Free Press
A Division of Macmillan Publishing Co., Inc.
866 Third Avenue, New York, N.Y. 10022

Library of Congress Catalog Card Number: 76-27153

First American Edition 1977

Printed in the United States of America

printing number

1   2   3   4   5   6   7   8   9   10

Library of Congress Cataloging in Publication Data

Mol, Hans   J.
    Identity and the sacred.

    Bibliography: p.
    Includes indexes.
    1.   Religion and sociology.   I.   Title.
BL60.M62   1977   301.5'8   76-27153
ISBN 0-02-921600-1

'Schijnt me, of 't raadselvolle leven droevig lacht met elk systeem.'

(It seems to me that life's mystery sadly smiles at each system.)

De Génestet (1860)

So I took the little scroll from the angel's hand and ate it; and in my mouth it did taste sweet as honey; but when I swallowed it my stomach turned sour.

Revelations 10:10

Contents

Contents

Introduction

This book is a sketch for a general, social-scientific, theory of religion. It is a sketch in the sense that it is incomplete and needs further filling in and rubbing out. Yet it is also a sketch in the sense that it provides tentative, plausible, coherence. It is an attempt to integrate anthropological, historical, psychological, and sociological approaches to religion into one conceptual scheme. It is also a stocktaking of years of extensive reading, research, and writing in the field. If my own previous work occasionally occupies centre stage, the reason is that this book grew out of a critical dialogue with that work. Hopefully, this book is an improvement!

This study also argues that existing categorizations in the sociology of religion are either inconsistent (the underlying assumptions of some of these classifications do not accord with others) or irrelevant for a systematic, comprehensive, sociological approach to religious phenomena. This bold accusation is sometimes articulated, but usually only inferred, as I believe that the burden of proof lies not in denigration but in construction.

Yet the conceptual scheme replacing such outdated categorizations as the sacred/profane, church/sect distinctions should not be over-estimated. Classifications should never be more than scaffolds for generalizations. True, scaffolds tend to determine the contours of the structures they surround and erect. But then one can choose one's apparatus with the larger goal in mind! I therefore tend to defend the conceptual scheme of this book (that religion is the sacralization of identity and that the mechanisms of sacralization consist of objectification, commitment, ritual, and myth) not on intrinsic grounds. What is the use of indestructible scaffolding, if one only intends to build a ramshackle hovel with it? However, I will defend it on the grounds that it directs attention to specific propositions about religion which I believe to be of strategic importance to the sociology of religion, which I hold to be consistent with existing anthropological, psychological, and sociological theories and which I feel to be most productive of innovative interpretations.

Yet even the best argument for a specific strategy does not cancel out the partiality, or even prejudice of one's conceptual scaffolding. With other scaffolding other edifices would have been erected! This relativization of one's assumptions and the awareness of arbitrariness of one's methodological departures seem to me a prerequisite for avoiding another dangerous pitfall: sociological reductionism, by which I mean the absolutization of a sociological methodology or the sacralization of a sociological perspective. I have consciously attempted to avoid this trap. It is for the reader to decide whether I have altogether succeeded. The advantage of at least trying has been that I have taken theological statements and religious expressions with more than usual seriousness. So serious in fact that throughout the book one can find veiled references to my conviction that theorizing *about* religion has little, if any, effect on the viability and sanity of self, group, society, etc., in contrast with *being* religious. The choice of mottos on page v reflects these sentiments. The Dutch poet, De Génestet, wrote the particular line after his visit to the liberal professor of theology Scholten at Leiden University. I am entirely sympathetic to the idea that intellectual systematizations are poor substitutes for vital religiosity. The quotation from Revelation can similarly be interpreted to mean that the consequences of a religious message for action and motivation are distinctly different from a superficial savouring of the same. Although I am not the kind of scholar who lives in the ivory castle of his illusory systems, I have the faint hope that this book is somewhat more acceptable to the religiously orthodox than similar academic ventures. This hope is founded on our common point of departure: that religion defines man and his place in the universe.

It is becoming a habit of scholars in the sociology of religion to present an autobiographical account of their ideologies in introductions. I think it is a good habit. It helps readers to understand (and explain away, if they so desire) whatever pro- or anti-religious biases they encounter. In my case it may help the reader to understand why identity and marginality figure so largely in this book.

The Dutch farmhouse where I was born in 1922 stood in a polder which had been sea in previous centuries. It is water again, for the town of Rotterdam decided to dig a deep channel for its Europoort harbour at the very spot where the farmhouse once stood. After I was born, my parents decided to have me baptized in the local Reformed Church, but I don't remember them going to church at any other occasion. By the time the last of my four brothers arrived, they had made up their minds that baptism was a hoax and he remains unchristened to this very day. Still my parents were not against religion. They loved to spar with the local minister whenever he ventured into our neighbourhood. They also sent me to Sunday-school when I was of primary school age, but I suspect that this was done for educational rather than religious reasons. On my return, I would have to retell the biblical story I had heard and before leaving for the next Sunday-school lesson my memory would be jolted again. This had incalculable effects on my village reputation. The Sunday-school teacher would invariably start the lesson by asking his large, sullen crowd of boys (the girls met somewhere else) what the previous story had been about. And just as invariably I alone would know. This, coupled with the fact that I could not speak the local dialect (by this time my parents had rented a farm in the centre of the Netherlands) and that by means of similar parental tactics I usually topped my classes at school, made me rather marginal to the crowd of little boys. As little boys can do so beautifully they gave me the appropriate nickname of 'blikken dominé' (tin-plate preacher).

By now the depression had descended with a vengeance on this little village of Ophemert in the middle of Holland. My parents had moved here in the middle twenties because of new economic opportunities in the area. The baron who owned most of the village, but hardly ever resided in the castle, had contrary to the local farmers, outgrown feudal thinking. So he decided that it would be much more profitable to introduce farmers like my father, who had been to agricultural colleges from more progressive areas of the Netherlands. He correctly foresaw that better farm management would eventually allow him to substantially raise the rent (which much later, according to local gossip, was squandered on safaris and loose living). These farmers occupied the best and largest farms, but remained a marginal layer in between the elite (burgomaster, minister, doctor, etc.) and the native small farmers and farmhands.

When the depression deepened, my parents began to accumulate huge debts. The farm rent was much in excess of the returns they received for the milk and the wheat. They borrowed from both grandparents and various uncles and just managed to avoid bankruptcy. It was at this time that I vividly remember my mother blowing up at the dinner table where all family business was discussed. The pious spinster sister of the baron who lived year round in the castle had been on her 'doing good' rounds through the village that afternoon. Usually she avoided my mother who was as irreligious as she was articulate. But this afternoon she had sipped tea at our house, which my parents secretly regarded as somewhat of an honour. In the course of the afternoon my mother had expanded on the calamities of farming. The spinster sister had made sympathetic noises which culminated in the statement 'Maybe it would help, if you were to pray, Mrs. Mol.' I am sure that Lady MacKay meant well, but it was entirely the wrong thing to say to my mother. And at the dinner table it rapidly became obvious that my parents expected much more from radical political action than from praying.

Both my father and mother had grown up on the south-western islands of the Netherlands, where farmers generally owned their farms and where liberal education and individual independence were highly valued. But in large families (my father had eight brothers and sisters) it was almost impossible for the younger children to acquire a farm of their own. Still the family spirit of independence remained and my parents were not the kind that would buckle under the exploitative power of an absentee landlord. They began to write what were for those days radical letters to national farmers' weeklies and these contributed to rent-control legislation for farmers.

About this time I was sent to the Gymnasium of the nearby town. It was enormously demanding. We were expected to translate Plato, Plutarch, and Tacitus for our final examinations without dictionary, not to mention four other languages. Yet more lasting than all the formal knowledge I received was an ingrained (much too ingrained!) faith in the goodness of rational truth and a similarly ingrained concern for any kind of underdog. This concern for the underdog was certainly helped along by spending all one's adolescence in the most elitist of possible Dutch schools where farmers' sons were barely tolerated socially.

There was a beautiful Reformed Church in the centre of the village. Part of it was built in medieval times. On Sundays in pre-World War II days a fair percentage of the population would walk there in black attire. The women would sit in the centre aisle. Those in front would have to crane their necks if they wanted to see as well as hear the preacher who would hold forth in the pulpit towering above. The men were better off. They could sit in the galleries and ogle both the women and the preacher. The poor would sit in the back of the church in the unrented pews. Also at the back above the main entrance was a beautiful small pipe organ. Both my parents played musical instruments when I was young and they let me have organ lessons. I developed quite a liking for baroque music for which the organ was very suited and sometimes I would play for services. I would probably have never darkened that church, if it had not been for the organ. Certainly the Barthian, highly theological sermons preached by the learned local minister had not the slightest attraction for me at the time and I could never understand what the locals could possibly get out of the drivel. It is even more mysterious that, in retrospect, this unintelligible preaching has had as much effect on later life as my upbringing in an enlightened, liberal household (where a very sensible combination of firmness and spontaneous affection gave me both the security and ambition which is so much at a premium nowadays). The section in this book on 'relevance A' and on the sophistication of the sin–salvation juxtaposition are groping attempts to sociologically account for this mystery on which most of my colleagues clomp more in a heavy-footed than sure-footed way.

After the Gymnasium I went to university, but the war had broken out and in quick succession many things began to happen. Towards the end of 1943 I found myself in a German 'Auffanglager', later prison and prison with hard labour for 'Rundfunkverbrechen' (offence against the broadcasting law—spreading news from the B.B.C.). The severest shock to my system was strangely enough not the refined Nazi cruelty, the gnawing hunger, or even the familiarity with death or the digging for unexploded bombs, but the gripping discovery that intellectuality was generally dysfunctional for morale and that deep commitment (whether to Nazism, the country, communism, or Jesus Christ) was correspondingly functional. And morale proved to be the sole prerequisite for survival!

In 1946 I accepted an assistantship to my uncle who was head of the administration of the largest co-operative sugar-beet factory and refinery in the Netherlands. My grandfather had been one of the originators of this flourishing enterprise and so the family had maintained long-standing ties of affection with this branch of industry in the southern part of Holland. The top management and most of middle management were Protestant and the workers were Catholic. I boarded in a nearby village for two years. Oud-Gastel was as different as could be from the village I had grown up in. The latter was individualistic, competitive, dour, and as respectful of Calvinist theology as it was illusionless about mankind. The former was a gossipy, happy, community of good, relatively un-ambitious Catholics where authority and cohesion were sternly main-tained by the Church. I resigned from my job in 1948 on the day I published all the vetoed articles of the factory paper. Although I was the editor, the technical manager, who had learnt to sharpen his autocratic wits on the Indonesian natives, had the final say in what was to be published. He had systematically weeded out all those articles which aimed at a mutual understanding of manage-ment and labour. However, without him knowing, I had kept second copies of the vetoed products. The clandestine edition was a howling success and was read by boards of directors as well as national union officials. Yet I thought it wiser to remove myself to the more promising shores of Australia, where other rebels in the past had been not inhospitably received.

In my case, rebellion consisted in studying theology at the United Theological Faculty of Sydney University. Ever since the war, theology had become an increasingly more absorbing pastime. I worked my way through college by working in a button factory and by waiting on tables in the University Hall of residence where I lived. It was in these theological courses that I began to avidly read Karl Barth and Reinhold Niebuhr. Through a series of scholarships I landed at Union Theological Seminary in New York, but not until after I had married an Australian girl (to whom after twenty years and four children, I am still very happily married) and after I had spent some time as chaplain to Dutch immigrants. Union and Columbia proved to be fascinating places where I could specialize in the very areas in which I had a long and abiding interest. Yet my practical knowledge of American society did not come from my Ph.D. work in the Department of Sociology at Columbia, but from a rural congregation in Northern Maryland. Here I learnt how important religion can be for the consolidation of a local hierarchy. Bethel Presbyterian Church consisted of independent efficient far-mers and a sprinkling of small-town shopkeepers. However, the imported, very rich aristocracy of the area played English country squire on their large estates and this meant large foxhunts and the blessing of the hounds at St. James Anglican Church. Neither did Bethel appeal to farmhands and other down-and-outers who would rather travel ten miles further to the Church of the Nazarene.

My first academic appointment was to the University of Canterbury in New Zealand. Here I began my studies of Dutch migrants and race relations which I completed at the Institute of Advanced Studies of the Australian National University in Canberra which offered me a fellowship in 1963. The Institute was a haven for those who wanted to write and do research. Ph.D. supervision was only a minor part of one's duties. Yet it was more congenial to those whose ethos was informed by British rationalism or Marxism and who had mastered the difficult art of the quick repartee and the cynical slapdown than to those with an interest in the sociology of religion. It was here that *Christianity in Chains, Religion in Australia,* and *Western Religion* were produced.

This book on the other hand has been written in a department where the study of religion is not only central, but where it also is analysed by a wide variety of disciplines. It could not have been written without close contact with historians, philosophers, psychologists, experts on Buddhism, Judaism, Christianity, and Hinduism. I therefore would like to thank the following colleagues and graduate students of the Department of Religion at McMaster University, Canada: J. G. Arapura, A. E. Combs, P. C. Craigie, G. P. Grant, L. Greenspan, H. H. Hiller, Y-h. Jan, D. Kinsley, M. A. Klest, S. MacIsaac, B. F. Meyer, J. C. Robertson, Jr., J. A. Ross, E. P. Sanders, K. Shinohara, K. Sivaraman, G. Vallee, I. Weeks, W. Whillier, and P. Younger. None of these have read the entire manuscript and yet all of them together have unknowingly emboldened me to paint in sweeping strokes across centuries and cultures with a broad brush. Without their cross-fertilizing and widely differing perspectives I might have felt more tempted to continue working in rather narrow empirical confines. This would have been less dangerous, but, as I read somewhere, who wants to be like the drunkard who had lost his keys in a dark alley, but kept looking for them under a lamp, because that is where he could see?

The outline of the book is fairly simple. Chapter I presents the basic argument. Yet before enlarging on the meaning (Chapters V–X) and foci (Chapters XI–XII) of identity, the dialectic between identity and differentiation (Chapters II–IV) is explored. It would have been just as logical to let Chapter V follow on from the basic argument. Yet I decided against this, as I wanted the larger theoretical setting for the argument to precede the detailed exposition. However, readers with a somewhat different taste from mine may want to plunge right into the discussion of the basic concepts in Chapter V. The book ends with an account of the mechanisms of sacralization.

HANS MOL

Hamilton, Ontario
March 1976

Identity
and the Sacred

Chapter I

Basic Argument

In this book the term 'religion' is used in a very wide sense—as the *sacralization of identity*. Before explaining this definition I should say something about the hazards of defining. There are many definitions of religion, and for a long time I refused to take any of them seriously. This was not so much because they were wrong, as because they were just window-dressing for the categories and generalizations that followed. Most of the time they were blinders or blinkers that restricted my field of vision. They preordained what was important and unimportant. And I wanted to see for myself. My fear was more of missing something crucial than of being swamped by a chaotic avalanche of impressions and data. I am essentially more interested in distilling essences than in refining them. For somewhat similar reasons (that they restrict one's field of vision or provide a false sense of comprehension and precision) Erasmus inferred that definitions tended to be dangerous, Hegel held that they were arbitrary, and Wittgenstein that they were impossible (Stark and Glock, 1968, p. 11; Findlay, 1958, p. 259; Wittgenstein, 1964, p. 112). Yet, any field of study (and religion is no exception) must of necessity be systematic. Conceptual delineations are the prerequisite for any system. The time for stocktaking must eventually come also for inductive scholars. The problem then becomes whether the definitions which are selected fit the actual situation and whether they facilitate the uncovering and description of the strategic elements of the field of inquiry. I hope that my definition will do these things, and will have a salutary effect on both the comprehensiveness and the truth value of the study of religion.

What then do I mean when I say that religion is the sacralization of identity? Let us take identity first. There is impressive evidence that for a large number of animals in general and for the primates in particular the place they occupy is of fundamental importance. 'There are few exceptions to the rule that the need for identity is the most powerful and the most pervasive among all species' (Ardrey, 1969, p. 361). Ethologists sometimes define this identity in respect of an animal's will to defend its territory: threats at the centre are vigorously rebuffed, but the further from the centre that a specific challenge occurs, the less energetic the defence. At other times, they define identity by the place which an animal occupies in the rank-order of the species. An animal defends its position with ardour and passion (Ardrey, 1970, p. 171; Lorenz, 1970, pp. 35-7). From chickens to tree-shrews, baboons, gorillas and man, a consistent status ranking can be recognized within each species, even though the defensive gestures by which rank is maintained change up the evolutionary scale, from overt threats to subtle cues and from physi-cal attacks to patterns of deference (Mazur, 1973, pp. 524-5).

When one turns to the way in which identity is used in relation to human beings one sees that the element of ardour remains, although the locations of identity greatly multiply. Erikson (1963, p. 240) mentions the way individuals defend their identity 'with the astonish-ing strength encountered in animals who are suddenly forced to defend their lives'. Klapp (1969, p. 146) sees enormous variety in the symbolic locations of identity—celibacy, sex, war, death, beauty, the sacred, the profane, reason, feelings, science, equality, women, nationalism, virginity, buffaloes, snakes, tea, peyote, alcohol, action, tranquillity, etc. One could easily add to this list, such items as money, ecology, psychoanalysis, Maoism, Christ, Vishnu, Allah, and totem. Man's creation of symbol systems facilitated man's adaptation of changing circumstances quicker than is possible in species that rely on genetic and organic changes (Lenski, 1970, p. 21). Con-sequently, identity may now be symbolically located in a great variety of forms rather than merely in territory or hierarchy. The Marxist suggestion that in capitalist society this location is confined to either property or class (Birnbaum, 1969) is becoming decreasingly true. It is likely that man's enhanced capacity for adaptation did not modify the initial driving force of the instinct for survival and the closely related need for integration and identity, however much their foci or concrete expressions have changed and multiplied. The post-tulate of this book is that the search for identity, which may culmi-nate in drug addiction for some adolescents in the 1970s, or in the Jesus Freak movements for others, is also recognizable in the most primitive of tribes who projected it on the totemic animal.

This, then, is the way in which the concept 'identity' will be employed. It differs from the sense in which Piaget uses the word: 'Is a square, placed on one of its corners, after 45° rotation, still identical to itself?' (Piaget, 1968, p. 143). It is not used in the sense of Gibson Winter's *Religious Identity* (Winter, 1968) which describes the organization and power structure of the major faiths in the United States. This does not mean that a religious denomination cannot be a focus of identity. On the contrary it often is. Still middle-class life-styles and values may be the actual focus of identity rather than a particular religious faith. Our definition attempts to make us aware of the latent and primary sources of identity, even if they cannot always be pinpointed operationally.

At this point I must elaborate my statement that man's enhanced capacity for adaptation has in no way modified his need for integration and identity. There is good reason to go somewhat further and suggest that there is a dialectic between adaptation and identity or between differentiation and integration and that religious organizations and orientations (but also art and play) are anything but impartial in this dialectic. My definition puts them squarely on the identity/integration side of the dialectic, where since Durkheim, empirical research has located them.

I am in good company when I postulate a basic dialectic between differentiation/integration or adaptation/identity. The ancient Chinese juxtaposed Yin (the static) with Yang (the dynamic). Toynbee (1946, p. 65) interprets the Fall to mean the acceptance of a challenge to achieved integration and the venturing out upon a fresh differentiation. Malinowski (1960, p. 38) distinguishes between a basic instrumental and integrative imperative. Talcott Parsons juxtaposes the adaptive and the integrative prerequisites of social systems, and some of his pupils, such as Clifford Geertz (1968, pp. 92–3), and Robert Bellah (1965 and 1970), have used and applied this basic dialectic to religious phenomena.

Religion always appears to modify or stabilize the differentiations it has been unable to prevent. More important, future differentiation appears to hinge on a baseline of existing identity and the guarantee of future identity. The elective affinity of the spirit of modern capitalism, modern science, and democracy for sixteenth-century Calvinism and seventeenth-century Puritanism hinges on the unique and almost self-contradictory sacralization of marginality of these religious traditions and their subsequent relativization of collectivism, social rewards, and nature. Historically, the function of specific religious organizations and orientations in preserving identity seems to be the strategically more important function for explaining social development. Yet this function is sometimes thought to be waning in modern societies. Richard Fenn argues, in a recent and influential article on 'A New Sociology of Religion', 'that conditions of advanced differentiation make it unlikely, if not impossible, for cultural integration to develop around any set of religious symbols' (1972, p. 16). Yet on the level of personality the craving for identity, the sacred idea of self-realization in psycho-analysis, existentialism, and humanism (or on the social level), the sacredness of democracy in the U.S.A., the millennial hopes of communism, the messiahship of the proletariat, and the free enterprise principle in economics can be viewed as integrative, unifying responses, and symbolic, commitment-demanding, rallying points for those who seek to limit the devastations of differentiation and disorder. It is not too difficult to find many more of these central beliefs integrating personal, group, or social identity right at the heart of modern industrial society, sometimes competing with, sometimes reinforcing one another. The problem of Fenn, and for others in the sociology of religion, is not so much that they deny the differentiation/integration dialectic, but that they work with strategically dysfunctional definitions of religion. To Fenn religion is confined to whatever is theocentric or super-natural. As a result he concentrates so much on traditional Christianity that he cannot see the emergence of a kaleidoscopic variety of sacralization patterns elsewhere.

The matter of definition plagues all scholars. If one insists on a supernatural definition of religion as, for instance, many Marxists do, the possibility that other dimensions of the sacralization mechanism (such as commitment) performing essentially similar functions altogether escapes attention. On the other hand, if one insists on awe or commitment for one's definition (as did Rudolf Otto and his following) one tends to overlook the contribution which objectification, myth, and ritual make to sacralization. The other problem which too narrow a definition of religion engenders is that of pre-empting the analytical possibilities of actual process (or degree of sacralization) and of historical change (or changes in historical dominance of one mechanism over another). The consequence of using these strategically dysfunctional definitions is that crutch-concepts such as secularization have to be employed in order to make up for otherwise unaccountable phenomena. Secularization, from my point of view, is the outcome of differentiations exceeding the capacity of religious organizations to integrate them in the traditional frame of reference, with the result that, on all levels, identities and systems of meaning are becoming sacralized by agencies other than these organizations. My larger definition allows me not only to link religion very closely to the differentiation/integration dialectic, but also enables me to treat conversion, charisma, and the rites of passage as essentially mechanisms for incorporating, rather than annihilating, change. All of them desacralize (or emotionally strip) a previous identity, and sacralize (or emotionally weld) a new one. Conversion does this for personal identity in a relatively unstructured situation in the same way that charisma does it for social identity. Rites of passage do the same thing in more structured settings. The basic point of this digression is to make clear that the basic contribution religion (as I use the term) makes to the dialectic with differentiation remains unrecognized unless (a) one's definition directs attention to process and response inherent in the concept of dialectic, (b) one's definition is wide enough to allow for parallel mechanisms, not all of which are necessary for the pattern all at the same time, (c) one's definition is narrow enough not to usurp the contributions that art and play, for instance, make to the integration side of the dialectic.

There is a close affinity between identity-defence and sacralization, as a more systematic discussion of the term will show.

By sacralization, I refer to the process by means of which on the level of symbol-systems certain patterns acquire the same taken-for-granted, stable, eternal, quality which on the level of instinctive behaviour was acquired by the consolidation and stabilization of new genetic materials. Sacralization, then, is a sort of brake applied to unchecked infinite adaptations in symbol systems for which there is increasingly less evolutionary necessity and which become increasingly more dysfunctional for the emotional security of personality and for the integration of tribe or community. To say the same in an over-simplified way: sacralization is to the dysfunctional potential of symbol-systems what antibodies are to the dysfunctional, cancerous, possibilities in physical systems. Sacralization produces immunity against persuasion similar to the biological immunization process (McGuire, 1964, p. 200). The concept comes close to the concept of institutionalization. The important difference is that I should like to use sacralization when institutionalization acquires other qualities such as untouchability and awe, qualities that reinforce the rock (or

better, which cement the sand) on which the house of identity is
constructed. Sacralization is the inevitable process that safeguards
identity when it is endangered by the disadvantages of the infinite
adaptability of symbol-systems. Sacralization protects identity, a
system of meaning, or a definition of reality, and modifies, obstructs,
or (if necessary) legitimates change. It is clear that the concept of
sacralization differs from what Durkheim called the sacred (Durkheim, 1954, p. 37 ff., 320). To Durkheim the sacred was completely
separate, even antagonistic to the profane. It was something given.
Although I agree with Durkheim that almost anything can be sacred,
the emphasis here is on the process, on the fluid transition from the
profane to the sacred. There is evidence that even in primitive religions the demarcation between the profane and the sacred was sometimes rather fluid (Eliade, 1967, pp. 136 ff.). It is our assumption that
the sacred, in Durkheim's sense, arises only when the crystallization
of specific primitive tribal patterns is left undisturbed for generations and when the strength and cohesion of tribal identity is a *sine
qua non* for survival. Yet I do not want to make the mistake of
Evans-Pritchard who, in his criticism of Durkheim, said that the
sacred and the profane 'are so closely intermingled as to be inseparable' and that the dichotomy was not much use (Evans-Pritchard,
1965, p. 65). Durkheim may have underrated the intermingling of
sacred and profane somewhat but their interdependence was very
much implied in his remark that God was society, and in his discussion of *mana*.

It is this conflicting but complementary relationship between the
sacred and the profane that I want to bring out by using 'sacralization' (the process of becoming, or making sacred) rather than 'the
sacred' (being sacred). It is the process of sacralization rather than
the state of sacredness which more readily conveys the dialectical
emergence of the integrative complement. Neither Durkheim nor
Evans-Pritchard are at all clear on this point and that is why their
conceptual frame of reference is inadequate *both* to account for the
emergence of sacrednesses in our time *and* for its objectifying,
separating characteristics once it has emerged. Both thought primarily in terms of primitive cultures where sacralization patterns
were full blown rather than embryonic. As scholars dealing with
past and primitive societies have led the way in the analysis of the
sacred, their definitions in terms of its ideal type or full-blown form
have been accepted rather uncritically, all the more so, since Western

evolutionary bias and assumptions of scientific superiority reject the thought that something which is mature in primitive cultures may be only embryonic in modern societies. For these reasons the widespread conclusion has been drawn that the sacred is on its way out. I do not think that this is so. Sacralization processes may be interrupted and prevented from maturing, but they are not disappearing: they appear to be as viable as ever.

Another reason for stressing the sacralization process rather than the separateness of the sacred is that 'change' or 'process' language is more appropriate for analysing 'changing' situations. For a sociological theory bent on developing generalizations in which both past and present, primitive and modern are adequately accounted for, it is necessary to have a conceptual apparatus geared to both stability and change, to similarities and differences. Treating the sacred as a fossil of the primitive past stresses the difference rather than the similarities between societies and cultures. In the fluid situation of modern western societies stability is precarious, and a definition which stresses 'process' rather than 'being' is more capable of dealing adequately with what appears to be an endless parade of stunted, discarded remnants of 'sacrednesses'. A conceptual apparatus derived from primitive conditions just will not do, and since my emphasis is on 'identity', rather than on 'society', I need a concept which allows for the analysis of a kaleidoscopic variety of these 'sacrednesses' in the same society. At the same time, it is my conviction that this set of concepts is still adequate to deal with archaic religions as well.

Finally, this definition is concerned not only with what religion is, but also with what it does. It allows for both conceptual analysis and for generalizations about religious functions. The definition and the exposition of its meaning are perspectives which make no claim to definitive comprehension. They have the bias of any perspective. If there is something unique about the bias, it is that it counterbalances the widespread pessimism about the viability of twentieth-century institutional religious expressions with an equal optimism about the future of religion in the wide sense in which the term is used here. The optimism inherent in the definition can be tempered only when it can be shown that the fundamental need of the human race for identity will succumb to an equally fundamental need for adaptation. I suspect, however, that both are essential for survival, and that neither will succumb to the other, which is another way of saying that things will probably stay the way they are. Still there are others (e.g. Toffler, 1970) who assume that the forces of adaptation will relentlessly cut down any obstacle (including the forces of identity) on the path of evolutionary progress, and for that reason authors like him have little time for religion and certainly underestimate its contribution to a saner world. I agree with sociologists such as Andrew M. Greeley (1969, p. 11) who hypothesize that there is a 'sacralizing tendency' in the human condition.

This excursion on the meaning of sacralization of identity has purposely lapsed into a discussion of issues, which are developed, explained, and illustrated below. It remains to ask in what way the need for identity manifests itself, and to inquire about the mechanisms for its sacralization.

Both in animals and in human beings, security is bound up with order. Unless all exigencies can be anticipated and responded to immediately and adequately, extinction is swift. For animals, order means the effective co-ordination of all the limited resources of aggression, defence, acute sense perception, food, and sex, not to mention the limited resources of the incredible physiological complexity of the body. To have a territorial or social location enhances the orderly maximization of these resources. Chaos endangers the specimen and the species and makes survival precarious. For human beings, order means all this plus the much more symbol-based elements, such as institutionalized reciprocity of feelings and cognitions, predictability of motivations and responses, common adherence to values and norms, common interpretations of existence and a common cathectic stake in these interpretations. The need for identity (or for a stable niche in this whole complex of physiological, psychological, and sociological patterns of interaction) is very much bound up with continuous regularity. Here, too, order means survival; chaos means extinction. Nevertheless, too much order, or too much hardening of the arteries can mean lessened adaptations. Thus, the New Zealand kakapo (a ground parrot) is threatened with extinction in its natural habitat because English settlers brought their dogs and cats, as well as their rats. Or the aborigines of Tasmania die out when Western culture in the guise of cruel Europeans begins to make inroads; or the older immigrant peasant pines away in the forgotten corner of a metropolitan slum area, because he cannot unlearn old patterns and adopt the languages and behaviour of the new country. Order (and the need for identity at the back of it) can become too much of a good thing, like too much sugar in one's tea. Similarly, innovation or creativity (and the need for adaptation at the back of it) can become destructive of order, like too many prima donnas under the one roof.

Religious practices give special underpinning to particular conceptions of order within a culture, thus making the security of the individual less precarious. Sometimes personal and social identity were too well sacralized, with the result that cultures became extinct when mechanisms for adaptation had become atrophied. At other times, such as our own, there are many complaints that there is too much change and that there are no traditions left to give continuity to one's identity.

Identity, order, and views of reality are all intertwined. In primitive societies, myth expressed the only valid revelation of reality and the sacred was the pre-eminently real (Eliade, 1967, pp. 23, 117). In the nineteenth century and the first half of the twentieth century, myth began to mean almost the opposite: whatever was opposed to reality. Sharp distinctions were made between reality and illusion (e.g. Freud, 1964). In the second half of the twentieth century, the biases of that distinction have been particularly brought out in the sociology of knowledge (e.g. Berger and Luckman, 1967). The number of scholars who believe that reality can be unconstructed and uninterpreted is dwindling. On the other hand, the conviction is growing that both scientific and Christian theological approaches to reality have common features, such as emotional commitment to assumptive departures and comprehensive explanations of existence. Durkheim (1954, p. 208) was one of the first to see the necessity for a faith in science. Both approaches to reality have crucial problems of fit. There is a tendency by one camp to neglect the re-enactment of the archaic, dream-like structures of the human psyche, or to underestimate the dysfunction of scepticism and observation for integration. The other camp either overestimates or underestimates the place of rationality in its own view of reality. The point is that an interpretation (*any* interpretation) of reality is necessary for the wholeness (and wholesomeness) of individual and society. The identity of either depends on a continuous, fitting, and consistent interpretation of features and events in one's surroundings. Still, the emphasis on the fit of the interpretation should not be misunderstood. There is good reason to believe that the transcendental aspects of many of these interpretations, and the otherness of the gods, also provided individual and society with leverage and psychic energy to pursue that change. The success of transcendental religions in evolutionary history is to be attributed to the combining of catalytic and securing functions.

Maximization of order and continuity in the interpretation of reality are prerequisites for identity. Moral rules in turn are the almost visible outlines and concretizations of that order. They are the living tissues covering the bones. They are the working bees busily engaged in resolving the practical inconsistencies, ambiguities, injustices, and above all, infringements. The master authority of order would be jeopardized if these yeoman services were not promptly performed. It is precisely because of their importance that traditional religious organizations sacralized the major ones such as the Golden rule or the Ten Commandments and their equivalent in the non-Christian religions. But still the master and servant should not be too closely identified as will be shown in a later chapter. It may be a case of the servant's rigidity allowing the master more flexibility, or on the other hand it may be a case of the order legitimating the rules. It is also to strengthen this legitimating role that specific social orders and specific views of reality tend to become sacralized. For all the major world religions have been the primary forces of legitimation not only of norms and values but also of the socialization processes, the family, the polity, the economy, etc. If this can no longer be said for all the major religious faiths, it is still true for the variegated foci of identity which have grown up simultaneously with the erosion of those faiths. A profession sometimes legitimates a person's practices, ethics, modes of behaviour; or a political ideology becomes the source of a person's value priorities. The waning capacity of universal religions to sacralize a social identity can be related to the decreasing extent to which highly differentiated societies are capable of being integrated. A successful muting, as well as motivating, of individuals; a successful constraining as well as of co-opting recalcitrant groups; a successful reforming as well as reinforcing of the social whole, depends on the cohesion of that social identity. Only to a certain extent can one expect sacralization mechanisms to heal a corrupt identity. On the other hand sectarian groups in these highly differentiated societies seem to derive at least some of their success from being buffers between the heterogeneity of the social whole and the threat of personal alienation.

There are at least four mechanisms of the sacralization process on both the personal and social level. Perhaps the most neglected one, I call objectification. It is the tendency to sum up the variegated elements of mundane existence in a transcendental point of reference where they can appear more orderly, more consistent, and more timeless. Under certain conditions, this transformed point of reference may in turn profoundly transform conceptions of existence or provide the leverage for transformation (Mol, 1968a, pp. 67 ff.). It was neglected for a long time because the atheistic biases, exaggerated individualism, or plain ignorance of philosophers, psychologists, and sociologists (from Feuerbach via Freud to Fromm and Peter Berger (1967, pp. 89, 90, 101) inclined them to look primarily at the negative dysfunctional side of the same coin. They called it the alienating aspects of religion.

Yet it can be plausibly defended that it was precisely this strong belief in objectified order that made science and differentiation possible in the first place. The condemnation of those religious objectifications (called reifications) that desacralized full individual self-determination in that they treated things as external to the mind shows only the bias of personality-centred humanism. The reification concept has no scientific utility for the explanation of religious phenomena: it is a monument to a humanistic ideology masquerading as a scientific construct.

Another closely related mechanism is commitment, by which I mean emotional attachment to a specific focus of identity. It is precisely through emotional fixation that personal and social unity takes place. Kenneth Keniston (Kaplan, 1970, p. 31) regards the fact of commitment as even more important than the object of commitment, and this allows him to speak about the fluidity of identity. However, the concept of identity should be wide enough also to allow for such items as commitment *against* the bigness in government and establishment values (which was typical for Keniston's sample of highly educated young people, on which his observations were based). Tolerance and open-mindedness can be close to the heart of a person's aspirations and commitments, and may therefore have similar centring functions which Christian salvation or the belief in Allah have for others. Identity in this sense cannot be regarded as fluid and flexible: a commitment to something which can easily be dethroned and replaced is not the kind of basic commitment that I have in mind.

This does not mean that commitment has to have a very specific concrete focus. It is possible to have a basic commitment to something as vague as the Buddhist Nirvana or God which Karl Barth has called 'that which we cannot think' (Barth and Thurneysen, 1932, p. 152) as long as this void of concreteness is in some way similar to the cloudlessness at the eye of the hurricane.

Commitment anchors a system of meaning in the emotions and, given time, develops into awe which wraps the system in 'don't touch' sentiments. Yet the holy also engenders commitment. This mutual reinforcement could easily lead to petrifaction, but for the differentiating and instrumental forces which encourage competition, scepticism, and rationality.

Commitment is of necessity closely linked with consistency and predictability. This is so because motivation for action resides in expressive orientations with strong commitment as a salient element, and not in cognitive orientation (in which rationality and technical reason are crucial). It is for this reason that the very popular rationalistic assumption of a universal, taken-for-granted *summmum bonum* in which sceptical, divisive reason determines its dialetical opposite (a unifying commitment), is both naïve and quixotic.

Sacrifice is a form of commitment which clarifies priorities in a hierarchy of potentially competing meanings. In pluralistic societies, the actual competition between a large variety of foci of identity has created dilemmas of commitment. Certain foci of identity are dislodged in the competitive battle, but those that survive tend to become stronger through successful boundary defence. Lack of commitment, lack of identity, meaninglessness, anomie and alienation are all very much related symptoms of societies in which definitions of reality are no longer taken for granted because competition has relativized each and all of them.

There is a tendency by various authors to overestimate the importance of some of these mechanisms at the expense of others. Neither Eliade (1967, p. 26) nor Max Weber (1952) pay a great deal of attention to commitment in this sense. Eliade is more interested in our fourth item (myth and symbol) and therefore calls the myth of Nazism inept without clarifying that Nazi Germany was kept together (long after the writing had appeared on the wall) by the strong commitment to national identity and to the Führer rather than by a myth of Nordic paganism. Weber was also too much interested in the cognitive affinity between systems of beliefs and

economic behaviour, to pay much attention to the crucial interven-
ing variable of commitment to these systems of belief.

Sociologists and anthropologists have fortunately paid far more
attention to the third mechanism ritual. Ethologists such as Lorenz
(1970, pp. 70–2) have observed that ritual is an ingenious way to
check the aggressive drive of animals without actually weakening its
species-preserving function. They believe that human rituals have
originated in an analogous way. Ritual maximizes order, reinforces
the place of the individual in his society, and strengthens the bonds
of a society *vis-à-vis* the individual. Through repetitive, emotion-
evoking action, social cohesion and personality integration are reinforced—at the same time that aggressive or socially destructive
actions are articulated, dramatized, and curbed. According to Durkheim (1954, p. 375): 'The traditions whose memory (ritual) perpetu-
ates express the way in which society represents man and the
world. . . . Through (ritual) the group periodically renews the sentiment which it has of itself and of its unity; at the same time, individuals are strengthened in their social natures.' Ritual also restores
identity, particularly when disruption has occurred, for example,
through death, or when rearrangements in marriage or family relations become necessary.

The fourth mechanism advancing the sacralization of identity is
a complex of phenomena often grouped under such headings as
myth, theology, and religious symbolism. Whether in primitive or
more advanced societies, myths interpret reality. Myths are often the
surface shorthand for much more basic experiences of human individuals and groups. They dramatize such primordial conflicts as that
between man's instinct for self-preservation and pressure of the horde
or group to curb this instinct for the social good. 'Myth is the
emotion-laden assertion of man's place in a world that is meaningful
to him, and of his solidarity with it. . . . It is a celebration of a
primordial reality rendered actively present. . . . Through it men
are related to their environment, to their ancestors, to their descen-
dants, to the beyond which is the ground of all existence, to what is
permanent beyond all flux' (O'Dea, 1966, pp. 42, 43). In other words,
a myth provides the fitting contour for one's existence, sublimating
the conflicts and reinforcing personal and social identity. It is thus
not surprising that there is so much structural similarity among
various myths. Myths of Paradise, of the Fall, or of Ascension can
be found in the most diverse cultures.

Myth sacralizes through recurrent narration. The further back in evolutionary history one goes the more the narration consists of concrete elements. Yet, even in primitive culture, behind these elements are fundamental notions of integration/identity and instrumentality/adaptation. Myths sacralize through the emotional anchorage of integrative reconciliations, but they can do so only through the presentation of the binary opposition with instrumental symbolism. The reconciling function of myth resides in repetitive presentations and representations.

Sectarian/evangelical theology also revolves around the analogous theme of sin and salvation, or alienation and integration, disorder and order. The effectiveness of this branch of Christianity may very well reside in its loyalty to this theme and the kaleidoscopic diversity with which the theme is dramatized over and over again.

The function of myth is not to explain the inexplicable (Frazer, 1922) or to sugar-coat the pill of harsh reality (Freud, 1964). It is true that by interpreting reality, a myth may satisfy 'Why' questions or make frustration more acceptable, but this is quite different from saying (as so many do both in psychology and sociology) that myth emerges as a response to problems, with the inference that myths will disappear as soon as these problems are solved. We are more inclined to regard myth as 'a statement of primeval reality' (Malinowski, 1954, p. 146) and thereby to stress the more enduring, reconciling, quality of myth.

SUMMARY OF CHAPTER

In the history of the human race there has always been an elemental concern with identity. A stable niche in a predictable environment has been crucial, but it has also been precarious and in consequence has evoked 'don't touch' sentiments. Even in the most advanced societies, the need for identity has been strong enough to perpetuate a demand for order and sameness, and an abhorrence of disorder and chaos. Here, too, man's redoubtable discovery of symbols has issued in the need for order in a system of symbols and, consequently, in taken-for-granted assumptions about reality. Here, too, it has proved to be necessary to safeguard order with rules, minimizing injustices and arbitrariness and to legitimate the niche of oneself or one's group in a complex arrangement of forces which threaten to change it.

Sacralization is the process by means of which man has pre-eminently safeguarded and reinforced this complex of orderly interpretations of reality, rules, and legitimations. The mechanisms of sacralization can be broken down in at least the following: (1) objectification (the projection of order in a beyond where it is less vulnerable to contradictions, exceptions, and contingencies—in other words a rarified realm where major outlines of order can be maintained in the face of temporal, but all-absorbing dislocations of that order); (2) commitment (the emotional anchorage in the various, proliferating, foci of identity); (3) ritual (the repetitive actions, articulations, and movements which prevent the object of sacralizations to be lost sight of); (4) myth (the integration of the various strains in a coherent, shorthand symbolic account).

Obviously there is a good deal of overlapping between these various mechanisms: there are objectifying elements in almost any myth, and without commitment neither objectification nor ritual is likely to be very efficacious. Still, all four are sufficiently different to warrant separate treatment. It is rather reassuring that the mechanisms of sacralization seem to be roughly congruent with such widely diverging concepts as Glock's dimensions of religiosity (1968, p. 19) and the ways Yoga (communion with the Supreme Being) is purported to improve in ancient Sanskrit writings (Soddy, 1961, p. 164).

Chapter II

Evolution, Differentiation and Secularization

Until recently the evolutionary approach to religion has been in justifiable disrepute. It suffered from too many exuberant, but premature speculations. Auguste Comte looked upon theology as illusory belief which science in general and sociology in particular would soon supplant (Comte, 1858). Spencer attacked Comte's ideas (Spencer, 1968, pp. 19–25) but took a similar position regarding religion. To him man's ignorance of causation in the scientific sense was responsible for his superstitions. 'Religion ignores its immense debt to Science', he said, adding that the latter was the agent of its purification (Spencer, 1896, p. 104). Like Comte, Spencer had a kind of paternalistic sympathy for religion: 'That seeming chaos of puerile assumptions and monstrous inferences, making up the vast mass of superstitious beliefs everywhere existing, thus falls into order when, instead of looking back upon it from our advanced standpoint, we look forward upon it from the standpoint of the primitive man' (Spencer, 1897, p. 423). This close link between assumptions of evolutionary progress and religious beliefs as a transitional mode of cognition permeated much of nineteenth-century thinking, and there was already a strong element of this in Hegel's identification of God with the Absolute, the spiritual with the rational, and religious consciousness with pictorial thinking (Hegel, 1967, p. 783). Edward Tylor's attempt to trace the origin of religion to man's wondering about his dreams and death, and Max Müller's similar effort to find it in the forms and forces of nature were variations on a similar theme (Durkheim, 1954, Chaps. II and III).

Durkheim and Freud had their own scientific biases, but they also regarded the cognitive explanations of religion as defective. To Durkheim religion was not primarily a set of beliefs, but a set of religious practices. They embodied the social traditions and social prescriptions. They strengthened the bonds between individual and society (Durkheim, 1954, p. 26). 'They are as necessary for the well working of our moral life as our food is for the maintenance of our physical life, for it is through them that the group affirms and maintains itself, and we know the point to which this is indispensable for the individual' (ibid., p. 382). What Durkheim did for the appreciation of religion as a social phenomenon, Freud did for it as a personal phenomenon. Religion for Freud was a way of coping, not with problems of cognition, but with problems of helplessness. It was 'born from man's need to make his helplessness tolerable and built up from the material of memories of the helplessness of his own childhood and the childhood of the human race' (Freud, 1964, p. 25).

There were traces of evolutionism in both Durkheim and Freud. After all, Durkheim attempted to throw some light on the nature of religion in general by studying the most elementary forms. Freud too speculated about the evolutionary origins of the Oedipus myth and the doctrine of the Fall (Freud, 1918). These traces were secondary and they were never sufficient to alienate the radically anti-evolutionist view which particularly emerged in anthropology (Boas, Lowie) and also effected sociology. Uppermost in the minds of those critics of the oversimplified notions of evolutionary theories was the uniqueness of cultures and the intricate fit of religion with other cultural traits (Parsons, 1961, p. 240).

In the second half of the twentieth century, the evolutionary approach to religion re-emerged, principally because to fit data into the best possible system of generalizations, chronological and cross-cultural sequences must be considered. Max Weber's scholarly reputation and influence in the sociology of religion up to the present time are based on the conscientious way in which he carried out research of this kind. Talcott Parsons elaborated Weber's framework in the theoretical, evolutionary direction by stressing social differentiation (the proliferation of increasingly distinct and specialized social structures). To him a critically important phenomenon was the emergence of the type of autonomous religion orientation which exerted leverage on social development (Parsons, 1961, p. 263). In Parsons' introduction to *The Sociology of Religion* (Weber, 1964, p. lx) he interprets Weber as attributing 'prime causal significance to the factor of "religious orientation" as an initiating factor and as a differentiating factor' in the development of human society.

ROBERT N. BELLAH

Robert N. Bellah has done most for both the revival and the respectability of the evolutionary approach to religion (1970). Bellah has traced the increasingly differentiated religious symbolism over time. In the earliest stage of religious development (Primitive Religion), man, through his capacity for symbolization, had already learned to transcend the limitations of his existence. The mythical beings, with whom the primitives become identified in ritual, represent ancestral progenitors, events, mountains, rocks, and trees. There is a hovering closeness of the world of myth to the actual world. The structure of the myth is fluid and allows for dream-like participation, easily leading to ritual innovation. Ritual may have both a personally invigorating as well as a socially reinforcing effect.

In the second, or Archaic stage, there is more differentiation. Mythical beings are more objectified and become gods. True cult emerges and worship and sacrifice become the means of communication between men as subjects and gods as objects. In the third or Historic stage there is a breakthrough to a monistic world-view. All historic religions, according to Bellah, share the element of transcendentalism and in this sense all are dualistic. Demythologization takes place in that the one God becomes a self-subsistent being, the sole creator and ruler of the universe. For the first time the central religious preoccupation becomes salvation, enlightenment, release, etc., and a clearly structured conception of the self emerges contrary to the identity diffusion of earlier religious forms. In the fourth, Early Modern, stage the separate identity of the self advances still further. Faith, an internal quality of the individual and the direct relation between the individual and transcendent reality become more salient. Only the Protestant Reformation, Bellah says, successfully broke through the mediated system of salvation and institutionalized immediate salvation. The fifth or Modern stage shows the final collapse of the dualistic world-view of the historic religions. An infinitely multiplex world replaces the simple duplex structure, which in turn replaced primitive monism. The symbolization of man's relation to the ultimate conditions of his existence is no longer the monopoly of any groups explicitly labelled as religious. Bellah is here guided by Tillich, Bultmann, and Bonhoeffer (rather than by Barth whom he thinks regressively reasserts 'the adequacy of the early modern theological formulations').

The value of Bellah's scheme lies in the way in which he traces the forces of differentiation in men's religions. At each stage, the self becomes increasingly more independent from environmental circumstances. This is possible only through an increasing objectification of the social order and 'by withdrawing cathexis from the myriad objects of empirical reality'.

We may criticize Bellah's scheme in similar terms to our criticism of Weber, whom both Parsons and Bellah follow closely. It is like talking almost exclusively about differential calculus in mathematics without paying much attention to its complement—integral calculus. The emphasis on differentiation in religious symbolization, however valid and true in itself, fails to account for identity or integration. Bellah's view of evolution ('as a process of increasing differentiation and complexity of organization that endows the organizations, social system, or whatever the unit in question may be with greater capacity to adapt to its environment . . .') inevitably leads to this one-sided approach, even though he follows the quotation by saying: 'so that [the unit] is in some sense more autonomous relative to its environment than were its less complex ancestors'. To Bellah, this autonomy is continuous with, rather than in contrast with, the forces of adaptation. However, we believe that for the continuing objectification to take place at all it is not only necessary for cathexis to be withdrawn from 'the myriad objects of empirical reality', but even more for cathexis to be attached to the new 'unit'. As soon as this occurs, further adaptation has to fight an uphill battle. An example from history: the importance of the Protestant Ethic in the sixteenth and seventeenth centuries did not just reside in the evolution of certain conceptions of salvation (or Archimedean point) as Weber would have it, but more in cathexis being attached to this new locus of salvation in such a manner that the previous 'mediated' salvation could be relegated (Mol, 1968a, p. 69). In other words, it is the capacity of commitment to be latched into another identity focus which appears to us to be the crucial theoretical variable. Unless the 'identity' and the 'differentiation' side of the evolutionary process are continually paired and juxtaposed, either rationalistic or irrationalistic biases inevitably creep into the analysis. If differentiation is stressed too much the forces of rationality and adaptation will be overestimated and the importance of the constancy and salience of emotional anchorage will be underestimated. On the other hand the opposite mistake is made when there is too exclusive an emphasis on identity and the forces which stress sameness and order.

Regarding the ability of the forces of differentiation to gain the upper hand over the forces of integration or identity, there must be traditional antecedents which lend the change both legitimation and, even more significant, a guarantee of a better fitting order and interpretation of reality. The Judaeo-Christian tradition had this potential in both its prophetic and Yahwhistic conceptions, but here it is sufficient to point out that differentiation is impossible unless consolidation of the new unit simultaneously takes place and unless this new unit can be visualized as in some way the better of two alternatives. The process of differentiation has an inevitable consequence for identity, the major outlines of which must already be present in embryonic form in earlier stages of history. Bellah remarks, following Voegelin, that all historic religions have mortgages imposed on them by the historical circumstances of their origins. From the point of view of identity exactly the opposite, but equally true, observation can be made: namely that the seeds for new foci of identity have to germinate successfully in the past in order to be viable options at a future stage. To be fair to Bellah, however, he points out that it would be hard to find anything later that is not already foreshadowed in the more primitive religious symbol systems.

From the 'identity' perspective one might almost want to reverse Bellah's appraisal of twentieth-century theologians. Barth's consistent, lifelong work was to theologize in terms of the Christian tradition. He attempted to carve out and reinforce a Christian identity, however sceptical one may be about this possibility within a highly abstract and intellectualistic theology. He, more than Bonhoeffer, Bultmann, and Tillich, reinforced a traditional baseline for the twentieth-century flux of accelerated differentiation, whereas they took their cues often implicitly from the flotsam of meaning which the flux casually deposited on the periphery. Tillich's compromises with rational secular scholarship and Bultmann's preoccupation with the higher criticism of Biblical literature cannot by any stretch of the imagination be deemed to have strengthened the faith. Neither may be effective as the Jesus Freaks, the ecology buffs, and Mao's missionaries in the creation of identity foci for some twentieth-century youths. At least Barth consistently encouraged those whose commitment was focused on traditional Christianity.

Also from the 'identity' perspective, one could question Bellah's postulation of the emergence of 'a dynamic multidimensional self capable, within limits, of continual self-transformation and capable, again within limits, of remaking the world'. If these limits are set by man's need for identity and order, the prognostication may be somewhat more acceptable. But since Bellah continues to write of 'man in the last analysis [being] responsible for the choice of his symbolism', we may regard him as coming close to denying a basic need for continuity of identity. The point is reminiscent of the Moral Educationists' article of faith that schools nowadays should help pupils *choose* moral standards (Wilson *et al.*, 1967, p. 30), as though almost anything—morals and symbols as well as Toffler's technical and social advances—is infinitely adaptable and self-revising without evolutionary progress having built-in strains towards conservation.

In other, later, work Bellah seems to counterbalance the emphasis on differentiation of religious symbolizations with an equally strong emphasis on identity. 'It is precisely the role of religion in action systems to provide ... a cognitively and motivationally meaningful identity conception or set of identity symbols' (1968). 'It is this stability, continuity and coherence provided by commitment to a set of religious symbols ... that give religion such a prominent place in defining the identity of a group or person' (1965). Obviously the relationship between differentiation and identity needs to be more systematically worked out in Bellah's system.

To us, the dialectic between differentiation and identity (integration) consist of both attraction *and* repulsion, mutual need *and* basic conflict. In the battle the conventional religious forces and organizations are very partial: they strengthen, through sacralization, the identity side of the dialectic. Yet, there is much give and take. Viable religious orientations and organizations develop sophisticated mechanisms to deal with change, as will be shown in the chapters discussing charisma, conversion and ritual.

There hardly seems to be a major discipline of scholarship in which this dialectic is not present in some form or other. In the physical sciences and economics (Maruyama, p. 174) it is sometimes described as morphogenesis (structure generation, deviation-amplification, the second cybernetics) versus morphostasis (structure stabilization, deviation-counteraction, the first cybernetics). In biology and anthropology (Róheim, 1930, p. 381) it is described as the tendency towards fission versus the resistance to fission. Some historians use differentiation/integration (Toynbee, 1957, Vol. II, p. 287), but others (Bryce, 1901, pp. 216–62) write about centrifugal versus centripetal forces. Sometimes the dialectic is described as change versus continuity (Firth, 1963, pp. 209 ff.), or dynamics versus statics (Comte, 1858), or homogeneity versus heterogeneity (Spencer, 1896, p. 371), at other times as innovation versus continuity (Lenski, 1970, p. 63). Although there are slight variations in the meaning of these concepts, the dialectic is usually regarded as crucial for the understanding of basic processes. We think that the dialectic as such has the basic function of facilitating both progress and order. Although religious structures and orientations are very much on the side of order, some of them have given the death-blow to progress, whereas others have indirectly facilitated it. This facilitation seems to have occurred only when the forces of differentiation and integration were roughly equal to one another, as they have been in Western civilization.

SECULARIZATION

The utility of most concepts in the sociology of religion depends on the frame of reference in which they are used. Later we shall have occasion to question the utility of the church/sect typology or the intrinsic/extrinsic categories for the identity frame of reference. Beyond the institutional or modern Western setting these terms may very well have to be reinterpreted.

The same challenge must be offered to the concept of secularization. Its utility is obvious when relatively simple answers are sought for such questions as to why religion in the West is becoming privatized, or why there is a decline in the traditional indices of church attachment, belief, and practice, or why the churches now have to compete with clubs and television, or why the legitimating potential of ecclesiastical institutions is weakening. The dabblers in the field would generally be satisfied with answers which in some form or other stressed the inevitability of secularization. The professional sociologist on the other hand is likely to remain unhappy unless he has linked the phenomena in question with concepts and generalizations of wider application. Within the institutional setting of the Christian Church a large variety of problems can be aptly summed up in the word 'secularization'. The utility of the concept diminishes when the search is directed to what lies 'behind' the term or to which sociological model would provide the best fit.

David Martin wants to eliminate the word 'secularization' altogether, primarily because it is 'a tool of counter-religious ideologies', to wit, rationalism, Marxism, and existentialism (Martin, 1965, p. 169). Peter Berger has also criticized the way the concept 'has been employed as an ideological concept highly charged with evaluative connotations' but has added that Christians and non-Christians have been equally at fault in this matter (Berger, 1967, p. 106). He continues to use the term after purifying it as follows: 'The process by which sectors of society and culture are removed from the domination of religious institutions and symbols' (ibid., p. 107). Dobbelaere (1973, p. 549) and Lauwers (pp. 529–33) also call attention to the ideological bias of the secularization concept. To us there seems to be only a thin line between religious biases, pointed out by these authors, and the bias of any theoretical perspective or frame of reference. At any rate Berger's definition coincides well with what we have called cultural secularization, 'or the forces whereby the influence of religion and religious institutions generally decreases in modern society' (Mol, 1970c, p. 183). It also fits in well with what Shiner finds acceptable in the various definitions of secularization (Shiner, 1967). Still, if this is all there is to secularization, it may be wiser to follow Parsons' example and look at the specific phenomena as so many applications of the much more general process of differentiation (Parsons, 1963). After all, what has happened to Christianity over the last 500 years is not different from what has happened to the family as economic, educational, welfare and many other functions have escaped from religious and family tutelage and acquired increasing independence of operation. Substituting 'differentiating' for this meaning of the word 'secularization' plainly makes sense: a good theoretical fit is guaranteed and the economy of our conceptual apparatus is advanced.

However, 'secularization' has also been used in an altogether different sense. To many authors it also means 'the forces whereby specific religious institutions and orientations themselves become part of and like the world'. Mol (1970c, p. 183) has called this 'institutional secularization'. But this cannot be regarded as a special case of differentiation, because this kind of secularization goes on independently of the forces of differentiation. If there were congruence, one would not find such considerable divergence within societies in which one can assume that the evolutionary/historical forces of differentiation have permeated equally. After all, in almost any country there are religious organizations that have become very much like the world, and others (often the sects) which have dug the deepest possible moat between themselves and their secular environment, and these groups are often also those religious organizations that have gained numerically at the expense of their more secular competitors. There is nothing here even faintly resembling the inexorable sweep of evolution towards further cultural secularization or differentiation.

Evidence for these generalizations comes from a variety of phenomena, findings and data, most of which were reported or summarized elsewhere (Mol, 1970c).

A. The Sects

There are many reports of sects (such as Pentecostalists) in Latin America which are increasing in influence at the expense of the more established Protestant, and particularly Catholic, churches. There are historical and other studies in the U.S.A. and Canada that show that the sects and the more evangelical and orthodox Protestant denominations have gained both in terms of influence and numbers at the expense of the liberal and adjustable churches (cf. Mann, 1961, p. 405; Wolf, 1959, pp. 3–6; Feuer and Perrine, 1966, pp. 367–82; Glock and Stark, 1966, p. 210; O'Dea, 1966, p. 62; McLoughlin, 1967, p. 43; Fallding, 1972, p. 109; Davies, 1961, p. 85). I think it is fair to conclude from these studies that some of the least secularized religious bodies tend to increase, and the more secularized to decrease, in strength within the same society.

Of course, this increase can partly be explained by the sect's appeal to the disprivileged and alienated, and not necessarily by an institutional variable. But then there is also amongst the churches and denominations an astonishing difference regarding the capacity to implement those norms (such as church-going). In the secular environment this is easily shrugged off as optional. By concentrating on the denominations we have to some extent controlled for this factor of disprivilege and alienation.

B. Dutch Migrants in New Zealand

The following research was carried out in Christchurch, New Zealand, in 1963 (Mol, 1965a). The sample consisted of 397 randomly selected adult Dutch immigrants. The number of refusals and no-contacts in the study was negligible. The changes in religious behaviour as measured by church attendance were remarkable: 21 per cent went to church less than they did in the Netherlands; 8 per cent had changed to more church-going; 49 per cent had kept to regular church attendance; and 21 per cent had retained habits of non-church-going. The most significant variable to account for these changes proved to be denominational affiliation: those who were Catholic in the Netherlands or who belonged to the strict Calvinistic 'Gereformeerde Kerk' were far less likely to have reduced their church-going (the percentages were 16 and 17 respectively) than those who had belonged to the Hervormde Kerk (Presbyterian former state church). Here the percentage was 40. The study concludes by saying:

... the Catholic and Reformed denominations continue fairly well to keep a hold on their membership; the Hervormd/Presbyterian group on the other hand seems to further decrease its tenuous hold. One can then say that there is from a sociological point of view an enormous difference in institutional posture between the Catholic/Reformed group on the one hand and the Hervormd/Presbyterian group on the other. The first group has the social characteristics of a tightly knit organisation: members do what is expected of them, return loyalty to the organisation for the desire of being accepted by the church. There is an important measure of social control. The cohesion or integration of these religious organisations in both the Netherlands and New Zealand is well established and it is this fact which makes them survive the emigration upset relatively unscathed. However, in the Hervormd/Presbyterian section, again from a sociological point of view, the situation is much more reminiscent of what Durkheim used to call anomie (lack of control by the group over its members, contacts between members which are both piecemeal and lacking in depth). Homans' description of Hilltown as an example of social disintegration is theoretically also akin to the phenomena of the downward spiral, which we have observed; the already low involvement of the average Hervormd/Presbyterian immigrant becomes even lower (Mol, 1965a; p. 42.).

C. Race and Religion in New Zealand

Another example of differences regarding the capacity to implement certain norms, which all denominations regard as important, this time not of church-going but of racial integration, comes from another New Zealand study (Mol, 1966; 1965b, pp. 140–9). Here, too, those denominations that were closely identified with the respectable middle classes had difficulties. On the other hand, those churches, such as the Catholic and particularly the Mormon Church, which were somewhat more independent from the secular order were less frustrated in their attempts to integrate Pakehas (white Europeans) and Maoris (Polynesians) into the one worshipping congregation. The study concludes:

> The finding that the Church of the Latter-Day Saints, and, to a lesser extent, Catholicism can implement a policy of integration points to the importance of internal cohesion (whatever the forces around which this cohesion structures itself) for ecclesiastical relevance in race relations.
>
> As long as some degree of independent implementation of norms is out of the question, the New Zealand Protestant churches will out of necessity have to follow the different functions assigned to them by the different races. The amorphous ecclesiastical structures of the New Zealand Protestant churches can theoretically be meliorated by an all-pervading unifying concern. Although the 'faith' is supposedly just that, in actual practice it is not even approaching this sociologically observable function. (Mol, 1965b; p. 148.)

D. Denominations in Australia

Similar evidence of large denominational differences in implementing religious norms comes from Australia. Anglican officials there say that they are in the unfortunate position of having to carry an enormous load of 'dead wood', people who are only 'Church of

England' on the census form, but who are in actual fact completely outside the church. They maintain that, if one compares church-going Anglicans with other church-goers, the Anglican Church's influence is not waning any more than, for instance, the Catholic Church's influence over its membership.

In the 'Religion in Australia Survey' (Mol, 1971a) the hypothesis was tested that there would not be any significant denominational differences in the church-going habits of the respondents, once parental church-going was controlled. In the survey, 1,009 respondents over 20 years of age (out of a total number of 2,640) reported that when they were growing up both their parents always or nearly always attended church. Of these respondents, 541, or 54 per cent, went to church as regularly as their parents did. The rest (468, or 46 per cent) reported that they now went hardly ever or occasionally, which proved to be about two or three times a year. However, there was a very significant difference between the major denominations: only 63 out of the 248 Anglican respondents whose parents were regular attenders attended regularly themselves (25 per cent). Of the 374 Catholic respondents whose parents were regular attenders, 281 (or 75 per cent) reported that they themselves went always or nearly always. Of the rest of the sample (387), consisting predominantly of Methodists and Presbyterians, 197 (or 50 per cent) said that they went to church as regularly as their parents had done. The hypothesis was therefore rejected. There were indeed very significant denominational differences even when parental church attendance was controlled.

To account for the differences, another hypothesis was suggested, that the differences between denominations were the result of greater 'turnover' (many leaving the flock, but also many returning) rather than of apostasy.

To test this hypothesis, the cards of the respondents who said that when they were growing up both their parents never went to church or went only occasionally (less than once a month) were lifted out to see how many respondents whose parents had been irregular were themselves regular church-goers. As Table 1 shows, neither in the Church of England nor in the other Protestant denominations is there any return flow comparable to the outflow: the 75 per cent of lapsing Anglicans was counterbalanced by only 7 per cent who were better attenders than their parents. In the other Protestant denominations the same was true to a lesser extent: the 50 per cent of the lapsed members was counterbalanced by 13 per cent who were better attenders than their parents. However, the Catholics again presented a different picture: 44 per cent were now attending usually or always although their parents never or only occasionally went. This hypothesis was therefore also rejected.

TABLE I

Percentage attending church regularly (once a month or more) in a random sample of adults in New South Wales, Victoria, and Tasmania by parental church attendance while respondents were growing up.

Respondent's denomination	Respondent's parents' church attendance	
	Regular	Irregular or never
Church of England	25 (N = 248)	7 (N = 475)
Catholic	75 (N = 374)	44 (N = 124)
Other	50 (N = 387)	13 (N = 317)

In all four cases, those religious organizations which had clearly delineated themselves from their secular surroundings rather than compromised with them, were more capable of implementing norms and had a better hold of their membership. Institutional secularization seemed to be bound up with shallow commitments, or to say it differently: the more secular the organization, the less it (or what it represented) appeared to function as a focus of identity. The very heterogeneity accompanying social differentiation seems to encourage its own opposite. The tightly knit, homogeneous sectarian religious movements appear to serve as islands of cohesion and pockets of meaning in a world plagued by incoherence and meaninglessness.

Here too an overemphasis on the forces of differentiation and a relative neglect of the countervailing forces of conservation and identity can lead to distorted analysis. It was only from the differentiation perspective that Peter Berger could so strongly predict the continuation of the secularization process (1967b). From the identity angle more or less the opposite could be said: in highly industrialized, strongly differentiated societies, the least secularized religious bodies are likely to increase more in strength than the more secularized ones. They provide better identity boundaries. And as will be discussed in Chapter XII, they are better able to provide a buffer between the amorphousness of the larger social whole and the anomie of self-orientations.

As a basic concept in the sociology of religion, secularization seems to be rather useless, but when it is related to a larger frame of reference the concrete phenomena it appears to cover do become meaningful. Certainly, the differentiation/identity dialectic accounts for both the decreasing dominance of religious institutions in the modern West, and for a simultaneous vitality precisely of those religious forms which demand single-hearted and single-minded commitment. In this explanatory account however, the concept of secularization is rather superfluous.

SUMMARY

Although evolutionary thinking about religion in the nineteenth century suffered from gross arrogance precisely when it was least comprehensive, it was granted a new lease on life in the latter half of the twentieth century. In the more recent approaches the cathectic as well as the cognitive functions of religious ritual, symbols and myth are given their due consideration. The contribution of scholars such as Parsons and Bellah lies in their tracing of an increasing differentiation of religion as a symbol-system, issuing in more objectification and greater independence of the self. The argument of this chapter has been that a differentiation perspective of religion is incomplete when it is not counterbalanced by an identity perspective. The transcendental point of reference which facilitated the emergence of new economic, political, religious, and social forms would have been impotent, if it had not been for an accompanying emotional detachment from the ecclesiastical structure which mediated salvation and an emotional attachment to a God who could be reached by faith alone. The gradual shedding by religious organizations of previous functions can indeed be explained by an evolution-instigated tendency towards greater adaptation and differentiation.

However, the vitality of precisely those religious organizations which delineate themselves most resolutely from their secular environment can only be explained if one gives a full hearing to the conservation or identity side of the same evolutionary process. The organizational strength of orthodox churches and sects in Christianity seems to lie in their provision of a clearly delineated identity which is palpably missing in the secularized denominations.

Chapter III

Marginality and Alienation

Our analysis of religious manifestations is set in the framework of the dialectic between differentiation and integration. Yet precisely because religion is not entirely impartial in this dialectic, favouring, as it does, the forces of integration, and because religion always reacts to the process of social differentiation, it is important to examine the character of this opposing force, which loosens the personal or social identities that traditional religions seek to stabilize. In the second half of the chapter we shall discuss the responses of viable religions to these forces of change, and in the next chapter we shall pursue the complicated question of response (it involves also a desacralization of defunct patterns of identity) in greater detail.

Painting with sweeping strokes, we begin with the most elementary of processes—man's evolutionary necessity to cope successfully with his environment. This process is itself dialectical, between, on the one hand, change/differentiation (that acquisition of a more invulnerable position in the environment) and on the other, stability/integration (the consolidation of that gain). Progressive mastery of the environment depends on both the complementarity of these forces and on their opposition to each other: they must therefore be roughly equal to one another. Adaptation to changing conditions and increased mastery of them may be impossible when integration has become petrifaction. Consolidation of the gain and pattern maintenance may be impossible when the forces of change have run amuck.

The primary means by which the forces of change have broken through the tendency towards consolidation, sacralization, and petrifaction has been what is called marginality, a term borrowed from the sociological literature on race relations. It refers to persons or groups who stand on the boundary of larger groups or societies, neither completely belonging nor suffering outright rejection. Migrants are often marginal people and sects are usually marginal groups. Generally, marginality is regarded as an undesirable state of affairs. Being treated as an alien or refusing to adopt the ways of a new country has an adverse effect on the sense of belonging (Stone-quist, 1937) and is an important reason why minorities have higher than average rates of mental problems (Malzberg and Lee, 1956). Marginality has often been regarded as a liability for the creation of a stable society or the establishment of a religion, but as an asset for, and even as the source of, innovation, rationality, objectivity, efficiency, and individualism.

Marginality can disrupt both human society and the animal kingdom. Chicken farmers avoid putting an outsider into a strange flock, since both the marginal chicken and the flock suffer from the disruption of existing stable status relationships. Etkin (p. 18) found this rejection of the stranger (xenophobia) amongst many animal species. In some primitive societies, such as the Lugbara in Africa, the more alien the stranger, the greater his rejection (Horton, p. 166). Traders, missionaries and conquerors (Murdock, p. 96) as the carriers of strange habits and customs, are major disrupters of stable cultures. They undermine stability and promote innovation. In ancient Greece, thieves and traders (both protected by the god Hermes) were in the same category of unreliability. The early latin *hostis* could mean both stranger and enemy (Gauthier, p. 20; Benveniste, p. 75). In both ancient Greece and Rome, the stranger had no access to worship, was not protected by the gods and he was even regarded as committing sacrilege if he happened to be present at a sacrifice. Only citizens were associated with the religion of the city. Strangers were not permitted to become landowners because the soil of the city had religious significance. (Fustel de Coulanges, 1882, p. 208).

The fear of the strange and the new was well illustrated by the trial of Socrates in 399 B.C. on the charge of non-belief in the gods of the state, and the introduction of new gods and the corruption of youth. Yet, the very Athenians who condemned Socrates to death had also encouraged the marginal (and with it the Trojan horse of change) when they allowed the Metics to settle in Piraeus. Trade with Ionia across the Aegean Sea was of mutual advantage. As Weber aptly remarks, 'Everywhere, scepticism or indifference to religion are and have been widely diffused attitudes of large-scale traders and financiers' (Weber, 1964, p. 92). The Metics were no exception and their philosophies strongly influenced people such as

Socrates who began to represent the most 'thorough-going rationalism the world had yet seen', championed 'the supremacy of the intellect as a court from which there is no appeal', while their individualism relativized the 'mandates of external authority' (Becker and Barnes, 1952, p. 149).

We see a similar cluster of forces breaking up the medieval synthesis. The increase in trade; the individualizing influence of printing (McLuhan, 1969, p. 248); the rise of a new bourgeoisie and capitalist entrepreneur; the mounting influence of an urban money economy at the expense of a rural primary industry (von Martin, pp. 1–5); new discoveries and conquests—all loosened the weave of society. Shrewd and rational activity became the hallmark of the trading and merchant class (Pirenne, p. 123). The money economy made relationships between people more objective and competitive (von Martin, p. 5). Instead of man being only conscious of himself as a member of a race, people, party, family or corporation, he began to recognize himself as a 'spiritual individual' (Burckhardt, p. 100). Machiavelli (p. 193) advised the prince to rely only on himself.

Similar to the Metics in ancient Athens the major entrepreneurs during and after the Reformation were marginal people. The new prosperity of Amsterdam, after 1600, rested on immigrants from Antwerp. The entrepreneurial classes of the new 'capitalist' cities of the seventeenth century consisted predominantly of migrants from Flanders, Jews from Lisbon and Seville, South Germans from Augsburg, Italians from Como, Locarno, Milan and Lucca (Trevor-Roper, p. 20). The important foothold which traders and entrepreneurs found in Europe round about the Reformation contrasts sharply with the exclusions and restrictions of trade in Asia. It is for this reason that 'a rational practical ethic and life methodology did not emerge from this (Indian) magical garden' (Weber, 1958, p. 336).

Marginality advances innovation and by implication weakens those forces (such as religion) which integrate systems of meaning. A Dutch historian of the town of Deventer explains the breakdown of a sense of community, the rise of individualism and the drop in church affiliation on the grounds of the foreign/native mixture of the town (Cannegieter, 1958, p. 129). Robert E. Park similarly held that the 'effect of mobility and migration is to secularize relations which were formerly sacred' (Park, 1964, p. 351).

Marginality can also contribute to more efficient production methods, to greater creativity and technical scientific progress (Mol,

1963), or to the expansion of men's horizons, to keener intelligence, and more rational viewpoints (Park, 1937). Simmel illustrates how marginality contributes to greater objectivity, in the example of Italian cities which called their judges from the outside 'because no native was free from entanglements in family and party interests' (Simmel, 1964, p. 404). For very similar reasons, the employment of Chinese officials in their home province was prohibited (Weber, 1964b, p. 48).

This capacity of marginal people to be detached from what is taken for granted by the natives furthers the scientific spirit of objectivity. The stranger questions what is unquestionable to the in-group. He examines what is self-explanatory to the natives. His objectivity is the direct result of the failure of his previous rules of guidance and his loss of status, all of which compel him to re-think instead of 'thinking-as-usual' (Schutz, 1960, p. 108).

The scientist, like the stranger, stands aside from the material to be investigated. Investigation is impossible when one takes for granted the matter that is to be investigated. In the same way as Socrates relativized the mandates of external authority and located it in the thinking self, so in the first half of the seventeenth century, Descartes used scepticism as his primary tool, thereby elevating objectivity and individual thought above obedience to existing modes of explanation. Marginality is closely associated with this stance of independence and scepticism. Tonybee (Vol. I, 1946, p. 394) therefore calls the intelligentsia 'born to be unhappy' and Charles Gillispie (1960, p. 44) blames the 'cruel edge of objectivity' for the fatal estrangement between science and ethics. Similarly, Kaufmann (p. iv) sees a correlation between knowledge and alienation: '... as freedom, education, and self-consciousness increase, alienation grows too'. Roszak (1973, p. 240) actually equates objectivity with alienation.

The assets and liabilities of marginality are brought out in a number of recent psychological and sociological studies. Hagen (1962, p. 96) makes the point that detached and anxious personalities are more likely to be innovators. Ralph Turner (1964, p. 6) observers that the great innovators in any era are likely to be marginal men, but that the negative consequences of marginality are 'rootlessness, absence of clear standards to guide behaviour, inability to make decisions, hyper-sensitiveness, inconsistency in behavior'. Erikson (1968, p. 88) contrasts marginality and a positive identity base.

ALIENATION

Weber's 'disenchantment' (Weber, 1946, p. 155) also belongs to this cluster of concepts and values that are associated with change. In Weber's mind disenchantment accompanied the progressive and inevitable rationalization and intellectualization of the world, in the face of which the ultimate and most sublime values had to retreat. This process has also been called alienation or estrangement. In the literature it is often used in the sense of 'whatever prevents integration and wholeness'. Unfortunately alienation has now become 'too much a concept of political theology' (Feuer, 1963, p. 146). Like 'reification', in present use, it serves as a monument to humanistic ideology masquerading as a scientific construct. Whatever is thought to have prevented *individuals* from becoming what they should be, is called 'alienation'. In almost diametrical contradiction to Weber, Feuerbach (1957) felt that man's alienation lay in the surrender of the self to the tyranny of religion. Erich Fromm (1957, p. 49) reflects the same thought when in almost identical words he says that man's alienation consists of projecting his own most valuable powers unto God. To the young Marx alienation consisted in man's submission to the tyranny of private property and the product of labour (Marx, 1963, pp. 124–5; also Kamenka, 1962, p. 75). To Marcuse it means incompatibility with the established forms of life (1968, pp. 60–1) or the social controls over a life of toil and fear (1968, p. 23). Others define alienation in terms of powerlessness, meaninglessness, normlessness, isolation, and self-estrangement (Seeman, 1959, and 1972). What is striking in these, generally psychological, conceptualizations (see also Schacht, 1972, pp. 259–66) is the implication that if man could only be free from economic, political, religious, and social oppressions, the problem would vanish. This, I think, is a rather serious fallacy.

The problem of man's alienation is much more cosmic and deep-seated. The self-perpetuating forces of change appear to be stronger than the countervailing forces of consolidation. To blame other (social) integrating forces for the frustration of the individual is rather myopic and naïve. A sacralized individualism may actually contribute to the incapacity of a society to reinforce norms and values or to provide a stable system of meaning. The problems of social integration are as severe as those of personal integration. *Both* are equally beleaguered by the disrupting forces of change and marginality. However, the complex dialectic between personal, group, and social identity will be discussed in Chapters XI–XIII. Here we confine ourselves to a few preliminary, general observations.

The major reason why the militant British Humanists, the Huxleys, Bertrand Russell and his followers, Fromm, and many other American psychoanalysts never had much of a mass following is that they grossly overestimated the solidity of rational individualism as a basis for identity and, ironically that they defined alienation in terms of the very religious and social forces from which, in the last resort, the therapeutic processes had to spring.

The greatest difficulty any believer faces is not to take his beliefs for granted. The strong beliefs of humanists and psychoanalysts in the value of individuality and rationality led them to define the ills which they saw in terms of the hunger for power, bureaucratic cul-de-sacs, mesmerizations with techniques, or religious corruption. In fact, man's alienation was more often than not the result of relativization and diminution of those values that demanded conformity and those patterns which were sacralized, the very values and patterns the humanists and most psychoanalysts defined as damaging man's dignity. Their utopianism consisted in assuming that the forces of change as such might be sacralized and thus become adequate platforms of identity. They assumed that social stability and order were so much given that they could be disregarded and that individual conflicts could be dealt with in individual rational terms. But individual self-awareness and personal self-realization have not been successful centring foci of identity, in spite of their potentially snug fit in the complex machinery of modernity. The attempt to relativize both a transcendental and social frame of reference leaves very little else around which to crystallize self-hood.

Durkheim made it clear that the goal of the individual could not be treated as independent of the norms and values of the society, but were given meaning by these values (Durkheim, 1964b).

Simmel saw the many dangerous possibilities of objectivity (and by implication of self-awareness (Simmel, 1964, p. 405). To him the bequest of modern rationalist individualism was man's inability 'to preserve a sense of the wholeness and identity of self against the very currents which were supposed to both liberate and emphasize this wholeness and identity of self' (Nisbet, 1967, p. 305).

To Weber rationality had its own built-in nemesis. 'From being a force of progress . . . rationalization becomes eventually the seed-bed of a tyranny greater, more penetrating, more lasting, than anything previously known in history' (ibid., p. 294).

De Tocqueville (1955, Vol. II, p. 5) attached great importance to the disposition of both the reformers and the eighteenth-century philosophers to subject the dogmas of the ancient faith to private scrutiny. Not altogether without justification, Nisbet (op. cit., p. 276) interprets de Tocqueville to say that all this, 'instead of enhancing man and magnifying the role of his individual reason, has actually diminished it. Reason is like happiness; make it the exclusive goal and we cannot achieve it'.

The problem is a relative one. If it had not been for the numerous sources of identity existing in our technological society, the situation would be much more intolerable than it is. Man derives a sense of belonging from his family, his peer-groups, his job relations, his hobby, his service or sports club, his church, and anyone of these has often become a major unifying focus of identity. If a sense of alienation persists it is because the self-sterilizing demands of education for objectivity, tolerance, and scepticism of premises, or the saliency of rational efficiency and individual ambition, all run counter to the successful formation of identities.

In the previous paragraph we mentioned some of the identity foci which in modern society counter the forces of change and instability. This counterbalancing dialectic can also be traced back to the very periods of history in which we discerned the strengthening impact of marginality.

Sometimes Judaism and Christianity are thought to be independent vehicles for change, and to 'challenge men to alienate themselves from nature, society, and themselves' (Kaufmann, 1970, p. liii). Yet I would rather defend the thesis that these religions sublimated and incorporated the marginal, the rational, the creative in response to the irremediable and irrevocable turn which differentiation and change had taken. This is *not* saying that religion is only reactive. A viable religion both initiates sacralization and defends stable patterns. The vitality of Judaism and those universal religions (Christianity and Islam) that were built on Judaic foundations lay in the sophisticated way they coped with change and marginality—the exodus, the conquests, the exile, minority status, and the experience of being a pariah people.

The emphasis on the revealed will of God who could both punish and love, drastically changed the cosiness of ethnic religiosity. In

Jahweh, a delicate, even uneasy balance was maintained as a crucial nexus between the forces of differentiation and marginality (His judgement and insistence on change in the status quo) with the forces of identity, order and integration (His promise of unrequited love for Israel). On the more mundane plane of social concretizations, coping with change became the domain of later prophecy, and the maintenance of the status quo the domain of priesthood. The result was that the marginal or prophetic protests were re-cemented into the tradition. The extraordinary success and influence of this tradition in both Christianity and Islam is to be attributed to the sacralization of an uneasy balance.

Christianity could not have arisen if the means of coping with marginality had not been created in Judaism. St. Paul's changed attitude towards unclean animals and the circumcision rites (Galatians 2) would have been difficult to imagine without the Jewish precedence of relativizing dogmatic and legalistic rigidities. His conversion can be seen as the culmination of inevitable previous tensions and their resolution in the identification with Christ, in whom God's marginality and love were concretely interwoven, and in whom also ethnic laws and rites had been 'fulfilled'.

The history of decay of the Roman Empire in the first four centuries of the Christian era can be seen as the rampage of the forces of change and relativization without the counterbalance of an Empire-wide solid source of identity which held it all in check. Emperor worship failed miserably: Christianity survived primarily because of the looseness of the social fabric and because it provided a fierce minority identity strengthened by both opposition and martyrdom.

The next ten centuries have often been seen by Christian scholars as the acme of Christian strength and consolidation. Such very different people as Christopher Dawson and Jacques Ellul have respectively written about the wonderful medieval synthesis (Dawson, 1949, pp. 201 ff.), and about this being the only specifically Christian era, before sheer technique had come to dominate society (Ellul, 1965). One may add that apparently this long period of recuperation was necessary to consolidate the slow gains of the forces of identity.

By the end of that era, the baseline was sufficiently strong for the latent forces of independent intellectual inquiry (the Renaissance) and of a more individual religiousness (the Reformation) to be resurrected and to acquire a new lease on life. In a situation of relative security and order, marginality and change can be tolerated some-what more easily. More importantly, however, the products of marginality, rationalism and individualism, inevitably remained as undercurrents in the secular (Greek) and sacred (Judaeo-Christian) traditions. The medieval cities were characterized by more indivi-dualism than any city of antiquity and even in the hierarchical scheme of Thomas Aquinas' *Summa* there was an intriguing inde-pendence of each institution and of each individual, rational creature. The consequence of the survival of the marginal in the distant past was its incorporation or co-optation rather similar to the biological cell busily restoring internal unity after the invasion of a foreign element. In contrast with sixteenth-century Java, where a sudden expansion of the trading classes signified the breakdown of Indic culture (Geertz, 1968, p. 39), Western society up to the Reformation had often enough learnt to cope with the marginal (for the sake of its contribution), so that societies became permanently more 'loosely woven'. This loose weave was to be further legitimated religiously at the time of the Reformation when the self's immediate relation with God was strengthened at the expense of his dependence on ecclesiastical mediation. Further innovation and industrialization now followed man's lesser reliance on the traditional pattern of closely knit communities: greater faith developed in man's inner-directed self. (For the use of this term see Riesman, 1955, pp. 28–32.) Particularly when the values of efficiency, and rationality that Weber associated with this-worldly asceticism (Weber, 1964a, p. 80) were socialized into this relative autonomous self, the resulting flexible unit could be only propitious for the economic and technological progress which was to follow.

However, this increased freedom of man from his social milieu was just another word for his greater marginality. The marginality would hardly have been taken as an alternative, if it had not been for the established precedence of the Old Testament God as a focus of identity in whom total reliance reposed through the relationship of faith. In Him, in contrast with the visible church on earth, there was no corruption. Why then aim at the man-made and the mun-dane, when real salvation was immediately available? The freedom from concretizations was a utopia, however much the uneasy balance could actually be maintained in God. For how could this faith be sustained and socialized unless there were some social and concrete means of judging that faith? The Church as a guardian had been relativized. Now there was a priesthood of all believers, but how could any group of people implement norms which were so exclusively personal and spiritual, unless there was also some stress on the fruits of that faith? Again the Judaeo-Christian tradition provided the embryonic and now elaborated answer: justification by faith was counterbalanced by sanctification. Faith without works was dead (James 2:17). And as Calvin said: 'God declares that rewards for virtue are treasured up with him, and none who yield obedience to his commands will labour in vain' (*Institutes*, Book II, Chap. viii, section 4). God was not only the forgiving, loving father who would reward good deeds, but also the judge who would punish wrongdoing. This increased emphasis on God as judge and determiner of existence seems only natural in the light of the decreased importance of the institutional church. The believer on whom now the whole onus of faith rested could be sustained only because he was constantly bludgeoned with the reassurance that Jahweh knew him, encompassed him, rewarded him, cajoled and punished him.

It is no accident that Weber's attention was drawn to the emergence of this Calvinistic new man as somehow important for the spirit of capitalism (Weber, 1952). The ascetic/rational attitude towards life was indeed propitious for economic development. Both he and Tawney were wrong, however, in explaining the entrepreneurial success of the Calvinists as a result of their sense of a divine call for mundane activities. Hudson (1959, p. 58) is essentially correct when he says that this explanation completely subverts the fundamental theological structure of Calvinism. We could add that it is indeed much more in line with authentic reformed theology to stress the marginality of the Calvinist, now less dependent on communal sustenance and reward and more capable of coping with the personal hardship of economic competition and the denigration of competitors (Mol, 1968a, p. 70). A system of strict ethics, such as honesty, truth, keeping one's word, appeared to be legitimated only as long as faith in a punishing and demanding, but also in a loving and forgiving, Jahweh, was maintained.

The strength of the Calvinist ethic lay also in its relevance for a rising bourgeoisie, which was both in need of religious legitimation for its freedom from feudal restrictions and of a religious justification for commercial independence. The energetic activity which had a striking affinity with the Old Testament God and which impressed Weber so much, also resulted from the marginality of the new classes who now had to consolidate their position in a not particularly hospitable world. It is for some such reason that Tawney (1937, p. 99) looks upon the doctrine of predestination as doing for the bourgeoisie of the sixteenth century what the theory of historical materialism attempted to do for the proletariat of the nineteenth— making it into a chosen race with a sense of destiny. This means that the Reformation sacralized the values of independence, rational- ism, and individualism already present in a 2,000-year-old Greek heritage, and now revitalized in the Renaissance. In both Renais- sance and Reformation, the marginality of a rising section of a stable society was an important factor for the increasing saliency of these values. In the ensuing consolidation of these groups these values were further institutionalized and sacralized, even though the forces of identity operating so strongly in the consolidating phases of a move- ment have always de-emphasized them. They could not be neglected, however, since they became so strongly embedded in the political and economic institutions of the succeeding centuries.

These values of independence, rationalism, and individualism were reinforced on the frontiers of the newly settled countries, such as the American colonies. There is evidence that, both then and now, mar- ginal people are more likely to move and migrate than those who have a great sense of belonging. Speaking about the new frontier of Nova Scotia in Canada towards the end of the eighteenth century, S. D. Clark (1948, p. 30) says that settlers tended to come from the least stable elements of the New England rural society where they had resented heavy social control. In their new environment these settlers stood for rugged individualism. In an extensive Dutch sur- vey migrants were shown to differ from non-migrants primarily in having weaker communal ties and in participating less in social affairs (Frijda, 1960, pp. 88–91). Like the settlers on the American frontier, they were both more marginal and more independent. One would expect that this self-reliance of the frontiersman would make him less interested in traditional religion, which particularly on the East coast of the American colonies often stood for social stability and reinforced the delicate status quo of the village status hierarchy. It was true that he often showed a disdain for this kind of religious- ness. Nevertheless, he also showed a remarkable sympathy for the fervent sectarian religious spirit which proved to flourish so well on the entire North American continent. One could speculate that both frontier and revivalist religion provided a gate of escape from the bondage of past frustrations. Both justified a change towards greater collectivism as rootlessness or marginality gradually made places for the rewards of social and religious legitimacy. Both provided an anchor against the insecure future of economic failure and human vicissitudes (Mol, 1969, p. 33). Simultaneously the democratic institutions which arose on the frontier and the non-elitist doctrines of personal salvation in sectarian religion safeguarded the frontiersman's independence and individualism. 'The Churches of the frontier tended to be voluntaristic organizations, in harmony with the other social structures of the individualistic society and in conformity with the conception of religion as immediate and individual experience' (Richard Niebuhr, 1957, p. 143).

Yet the very fact that these churches were social institutions (however much they safeguarded individual salvation and equality) also meant that they took the sting out of marginality. The more the churches helped the frontier farmers to belong, the less marginal they became; the safer the individual felt in his communal niche, the more sectarian fervour diminished. The forces of identity and stability closed in on the forces of differentiation and change. Marginality represented change; sectarianism paved the way to new personal and social identities; denominationalism represented stability.

Urban technology institutionalized individualism, objectivity and rationality even more strongly than the rural frontier. Here the forces of identity had a more difficult struggle. In the city, man could better maximize his economic security, but closely involved with this security was the viability and technical efficiency of industry. In the cities, too, sheer numbers weakened social control and strengthened anonymity. It is in this kind of environment that one can expect society to be anything but homogeneous, and consequently those religious bodies which sacralize social identity are not particularly likely to flourish. And yet, as we will see later, it is in this ostensibly barren ground that we can find a great variety of identity foci, all being sacralized, or, at least, being potentially sacralizable!

SUMMARY

Marginality, arising from contact with other cultures, societies, and groups is a major source for social differentiation. The ancient Greek and Roman religions were the most important bulwark for the preservation of national and local identity. Still they could not stem the tide of individualism, rationality, and objectivity following in the wake of culture conflict. The Judaeo-Christian-Islamic religions legitimated marginality by incorporating prophecy in their sacred traditions and by emphasizing Jahweh/God/Allah as the transcendental judge. In consequence, these religions were better able to deal with change and to provide a baseline for the construction of new forms of identity. The Reformation may be regarded as a successful attempt to re-emphasize these notions from the past, thereby consolidating changes brought about by Renaissance thinking, commerce, and entrepreneurial activity within better-suited foci of identity. It legitimated these changes because Christian traditions anticipated these more individualistic forms of identity as viable patterns for socialization. That viability depended far more than is generally realized on the legitimacy of the extra-individual, transcendental source.

If, at the end of the twentieth century, the traditional religious categories of the Judaeo-Christian heritage seem to be less successful in providing the major platform of identity construction, it may be because they have to share this function with numerous other foci of identity that have emerged in the wake of the unprecedented success of the forces of differentiation, rationality, individualism, which make man the undisputed master and manipulator of his physical environment. Still, some of these competing foci of identity, particularly those which sacralize self-hood, are in greater functional trouble than appears from their exuberant confidence. Certainly the problems of alienation are unlikely to be resolved when philosophers, psychoanalysts, and sociologists continue to presume that forms of religious and social conformity are the source, rather than at least a part of the solution, of these problems. The tragedy of the situation is that although the forces of identity are everywhere visible, they operate only slowly. In the eagerness to catch up, identities are structured around rather unlikely objects, and one is sometimes struck by the similarity of these private enthusiasms for limited causes and escapes to the efforts of those misguided animals in artificial environments which attempt to mate with their caretakers.

Chapter IV

Charisma and Conversion

In the previous chapter we began to discuss the integrating/sacralizing response of viable religions to the forces of change. The problem for religion is much more complicated than that of merely finding an appropriate response. After all, to respond and change rather than to stabilize and sacralize goes against the basic function of religious orientation. The question therefore becomes: what mechanisms have religions evolved to control the way in which existing patterns of identity are broken down and new ones crystallize?

CHARISMA

Charisma is to identity what marginality is to change. Marginality contributes to the loosening of the social fabric, charisma draws together the strands again and reinforces a new identity. The term 'charisma' is from the vocabulary of the early Christian church, where it meant the 'gift of grace'. It was a fundamental concept for St. Paul, for whom it expressed God's spontaneous, unmerited gift of divine love which was necessary for man's redemption. Weber (1952, p. 294) also defined it in that sense: '... prophetic charisma ... is a free gift of godly grace', but then in his actual use of the term the transcendental reference disappeared and became a human psychological quality of almost magical power over others (1964a, pp. 358–9). From an attribute of God it became an attribute of leadership, of the kind which relies on emotional rather than rational response of the followers. It was a quality of inspiration and enthusiasm possessed by certain religious as well as military and political leaders. It was a direct antithesis to rational, bureaucratic authority. Weber called it the greatest revolutionary force in traditional societies. Quite contrary to the equally revolutionary force of reason, it resulted 'in a radical alteration of the central system of attitudes . . . with a completely new orientation of all attitudes' (p. 363).

The contribution of charisma appears to lie in anchoring change in the emotions of men. Perhaps for this reason, Weber regards it as so radically different from reason. In contrast to the marginal migrants, strangers, traders, and philosophers who come from outside a given community, the charismatic leaders usually come from within. They act as catalysts. They respond to the tensions that emerge inside a society, and their vision induces men to become emotionally detached from the old order, and ready to commit themselves to a new one. The successful leaders of cargo cults who were often native police-boys or mission helpers (Christiansen, p. 118) well acquainted with both the traditional and the contact culture, performed this catalytic role.

Unlike charismatic leaders, marginal outsiders relativize the bases for identity without putting anything in their place. Reasoned and objective detachment is their characteristic stance. The futility of transferring an alien identity to a new country soon becomes apparent, and the longer they live in a new situation the less certain they become about the absolute value of their previous identity. In other words, the marginal man is often an ineffective leader precisely because he is uncertain, both about the world from which he comes and the new one in which he now finds himself. Often he goes through an identity crisis, and, for this reason, I do not want to link charisma with social marginality, as Berger does (1963, p. 950).

By contrast the charismatic leader's strength is his certainty and his capacity constructively to guide a change of identity by processes of emotional stripping and welding. The psychologists call this 'transference' (Wheelis, 1958) and the anthropologists 'revitalization' (Wallace, 1966). In the first instance, the charismatic leader becomes a father figure, a new authority from which the follower eagerly accepts a new interpretation of both the past and the future. In the second instance the charismatic leader legitimates protest against the incompatible or frustrating elements of the old culture, which he revitalizes by articulating a new synthesis.

Precisely because charisma is of such cathectic importance I think it mistaken to emphasize the revolutionary innovative character of charismatic figures, as is often done in the literature (Wallace, 1966, p. 209; Weber, 1964a, p. 326; Berger, 1963, p. 950; Parsons, 1964b,

p. xxiii). At the most, one may say that they contribute to the success of an innovative movement. However, contrary to marginal people they are not so much the instigators as the catalysts for the kind of change that, for numerous other reasons, is already in the air.

The secret of all charismatic leadership is to hear what the masses are ready to hear, as Erikson (1969, p. 403) observes with reference to Gandhi. The sixteenth-century Javanese charismatic leader, Kalidjaga, and the seventeenth-century Moroccan charismatic leader, Lyusi, were hardly innovating revolutionaries. Geertz (1968, p. 35) calls them 'profoundly conservative' as they defended received forms of religious consciousness in the face of radical social and political challenges. And yet they were both catalysts for change. Lanternari (p. 315) in summing up his research on native, charismatic, movements stresses that the purpose of the latter is 'to make a positive contribution to the regeneration of society as a whole'.

Hebrew prophecy is a good example of charisma reintegrating rather than revolutionizing society. Particularly in the earlier period the prophets were obviously charismatic leaders, vital to morale and to the successful outcome of war and conquest (Moses and the Judges). The later prophets, on the other hand, were characterized by Weber (1952a, pp. xxiii, 292–3) as outsiders, lonely men, heroically swimming against the stream, hated and misunderstood by their listeners, always unloved, often ridiculed, threatened, spit upon, slapped in the face. This characterization is, however, somewhat one-sided. The prophets from Elijah through Malachi saw themselves as standing firmly within tradition. Those whom they attacked, whether king or people, were viewed by the prophet as 'marginal', in the sense that they had deviated from the norm, and were acting in a manner that was at best peripheral to, and at worst contradictory of, the tradition. More recent studies than Weber's have confirmed that the prophets stood within the cult as unquestioned authorities, representing both the will of deity and the welfare of the people (A. Johnson, 1962, pp. 59–60, 75). Precisely because they were seen as normative, as the authentic representatives of the ancient communal tradition, they were despised by the forces that sought to convert 'marginal departures' into the law of the land. At the same time, they reinterpreted catastrophic events (conquest, exile) as meaningful in the light of ancient tradition and by so doing they sought to restore Israel. Thus we agree with Shils

(1965, p. 200) when he says that charisma conserves social order through its 'awe-inspiring centrality'.

The utility of charisma for emotional anchorage can be illustrated from a variety of sources. Weber mentions the shaman as a charismatic type (1964a, p. 359). In a large number of cultures the shaman deals with the supernatural world on behalf of his community. He is often afflicted with serious mental and physical disorders, which sets him apart from his community, but which also makes him valuable, in that he is thought to be above the ordinary. Wallace (1966, p. 152) suggests that societies all over the world cure a hysterical or schizophrenic person by ritualizing his transition from a collapsed secular identity to a new identification as a supernatural being. The shaman, whose nervous instability is now socially legitimated and even rewarded, consoles and comforts his community through his ability 'to see what is hidden and invisible to the rest and to bring back direct and reliable information from the supernatural worlds' (Eliade, 1964, p. 509). The personal change is brought about in a painful and tortuous way: shamanic initiations are often hair-raising—the Manchu require that the candidate dive into the first of nine holes in the ice, come out through the second and so on to the ninth hole (p. 113). This is thought to pave the way for potential social and personal changes in clients. The shaman re-establishes communication between earth and heaven that was interrupted by 'the Fall' (Eliade, 1967, p. 72); he repairs the emotional tension between 'id' and 'superego'. Vital to this process is the mechanism of ecstasy, which to Eliade is the defining characteristic of shamanism (1964, p. 4).

It is particularly through this capacity to 'stand outside oneself' (the original Greek meaning of ecstasy) that we can see the link with Weber's charisma, 'the extraordinary, divine, unmerited gift of grace'. In both instances the force that moves and reintegrates humans and communities is perceived to be entirely outside human control. It purifies, inspires, and 'welds' emotions. Faith, on the part of leaders and participants, is necessary in both cases to obtain this mystic sensitivity. To create a sensory condition that is open to the supernatural, shamanism attempts to destroy profane kinds of sensitivity through monotonous chants, endlessly repeated refrains, fatigue, fasting, dancing, narcotics, etc. (Eliade, 1967, p. 86). In this sensory vacuum, the capacity for canalizing disorders into socially acceptable syndromes (Nadel, 1946, p. 36) and for redefining the social situation is maximized. The zeal of the charismatic leaders and shamans can refocus disparate and divergent sets of meaning by creating an external vantage point (Mol, 1969, p. 50).

A very good example of the 'stripping' and 'welding' effect of charisma is provided by the Ratana religious movement in New Zealand. When, in the first half of the nineteenth century, British whalers, traders, and ex-convicts arrived in New Zealand, alcohol, muskets, and new diseases reduced the warring Maori tribes by half (Henderson, 1963, p. 1). In the treaty of Waitangi, in 1840, the Maori chiefs accepted the law of England, but subsequent wars led to further confiscation of the best Maori lands. Christian missionaries inspired new supra-tribal religious movements sometimes to their own detriment. One missionary at Opotiki was murdered, and his eyes were eaten while the congregation drank his blood. The fanatical Hau Hau cult which was responsible for these and similar atrocities was soon put to an end by military campaigns (Babbage, 1937). However, other native religious movements combining Christian and Maori elements persevered for more than a century. At the 1961 census the Ringatu religion, for instance, still claimed three per cent of the Maori population (Mol, 1966, p. 38).

The most successful native religious movement did not begin until 1918. It centred around Tahupotiki Wiremu Ratana, born in 1873. He was very much in demand as the champion ploughman and wheat-stacker of the district, but often 'he would stand, brooding, gazing at nothing and then throw himself into the work again' (Henderson, p. 22). Ratana 'heard voices', and some of his relatives wanted to take him to a mental hospital. A large majority of his relations died in the 1918 influenza epidemic, and soon after Ratana saw a vision of a small round cloud rising from the sea, and he heard the Holy Ghost commanding him to unite the Maori people and to turn them to 'Jehovah of the Thousands'. Later, he saw an angel standing in front of a window repeating the message, exhorting him to destroy the power of the tohunga (Maori witch-doctor) and to cure the spirits and bodies of his people. On this Ratana threw all his beer out of the house and smashed the telephone over which he was said to have operated as the local bookmaker. 'He preached vigorously against drink henceforth' (ibid., p. 25).

Soon he became famous as a faith-healer, and bus and train loads of Maoris would arrive at his door pitching their tents round the farmhouse and giving the place 'the appearance of a shanty town or the transit camp of an army on the march' (ibid., p. 26). At the Christmas gathering of 1920, there were 3,000 followers congregated for the opening of a new interdenominational church. The creed of the new church generally followed orthodox Christianity, but the services, even to this day, are a mixture of sectarian informality and Maori ritual. The movement grew from strength to strength. At the 1936 Census, almost twenty per cent of the 82,326 Maoris belonged to the Ratana movement, but numbers declined before Ratana's death in 1939. At the 1961 Census, the percentage had dropped to fourteen (Mol, 1966, p. 40). The significance of the Ratana movement was its capacity through charisma to rally a depressed people and to provide them with the *mana* necessary for a new identity. This identity also had a political side. Through its alliance with the Labour Party and its representatives in Parliament many Maori causes were advanced. Still it was primarily the religious zeal and conviction in the early days of the movement by which the Maoris became emotionally detached from their former state of depressed and decadent lethargy, and attached to a new identity of existential purpose.

Charisma has achieved similar results for such diverse groups as Black Nationalists (Essien-Udom, pp. 64 ff.; Lincoln, 1961), the Indian tribes practising the Ghost Dance (Mooney, 1970, p. 25), and separatist movements in Africa (Herskovits, 1962, p. 418).

Similar evidence for the stripping and welding function of charisma comes from some of the migration literature. In the first half of the eighteenth century, the evangelical and pietist clergymen of the Dutch Reformed and German Lutheran Churches adjusted better to the new conditions of the American colonies than their orthodox and conservative colleagues. They were more independent of their mother churches in Europe; they were also less inclined to sacralize Dutch and German traditions; they adopted English more quickly in their services; and they favoured much more the training and ordaining of ministerial candidates locally. Their fervent religious beliefs contributed strongly to their capacity to relativize the traditions of their old country and to detach themselves from past patterns. Their charisma detached the ancient Christian symbols from their old-world cultural setting. New values and new ways of acting and reacting were now crystallized in the highly charged, emotional cauldron created by revivalist religiosity. As a result the evangelical faction in the Dutch Reformed Church became much stronger than it was in the Netherlands. In the German Lutheran

Church the pietist section, led by Henry Melchior Muhlenberg, actually completely supplanted the orthodox, New York-based, organization led by Wilhelm Christophorus Berkenmeyer (Mol, 1968a).

The anthropologist, Anthony Wallace, gives other examples of enthusiastic religious movements promoting adjustment to social and cultural change. He calls all these movements (such as cargo, nativistic and messianic cults) revitalization movements, because as he says they are 'conscious, organized efforts by members of a society to construct a more satisfying culture' (1966, p. 30). They can resolve identity crises of entire communities (p. 157) by crystallizing old notions into a new pattern (p. 212). Wallace's theory is certainly an advance over more sociological approaches which have not made much theoretical mileage out of the concept of charisma. Still, Wallace's rationalistic biases (to him the future of religion lies in its 'desupernaturalization' because 'science always wins', p. 261) prevent him from seeing that in modern Western societies the forces of rational individualism have aggravated anomie. Certainly one of the few and feeble attempts to remedy anomie with scientific methods (psychoanalysis) has been much less successful numerically than the enthusiastic movements Wallace describes so well. Because of his rationalistic bias, Wallace's revitalization theory fails to address itself to the issue of detachment. Where we would maintain that the very 'heat' of ecstasy or charisma detaches individuals and groups from a previous identity, Wallace speaks only of the disallowance of trait complexes (pp. 210–11). He underestimates man's emotional attachment to even unsatisfactory patterns of behaviour and culture.

CONVERSION

Detachment from any established identity pattern is painful and this is particularly well illustrated in the literature on conversion. Most accounts of conversion experiences retail the anguish that converts suffer before the new orientation is accepted (James, 1902; Boisen, 1936).

Conversion is to the person what charisma is to the social group. It is the means by which a new perspective becomes emotionally anchored in the personality, which is unified in the process. The convert feels that he has obtained a new identity, and very often he strengthens his new assumptive world by repeating over and over again how evil, or disconsolate, or inadequate he was before the conversion took place. Conversion then is the adoption of a new orientation, a re-ordering of priorities and values.

It may take many forms. Sometimes, as with satori in Zen Buddhism, or the slow ripening of a Christian conviction, the transition to a new identity is gradual, and in this case, with ideas and orientations gradually falling into place, there is less need for emotional stripping. But something new is happening, with its climax as the culmination to a long search. Satori too, however restrained and intellectual, is 'the unfolding of a new world hitherto unperceived in the confusion of a dualistically-trained mind', 'the remaking of life itself', 'the harmonisation of all the world's opposites and contradictions' (Suzuki, 1962, p. 154). It is a distinct resolution, similar to the one articulated by the drug addict, who had been looking for 'something' all his life, and who finally saw the last piece of the jigsaw fall into its place (Winick, 1963, p. 271). Gradual conversion may also follow successful psychoanalytic treatment. The psychoanalytic cure, as Lévi-Strauss (1967, pp. 183, 202) remarks, hardly differs from the conversion brought about by sorcerers and shamans. The gradual change to a new and better-fitting paradigm in scientific thinking is called 'conversion' by Kuhn (1970, pp. 157–9). The intriguing characteristic of this kind of conversion is similarly a transfer of basic allegiance to a new framework of commitments.

Generally, however, conversion experiences stress the break between the past and the present. The drug addicts who have joined the Jesus Freak movement strongly dissociate themselves from their previous addiction. Jesus really turns them on, they say: drugs were only a crutch or a pseudo-device for unification. And when Arthur Koestler described his conversion to communism in similar words, it was more like St. Paul's or St. Augustine's experience than a gradual enlightenment. After reading Marx, Engels, and Lenin he believed that something clicked in his brain and it was as though a mental explosion shook him, producing mental rapture, a new light, which seemed to pour from all directions, 'the whole universe falling into pattern like the stray pieces of a jigsaw puzzle assembled by magic at one stroke' (Koestler, 1951, p. 32). This is all in strong contrast with the 'tortured' past, full of doubts, conflicts, and confusion, 'the tasteless, colourless world of those who don't know'. The only link with the past is the fear of 'losing faith again, losing thereby what alone makes life worth living, and falling back into the outer darkness, where there is wailing and gnashing of teeth'.

Van der Leeuw (1964, p. 533) finds great similarity in the conversion experiences of all religions: 'a second self stands over against the first: a completely new life begins: everything has become different'. This was also true according to him for certain initiation experiences whether of primitive negroes or Hellenistic Greeks. All initiates were new men with new names (p. 531) who looked upon themselves as different and were treated as such. In order to emphasize the new life, the death of the old man was sometimes very vividly re-enacted in primitive religions. In some, neophytes were buried under branches in newly dug graves, where they had to remain motionless for days. In others the initiates were actually tortured and mutilated (Eliade, 1967, p. 198) to stress the dying of the old self.

In all these instances, the old identity is forcibly obliterated and emotionally defused, in order that a new identity can come to fruition. This may be called by many names: 're-orientation of the soul of an individual' (Nock, 1933, p. 7); 'redefinition of a patient (in psychoanalysis) from a new standpoint' (Burke, 1955); 'personal reorganization brought about by identification with the new group and its values' (O'Dea, 1966, p. 62); or 'mystical regeneration' (Eliade, 1967, p. 199). There are slight conceptual differences underlying these formulations, that are for our purposes unimportant.

The mechanism of conversion also reveals an underlying similarity in a great variety of cultures and ages. First there is detachment from former patterns of identity. 'And You set me there before my own face that I might see how vile I was, how twisted and unclean and spotted and ulcerous. I saw myself and was horrified; but there was no way to flee from myself' (Augustine, 1945, p. 134). At the meetings of Alcoholics Anonymous, members repeatedly witness about the damage they did to their jobs and families because of alcoholism. In psychotherapeutic sessions, the patient is always encouraged to dig into the unconscious and to unearth from the past even the most painful episodes, as the analyst believes that an articulation of these episodes is necessary for a more successful personality reintegration. The Chinese communists who brainwashed the American civilian prisoners had to first 'unfreeze' the existing personality equilibrium in order to give change in motivation a chance (Schein, 1961, p. 119). Unfreezing consists in mobilizing guilt, repetitive confessions, and reviews of the past. The stripping process always involves a loosening of previous allegiances (Strauss, 1959, p. 123) and a mortification of self (Goffman, 1960, p. 454).

The next stage is the never-never situation of meaninglessness and anomie. The individual is neither here nor there. Old beliefs and orientations are on the verge of vanishing and a new focus of identity has not yet taken its place. 'Nothing is more anxiety-producing than uncertainty' (Frank, 1961, p. 32). There is a vacuum resulting either from the confluence of circumstances or from manipulative techniques, as in the physical exhaustion of tribal dances and ritual; the emotional exhortation of revival preachers; the probings of psychiatrists; or the withdrawal of trusted people by communist brainwashers. This period of indecision and instability is highly disturbing and disconcerting. Confusion increases suggestibility (ibid., p. 159).

The contrast with the next stage is so great, that converts in their recollections speak about a flash of light, a sudden sound, an overwhelming warmth. In this stage, this attachment to the new focus of identity occurs. If the previous stages were manipulated, the new attachment is greatly strengthened by the reference group.

'The sympathetic support of other people is a crucial part of all conversions' (Shibutani, 1961, p. 528). The initiated of the tribe surround and comfort the initiate. The Christian believers praise the Lord together with the convert. The members of Synanon (former drug addicts) or Alcoholics Anonymous give time and effort unstintingly to neophytes. Gurus guide psychedelic trips and Chinese brainwashers and their fellow-believers benevolently shower their converted victims with affection. The psychotherapist provides the well-behaving patient with the acceptance he craves.

The process of conversion sometimes becomes a substitute for the new identity. The two may become so closely associated with one another that the conversion experience as such is looked upon as sacred. The more communicable or visible aspect of the experience becomes the symbol for relationship to the new faith. The process of change itself is sacralized rather than the goal to which change leads. Because it made this point clear, William Sargant's *Battle for the Mind* (1963) was sometimes regarded as an atheistic plot against which the evangelicals in Protestant Christianity had to defend themselves (Mol, 1969, p. 33).

It should be granted that charisma and conversion are important mechanisms which consolidate change. Without them, the forces of marginality and rationality could have been a liability rather than an asset for human survival. Even so, their actual contribution lies not in the mechanism as such, but in their contribution to the consolidation and integration of assumptive worlds, now better attuned to changed situations.

SUMMARY

Charisma on the social, and conversion at the personal, level are examples of the strength of the forces leading to identity formation. Strong emotional efforts and much psychic energy go into the stripping of one pattern and into the welding of another one that is more suited to the conditions of societies, groups, and individuals.

Both charisma and conversion are means by which religions continue to integrate, even though the results of their operation are recurrently neutralized by the forces of adaptation and differentiation. Those religions in the past which did not develop these mechanisms (such as the religions of Greece and Rome) did not survive.

If Western Christianity sometimes appears inept and behind the times, it is more often because it attempts to sacralize change as such than because it hides itself in obsolete patterns of identity. Of course, the latter tendency is not altogether foreign to those sections of Christianity that have a stake in the maintenance of the status quo. However, the war cry to adjust is often a surrender to the very forces which keep religious organizations in this in-between stage of instability and confusion.

It is true that sectarian religion, together with Marxist, psychoanalytical and other group-therapeutical conversion techniques, continues to battle for pertinent forms of identity. It is also true that, in comparison, mainstream Christianity seems rather lethargic in this battle. Still the entire Judaeo-Christian-Islamic tradition (and not just their sects) has a rather enviable historical record of vitality, capacity for absorption, and depth of understanding of the human condition. Its present-day confusions and altercations remind one of the forlorn, anxiety-ridden poker player who holds a respectable number of aces.

Chapter V

The Fragile Frame of Identity

The relations between the forces of adaptation (differentiation, change) and the forces of identity (integration, consolidation) oscillate. In (human) history man's need for a sense of identity, a stable niche in a predictable environment, has been both crucial and yet precarious. The precariousness of human identity has led man repeatedly to wrap it in 'don't touch' sentiments.

There are as many definitions and uses of the word 'identity' as there are theories employing it (de Levita, p. 3). Erikson, who has made the concept into the cornerstone for his theoretical model (to him it has the same strategic importance sexuality had for Freud), confesses that the more he writes about it, 'the more the word becomes a term as unfathomable as it is all pervasive' (Erikson, 1963, p. 282; 1968, p. 9). A social psychologist who uses the term as his main organizing concept calls it ambiguous and diffuse and, 'fully as elusive as is everyone's sense of his own identity' (Strauss, 1959, p. 9). Although this may seem as a crushing indictment to those whose faith in scientific watertight compartments is boundless, those of us who recognize that there is nothing absolute about one's categories of analysis, and that every classification contains implicit hypotheses, can accept the large variety of uses. Judgement about a particular usage cannot be postponed indefinitely, however, and must depend on its explanatory power for the wider field of investigation. Avoiding the Eriksonian and Straussian uncertainties, we shall try to clarify our use of the concept by contrasting it with other usages.

In its literal derivative sense of 'absolute sameness', identity is nowadays used only by mathematicians and logicians. In the older literature it is generally linked with consciousness. Locke related the concept to the thinking, intelligence, and reflection of a person, but this in turn could be summed up as 'consciousness', which, he said, 'makes personal identity'. On the same page he also described it as 'the sameness of a rational being' (Locke, 1801, Vol. II, p. 52; Book II, Chap. 27, paras. 9–10). For Leibnitz, too, personal identity consisted in the consciousness of the thinking self: this consciousness was evidence for (the existence of) moral and personal identity (Leibniz, 1961, Vol. I, p. 405). For Kant (1965, p. 343), only that of which we were conscious belonged to our identical self, although he warned that identity was not an objective property of the observing self. A related emphasis on self-awareness is found in Kierkegaard's view of identity (1941, pp. 112, 299), in Jaspers (1963, p. 125) and in Bronowski (1965).

Philosophers have continued to think about identity in terms of such questions as 'When Mr. Brown's brain is successfully grafted into Mr. Robinson's head, is Mr. Robinson still Mr. Robinson?' (Wiggins, p. 50). 'Is the river into which I step at two separate occasions, still the same river?' (Herbst, p. 159). Heidegger, however, seems to have gone much beyond the earlier formulations. He questions the principle of identity as a principle of thinking (Heidegger, 1969, p. 25). Instead he links identity with the Being of beings, a fundamental characteristic of which is the unity within itself, a belonging together. Generally in existential literature the word 'being' is often used where we prefer 'identity'; and 'becoming' where we think 'change' is more appropriate. The same applies to the Sanskrit *Sat* which is usually translated by 'being' (Arapura, 1974, p. 1), but which has interesting connotations of identity as a taken-for-granted reality and of concomitant motivations and sacralizations of that identity.

From the vantage point of the social sciences in the latter half of the twentieth century, it can be seen that the concept has changed since the early definitions. It has almost made a full turn about. To us, rationality has a toxic potential and consciousness or awareness of the self, we feel, does not automatically lead to the integration of the self. To us, identity is a taken-for-granted, rather than a reflected-upon phenomenon. To us, identity is often sacralized by commitment and ritual rather than by observation and analysis, and we feel that this is a major reason why the principal religions of the world have tended to say that a person would find his identity 'not by accentuating and concentrating on his ego, but by losing, subduing, or denying it' (Klapp, 1969, p. 326). In psychoanalytic circles there is similarly an admittedly still feeble realization that at least some reflections about the self are pathological (de Levita, p. 159).

Jung and religious mystics maintain that to find a higher, non-personal identity, it may be necessary to avoid thought and wilful choice (Klapp, p. 35). Goldmann (p. 48) even goes so far as to say that it is the sick organ which creates awareness.

The modern psychological views of identity began with William James. To him the consciousness of personal identity reposed in the sense of sameness (James, 1890, Vol. I, p. 459), and arises from the resemblance and continuity of our feelings (p. 336) rather than of facts. This would not differ greatly from Kant's formulations were James not to include within 'consciousness', the experiences of the individual, and within 'feelings', such matters as self-esteem and recognition by others.

Erikson further developed the social aspect of identity. 'The term identity . . . connotes both a persistent sameness within oneself (self-sameness) and a persistent sharing of some kind of essential character with others' (1960, p. 30). This persistent sameness within oneself can be conscious, but there is also an unconscious striving for continuity of personal character (1960, p. 51; 1968, p. 208). The persistent sharing with others involves an inner solidarity with a group's ideals and identity. Erikson is aware of the importance of collective identity as separate from personal identity. If, as with the Sioux Indians whom he studied, the basis for collective identity formation is denied, the 'reservoir of collective integrity from which the individual must derive his stature as a social being' is also in jeopardy (1963, p. 154). There are kinds of collective identities, however (such as class, nation, culture), which Erikson likes and which he therefore regards as leading to true identity, and others (such as extreme nationalism, racism or class consciousness) which he dislikes and which he calls 'synthetic identities' (1964, p. 93). The former emphasize wholeness (a sound, organic, progressive mutuality between diversified functions and parts within an entirety, the boundaries of which are open and fluent); the latter stress totality (given a certain arbitrary delineation, nothing that belongs inside must be left outside, nothing that must be outside can be tolerated inside) (1964, p. 92). One can share Erikson's private values (and similar ones of those social psychologists who worked on the authoritarian personality) without feeling compelled to cloak them with scientific categories such as true and synthetic. For it is quite reasonable to suggest that it is precisely the boundary (any boundary—of the Boy Scout Movement, a monastic community, the American

Way of Life, the Ku Klux Klan or the John Birch Society) which provides the sense of identity, and which has the desired integrative effects irrespective of the 'truth' of the identity focus. It is also reasonable to suggest that precisely when, through economic, military, political, or other disruptions (for example the Weimar Republic), one set of boundaries for a national identity lose their viability, a new countervailing set (Nazism) will prove their viability by overstressing exclusiveness. In other words, 'wholeness', in Erikson's terminology, may have structural weaknesses which lead to 'totality' and vice versa, but an analysis of these functions and structures is endangered by an irrelevant value distinction. If scientific categories are spawned by value judgements they are likely to stand in the way of an understanding of the very situation which produced these judgements.

This is also true for another pair of concepts which Erikson uses: identity-diffusion (comparable to an excessive other-directedness), and identity-foreclosure (which I interpret to mean the refusal to integrate new events and experiences in a given identity) (Stein, 1960, p. 19). What diffusion and foreclosure consist of, in concrete terms, very much depends on a particular society and the values of a specific psychoanalyst. But behind it all (and certainly of more general interest) is again the problem of boundaries for identity formation. I suggest that what occurs in all societies is that bulwarks are erected around personal and group identities, and that only in highly advanced technological/democratic societies does the problem of over-choice and consequent indeterminacy of a given focus of identity arise. Simultaneously, in these societies, there is likely to be an artificial guarding and overprotection of whatever centre has been arrived at: the word 'foreclosure' is a good term for this phenomenon. However, it is only in societies such as the U.S.A. that the finding of an ever-changing balance between the stability and flexibility of one's identity becomes a major psychological enterprise. A comprehensive theory of how personal or group identity is formed and maintained on the other hand should be cross-cultural. This means that we reject the true/synthetic or diffused/foreclosed dichotomy as useful for a general theory of identity, however much the distinctions illustrate the predicament of particular societies where boundaries of group identity have become threadbare or where over-choice makes them precarious. We also reject Erikson's view of religion as a source of ideologies for those who seek identities

(Erikson, 1962, p. 20). Yet this disagreement is only a matter of definition. If one uses religion in the wide sense in which we are using it, any sacralized ideology is a religion, and religion sacralizes *any* identity. If, however, one uses religion in a restricted sense, e.g. of a specific organization, it indeed becomes one possible choice amongst others. Our problem of course is that there are no separate words for these two usages of the word 'religion'. Occasionally we too have used the word in the restricted sense. We could have made use of an artificial device such as calling religion in the wide sense 'religion$_1$' and in the specific sense, 'religion$_2$'. Generally the context will make clear in what sense the word is used, and we have minimized the confusion by often describing 'religion$_2$' as religious organization, universal religion, sectarian religion, etc.

Identity is approached in yet a different way by a group of scholars who see it as a product of interaction with others in social groups. Foremost amongst them are the social psychologists. To Strauss, everyone sees himself in the mirrors of judgements of others, and a particular brand of mask or identity is fashioned by an anticipation of these judgements (Strauss, 1959, p. 9). To Berger and Luckmann, identity is a phenomenon that emerges from the dialectic between individual and society (1967, p. 174). Yet they also occasionally use it in the more acceptable sense of 'a definite, stable and socially recognized identity', or as anchored 'in a cosmic reality protected from both the contingencies of socialization and the malevolent self-transformations of marginal experience' (1967, p. 118). Soddy, presenting the materials of the Conference on Identity of the World Federation for Mental Health in 1957, defines identity 'as an anchorage of the self to the social matrix', but feels that this definition should stress more fully the reciprocity of the relationship (1961, p. 4). Klapp (1969, p. 39) refers to identity as 'a functioning system of three variables: (1) what a person thinks about himself introspectively, (2) what he projects or sees imaged or accepted in the eyes of others (his social identity); and (3) his feelings validated when "real to me" and when shared with others'.

There are two problems with these definitions. They stress interaction too much and the framework which makes this interaction possible too little. Most social psychologists tend to think of identity as the conglomeration of roles which are the product of social expectations and personal response. What we have in mind, however, is the stable setting in which these exchanges can successfully take place, and which by definition is more enduring than a galaxy of roles and phases of maturation.

We therefore have more sympathy for those who think of identity as 'the most essential nucleus of man which becomes visible only after all his roles have been laid aside' (de Levita, p. 131), or as Wheelis (p. 200) has it: 'Identity is founded . . . on those values which are at the top of the hierarchy—the beliefs, faiths, and ideals which integrate and determine subordinate values' (p. 200). Bellah's definition (1965, p. 173) of identity as 'a statement of what a person or a group is essentially, and, as it were, permanently', is also much more acceptable. Christian too uses identity in this sense, as e.g. in 'These shrines correspond to levels on which the people form a community, or have a sense of identity (nation, region, province, vale, village, barriada)' (1972, p. xii).

Another problem with the social psychological set of definitions is their emphasis on close interdependence of personal and social identity, at the expense of the potential and actual conflict between them. The stability and continuity of the social order have repeatedly been undermined by the 'id' forces of the individual, around which personal identity could rather naturally crystallize. And the other way round: personal identity and the flowering of individual creativity and independence have often been grievously inhibited by monolithic social forces. The point is not that there is no reciprocity between personal and social identity. On the contrary: religious organizations have often tenaciously survived precisely because of their significance in the interaction and the interdependence of society and individuals. However, for a full picture neither their failures nor their successes in resolving these conflicts should be overlooked. If they are overlooked, and a predominant social psychological view prevails, man will appear too exclusively as a manipulator of roles and a manager of impressions rather than as the rebel brought to heel by a society which insists that he *is* good instead of only appearing to be that way (Mol, 1971c, p. 222).

Partly because of this conflict between personal and social identity or because of the predicament of modern society, where 'neither ego nor superego can be confident of control of the id forces' (as Ruitenbeek, p. 10, has it), identity is rather fragile and constantly in need of protection. How fragile it is can often be best understood if one 'thinks away' whatever a person or a society takes for granted. This is not easily done, and it may be impossible to do it for one's own society. Even the few sentences of this paragraph take for granted a whole universe of thought connections which in turn rest on the slowly accumulated tradition of Western civilization.

It is somewhat less difficult to 'think away' whatever primitive or non-Western societies take for granted. One has a different perspective—a different bias in approaching it. A good example are rites of magic. If magic did not exist in those societies what would happen? Or what function do they actually have? From the Western point of view it was only natural to regard these rites originally as erroneous science. More thorough anthropological research has now led to the conclusion that an important function is their capacity to improve confidence and to reduce anxiety, fear, and doubt about having made the best choice among the available alternatives (Wallace, 1966, pp 173–5). Similarly with witchcraft. The same strongly held beliefs that man's identity consisted in the sameness of his consciousness and rationality made scholars presume that witchcraft was just an aberration of the less advanced, irrational, mind. But closer investigation has shown that it prevails particularly 'when people must interact with one another on important matters in the absence of legitimated social controls and arrangements' (Swanson, 1966, p. 151). We can say the same in our terminology: the rites of magic and witchcraft make one's place in the configuration of social and physical forces less fragile.

Other examples of the fragility of identity and of the religious attempts to strengthen the fragile frame are furnished by specific rather influential, sociological theories of religion. Some sociologists have seen religion as the response to the brute facts of contingency (the uncertainty context), powerlessness (superordination and subordination in the relations of men) and scarcity (frustration and deprivation) (O'Dea, 1966, p. 5). Weber (1964, p. 113) finds that a theodicy of disprivilege is always in some form 'a component of every salvation religion which draws its adherents primarily from the disprivileged classes'. Nietzsche postulates that all great religions 'counteract a certain epidemic malaise due to unreleased tension' 1956, p. 267). Berger says that theodicy 'constitutes an essentially sado-masochistic collusion on the level of meaning, between oppressors and victims' (1967a, p. 59) and that the sufferings of the Black Death and the social displacements of the Industrial Revolution issued 'in a number of violent millenarian movements' (p. 68).

All these theories regard specific existential problems as closely related to types and functions of religious belief, or even as their causes. These ideas can be subsumed more comprehensively in the generalization that there is a tendency for personal and social identity to become sacralized and that this is particularly so when changes, upheavals, injustices, and uncertainties make a specific identity both fragile and precarious.

Contrary to the approaches mentioned above, the larger theory also has the advantages of being able to account for religious behaviour when problems are less obvious or when the affluent, educated, and urbanized baffle the atheists by religious propensities. An example of a case that does not easily fit into other theories is that of intellectuals who undergo severe identity crises. A sense of aimlessness has gripped them and is re-enacted often effectively in the theatre of the absurd. Still the sublimation of deep-seated problems achieved by the best of novels and plays of the absurd is in itself strong evidence for man's overarching desire to fit these experiences of meaninglessness into a composite picture that permits him to 'cope', 'endure', or 'resign' more serenely. It is through sublimation that these experiences of meaninglessness become more meaningful. Play through re-enactment, art through sublimation, and religion through sacralization, all in their various ways contribute to the strengthening of the fragile frame of identity. How intellectuals are more likely to suffer from identity problems is beautifully brought out in the story of the intellectual Nerzhin in Solzhenitsyn's *First Circle*, who drinks up the autobiographical story of the semi-literate Spiridon. The taken-for-granted, solidly established, identity of the latter is a source of inspiration for the former who has vainly sought similar integrity and genuineness. How religion can have a similar effect in intellectuals becomes clear when one compares T. S. Eliot's first major poem *The Wasteland*, recording his sense of dereliction and lack of meaning, with the *Four Quartets* which he wrote after his conversion to Christianity. It would be rather difficult to 'explain' Eliot's conversion in terms of the theories outlined above. However, it makes sense if one postulates an innate search for the kind of identity which best fits a specific situation of time and tradition, and if one further postulates that the fragility of any of these possible foci of identity is an important impetus for providing it with a strong emotional anchorage.

A third advantage of the larger theory is that it minimizes the justified objections of religious practitioners that so many theories about religion assume naïve anachronisms or puerile projections. These religionists accept the view that religion defines man and his place in the universe which is essentially what we are also maintaining. The premise that to reinforce a specific identity (what is what religious practitioners do) leads to greater sanity than to observe and analyse other identities (as we do), which is affirmed in our larger theory, favours rather than disfavours any religious orientation. The observers of a specific religious orientation usually emphasize those variables that have an effect on religion, whereas practitioners of religion stress the factors upon which religion has had an effect. Observers tend to take religion as the dependent variable, the practitioners as the independent one. Any good sociological theory of religion and any good religious belief should have in common that they establish a close correlation between the system of interpretation and the data to be interpreted. Otherwise either or both will be irrelevant. If the data do not fit the theory, or conversely if the beliefs do not interpret man's world, both are irrelevant.

Lest it be presumed that the larger theory is primarily oriented towards Christianity, let it be said that in Hinduism, one of the world's oldest religions, the problem of identity has always been the fundamental question (Ross, 1953, p. ix), and its goal is for man fully to realize the identity of Brahman and to be reunited with his divine essence by means of Yoga (Needleman, 1970, p. 24). Almost any of its major tenets can be analysed in terms of the counterbalancing function it has for the various fragilities in the frame of identity.

One does not always have to 'think away' what is taken for granted to discover the fragility of identity. Often personal or group identities actually collapse after contact with a different civilization. What was taken for granted has now become debatable. One's religious orientation provides less of a 'fit', and is even questioned. And so Natsume Soseki, the modern Japanese novelist, speaks of the spiritual breakdown of Japan; Hasanal Banna, founder of the Muslim Brotherhood, decries the spiritual disintegration in Cairo after World War I; and an 'Indonesian intellectual, Soedjatmoko, speaks of a crisis of identity', all following contact with the modern world (Bellah, 1970, p. 65).

However, within the technologically advanced Western societies, one can also observe just how fragile the niche is. Here the rebelliousness of the young is more than just an inter-generational problem.

The older generation is accused of leaving behind an unhinged world in which there are no reliable reference points. What has been handed down, say the young, is an indigestible mixture of largely instrumental values (how to be successful in achieving concrete goals) with a few spiritual sops for those weaklings who cannot do without them. What they miss is a stable context for any action or value that rises above the merely acquisitive and technical. And so they proclaim an overarching faith in the power of love and a preference for quality over quantity. To them ecology and the poor are more important than highways and moon exploration. The niche they want to occupy consists of integrative rather than instrumental values. Emotional anchorage is preferred to technological progress. All the elements that in the past made for economic progress (the profit motive, rational calculation, the interplay of power, and ambition) take second place to such elements as the common good, understanding of others, and freedom of expression.

The International Youth Conference on the Human Environment, held at McMaster University, Canada, in 1971, advocated a people—rather than profit—orientation. It declared itself against military technology and for a re-ordering of priorities so that innate ecological characteristics and human needs would come first, with economic assessments second, and technological feasibility last (Hailstone, p. 22).

These movements make it clear that the specific patterns of identity of the previous generation are fragile and tend also to be obsolete, primarily because, in the final resort, instrumental values conflict with an adequate integration of self and society. Often a nostalgia for the security of the square world can be detected in these movements, but this arises from the search for a new basis of identity which occurs simultaneously with the demand for a break with the past, which destroys existing traditional forms. All this leads to the further liquefying of an already fluid sense of identity, thereby increasing anxiety. This process has been aptly summed up in the title of Klapp's very perceptive and informative book, *The Collective Search for Identity*. To Klapp (p. 329), identity problems creep up like air pollution in advanced technological society, but he also observes that cults are often the natural response for this search (pp. 139–45).

Erikson links the identity crisis of youth with specific biographical events, although he is not unaware that 'conditions of economic, ethnic and religious marginality provide poor bases for positive identities' and indeed can lead to a negative identity (1960, p. 85). Adolescents, he says, prefer a negative identity to no identity at all (1968, pp. 83–4), but to him this identification with asocial gangs and groups is both malignant and pathological. Even so, this negative identity of some modern youth may also have its functions. On the personal level, to be strongly against something can also integrate the personality, particularly when there is social support (through a deviant group) for the stance. Radical protests against the basic structure of modern industrial societies may also have the important latent function of restoring the balance between integration and adaptation. One would be hard put to call this malignant and pathological.

SUMMARY

Identity on the personal level is the stable niche that man occupies in a potentially chaotic environment which he is therefore prepared vigorously to defend. Similarly, on the social level, a stable aggregate of basic and commonly held beliefs, patterns, and values maintains itself over against the potential threat of its environment and its members. 'Consciousness' and 'awareness' are less central to the usage of the concept than 'boundaries'.

Personal and social identity very much depend on one another, but there are also numerous possibilities for conflict between the two. Even so, conflict is only one of many reasons for the fragility of the frame of identity. Death, diffidence, conquests, economic disasters, injustice, and, in modern societies, an excessive emphasis on instrumental values, relativization, and over-choice of identity foci are some of these other reasons.

Art, play, and sacralization are all means to strengthen the fragile frame of identity. Various theories have attempted to account for religious behaviour and phenomena, but all of them fall short of comprehending the admittedly heterogeneous field. Of course, by attempting to be more comprehensive there is the constant danger that one's organizing principle becomes fuzzy and elusive. This disadvantage may, however, be balanced by the potential for theoretical reconstruction and interpretative innovation of our identity frame of reference.

Chapter VI

Kindred Concepts and Relevance

The concepts that sociologists and psychologists use to make sense of religious phenomena are all related to one another. It should therefore come as no surprise that strong links exist between identity as used here and such terms as integration, interpretation of reality, meaning, order, and security. All deal with what we have called the identity as over against the differentiation perspective: they deal with what unifies rather than what separates. The major reason why we prefer identity is its connotation with boundary and place.

Human beings want 'to locate themselves in a "system", a "universe", a "process" transcending the immediate give-and-take between the individual and his environment' (Brinton, 1958, p. 11). Or, as Gabrielle Roy (p. 35) has it about Alexandre Chenevert, the cashier, in her novel of that name: 'He had entered the savings bank and there he had stayed, as almost all human beings tend to stay once they have found a safe refuge.' The German poet, Rilke (Laing, 1971, p. 134), puts it, if anything, more strongly when he says: 'Where you are, there arises a place.'

Inevitably this place is bounded and the more precarious the place is, the more essential boundaries become. Boundaries also serve to provide humans with 'images of limits and restraints, if only to help us grasp what we are transcending' (Lifton, p. xii). This is as true for groups and societies as it is for individuals. 'Boundaries define a group, set it off from its environment, and give it a sharp focus, which facilitates commitment' (Kanter, p. 169). Religious organizations have traditionally reinforced these places and boundaries. In Northern Spain, Christian (p. 99) observes: 'The more clear-cut the sociographic unit, the sharper its boundaries, then the more likely it was to have a cultural symbol, a protector, a patron in a shrine image.'

Yet there are instances (which we discuss in the chapters on identity foci) when the concept of *integration* is more appropriate because the unification under discussion has little to do with simultaneous delineation. Admittedly this is more the exception than the rule, particularly in modern societies. However, even the identity of a primitive tribe with no outside contact whatsoever has a distinct outline. It is a construct and a system in no-construct and no-system. However, we may concentrate discussion on what unifies a system from within, rather than what separates it from without.

Durkheim (1951, 1954 and 1964) did this, and consequently the term 'integration', or whatever reaffirmed collective sentiments, emerged as a major organizing principle in his work. Anomie (the state of normlessness and social disorganization) was to him the exact opposite of integration. Anomie decreased the bonds of a moral community, while integration was another name for the centripetal forces that strengthened those bonds. Religious ritual pre-eminently united individuals to their groups. That this very integrating force could simultaneously have consequences of distantiation, or might even imply conflict with other groups, was not one of Durkheim's major concerns. To us this is important and we therefore use identity and integration according to whether maintenance or unification needs to be stressed.

An agreed-upon and commonly held *interpretation of reality* is a prerequisite for social identity. It is also the constructive link with personal identity. From birth, the individual is persistently and unwittingly socialized into specific appraisals of his surroundings. What is 'real' to people is, in the final resort, whatever previous generations defined as real. It is a construct in the face of a shapeless nothing. It is a perspective both crucial and precarious, and is therefore surrounded by buttresses. It postulates coherence between phenomena. However reality is *not* independently given—something man's laborious search for knowledge can gradually unfold, visualize, and clarify.

Naïve realism ('the literal representation of the world, a reproduction of objective reality as it is in itself', Barbour, p. 35) was the article of faith of many scholars and philosophers up to the second half of the twentieth century. It is now increasingly demoted as one perspective among others. Modern physics regards the atomic world as 'not only inaccessible to direct observation and inexpressible in terms of the senses', but even beyond imagination (ibid., p. 157-8).

The postulation of a taken-for-granted objective reality has indubitable advantages for the progress of science. To many it has become the sacred legitimation of the entire scientific enterprise, and thereby guarantees its progress. The guarantee is all the more safe if the postulate is allowed to become an act of faith, a source of commitment, a universal and exclusive definition of reality, an eternal truth. Yet the fact that the sacralization of the postulate has this advantageous effect does not therefore oblige us to become its worshipper. Unless we relativize this sacralization pattern as well, we do even more injustice than we already and inevitably do to the other religious beliefs that we wish to analyse. It is for this reason that we agree with Winch (1971, p. 81) when he criticizes Evans-Pritchard and Pareto for regarding 'the conception of "reality" as intelligible and applicable outside the context of scientific reasoning itself'. The anthropologist Castaneda (1972, pp. 9, 14) had to break the dogmatic certainty of his scientific perception of reality in order to do justice to his analysis of the world of sorcery of Don Juan.

There is no such thing as uninterpreted reality. Religious beliefs and rituals met and meet the need for order and identity by providing specific interpretations of reality. The macrofunction of religion is the 'symbolic affirmation of social reality' (de Waal Malefijt, p. 359) or as Geertz (1968, p. 98) says: '. . . religious patterns . . . are frames of perception, symbolic screens through which experience is interpreted . . . blueprints for conduct'.

The concept of reality definition, however, relates generally to socialization and symbolic interaction, and is therefore less suitable for dealing with boundary conflicts of established or emerging personal and social foci of identity. Because of its emphasis on interpretation and cognition it leads generally to disregard of man's biological nature. It is therefore a narrower concept than 'identity' which we wish to employ when we have in mind a stable niche in a whole complex of physiological, psychological, and sociological patterns of interaction. We use it interchangeably with identity only when we deal with symbolic interaction and cognitive interpretation. (For the use of the concept, see Berger and Luckmann, 1967. Also Holzner.)

Some of these remarks similarly apply to *meaning*. I don't have in mind 'meaning' in the sense of the meaning of a word by itself (in German: *Bedeutung*), but meaning in the sense of the place a word or event has in a given context (in German: *Sinn*—see for the distinction Nygren, 1972, p. 230). John Dewey and Ernest Becker (p. 183) use the term in this way: the connection of events and objects in an interdependent, self-consistent scheme.

Like the concept of identity, meaning is rather diffuse. Some (Nygren, p. 169) regard the concept as 'too open'. Like identity, meaning deals with taken-for-granted interpretations. Weber, for whom this concept was particularly important, postulates a basic need on the part of man to eliminate meaninglessness of any kind. Whatever happened had to make sense, he thought, and consequently meaning is attributed to events in continually more 'ultimate' reference points (Weber, 1946, pp. 351–4; Weber, 1964a, p. 99; Parsons, 1964b, pp. xlv–xlix). This leads to either a progressively greater extension of the time span (Karma and Hinduism) or to the assumption of an inherently destined creation (Christianity). Meaning to Weber was primarily the answer to 'why' questions. Identity as we use it refers to a stable frame of reference for both the 'what' and the 'why' of existence. There is also a sense of emotional anchorage in the concept that 'meaning' does not ordinarily carry. The latter leans more towards the cognitive perception of phenomena. Another advantage of identity over meaning for our purposes is its greater comprehensiveness. It includes the identity of animal species, for instance. If, in this book, 'system of meaning' is used instead of identity, it is often when both the exigencies of style demand it, and when there is less emphasis on boundary and more on belief. It is easier to say, for example, that rites act out a system of meaning than that they act out an identity.

A concept which the Javanese borrowed from India, and which combines both meaning and identity, is *rasa*. It means both 'feeling' and 'meaning' and is best translated with 'identity' in some passages from religious literature where it refers to the feeling for one's native country, or to the Jews, who were exiled from their own country, but kept their *rasa*. It conveys an underlying feeling of unity with existence, an emotional place and a subjective experience 'to which everything else can be tied' (Geertz, 1969, pp. 238, 239, 334).

Both animals and human beings have a strong proclivity for *order* (Lorenz, p. 60; Erikson, 1963, p. 268). Habit has a species-preserving function for animals. For human beings order is even more important because the adaptiveness of their symbol systems has by implication a greater potential for disruption. Naturally, what, concretely, order consists of, differs from culture to culture.

The *prijaji* (Javanese cultural elite) are convinced that animals (and many non-prijajis as well) don't know order, because they do not have the formality of bearing, the restraint of expression, and bodily self-discipline (Geertz, 1969, p. 247). But in other cultures spontaneity is not necessarily seen as always a threat to social discipline and, by implication, order. Plays and art forms are good examples of the ways order is reinforced. Huizinga (p. 29) even insists that play creates order and *is* order. Through sacralization religions do the same.

In early Hinduism the concept of *rta* refers to both a cosmic and moral order. In later Hinduism this word was replaced by *Dharma* emphasizing man's supporting role of the cosmic and moral order. 'It can mean the principle of eternal order, the good society for which men should strive, the laws governing society, or the moral energy with which an individual relates himself to his universe. . . . *Dharma* refers to order as it is manifest in all these forms' (Younger, pp. 34, 35).

In many religions (both primitive and modern) order and chaos are continually contrasted. Paradise or Heaven represents undifferentiated order and wholeness. The Fall represents the situation when this order cannot be taken for granted any longer. The potential for evil, or whatever disrupts, is real, but God's creation once for all, or God's offer of salvation now, minimizes chaos because in God's existence and action, order is summed up. In the rites of some primitive religions (for example those of the Oraons of Central India) chaos is re-entered symbolically and confusion is re-enacted in order all the more to assure its opposite (Eliade, 1967, p. 186, interprets the example somewhat differently). To Berger, chaos is the oldest antagonist of the sacred. It is an all-embracing sacred order which reinforces the solidarity of every human society in the ever-present face of chaos (Berger, 1967a, pp. 39, 51). To Firth, religious beliefs represent man's attempt to order his universe of relations (1964, pp. 258, 259). Similarly to Horton (1970, p. 134), 'gods serve to introduce unity into diversity, simplicity into complexity, order into disorder, regularity into anomaly'. To Nadel (1946, p. 34), 'religion offers, in whatever disguise, the certainty of a physical and moral order'.

It is obvious that the proclivity of man and society for order is closely intertwined with the need for identity. Identity presumes the sameness of order. The stable frame of reference, the chronological and spatial continuity of identity, are all basically derived from, or certainly strongly advanced by, the veneration of order and abhorrence of chaos. Identity, however, has the advantage of drawing the attention to a crucial delineation of concrete forms of order, and to the conflict that disorder produces when these delineations are eroded by competing 'forms of order' operating equally under the internal driving force of maximum integration.

Security is the vaguest and most ambiguous of terms in this group of kindred concepts. It straddles an entire universe of personal and social motives. The lack of popularity of the term in the scientific analysis of religion seems to be compensated by its prominence in the literature written by and for believers. Amongst the observers of religion, Radin appears to see a closer link between economic insecurity and religion than others. To him religious feelings are compensation fantasies of the struggle for existence in an insecure physical and social environment. To say that religion permeates every phase of primitive culture is really saying that the struggle for existence permeates every phase of life there (Radin, 1957, pp. 5, 8, 40, 192), but there are dangers in thinking about religion in terms of compensation fantasies for economic insecurity.

The first is the premature exhaustion of theory, leaving many cases unexplained. Present-day American society is a good example of the data not fitting the theory. One does not have to accept Philip Slater's eccentric and ethnocentric theories that seek to explain basic changes in American value priorities by changes in scarcity (Slater, 1971, pp. 83, 90–1, 106–7, 180) to agree with the implication that there is very little left of the struggle for existence which struck Radin in primitive societies. Nevertheless, it is precisely amongst the privileged that one can find an extraordinary collection of cults, sects, and religions.

The second danger is that the forces leading to greater economic security through better adaptation to the environment (better tools, more efficient production methods) tend to conflict with the forces consolidating identity (such as religion). There are many examples of primitive cultures and religions disintegrating as the direct result of a new technology. This means that we have to be doubly careful with the use of the term, because one kind of security can lead to its opposite in another kind. The term is appropriate only when we deal with the most basic motive for evolutionary progress. Man's security hinges on both better adaptation to his environment and on consolidation of the gain. But either force can lead to destruction of the other, making a perpetual redressing of the balance a prerequisite for survival. Only by a constant balancing act can the disadvantages, or the complex of dysfunctions, of either force be minimized and their advantages, or functions, maximized. For detailed analysis of this basic process the term 'security' is therefore too broad and ambiguous.

To be fair to Radin, however, he later somewhat inconsistently reinterprets his previous remarks by saying: 'religious beliefs and attitudes were assuredly not created either by methods of food production or by some mechanism or exchange. But they did grow up together with them, and it was the economic system that made certain constituents and certain forms of religion relevant at one period and others relevant to another' (pp. 40, 41). This one can agree with, as the relevance of religion is tied in with specific and concrete fragilities of the identity frame of reference. These fragilities may consist of a precarious economy at one time and of an over-choice of identity foci at another.

RELEVANCE

The previous paragraph has led us right into the heart of the relevance problem of modern religions. In the same way as there should be a close fit between data and theory, so too the relevance of any religious orientation depends on the fit of its interpretative frame of reference. Fit, or congruence, does not necessarily mean explicit similarity. A faithful and factual reconstruction of symptoms and events leading to death, disaster, or frustration is a far cry from fitting the event in a cosmic drama of good and evil. However, this cosmic drama may, by its very oppositeness, provide the better fit. It may provide the coherence, continuity, and emotional anchorage in time and space which the actual events have put into jeopardy. If this is so, the cosmic drama fits and the factual account is irrelevant.

Fit does not exclude otherness. On the contrary, it is precisely the otherness, rather than the factuality, which restores the jeopardized equilibrium. This is, I think, what Karl Barth (Barth, 1936, p. 160; Arapura, 1970, p. 153) had in mind when he wrote that it is God's otherness which is yet related to us. Relevance depends on the capacity for integration, rather than on the faithful representations of facts. But capacity for restoration and integration depends in turn on the fragilities of a specific identity frame being both recognized and accounted for. Religious forms can be relevant only when they grow together with the culture in which they find themselves, while at the same time remaining altogether different in order to perform their functions better. It is inevitable, therefore, that particular fragilities of particular times and cultures are prominently reflected in religious manifestations. But in all cultures, the essence of the religious function is to reinforce by sacralization personal, group, or social identity. The relevance of religious organizations should therefore be judged *both* in terms of the maintenance of otherness, a prerequisite for the execution of its essential function, *and* in terms of its sensitive reflection of the specific fragilities of a specific identity frame.

In successful or, at any rate, in surviving religions an implicit congruence is to be expected between the sacred abstractions and profane manifestations. At the same time the configuration of beliefs, rituals, and myths must be sufficiently separate, self-contained and stable successfully to absorb mundane threats to identity.

Max Weber used the words 'elective affinity' to indicate a relation of mutual adjustment of otherwise fairly independent units. He says that the strata of artisans and traders showed an elective affinity for active ascetic religions (1946, pp. 284, 285). One could similarly use 'elective affinity' to denote the congruence between totemic rituals and environmental risks, or between beliefs in the imminent end of the world order and disprivileged status in Western societies. (Clark, 1937; Wilson, 1961). Beliefs and rituals are both affected by, and in turn affect, concrete situations and the way they are regarded: they are relevant for one another.

Schisms are an interesting example of the pressure on religious organizations to be relevant. With the rise of independent nationhood, national churches split off from the universal mother church. In advanced pluralistic societies, with few impediments to organizational proliferation, the exclusion of those with different styles of life, different views on the slavery issue, or different preferences for the language of the sermon, made for greater homogeneity and relevance of new ecclesiastical forms, as in the nineteenth-century schisms in the U.S.A., dividing the major Protestant churches in separate Northern and Southern denominations. Thus the bitter controversy between German and English-speaking Lutheran churches resulted in separate branches and buildings. Thus, the tendency of local congregations in America was to become representative for one rather than a variety of life-styles. In all these examples, heterogeneity, particularly with respect to what were perceived to be basic girders in the group or within the social frame of identity, made place for homogeneity or like-mindedness. Organizational exclusion reinforced group identity, but often some latent reasons for schisms were hidden behind manifest doctrinal controversies. A good example was the ideological disputes about the addition of *filioque* (the Holy Spirit also proceeding 'from the Son') to the Creed, which was the ostensible source of schism between the Eastern and the Roman Church. Many scholars are convinced that the cultural differences between Hellenic East and Roman West was the more authentic reason (Niebuhr, 1957, p. 114).

If the Catholic Church managed to avoid many schisms, it was because it allowed considerable leeway to divergent expressions (the monastic orders) and national sentiments. As soon as these divergent and subsidiary forms of identity became visible to, or intertwined with, one another, the conflicts were difficult to settle. Towards the end of the nineteenth century, the movement to establish dioceses in the United States along national rather than geographical lines (Cahenslyism) came to nothing, primarily because, with the increasing Americanization of the immigrants and their children, the need for national churches decreased (Mol, 1961, p. 44). At any rate the Catholic Church, up till the 1960s, is an example *par excellence* of the enormous effort expended on the preservation of a unitary identity in the face of strong pressures to become relevant in terms of a different set of variables.

Schisms and religious conflicts are often regarded with regret by those sympathetic to Christianity, or with derision by its opponents. Both have falacious notions regarding the integrative, conflict-resolving functions of religious organizations. The identities that are sacralized vary profoundly from one culture or group to another. Their conflicts can often be resolved only by either their complete separation or their dissolution in a new larger commitment. But this means change and relativization of the existing identity which is the exact reversal of the sacralizing process.

Richard Niebuhr very much regrets the identification of religious organizations with class, nations, and racial lines of divisions (1957, pp. 264 ff.). But the universal brotherhood he advocates is only another frame of identity with different girders.

Talcott Parsons finds it difficult to justify religious resentment and the religious wars of the seventeenth century (1952, p. 18) but again these conflicts can be effectively analysed in terms of the boundary clashes between different frames of identity.

Bertrand Russell sneers at the distinction of Christianity to be more ready than other religions to persecute. He scoffs at the Christian fervour of the Crusades 'which led to pogroms in Western Europe' (Russell, 1964, p. 202). However the specific fragilities of the Christian frame of identity in those times made specific responses of defence and fervour more relevant than the open-minded tolerance which is the sacred element of Russell's system of beliefs, defended with commensurate fervour. The utopian fallacy in Russell's notions is that the fervent belief in open-minded tolerance is a regrettable contradiction and is potentially destructive of the very tolerance it seeks. More important is the simple-minded illusion, (a) that one value such as brotherly love (rather than a host of psychological, sociological, and other variables making for unique constellations of relevance in each instance) should and could always predominate; (b) that there is a straight line between this one ethical principle and its unambiguous implementation; and (c) that rational open-mindedness rather than fervour can be the binding force for group and social identity. All these assumptions are profoundly questionable.

We have already said that the relevance of religious organizations should be judged *both* in terms of the maintenance of otherness; a prerequisite for the execution of its essential function (we may call this relevance A); and in terms of its sensitive reflection of the specific fragilities of a specific identity frame (relevance B). The reason for labelling both facets is the need for shorthand terms in the analysis of the present-day problems of relevance in Christianity. In other religions, the two facets are often not even separable. But in the differentiated societies of the West, the deepest divisions within the ecclesiastical bodies run exactly between these two diverging conceptions of their function. On the one hand are the conservatives/evangelicals/fundamentalists (in Protestantism), or verticalists (in Catholicism) whose concern is primarily with relevance A. On the other hand are the liberals/modernists (in Protestantism) or horizontalists (in Catholicism) who think almost exclusively in terms of relevance B. David Moberg (1962, p. 285) observes correctly that there is often 'closer fellowship between churches of different denominations united on the basis of common fundamentalist or liberal faith than between divergent churches in the same denomination'. It could be added that the crystallization of separate identities around each divergent function has a history as long as the ensuing conflict is deep. The conflict comes as no surprise if one assumes both the brittleness and the boundary-defence of any identity.

The protagonists of relevance A speak about sin and salvation; God's will and man's obstinacy; surrender, and reconciliation. The protagonists of relevance B have effectively monopolized the very term relevance (so that the first group is loath to touch it) and speak about concrete injustice, the war on poverty, the exploitation of man by man, political action, and social problems. The first group correctly and implicitly expects that by submergence in, and dedication to, a specific transcendental frame of reference man will contribute to greater sanity and meaningfulness of the secular order. The second group correctly and explicitly wants the world to be a better place in which to live, by organized social action and by Good Samaritan types of personal motivation.

The battle goes on. There are occasional moves to take cognizance of the other point of view. At the first U.S. Congress on Evangelism (Moberg, 1972, pp. 163–5) apathy towards social action in the U.S. was strongly attacked. About the same time the prominent liberal theologian, John C. Bennett, then president of Union Theological Seminary, felt that those Christians who were heavily committed to radical social action could do with a little more God-talk in their religious diet. He advocated a healthy sense of the transcendence of God which would be an antidote to the self-righteousness of those who think they are waging holy warfare in a noble cause (Bennett, 1969).

Generally however, one view is adopted and the other criticized. It is ironic that the critique of relevance B is now increasingly launched by philosophers, intellectuals, sociologists, or non-Christians—the very people whom the liberals regarded as securely in their camp. The philosopher Needleman asks the provocative question:

As Church and synagogue turn to psychiatry, the scientific world-view, or social action, are they not turning toward what has

failed and is failing?... Men turn to religion and find, to their
ultimate dismay, that religion turns to them, to their sciences,
their ideas of action and accomplishment, and their language.
(Needleman, p. 10.)

C. S. Lewis heartily approved of the man who pointed out that
the charge to Peter was 'Feed my sheep' and not 'Try experiments
on my rats, or even, teach my performing dogs new tricks' (Lewis,
1964, p. 13). The sociologist, Peter Berger, approves of Dean Inge's
remark that a man who marries the spirit of the age soon finds himself a widower and aptly remarks that these kinds of relevancies are
'extremely vulnerable to changing fashions and thus of generally
short duration' (Berger, 1969, p. 29). Andrew Greeley (1969, p. 110)
criticizes as 'conspicuously unsuccessful' the attempt of theological
liberals to rewrite Christianity, so that it will be acceptable to
modern science. Some of those who look at the West through Eastern eyes similarly dislike the agile adjustability of the American
churches with their orientation to social action. The Protestant
churches are accused of not giving 'spiritual food', but instead of
giving religion, they 'protest against the Vietnam War' or advocate
'social involvement'. It is interesting that these very critics of
Western pragmatic religiosity tend to advocate relevance B in
poverty-stricken Calcutta (Ranganathananda, 1970, p. 435; French,
1972, pp. 284, 289 ff.).

But then there are also the formidable proponents of relevance B
and critics of relevance A. The Bishop of Woolwich, whose *Honest
to God* became one of the bestsellers of the 1960s, took as his point
of criticism for truth 'what modern man could or could not believe',
and attempted to find God 'from what actually is most real to people
in everyday life' (Robinson, 1963a, pp. 160, 277). Consequently the
God 'out there' was to be replaced by the God 'down here' (Robinson, 1963, Chap. 1). Harvey Cox eulogizes the secular city as representing the same eschatological reality once expressed by the idea of
the Kingdom of God (1965, p. 110). One ought to speak about God
in a secular, political fashion, e.g. standing in a picket line (ibid.,
p. 256). He heralds the new post-Barthian era when man's experiences take again the centre stage (1969, p. 165). The French socio-
logist/theologian, Jacques Ellul, who maintains that God, revealed
in Jesus Christ, should occupy this position, is severely criticized
because of his 'neat chic-radical excuse for doing nothing at all. He

serves best who merely sits and bitches ...' (Cox, 1971; Temple, 1972, p. 183).

It is true that relevance A has the advantage of issuing from an independent, time-honoured tradition, whereas relevance B is sometimes so attached to a specific concrete action-strategy that it succumbs with the cause. But on the other hand, too much independence of A augments risks of ineffectiveness through isolation and the social actionists can rightfully claim that they too are guided by a long respectable tradition beginning with the prophets (Mol, 1969, p. 48).

Ultimately however, there is no escape from the relevance of independent identity.

It is not true that one can only be relevant if one communicates in terms of the expectations of a secular society, granted there is such a thing. One can influence by what one is as well as by what one is expected to be. An independent initiative may be particularly fruitful in an age of rapid change when a changing system of values leaves people with the uncomfortable feeling that nothing is secure and that even institutions which claim to be vitally concerned with ultimate meaning and eternal values, are in reality conforming to a situation not defined by them but defined for them. (Mol, 1969, p. 13.)

SUMMARY

The boundary of the frame of identity has developed into a major tool of our analysis. Primarily on the ground that we do not want to lose sight of this facet, we have favoured identity over many other useful concepts such as integration, interpretation of reality, meaning, order, and security. The brittleness and frailty of a specific frame of identity directs the attention to the many mechanisms that may strengthen and reinforce it.

Not only the boundary, but also what is within the boundary is constantly tested on the soundness of its strength. In spite of the great differences between and within social, group, and personal identities, they all have in common a tendency towards internal unity and the meshing of parts.

This is where the problem of relevance comes in: for in this meshing or integrating the various parts are under pressure to adjust to one another in order to minimize friction, and to maximize function. The first (minimization of friction) may lead to amalgamation, the second (maximization of function) to independence, and optimum integration is reached when neither force succeeds in fully reaching its goal, but is held in check by the other.

The history of both archaic and modern religions furnishes examples of this theorizing. The correlations between forms of religious beliefs and ritual, and the economic, political, and kinship patterns show how within the tribal unit the successful meshing contributes to the strength of the identity. In modern societies (e.g. the U.S.A.) economic frictions (slums and poverty versus affluence), political friction (establishment-power versus radical powerlessness), and racial frictions (negro versus white) are feverishly patched over by the ecclesiastical and other social activists. These activists contribute to the relatively greater justice and unity of the society. This is relevance B: an interdependence of units and a sensitive repairing of fragilities.

However, relevance A denotes the contribution of the otherness or the independence of the religious sub-system. It interprets the total system by its own criteria rather than by those borrowed from elsewhere, and it has the advantage of sacralizing expertise, the capacity for emotional anchorage, and the resolution of numerous frictions and fragilities by placing them in a larger, more cosmic setting. The result is the relativization of the threat and mitigation of anxiety. This is the latent function and essential relevance of religion from the most primitive ritual to the most awe-inspiring cathedral sermon on sin and salvation.

Chapter VII

Cohesion and Prejudice

Whether or not specific frames of identity are viable depends on their fragility, their relevance, and also their cohesion.

Conflict, conquest, death, differentiation, diffidence, disaster, frustration, injustice, over-choice, rationality, scepticism, etc., can all weaken specific frames of identity. And these are therefore defended by sometimes subtle, sometimes brutal, counter-attacks. Sacralization and sublimation are among the more subtle ways of rendering the eroding forces impotent. Murders, persecutions, and wars are more ruthless methods of defending a specific personal or social identity.

Relevance and viability similarly depend on one another. The place an individual can continue to occupy amongst other individuals, or the place a society, or group in that society, can continue to occupy amongst other groups and societies, depends on the relevance these places have for their occupants. Frames of identity can become obsolete and provide façades for more viable forms of identity. But they can also become stronger through mutual need and sustenance.

Just how cohesive a frame of identity is, depends on where it is fragile and how challenge is met. Challenge itself can lead to complete disintegration. The Aztec empire crumbled before the energy and civilization of the Spanish invaders. The old lady whose entire existence revolved around her husband died soon after he did.

But then the challenge can also be a blessing in disguise. The British rallied around Sir Winston Churchill when the German invasion was imminent. Similarly the cohesion of the Catholic Church improved greatly after Pope Pius IX in 1864 accepted the challenge of pervasive liberalism in the encyclical *Quanta Cura*. The enormous and costly effort to provide Catholic schools was a boon to the morale of Catholics and heightened their interest in their Church (Greeley and Rossi, 1966; Mol, 1971a, pp. 177, 178,

183). The challenge of adversity has often had an invigorating and integrating effect on individuals.

Historians, more than other scholars, have drawn the attention to the importance of challenge. Arnold Toynbee (1946 and 1957) made the theme of challenge and response the major axis around which the rise and fall of civilizations revolve. Much earlier, Ibn Khaldun (1332–1406) astutely observed how the challenge of life in the desert strengthened the cohesion of Bedouin tribes, and how the softness of the urban environment weakened it (Vol. I, p. 263).

Religious forces do not altogether stand idly by in this challenge/response or differentiation/identity dialectic. Khaldun fully confirms our expectation that these forces strengthen the cohesive side. Religion, he said, sometimes increases solidarity 'many times over' (Vol. I, p. 322) and he attributes the rapid and sweeping conquests of the Muslim Arabs in the seventh century A.D. to the formidable combination of religious and tribal solidarity. In one of his other volumes of the *Muqaddimah*, Khaldun confirms our theorizing about fit and relevance. He says that group-feeling is also a prerequisite for religion (Vol. II, p. 195). In other words, religion effects, but is also affected. It is strengthened, but also strengthens.

How it can strengthen is well brought out in the studies of utopian communities: religion contributes to the stability and the survival capacity of these groups (Stephan and Stephan, p. 94).

In modern Western societies, the problem of sacralizing identities is compounded by the emergence of separate religious organizations. The need for consolidation of the independent religious function is an important factor in this development. In the analysis of cohesion one ought therefore to distinguish between the cohesion of specific frames of identity and the cohesion of the religious organizations. A political movement intent on eliminating particular injustices develops its own sacralizing mechanisms because the religious organizations cannot afford unambiguously to legitimize the movement without antagonizing (therefore *not* legitimizing) those with contrary beliefs and programmes. The religious organization thus loses some of its effectiveness, since it cannot any further straddle the deepest emotions of its entire constituency, but it counters this loss of effectiveness by internal organizational strengthening.

One of the most essential reasons for the strength of recent, as compared with older, religious organizations is the as yet uncompromised fit with the identity needs of their constituencies. The younger sects are always more cohesive than the older churches. Their effectiveness does not as yet depend on straddling a variety of life-styles, interpretations of existence, and occupational experiences. Instead they cater to one specific, rather homogeneous segment of a much larger population, the heterogeneity of which does not obstruct organizational proliferation.

CHURCH ATTENDANCE

Church attendance can be used as a rough indication of the hold of a church or sect on its constituency. We suggest that there is a correlation between church attendance and the capacity of that church comprehensively to reinforce the identity of its membership. When, in Ireland, church attendance on an average Sunday hovers around 95 per cent (Ward, pp. 297–8), one does not go far wrong by attributing this, at least in part, to the ability of the Catholic Church to express the aspirations of the entire population as the fulcrum of Irish and local identity when this was seriously threatened by the British. But it is also a tribute to the vigilance and viability of the internal identity of the Catholic Church. Through dedicated celibate clergy and their kinship links with the peasant population, the church can maintain its hold. When on the other hand in Scandinavia church attendance on an average Sunday hovers around 5 per cent (Thorgaard, p. 136; Seppänen, p. 155; Vogt, p. 393; Gustafsson, p. 496), one can partly explain this by the incapacity of the Lutheran state church strongly to reinforce Danish, Finnish, Norwegian, and Swedish identity needs. Apart from the fact that organized religion never became the rallying cry of these nations when endangered, the Protestant stress on personal salvation, rather than on corporate mediacy, diminished ecclesiastical cohesion. When, in almost any country (see entry 'church-attendance, rural-urban' in Mol, Hetherton, and Henty, 1972), country dwellers are more loyal to their churches than city people, an important reason is the incapacity of urban churches to straddle a heterogeneous population with diverging life-styles and experiences. In the country, on the other hand, a communal identity provides a viable basis for sacralization. The strength of urban religion in the U.S.A. (contrary to most European countries) has much to do with the capacity of a variety of denominations to sacralize separately a variety of homogeneous identity clusters. The liberal theologians in the U.S.A. who are oriented to social action, have been particularly inept in ignoring this major function.

Colin Williams (1963, p. 10) decries the incapacity of local congregations to fulfil their mission in the world, because they are segregated on the basis of residence 'into different communities of colour, class, culture and race'. The utopian assumptions on the part of many ecclesiastical officials with respect to the role of religion as an agency primarily sanctifying national or international goals and values, rather than group identities, has led to considerable alienation in the U.S.A. between local congregations and denominational headquarters. Gibson Winter's schemes to make the local congregations more heterogeneous, and his lament that the isolationism of the church helps it to become an adjustive rather than a creative force in a technical society, is another example of a rather narrow perspective on the function of religion (1961; 1963, p. 13). John C. Bennett (1964, p. 105) belongs to the same category of national ecclesiastical leaders and educators in the U.S.A., whose perspective has led them to neglect the grass-root bases for religious vitality in that country for the sake of patching up a national or international identity which appears to be experiencing erosion. Compared with other countries, the strength of local American Protestantism lies in the accidental but fortuitous circumstance of denominational proliferation running parallel to the proliferation of separate frames of identity which in turn accompanied industrial and urban segmentation. The pragmatic alacrity of the local American congregations to take up the cudgels of competition has had a salubrious effect on the strength of these separate identity clusters.

How strong these latent forces are in American religion can be shown by the way in which they overshadow the forces of technology, urbanization, industrialization, and individualization, all of which push in an entirely opposite direction. In most other, older, countries (even in Ireland—Ward, 1972, p. 298) there is impressive evidence that decrease in church attendance accompanies the industrial, urban spread. This is so, I suggest, because an ecclesiastical organization which has emerged in the past as the sole sacralizer of a larger national identity has few means to be in advance of the newly emerging frames of identity. Its entire basis for being is the integration rather than the differentiation of existence, and in modern societies the latter tends to be chronological prior to the former. It comes as no surprise, therefore, that the mainstay of these bodies was the least changing sections of society, such as the older bourgeoisie. However, in the U.S.A., at least four structural components countered this tendency: (a) voluntarism (parishes depended on the financial contributions of the membership guaranteeing both fit with group identity needs and greater loyalty of membership); (b) competition (the success-ethic dictated the urge to vie for organizational strength and viability *vis-à-vis* other parishes even within the same denomination); (c) residential homogeneity (the American sociologists of religion all bark up the wrong tree when they continue to stress the occupational profiles of entire denominations rather than the occupational homogeneity of the local parishes); (d) prominence of revivalistic change-orientation (since the inception of the American colonies, and subsequently on the westward moving frontier, American religiosity has stressed charisma and conversion, which are *par excellence* mechanisms to consolidate new identities). It is for these reasons of fit and cohesion that in the U.S.A. Protestant church attendance and religious interest in general are so much higher than for instance in England, where the Church of England in the industrial districts fares little better than in Scandinavia (Martin, 1967, Chap. 2; 1972, pp. 232–3; Wickham, 1957; Scharf, p. 162; Inglis, 1963).

Our emphasis on the way in which religion fits identity needs, as a major explanatory variable, finds confirmation in what, to those who use inherent characteristics of industry and rationality as their sole explanatory basis, must be an embarrassing exception. In the least industrialized, poverty-stricken, southern areas of Portugal church attendance is very small (8 per cent) as compared with the more urbanized, relatively wealthier diocese of Lisbon (17 per cent) (Querido, pp. 427–8). In the southern section poor peasants toil on the soil belonging to the *Senhor*, owner of large estates. They form a discontented social class which 'tends to reject all the values of the society of which it forms a part and which it identifies with the values of the dominant class. If the total society is Catholic at least sociologically, then Catholicism is rejected' (ibid., p. 435). In other words, the state church cannot straddle the very divergent identity needs: it has opted for the status quo. Although it may not be the case in southern Portugal, in such conditions revolutionary Marxism or fervent Pentecostalism typically provide both the fit and the cohesion for an alienated class.

Our analysis indicates that the viability of specific frames of identity is very much bound to their cohesion, and that the basic dilemma of religious organizations is how to fit the proliferating crystallizations of identity when the sacralization of previous undifferentiated, now relatively obsolete, forms have become less relevant. If our theory holds, we may expect certain consequences from the many ecumenical efforts in the twentieth century.

On the international level, one would expect the success of these movements, such as the World Council of Churches, to be dependent on their congruence with an increasing sense of international identity. But since an increasing sense of international identity has scarcely arisen, it comes as no surprise that the World Council of Churches, like the United Nations and the former League of Nations, should suffer from grass-root powerlessness. Etzioni (1971, p. 565) explains the collapse of the United Arab Republic or the Federation of the West Indies by the absence of a supranational community. The thrust of both political and religious movements is confined to small coteries of dedicated intellectuals. Dormant within the major religions lies the universal message that might equally well sacralize either the world or more restricted social, group, or personal identities, but its revivification depends on the grass-root support it can marshal. In the past the unity of a nation often emerged only in the face of concrete external threat. A parallel threat at the international level would occur only in the unlikely event of invasion from outer space, since the international problems of ecology, poverty, nuclear threat, and war do not appear to issue the same sort of challenge or to create international unity as a response.

The Catholic Church has, of course, maintained its international character. Even so, this character survived only by vigorous internal organization, and by numerous compromises with strongly entrenched national, regional and group peculiarities. How well Catholicism is entwined with local identity is brought out by Christian (p. vii) when he says of an area of northern Spain that the 'rise in popularity of some shrines and the decline of others coincide with shifts in identity of the people of the valley'. Although the Catholic saints are universal, in the mind of the villagers they are identified with the local scene. Even the emigrants who leave the area to amass a ruthless fortune in the cities usually make the first stop on their return at the village shrine image, especially that of Mary. Christian (p. 162) explains the function of the shrine in these instances as 'a cleansing station where a ritual purification (a kind of debriefing) takes place . . . a redemption center that permits re-entry into the village society'.

On the national level, ecumenical efforts and mergers have succeeded somewhat better. The disappearance of major distinctions in the past (the slavery issue or ethnic identity, in the U.S., for instance) opened the way for inter-church co-operation. More efficient use of manpower, lesser prominence of doctrinal distinctions, the morale of churchmen (Wilson, 1966, p. 176) were some of the internal reasons for the merger of ecclesiastical bodies. Simultaneously, other internal factors militated against this process, particularly where differences occurred in the perception of religious function (relevance A versus relevance B—predominantly fundamentalist bodies never merged with predominantly liberal bodies); or in class structure (predominantly middle-class bodies hardly ever merged with predominantly lower-class bodies). On the other hand differences in geographical distribution might assist ecumenism—the major reason why, in 1957, in the U.S.A., the ethnic Evangelical and Reformed Church could merge with the Anglo-Saxon upper-middle-class Congregational Christian Churches was their geographical separation.

Some of these internal factors (ethnicity, class, perception of function) operate strongly on the local level and explain why there has often been more resistance to amalgamation at the grass roots than in the denominational headquarters. Both in an Australian and a Canadian study, it was found that opposition to mergers had little, if anything, to do with theological or other religious variables (church attendance, prayer, beliefs, experiences), but was strongly related to authoritarian character traits (Mol, 1969a, p. 28; Kaill, 1971, p. 154). Merger attempts appeared to undermine the fixed localized authority which provided the security of an established order in a world by which one felt threatened.

PREJUDICE

The need for discernible identity boundaries appears to be an important factor behind the negative attitudes towards the mergers of ecclesiastical organizations. The same need has proved to be crucial in the studies of prejudice. Since we have assumed that the need for identity boundaries is both universal and closely linked with the essence and function of religion, do we therefore imply that religion fosters and reinforces prejudice?

The answer is yes, provided that prejudice is taken in its literal meaning of prejudgement: judging our environment (and events and groups within it) in anticipation and from a certain vantage point. Using this wide definition one is actually led to stress the inevitability, universality, and even necessity of prejudice. Our Western and, even more, our scientific cultures frown on this usage, but even so, let us see what happens when we think about prejudice, or closed-mindedness as a function rather than a dysfunction. Prejudice can be an important method of protecting and strengthening a group. It inhibits the possible influence that one group can exert on another. It spontaneously conserves a particular social order and its distinctions. It makes up for the insecurity of open-mindedness. It maximizes cohesion and minimizes amorphousness.

There are much narrower definitions. When the authors of *The Authoritarian Personality* (Adorno *et al.*, 1950) began their research in 1943, the problem of anti-Semitism in Nazi Germany was of crucial importance. Consequently they concentrated on prejudice against minorities. Edward Shils (1954) suggested that there were also left-wing authoritarians, and Milton Rokeach (1960) went from there to do research on intolerance or closed-mindedness in general. He substituted the categorization of a belief criterion (how much we like and dislike those whose belief-disbelief systems are similar to, or different from, our own) for an ethnic or racial criterion (how much we like and dislike Jews, Negroes, foreigners, etc. (ibid., p. 394)). However, Rokeach too, failed to see how the open-minded person is open-minded relative only to a particular cultural context and that he too moves within specific identity boundaries which will be ardently defended when challenged. Although Americans are accused of bragging at all times, foreigners have noted that the rate goes up when they are in foreign countries: there is a greater need for the open-minded to vocalize the goodness of their Americanity, more so when it is no longer taken for granted. An altogether different example of the boundaries of open-mindedness are classifications. Open-minded scientists may smile about the universal taboo reactions to events and actions that occur in primitive societies and that seriously defy the classificatory boundaries (Horton, p. 165; Douglas, pp. 4, 95, 113, etc.). And yet the outcries against those who defy specific, taken-for-granted scientific classifications have exactly the same function as taboos. The difference between the open-minded and closed-minded person from our point of view is that the closed-minded seems to be in greater need of 'discernible', close-at-hand, more concrete boundaries, whereas the open-minded finds his security in larger, culturally more diffuse, less concrete delineations. These delineations are just as real, but they are less obvious, less controversial, and much more taken for granted. Similar observations were made by Sartre (1960a) when he typified the anti-Semite as a person who was frightened of change and who longed for a concrete reality with very definite rules, and also by Gregory (1957, pp. 226, 231) when he wrote about the authoritarian's demand for concreteness and his strong rejection of all that distinguished outgroups from ingroups.

This brings us back to the adjective 'discernible', used in the first paragraph of this section. Those who oppose amalgamations with other denominations seem to be more in need of concrete, discernible boundaries between us (Presbyterians, for instance) and not-us (Catholics, for instance). On the other hand, the identity of those who favour mergers appears to be structured around more abstract ethics and beliefs. Here the boundaries may be between us (all Christians, for instance, for whom Christ's love ethic or view of salvation is important) and not-us (bigots, or unbelievers, who are guided by a non-transcendental belief, or individual-based morality).

It is possible also to subsume the celebrated extrinsic/intrinsic dichotomy in the psychology of religion under this discernible/indiscernible distinction. Gordon Allport (1963) who developed this concept thought of the extrinsic religious person as someone who used religion for his own selfish ends. This might be salvation at the expense of outgroups, or individual security and status. On the other hand, he defined the intrinsic religious person as living his religion and regarding self-oriented needs as of less ultimate significance than religious beliefs (Hunt and King, 1971, p. 341). The former was more prejudiced—the other less.

Thus we may say that the extrinsic person is more likely to defend and sacralize a personal or group identity. The intrinsic person is more likely to defend and contribute to the sacralization of a larger social identity, and to see the self in a more cosmic perspective. The boundary conflicts, about which the researchers in this area are *actually* talking, correspondingly differ from the extrinsic to the intrinsic person. The former stresses specific intra-societal divisions, the latter more general, extra-societal ones. Culture-bound as most researchers of necessity are, the intra-societal divisions are stressed because they increase rather than decrease tension. The intrinsic person on the other hand relativizes these divisions from the perspective of his larger vision and thereby mitigates them. These internal divisions draw the attention, because they sharpen internal boundaries at the expense of social integration. They are therefore more discernible. It is for these reasons that the term prejudice is almost always used by both the public and scientific researchers in the pejorative and narrower sense. Within this frame of reference of a specific society and culture, it now becomes self-evident why the contribution that prejudice, in the narrower sense, makes to personal and group identity is just as unresearched as the contribution that prejudice in the larger sense makes to social identity. It is precisely because prejudice here becomes almost synonymous with continuity of the definition of the situation, and with consolidation of a view of reality, that we make sparing use both of this concept and those related to it, such as the distinctions between intrinsic and extrinsic, open-minded and closed-minded, authoritarian and tolerant personalities.

In passing it may be said that over against the many philosophers, psychologists, and sociologists who assume that tolerance can be only unmitigatingly functional, there are a few who occasionally also mention its dysfunctions. In ethology, some scholars look upon xenophobia as guaranteeing the integrity of the group (Ardrey, 1970, p. 236), and even upon a touch of paranoia as 'inevitable if members of a sub-group are to test their strength against the weight of a majority' (ibid., p. 286). In psychology, Erikson (1963, p. 419) perceptively remarks that the tolerant appraisal of other identities endangers one's own. In sociology, Fallding (1969, p. 98) criticizes the emphasis on the virtue of tolerance, and is prepared to accept it as a virtue only 'if it is a temporary truce to compare differences'. To Gilbert Chesterton, tolerance was the virtue of people who did not believe anything. In a more historical vein, Seymour M. Lipset comes close to explaining the numerous sources of prejudices in the U.S.A. as so many defences of embattled forms of self-identity (Lipset, 1970, p. 92).

However, most research begins with the assumption that prejudice is dysfunctional (which of course it usually is for those individuals, groups, or societies against which the discrimination is directed). It is unlikely that the Anti-Defamation League of B'nai B'rith would have parted with $500,000 for Glock and Stark's research (1966, p. xii) if the Berkeley scholars had not shared dysfunctional assumptions regarding anti-Semitism and instead had wanted to study the utility of anti-Semitism. To be sure, Glock and Stark admit the two-sidedness of the militant particularism of religion in which they locate prejudice and Anti-Semitism (ibid., p. 208). They call it 'harmful' against the background of a larger society, but 'a positive mobilizing and energizing force' when viewed from within any religion (ibid., p. 210). Yet the brunt of their approach is guided by an ethical mission to eradicate bigotry.

As with Allport's extrinsic/intrinsic dichotomy, and Rokeach's open-minded/closed-minded dichotomy, one can here too translate Glock and Stark's particularism index in terms of boundary variations. In their surveys, those who are most prejudiced are also those who have erected the clearest boundaries around their particular, parochial, orthodox views of salvation (ibid., pp. 24, 208). On the other hand, those who are least prejudiced are the liberals (the 'real Christians' in their research) for whom the brotherhood of man is fundamental and for whom the identity boundaries are much wider and much less exclusive.

To Glock and Stark, it was a major surprise that an exclusivist theological emphasis was a *raison d'être* for bigotry (ibid., p. 207). Still one can expect a congruence, correlation, or fit (*not* a causal connection as Glock and Stark imply, but which their data do *not* support) between kinds of religiosity and specific frames of identity. One may expect an exclusive theology among those believers and sects that have delineated themselves quite decidedly from their environment, just as one can expect the millennial dreams of dis-privileged sects. There is a fit between religiosity and situation.

Yet, precisely because of the abstract nature of religious belief, it would be folly to expect only one concrete set of socially manifest consequences of particular items of belief. The 'Chosen Race' concept of the Judaeo-Christian tradition happens to be the one which in the past has admirably reinforced Jewish solidarity, but it did exactly the same for those Bible-oriented Christians for whom the Messiahship of Christ was central. Yet there are many concepts in the same tradition which lend themselves less to accentuating the Jewish/Christian boundary. It is only by this type of theorizing that one may come to terms with findings which at first sight seem to contradict those of Glock and Stark. (For other criticism of Glock and Stark's work on anti-Semitism see Moberg, 1972, pp. 61–3; Middleton, p. 33; Strommen *et al.*, 1972.)

In the large Australian survey mentioned earlier it was found that the orthodox believers (who attended church regularly, prayed daily, and believed in God without doubt) had much more positive and less negative feelings towards Jews, than had the secularists who did or believed none of these things. On the other hand, in this same study a larger percentage of respondents with the majority of their best friends in the local church had negative feelings towards Jews than of respondents who had the majority of their best friends outside the local church (Mol, 1971a, pp. 160, 161). This suggests that cross-cultural comparisons are likely to support Lenski's conclusion that those who have an associational involvement in religion (primarily church-goers) are less prejudiced and that those with a communal involvement (primarily those who have most of their friends in the local church and derive a sense of belonging from this fact) are more so (Lenski, 1961, p. 67). Glock and Stark similarly found that church attendance had little to do with anti-Semitism and, if anything, often tended to decrease it (pp. 137, 138). They concentrated, therefore, on specific religious beliefs.

On balance and in a very general way, Christianity seems to make identity boundaries more inclusive through encyclicals, literature, preaching, the love ethic, etc. Yet there is no guarantee that specific Christian beliefs (such as 'the Chosen Race') or Biblical stories (such as Ham being cursed by his father Noah to become a slave of slaves) are not accentuated in order to sacralize certain identities and to mark specific boundaries. These things may occur with or without the sanction of ecclesiastical officials.

The specific content of a religious tradition and its vigorous promulgation are only some of the factors reinforcing specific frames of identity. Preaching against prejudice is relatively useless when specific forms of prejudice and scapegoating fulfil basic functions for personality and group integration, and when national, social, group, or personal identities are fragile. Minorities have the advantage or disadvantage (whatever the point of view) of visibility and discernibility when the actual reasons for fragility are invisible, inevitable,

and worse, irremediable. Compensation and projection actually minimize the fragility, whereas a rational, efficient attack on the real
cause would only maximize the awareness of its irremediability.

SUMMARY

If only a viable frame of identity can be sacralized (and religion
depends on *it*), then it follows that the cohesion of any frame of
identity is advanced by sacralization (*it* often depends on religion).

The contribution of religion to greater cohesion is not through
actual, efficient, reparation of fragility. On the contrary the direct
attack usually leads only to a greater awareness of the inevitability
and irremediability of the situation. By contrast, sacralization can
indirectly compensate for the breaches by reinforcing cohesion and
projecting order in an ultramundane realm. Here it is less vulnerable to a constant bombardment of mundane disorderly elements.

In order to safeguard its independence the sacralization function
becomes embedded in separate organizational structures. This guarantees its perpetuation but also further jeopardizes its capacity to
remain congruent with newly emerging frames of identity. It is for
these reasons that older religious organizations tend to rely most on
the least changing segments of their constituency (e.g. the older bourgeoisie) and that the faster changing segments develop their own
sacralizing tendencies (late nineteenth-century labour movements).

The incapacity of older religious organizations to straddle too
broad a span of identity clusters is reflected in decreasing church
attendance. This functional disadvantage may be (and often is,
in the case of Catholicism) countered through mechanisms that
strengthen internal organizational (celibacy, separate school-system,
mediacy of salvation) and compensate for lost cohesion. Although,
in the case of all universal religions, the potential for sacralization of
a supranational identity is abundantly available, in actual practice
the weakness of the ecumenical bodies lies in their grass-roots powerlessness, and, beyond this, in the general tendency of identities to
crystallize around more discernible, closer-at-hand elements. Prejudice (in the narrower sense of identity crystallization around these
more discernible elements) is a good example of how the cohesion of
group identities weakens social or universal solidarity.

Given a chance, any of these identity frames (whether personal, group, or social) will develop their own sacralizations, thereby increasing both internal cohesion and external tensions for the larger unit of which each is a part.

Large-scale cohesion may be attained only at the expense of lesser cohesion elsewhere, and religious organizations cannot avoid the predicament of sacralizing one identity at the expense of another. To say all this more simply, obscurely, and vulgarly: religion *can* create pies in the sky, but it *cannot* have and eat them as well.

Chapter VIII

Morality*

Identity states what a society, group or person is. Morality, on the other hand, emphasizes what is expected. Through the former, existence is interpreted and infused with meaning. The latter oils the machinery of human interaction by rewarding correct, and punishing incorrect, behaviour.

When identity is sacralized it sometimes becomes more abstract: what the society, group or individual *really* is depends on a more ultimate reference point: a tool in God's hand; a stage in a cosmic process; a vehicle for human betterment; a part of the universal atman, etc. This is less true for primitive societies, in which the world of myth and the actual world often seem inseparable, but it becomes increasingly true of more advanced societies.

On the other hand, rules of ethics are discernible and implementable. Conduct, norms, and values can be judged and therefore punished and rewarded. Yet they can be more readily implemented if there are mutually consistent criteria for goodness, decency, discipline, etc., which are taken for granted. They often need the sanction of fitting into a particular conception of order or a higher level principle (for instance, a Golden Rule).

There are good reasons for the historical differentiation between a system of 'ought'-ness and a system of 'is'-ness, or in more formal language, why a normative system became separated from a cognitive system. The more complex a culture, the more remote and general an over-arching belief system has to be, if it is to continue its sacralizing and integrating function. Yet, simultaneously the need for concrete prescriptions and specific rules also increases because of the greater variety of relationships. This may explain why in primitive, undifferentiated, societies the identity fragilities tended to consist

* Some passages of this chapter have been taken from Mol, 1969, Chap. 6.

somewhat more of survival problems, in later societies more of moral problems (Robertson, 1970, p. 106). Some scholars (Tylor, 1871; Wallis, 1939) go so far as to say that primitive religion hardly dealt with morality, if it did so at all. Yet this is only true when morality is taken in the narrow sense of relationships between individuals (Swanson, 1966, p. 158). When it is defined in social rather than in individualistic terms (the relations between group and members) then, in any society as Malinowski said (1936), personal comfort may have to be sacrificed for the common weal (Swanson, ibid.). A potential for social disruption in personal aggression and self-assertion has always existed, and religion has always amended these essential moral relationships through common worship, ritual, objectification, commitment, and myth.

Such amendment did not necessarily lead to the separation of the cognitive from the normative system. Neither those religions which lacked an elaborate transcendental frame of reference (Confucianism) nor religions with an entire pantheon of gods (Hinduism) found need for much distinction between the two, as long as the societies which they served remained relatively undifferentiated. The following conceptualizations are therefore more appropriate to the West and to Christianity. In any society, identities tend to include the moral order, but only in advanced societies does a dialectic arise between the cognitive and normative system. This dialectic can best be described in terms of functions and dysfunctions.

Religion appears to have a twofold effect on morality. The first, more functional, effect is stabilization and integration. The second, more dysfunctional effect, which is most evident in societies in which keeping up with change is necessary, or at least an advantage, is rigidification.

INTEGRATION

By differentiation, we have maintained, emerging religious organizations could perform their function more adequately. They could now concentrate on the more enduring stable elements of identity instead of having also to encompass those roles and norms that were more subject to change and that were incidental to frames of identity. This is the essential reason why the universal religions moved their reference points in a more ultimate, ultra-mundane direction.

None the less, the integration function inevitably meets its limits when the units to be encompassed become so independent that they begin to develop their own sacralizing tendency. This independence may be caused by deep conflicts within the social fabric (e.g. the proletariat versus the entrepreneurial classes) or by other clashes of identity boundaries. The ensuing plausibility problem (see for this term Berger, 1967a), or the competition that universal religions encounter for their previously taken-for-granted interpretations, may lead to a de-emphasis of their ultimate justifications. After all, below these ultimate justifications and above the house and garden variety of mundane norms and rules are the middle axioms to which both universal religions, some of their offspring (e.g. situational ethics) and their adversaries (e.g. rational humanism) pay equal tribute.

The Golden Rule is an example *par excellence* of middle axioms which sum up as a terse maxim what is basic for oiling the machinery of human interaction. Reciprocity—seeking the closest possible similarity between treatment of others and expected treatment of oneself —is the essense of the Golden Rule. All universal religions sacralize this rule in their scriptures (Browne, p. xv).

BRAHMANISM: This is the sum of duty: Do naught unto others which would cause you pain if done to you. (Mahabharata, 5, 1517.)

BUDDHISM: Hurt not others in ways that you yourself would find hurtful. (Udana-Varga 5, 18.)

CONFUCIANISM: Is there one maxim which ought to be acted upon throughout one's whole life? Surely it is the maxim of loving-kindness: Do not unto others what you would not have them do unto you. (Analects, 15, 23.)

TAOISM: Regard your neighbour's gain as your own gain, and your neighbour's loss as your own loss. (T'ai Shang Kan Ying P'ien.)

ZOROASTRIANISM: That nature alone is good which refrains from doing unto another whatsoever is not good for itself. (Dadi-stan-i-dinik, 94, 5.)

JUDAISM: What is hateful to you, do not to your fellow-man. That is the entire Law; all the rest is commentary. (Talmud, Shabbat 31a.)

CHRISTIANITY: All things whatsoever ye would that men should do to you, do ye even so to them: for this is the Law and the Prophets. (Matthew 7, 12.)

ISLAM: No one of you is a believer until he desires for his brother that which he desires for himself. (Sunnah.)

The importance of the Golden Rule lies, (a) in its general contribution to an orderly society, leaving aside the problem of specific prescriptions differing from place to place and time to time; and (b) in its provision of a discernible and practical axiom that nevertheless integrates a whole body of rules, and which, in the process, furnishes a mutually consistent criterion.

Yet if the middle axiom becomes elevated as its own final justification, order is not maximized. Its full implementation depends on its being believed for other reasons. Reciprocity in human relations, and the confidence that flows from the assurance that one's expectations will be met, are endangered when only discernible rules are rewarded or backed by punishment. It is less comfortable to live in a society in which people are honest only so long as one cannot get away with dishonesty, than it is to live in a society where there is a basic intention and motivation to be honest. Social motivation is also more positively advanced by a mechanism sacralizing forgiveness which (as we shall see later) can have anomic or rule-relativizing consequences.

A society in which the basic motivations have a less discernible, perhaps more sacred, source is also likely to be the more orderly one. In Islam, this is well expressed by the Sufi symbol of the walnut, the shell of which is compared with the *Sharī'ah* (Divine Law) and the kernel with the *Tarīqah* (Spiritual Path, the inner source of life of Islam). Without the kernel, it is maintained that the walnut and its shell have no end or purpose (Nasr, pp. 121–4; Needleman, p. 31). One could interpret this also to mean that an important function of the esoteric core of the major universal religions is to provide the justification for the more discernible and implementable rules.

By now it is clear that we look upon this function as one of several, contrary to Immanuel Kant who valued religion *only* for the moral doctrine it contained and regarded the rest as 'mere delusion' (Körner, p. 170). Much more insightful are the remarks of Oman (p. 62) that without religion morality cannot penetrate from good form to goodness, from manners to morals; of Geertz (1959, p. 421) that religion grounds the most specific requirements of human action in the most general contexts of human existence; and of Roubiczek (p. 96) that religion gives objectivity to moral values.

The assumption that religion sustains morality is remarkably widespread. In Buddhism, the fundamental problem as to how one ought to live is answered in relation to the cognitive framework of the Four Noble Truths. The Ten Commandments of the Judaeo-Christian tradition are described as God's gift to man. Socrates invented the noble falsehood of man's origin in order to preserve the rules of his ideal state (Plato, p. 120 ff.). The Greek historian Polybius (pp. 505–6) maintained that religion kept the Roman commonwealth together, checked 'lawless desires, unreasoning anger and violent passion'. Thomas Aquinas articulated the stabilizing effect of religion on moral laws in the *Summa Theologica* as follows:

> . . . by reason of the uncertainty of human judgement especially on contingent and particular matters, different people form different judgements, on human acts; whence also different and contrary laws result. In order, therefore, that man may know without any doubt what he ought to do and what he ought to avoid, it was necessary for man to be directed in his proper acts by a law given by God; for it is certain that such a law cannot err. (Aquinas, p. 753.)

In the American colonies, George Washington doubted that national morality could prevail 'in exclusion of religious principle' (Bellah, 1970, p. 173).

Similar sentiments were expressed in England in 1818, when a Bill was introduced to build more churches in the industrial cities. The Prime Minister, Lord Liverpool, defended the Bill strongly because he expected religion to safeguard public security and private morality (MacIntyre, pp. 18–19). In 1820, Catholic priests were reluctantly allowed to minister in Australia, which served Britain as a large and uniquely isolated jail at that time. The primary motive for their appointment was the administrative conviction that religious functionaries would improve the deplorable moral conditions. It was therefore only natural that the priests' salaries were paid from the Police Fund (O'Farrell, p. 16; see Mol, 1971a, pp. 47–50 for other examples in Australian history). Later in the nineteenth and twentieth centuries, those who tended to sacralize a scientific world-view also felt that this perspective could integrate the moral order. (Freud, 1964, p. 67; Rieff, 1961, p. 325; Ben-David, 1971, p. 128). In any of the Marxist countries a large variety of ethical rules are ultimately justified in terms of the Communist vision of the good life and the good society. To Lenin, sexual restraint was the hallmark of the dedicated Marxist (Stafford, p. 8).

The general acceptance of the integrating function of religion for values is well summed up as follows: 'Religion has accounted in large part for the fact that values in almost all human societies are not a mere hodge-podge, but constitute a hierarchy' (Nottingham, p. 14).

All this is not achieved, as adversaries of orthodox Christianity often assume, by the postulation of an avenging judge or the threat of hell in the hereafter. A moral veto is insufficient to curb, for instance, aggressive or sexual instincts. Attempts to control men by condemnation is like tightening down the safety valve more securely in order to counter the increasing pressure in a boiler. Religion integrates the moral order also by redirecting possible forces of disorder into safer channels, such as ritual dance or single-hearted commitment.

Earlier we implied that in modern advanced societies the esoteric core of universal religions has lost some of its plausibility through competition. Yet one should always be careful not to assume too readily that the alleged erosion of religious practices and religious motivation for mundane conduct also entails that entire cultures are now devoid of a sustaining (e.g. Christian) tradition. In Australian research, an unexpected correlation was found between the belief in God and ethical opinions. The believing secularists who did not go to church or pray (16 per cent of the population), but who believed in God without doubt, were decidedly different from the more consistent secularists whose opinions were, in contrast, heterodox and secular, and who were much more likely to be permissive and to leave open the options for conduct. On the other hand, the believing secularists were the 'modal' Australians who appeared to dislike equally the very religious and the very unreligious, but who assumed that religion was necessary to support morality (Mol, 1971a, pp. 45, 49, 52).

They have their equivalent in the U.S.A., where they complain about the corruption of the New York Police force and the lack of law and order in terms of a fading moral consensus and a similarly fading religious rationale for morality. Their assumptions should not be too easily discarded: it is much more difficult for a police force to maintain standards of integrity and honesty when the prevailing standards of the community it serves are based on 'what one can get away with' rather than on absolute standards of good and evil.

It is with the American situation of weakening transcendental support in mind, that Glock has come to the conclusion that the 'capacity of religion to inform the secular normative structure seems to be largely a thing of the past' (Glock, 1960, p. 59). He speaks here about organized religion and not the 'secular' religions such as the American way of life (Herberg, 1955, Chap. V) or civil religion (Bellah, 1970, Chap. IX) which undoubtedly reinforce values of democracy such as egalitarianism. Of course, the 'organized' religion of the sects and denominations still reinforces specific norms, values, and beliefs. Glock would not deny this, but (somewhat unrealistically) expects organized religion also to direct and change instead of merely to reinforce.

Glock has a valid point when he says that organized religion has a diminished influence, because 'the level of abstraction at which the topic is pursued has the consequence of leaving to other sources the final say in determining everyday norms and values' (Ibid., p. 60). This level of abstraction, as we have seen, is both a necessity and a predicament. The predicament may consist in a tendency for the more visible, discernible middle axioms to become independently sacralized. Or it may consist in these middle axioms becoming the sacred substitutes for the more abstract core within organized religion. This will be discussed in the section on the dysfunction of moral systems for religious ones (distortion). Here, however, we should pay some attention to a different predicament: that religious systems tend to rigidify moral ones.

RIGIDIFICATION

Each particular institutional segment of society has not only advantages for institutional orders, it must also have disadvantages or dysfunctions. Generally, the survival, within a conglomeration of interlocking systems, of one such system, depends on the sum total of its functions to outweigh the sum total of its dysfunctions. So it is with the interaction between the subsystem that sacralizes identity and the subsystem that adjusts the network of mutual expectations. The sum total of dysfunctions that religion has for morality can be aptly, and more or less comprehensively, expressed by the term 'rigidification'.

In an ancient Greek legend, the Phrygian King Midas turned everything he touched into gold and consequently even his food became rigid and indigestible. So with religion. Whatever it touches may similarly acquire sacred characteristics. Durkheim observed this in the primitive totemic religions that he studied, and he called it 'the contagiousness of religion' (1954, pp. 222, 237). In so far as religion integrates moral standards, it simultaneously lends them a 'don't touch', or 'don't change' quality.

In India, change in the system of social expectations is said to be severely hampered by Hindu sacralization of caste. Sri Aurobindo says that religions have too often been a force for retardation, burning a Giordano Bruno, imprisoning a Galileo, and supporting a rigid social system (Gandhi, 1950, p. 35–8). In the West, Herbert Spencer observed in the last century, ecclesiastical institutions were conservative in the double sense: they strengthened social bonds and so conserved the social aggregate, but they also offered extreme resistance to change (1897, Part VI, Chap. IX, pp. 770–1). In *The Future of an Illusion*, Freud maintains that commandments and laws would lose their rigidity and unchangeableness if the religious superstructure were abolished (1964, pp. 67, 68).

More recently, those Western theologians who hope to make Christianity more relevant through social action have also complained about the rigidifying consequences of traditional Christianity (Robinson, 1963, Chap. 6). The solution which they advocate is to reduce the supernaturalistic metaphysic, to emphasize the 'built-in moral compass' of the love ethic (p. 115), and to answer 'ought' questions 'in terms of the intrinsic realities of the situation itself' (p. 113). Tillich's remarks about love transcending the alternative of absolute and relative ethics (1951, p. 173), and Fletcher's practical concern with the uniqueness of each situation (1966, 1967; Robertson, 1968, pp. 65, 66) are central to this orientation.

The new morality, or situational ethics, is the almost perfect example of the attempt to resolve the structural predicament of Christianity in highly differentiated societies by maximizing its functions for morality (Christian love is an important integrating principle) and minimizing its dysfunctions (by retaining sufficient flexibility to judge each situation in terms of its own merit).

There is a good reason why the new moralists are almost without exception also social activists. Basically both movements assume that Christianity must cast a very wide net, ceaselessly integrating, repairing, and straddling the larger social identity. By contrast, the advocates of relevance A (the orthodox/evangelicals/verticalists) tend to confine their attempts at integrating morality to the much smaller segments of believers who are pitched against the vast evil world. They can therefore afford to be specific and concrete and, indeed, to relish it. More important, by preserving the transcendental super-structure they can also better use it for motivation and value maintenance.

The 'it depends' stance of situational ethics tends to leave unclear the identity boundaries of both the group and the individual. Instead of clarification and delineation, this approach accepts the abstractions that facilitate the functions of encompassing a differentiated society. Sexual relations before marriage is the issue through which situation ethics has understandably drawn much attention. Those who adopt this position neither approve nor disapprove, very much reflecting society at large in this regard. They maintain that the relationship between the unmarried partners (deep love or casual appetite outlet?) should be the guiding rationale, since either blanket approval or disapproval might be interpreted as partisan justification. They do not want controversy, but an integrative interpretation of action. The hidden consequence of the 'it depends' stance is a lesser integration and a diminished authority of the superego. In the somewhat different context of writing about the dysfunctions of the diverse and conflicting mores within the same culture, Wheelis comes to very much the same conclusion (1958, p. 126).

What happens in such cases is that the middle axiom of the Golden Rule, or in this case the love ethic, tends to become its own justification. The cosmic couch for the ethic becomes a ramshackle, somewhat irrelevant structure. Yet it is precisely this context which has the potential for social motivation, value maintenance, and therefore for identity delineation.

Throughout, we have assumed the principle of mutual inter-dependence between religions and other sub-systems. This means that we expect religion to be also affected by morality. Here too we can distinguish between a positive, functional, helping effect and a negative, dysfunctional, hindering influence. We shall name the first 'concretization', and the second 'distortion'.

CONCRETIZATION

The Sufi symbol of the walnut kernel providing the shell with a reason for being can also be turned around. After all, the shell (divine law) protects the kernel (the inner source of life of Islam) and helps it to survive.

In Buddhism, too, the moral commandments are seen as an aid to greater spiritual development. Avoiding the doing of all evil, the accomplishing of good, the purifying of the mind, are, according to the Buddha, all essential conditions for attaining Nirvana (Saddhatissa, p. 185).

In Christianity, too, moral standards have often formed the channels for the finite expression of the system of ultimate meaning. The faith of the Christian, with all its basically intangible, unprovable, almost incommunicable, and therefore socially insecure facets, could be concretely anchored in moral standards. By this alliance between the Christian faith and moral standards of a particular time and place, the former was prevented from dying the death of social irrelevance and sterile isolationism. Moral standards were used as an expression, a vehicle, or even as a measurement of the dedication of the followers. Through these moral standards and the quality of commitment to a particular moral system the Christians hoped that their faith or their system of ultimate meaning would be more visible, and therefore more accessible, to others.

The biblical injunction of James 2:17—'So Faith by itself, if it has no works, is dead'—is an illustration of this point. Sects from the early church onwards have attempted to realize the ethic of the Sermon on the Mount in actual communities. The monastic orders came into being primarily to protect and concretize the faith in communities of like-minded Christians who upheld ascetic moral standards. Here this faith could be given more finite expression than in the rough morality of the secular communities.

In modern times, Paul Tillich stressed the importance of the moral expression in religion when he said, that without the moral act religion would deteriorate into an emotional distortion of mysticism (Tillich, 1964, p. 18). The widespread pressure of modern society on the churches 'to be socially and morally relevant' is another illustration. The churches have responded with numerous pronouncements on marriage and sex, on property and usury, on alcoholism and delinquency, on war and peace, on power and corruption, etc. The problem in modern times seems to be that Christians, although they have written and spoken voluminously on these issues, cannot bridge the divergences and cannot keep up with the changes of opinions, attitudes, and events which move too fast for crystallization.

However, during the slower pace of earlier centuries, Christianity concretized its message in the doctrine of sanctification. This doctrine stressed the importance of moral fruits as a way to express one's faith in God. Its counterpart was the doctrine of justification, which stressed unmerited grace and by implication emasculated the emphasis on fruits. Dittes expressed this dilemma of Christianity well when he said that 'for the religious spirit expression in forms, in a body, is necessary, and for the religious spirit, expression in forms, in a body, is defiling' (Dittes, p. 379). John Oman (p. 63) expresses a similar dilemma by saying that depth and reality are destroyed when religion and morality are either yoked together or divorced from one another. He implies that they both oppose and complement one another: '. . . if religion without morality lacks a solid earth to walk on, morality, without religion, lacks a wide heaven to breathe in' (p. 62).

DISTORTIONS

The alliance between moral systems and religion can concretize the faith, as well as obscure it, indeed, the very concretization of the infinite tends to distort it.

Buddhism, as if aware of this danger, asserts that Nirvana (the inconceivable, transcendental, reality—Dutt, p. 281) is much more than moral perfection, and is not produced by the eightfold paths or the thirty-seven practices leading to full enlightenment (ibid., p. 290). It is unconditional and unconstituted (p. 294), and thus, identification with rules and precepts would distort its meaning.

As soon as historically finite solutions to finite moral problems were advocated and adopted by the churches, these solutions inevitably acquired sacred sanctions. To many, the moral rules themselves became the content of the faith. After all, these rules were visible, could be implemented, and could be subject to sanctions. Moral rules advance the smooth operation of communities and societies. However, precisely because of the alliance with a particular set of moral standards in specific periods of history, Judaism and, later, Christianity tended again and again to upstage law. Moral conservatism took the place of an essentially radical system of ultimate meaning. This was all the more so when the churches became established state churches and began to reinforce and stabilize national rather than minority moral standards. A church is nearly always much less legalistic in its early stages of development than in the later stages of its existence. The distortion of religion by the requirements of moral communities is forcefully brought out in the New Testament. Jesus time and again denounces the Pharisees for whom an extensive system or moral rules was of crucial importance. St. Paul, in his letter to the Romans, also stresses freedom from the Law (Torah) in order to minimize its distortive tendencies.

The Reformation, too, can be seen primarily as a questioning of institutional rules and prescriptions. The reformers felt that the emphasis on prescriptions and institutional loyalties obscured the primacy of the transcendental element. Nevertheless, Luther's emphasis on salvation by faith rather than by works, however true it was to the original theology of the early church, also had debilitating consequences; as faith was emphasized, so good works were correspondingly less insisted upon. A vaguer, more ethereal, invisible norm took precedence over a norm which strengthened the existing moral order. An important prop for the satisfaction of social and ecclesiastical acceptance was now weakened. Man was now somewhat less assured that certain concrete actions would lead to heavenly and earthly favour. He was now less confident in making distinctions between human beings. It is more difficult to judge others on faith, and much easier to judge their behaviour and conduct.

The greater proclivity of the Protestant churches to become secularized may be partially attributed to the invisibility, and therefore the social uncontrollability, of the norm of faith. Protestantism has been justifiably associated with the rise of individualism: the Reformation threw the individual back on himself as the norm of a strictly personal relationship with God was given greater emphasis. On the other hand, the social need for the rewards of conformity to clearly visible and workable prescriptions became proportionally less important. Secular humanism, with its overemphasis on the individual, is in many respects a legitimate child of the Reformation.

Thus, by attempting to minimize the distortion, the reformers had to accept a lesser degree of concretization. But the necessary ambiguity between institution and salvation by faith could never be

suspended. It was therefore natural that all through the history of
Protestantism the churches were tempted to upgrade religious forms
and consequently to sanction the relative. There was always pressure
to allay man's anxiety by concretely localizing the sacred, and
thereby providing the means for socializing and controlling man's
attitudes towards the sacred.

Another way to resolve the ambiguity between institution and
salvation by faith was to minimize the absolute demands of a jealous
and sovereign God and to re-emphasize His divine characteristics
(such as love and charity) which were intrinsically integrative.

In spite of—perhaps maybe in reaction to—the Reformation's re-
emphasis on faith, Western civilization, particularly in the predominantly Protestant countries, has increasingly defined the visible
or communicable as real. Man is, after all, social; his attitudes, values,
and beliefs are formed by the cues, the punishments and the rewards
of others in so far as these cues, punishments, and rewards are communicable. This belief that only the visible or the communicable is
real has had significant repercussions on the sense of meaninglessness of existence, since it becomes much more difficult to create a
projected unity, and on the authority for motives (if one is judged
only by appearances, why should one make life more difficult by
bothering about the authority of the invisible?). That this view of
reality has its own peculiar disadvantages for society is increasingly
realized (Inglis, 1964).

The distortion of religion by the requirements of moral communities (e.g. the church) is also brought out by Kierkegaard, who points
to the distortion which ethical or natural religiousness perpetrates on
Christian religiousness (Martin, 1950, pp. 102 ff.).

Feodor Dostoievsky in his narrative 'The Grand Inquisitor' from
The Brothers Karamazov is sociologically more perceptive, however, in portraying the contrasting effects in the parable of the second
advent of Christ to Seville during the Inquisition. In the story the
concretization is the church's response to man's need for someone
to keep his conscience, for someone to unite him under one authority.
This distortion is the transvaluation of 'the heavenly bread' into 'the
earthly bread', or as Kimmel and Clive put it:

In the episode of 'The Grand Inquisitor' the crucifixion—the
possibility (inevitability?) in life of a demonic distortion of truth
in the name of truth, of the good in the name of goodness, of

freedom in the name of freedom—is given its most powerful modern expression. (Kimmel, 1960, p. 239.)

All this could lead to a misunderstanding, namely that in attempting to escape the distortion of social and moral requirements the religious core transcends social functions, or, rather, becomes irrelevant to them. This is not the case. The Lutheran doctrine of grace and justification by faith lightens the burdens of the past (sins are freely forgiven, the past is decidedly relativized) and provides motivational energy for unimpeded social participation in the future, since God's support can be relied upon, even if it is entirely undeserved. The doctrine of sanctification can be seen as an attempt to minimize the anomic potentialities of grace by its stress on moral fruits as a way to express one's faith. From the sociological perspective, the perpetual paradox of sin and grace, or sanctification and justification, is a unique attempt to maximize both social motivation and the validity of values, and to minimize their intrinsic discrepancy. In a viable social environment, an overemphasis on sanctification creates problems of social motivation, and an overemphasis on justification produces problems of value maintenance. It is for this reason that both emphases are necessary and are kept in an uneasy, sociologically eminently sensible, but logically equally repugnant, balance.

SUMMARY

There is an intricate interaction between man's instinct for mastering his environment, the increasing complexity of the results of this mastery, and the increasing abstraction necessary to encompass and integrate proliferating elements in this complex whole. Scientific and rational thinking, as we know it today, are one consequence of the sacralization of these abstract points of reference.

The development of differentiation and abstraction also had inevitable consequences for the interaction between the emerging systems that sacralized identity (religion) and the systems that oiled the machinery of social relations (morality). In undifferentiated societies the two were often indistinguishable, but in modern societies, a twofold development took place:

(a) The task of encompassing very large, heterogeneous frames of identity (nations and national value systems) tended to be sacrificed for more manageable homogeneous units (sects or orthodox denominations, political ideologies, commitment-requiring causes) that could maintain both plausible points of ultimate reference and concrete value prescriptions for selected memberships. On the other hand, those who continued to think in terms of a universal or a national frame of identity, such as the proponents of situational ethics or the new morality, were obliged to add water to their wine, diminish the significance of the transcendental, and elevate the love ethic, in order to avoid giving blanket approval or disapproval of specifics that, in the complex heterogeneous larger entity, were controversial. The weakness of this 'it depends' stance is the absence of a stimulus for social motivation, and poor capacity for value maintenance and concrete identity boundaries.

(b) This weakness is avoided in the more isolated, smaller, more cohesive frames frames of identity. In both this case and in the past, that of the universal religions, which could then still successfully encompass larger entities, a relationship of functions and dysfunctions developed. Christianity, for instance, contributed to the integration and internal consistency of specific moral standards (function). However, precisely because these standards became more sacred, they also became more rigid (dysfunction). Things also occurred the other way round: both in Buddhism and Christianity moral standards often provided the channel by means of which finite expression could be given to a system of ultimate meaning (function), but this very concretization of the infinite or unconditional also distorted the same system (dysfunction).

This dilemma of balancing functions and dysfunctions is well illustrated by the sociologically sensible, but logically repugnant, paradox between sin and grace, or between the doctrines of sanctification and justification by faith. Sanctification provides the need for a stable moral system. Justification provides the need for maximum social motivation and acceptance, which the more esoteric core of a system of meaning promises in exchange for greater commitment.

Chapter IX

Legitimation: Economy, Polity, Science

Legitimation is generally used in the sense of justification, and often one word can be substituted for the other. Thus: Etzioni (1971, p. 565) writes that the only legitimation for the supranational state lies in a supranational consensus and focus of loyalty, and Weber (1946, pp. 78, 79) says that traditional charismatic or legal authority legitimates the exercise of power over others. Very often an event, or norm, is legitimated or justified by a higher order principle. Even the modern atheist legitimates death 'in terms of a Weltanschauung of progressive evolution or of revolutionary history'. Death is always integrated 'with a reality spanning symbolic universe' (Berger and Luckmann, p. 119).

In the not so distant past, venerable religious institutions provided most of these legitimations. The sacred represented the apex of higher order principles, and a hierarchical network of links provided the rationale for action. The taken-for-granted identity of a person, group, or society was a higher court of appeal. Personal experiences as well as entire institutions were explained and justified in terms of a time-honoured system of ultimate meaning. As long as these experiences were adequately confirmed by the system of ultimate meaning, this system tended to become sacralized and encrusted with the awe of perpetuity.

Recently, however, the traditional sacred mould for these legitimations has become somewhat tarnished. In the previous chapter, we noted that religious traditions could be better characterized as standing in a dialectic relationship with morality than as providing overarching protection and legitimation for it.

This is also true for the other sub-systems of modern society, such as the economy, polity, science, class, and family. In the not so distant Christian past, all of these sub-systems depended on legitimation by religious institutions. In the Middle Ages, such minor matters as interest rates came under religious scrutiny. Up till the middle of the nineteenth century, education came under ecclesiastical tutelage. Even now the world's few remaining monarchs are crowned in religious ceremonies, presidents are sworn in on the Bible, and the Christian churces legitimate specific family socialization patterns and distinctive styles of life. Yet in the West, the increasing social differentiation of society and the accompanying independence of emerging sub-systems has led to a dialectical, rather than to a legitimating relationship. Man's mastery of the environment through economic and technical manipulation could better be accomplished without the burdens of sacred prescriptions. Nevertheless, problems of meaning and ultimate goals could not be solved by these newly autonomous sub-systems. Nor could they consolidate and anchor individual, group, and social identities. In other words, modern societies use the advantage of the independence of their sub-systems for the more complete mastery of their environment while remaining sceptical about their self-sacralizations. Sacralization would maximize independence, but it would also handicap instrumental functions. A dialectical, rather than a legitimating or a repudiating, relationship with the religious sub-system appears to approximate the balance at which functions are maximized and dysfunctions minimized. None the less, there are examples of self-sacralization of sub-systems: a profession sometimes legitimates a person's practices, ethics, and modes of behaviour; a political ideology becomes the source of a person's value priorities; or scientific objectivity becomes the all-absorbing faith of the devotee.

One final introductory point must be made: there are crucial differences between the major sub-systems of modern societies. The economic and science/educational sub-systems tend to favour the forces of change and differentiation. On the other hand, the family and social strata tend to favour the forces of consolidation and identity. The polity appears to be in the middle, creating and maintaining order, but innovating expediently when the situation demands.

Both the traditional religious institutions and their modern counterparts do little legitimating for the economy and science. They counterbalance and complement. They may sacralize some of the values (honesty, reliability, responsibility) crucial to the functioning of the economy, polity, and science. On the other hand, they sacralize emotional bonds of love and protection or particularistic values that are crucial for family life but dysfunctional for industrial and political bureaucracies. Traditional religious institutions, hippie communes, sectarian groups, and weird cults all serve as antidotes to the cold anonymity of a complex urban society and bolster the forces of identity and integration at the expense of those of adaptation, change, and manipulation. Each major sub-system must be examined separately, since each has its own set of dialectical relationships with religious forces.

ECONOMY

Parsons correctly puts the economy in his adaptation segment of the functional prerequisites for any social system (1971, p. 11). To translate this into our terms, economic forces are *par excellence* forces making for change, differentiation, and manipulation. The division of labour, and the profit-motive, issuing in the efficient, rational uses of resources decrease man's dependence on his environment by providing him with a higher standard of living, and therefore maximize his ability to survive. What they do *not* is integrate man, groups, and societies.

Although we expect religion in the large sense we are using it here to fill the complementary or distinguishing role, there is, *mirabile dictu*, a much larger amount of literature on the contribution Christianity made to the very forces which in the last resort undermined it or at least made its existence uncomfortable.

It was Max Weber, whose essay, *The Protestant Ethic and the Spirit of Capitalism* (1952, first published in 1904) started a veritable avalanche of books and articles on this topic (to name a few major ones: Robertson, 1933; Fanfani, 1935; Tawney, 1937; Fischoff, 1944; Parsons, 1949; Birnbaum, 1953; Green, 1959; Samuelsson, 1964; Eisenstadt, 1968; Demerath and Hammond, 1969). Weber argued that Calvinism provided an inner support or an intellectual moral vertebra which facilitated the vigorous development of modern capitalism. By the latter he meant a rational industrial organization, using to the full any opportunity for profit-making, separation of business from household and rational bookkeeping (Weber, 1952, p. 21).

The spiritual support took place through the Calvinist emphasis on worldly asceticism. The spur to economic growth lay in the accumulation of capital through ascetic compulsion to save (p. 172). But why work at all when Calvinism also taught through the doctrine of predestination that the fruits of one's work could not possibly lead to salvation? Weber's answer was that Calvinistic man saw himself as a trustee of the goods which God had provided. Like the good servant in the parable of the Talents (Matthew 25:14–30) it was his individual responsibility to account for every penny entrusted to him and it was 'at least hazardous to spend any of it for a purpose which does not serve the Glory of God, but only one's own enjoyment' (p. 170). Yet why was Calvinism so different in this respect from Catholicism or even Lutheranism? After all, the same doctrines went back to the beginning of the Christian era. Weber's answer was that medieval Catholicism had incarcerated asceticism within the monastery walls, whereas Protestantism let it stride 'into the market-place of life' penetrating the 'daily routine of life with its methodicalness' (p. 154). And as to Lutheranism, it 'lacked a psychological sanction of systematic conduct to compel the methodical rationalization of life' (p. 128). To the Calvinist every social activity in the world was legitimated solely in so far as it led to the greater glory of God whereas Luther tended to justify it in terms of brotherly love (p. 108). Calvinism too developed a different conception of calling, 'proving one's faith in worldly activity' (p. 121) or as Yinger in an excellent chapter on this topic says so well: 'For ordinary men the recognizability of the state of grace was of supreme importance: all men did not have Calvin's self-assurance— they wanted a visible sign of salvation' (1970, p. 383). Success in this world's activities became the locus for self-assurance and proof of divine grace.

Contrary to the imputations of some of his critics (e.g. H. M. Robertson, Samuelsson, p. 96) Weber was adamant that Calvinism did not *cause* the Spirit of Capitalism. He was only concerned with treating one side of the causal chain he said (p. 27), and in his other works (see *The Sociology of Religion*, 1964) insisted that theological doctrines were also on the receiving end. To him religious and economic phenomena were interdependent.

Yet he was more interested in religion as the affecting or independent variable and his studies of other religions were primarily undertaken to discover why the latter did not encourage the spirit of rational capitalism.

In Confucianism, which at first sight seemed more congenial to this-worldly enterprises than other religions, he found that rationalism was a rational adjustment *to* the world, whereas Puritan rationalism meant rational mastery *of* the world. The Confucian emphasis on the sacredness of tradition and on the refined administrator steeped in the classics and literary intellectuality went against the entrepreneurial rationality typical for the spirit of capitalism (Weber, 1964b, pp. 104, 132, 235, 236).

Even less encouragement did Weber find in the other religions he compared. Hinduism, for instance, he found much too escapist and other-worldly and therefore not leading to preoccupation with rational mastery and entrepreneurial exploitation of the world (Weber, 1958; Parsons, 1949, pp. 552–6).

Appraising the Protestantic Ethic thesis: given Weber's important notion of interdependence, there can be no surprise about the fit between a particular religious emphasis (the Calvinist ethic) and a newly emerging economic orientation (the spirit of rational capitalism). Neither can there be any surprise about the lack of fit between this spirit and religious orientations of other times and cultures. In terms of our basic hypothesis: if religious forces fail to interact with, or be relevant for, specific personal, group or social identities of a specific time in a specific culture, they are not likely to survive. Of necessity, therefore, one can expect Confucianism and Hinduism to fit with a specific situation in China and India and *not* in Europe.

In Europe, on the other hand, a rising commercial bourgeoisie felt ill at ease in a setting where feudal constraints were sacralized and again it is only natural that the identity of the new movements was better served by new sacralization patterns. True, Catholicism itself was the product of its own continual absorptions of basically antagonistic elements, resulting in more individualism and cold rationalism than any of the other religious organizations (Judaism excepted)! Yet the new religious movements had the advantage of a new closely fitting baseline, even when in their actual doctrinal presentation very little had changed. Justification by faith, predestination, election, conversion, etc., all had a venerable history going all the way back to the New Testament scriptures and St. Augustine amongst others. What was relatively new was the change in emphasis from ecclesiastical mediacy to direct personal commitment, from earning one's salvation through visible implementable action to the undeserved gift of grace. This, together with the

advantage of any fresh start unencumbered with previous ecclesiastical traditions and fortified with charismatic syntony, made Protestantism such an attractive option. The identity of the commercial
and entrepreneurial classes was bound to a high degree of individual
freedom, personal faith, and a prosaic view of man (all are sinful)
in order to survive the competition. Similarly the poorest classes
often found in Calvinism an agreeable downstaging of the ultimate
significance of power and wealth (Hyma, p. 340; Samuelsson, p. 105).
Also needed was a future orientation (the parousia and heaven) at
the expense of the past (forgiveness of sin) and the present (life in the
flesh is misery) in order to free emotions and galvanize energy. Yet
all this individualism and capacity to cope with negative social
evaluations should never endanger a high degree of mutual confidence (the common brotherhood of faith), moral stability, honesty
and sobriety (God's omniscience and judgement) in one's community.

Throughout this interpretation (which is consistent with our
fundamental assertion that religion sacralizes identity rather than
creates it) we have implicitly modified Weber. The latter staunchly
maintained that Calvinism had its own independent effect and
would have heartily agreed with Trevor-Roper (pp. 2–4) that
religion was the crucial variable for the political, economic, and
intellectual change in Europe from 1520 (when Spain and the
Empire, Italy, and the Papacy were the centre of power, wealth,
industry, and intellectual life) to 1700 (when this centre had moved
to Protestant England, Holland, Switzerland, and the cities of the
Baltic). We maintain, however, that this change could only take
place because the available economic and other opportunities could
be maximized through a close fit with a religious re-emphasis,
minimizing diffidence and insecurity about change. The reassertion
that there was nothing sacred about the world and its inhabitants
and even the visible church paved the way for rational mastery,
manipulation, and a competitive, illusionless, view of one's fellow-
beings. A new religious movement with fresh energies had by
definition a better opportunity to become the integrative counterpart
to an emerging instrumental sub-system than the traditional religious
institutions with energies dissipated by self-maintenance and defence
of the status quo.

It is the changeover from a legitimating to a dialectical relationship between the economic and religious sub-system which Calvinism

facilitated. And yet the latter in its early phases remained highly critical of independent instrumental values, the growth of which it facilitated. Weber's critics, such as Samuelsson, have failed to see that there can be (and actually was) congruence or affinity between essentially opposite religious and entrepreneurial camps (Samuelsson, 1961; Gellner, pp. 19–20). By pointing out the contrasts and by denying the complexity of latent functions, Samuelsson assumes to have refuted Weber's argument in the Protestant Ethic and the Spirit of Capitalism. Weber's rationalistic bias (Campbell and Fukuyama, p. 182; Marcuse, 1969, p. 204) is partly to blame for this confusion of tongues. Yet Weber's view of the saliency of the affinity of the two spirits can be suitably maintained, provided one is also aware of the essential contrast in functions between the religious and entrepreneurial movements.

Weber maintained that the impetus for a unique spirit of capitalism ultimately lay in a unique Calvinist sense of calling. This is plainly not so. As mentioned in a previous chapter there is good evidence that this specific emphasis on calling or proving oneself in one's vocation 'fully developed only in the seventeenth century' (Borkenau, p. 287) and actually 'completely subverted the fundamental theological structure of Calvinism' (Hudson, p. 58). It obviously was a bending of theology to fit an already flourishing 'spirit of capitalism' rather than a necessary condition for this spirit to develop. In addition the emphasis on calling is unnecessary as there are more crucial variables (such as charismatic fervency) to link both 'spirits' (Mol, 1968a, pp. 69–70).

Weber was right (and sociologically very perceptive) when he emphasized the elective affinity between the spirit of Calvinism and capitalism. However, he was wrong (because he was religiously unmusical, as he admitted) when he explained this affinity by means of the doctrine of calling. He failed to see that the upgrading of God's judgement and election was the direct consequence of the relativization of the church as mediator of grace. Or to say this more sociologically, he failed to see that the downgrading of the more recognizable organs of social control was compensated by the upstaging of the less recognizable (and therefore fanatically emphasized) transcendental source of ethical judgement. This doctrinal change in emphasis enhanced the forces of individualism and austerity and decreased the forces of corporateness and social dependence, the shelter of mutual trust and love. This loosening of the social fabric

enabled the economic (or manipulative) system to become gradually
more independent from the religious (or integrative) sub-system. And
as we will see later: the emotional acceptance of man's marginality
in the sight of God had a propitious effect on the marginal, rational,
manipulative stance man adopted towards his environment.

An interesting, modern, example of certain forms of Protestantism
loosening the social fabric can be found in Latin America. From
1960 to 1967 the annual evangelical growth rate in this area of the
world was 10 per cent, although the population grew by only 3 per
cent in the same period (Read, Monterosso and Johnson, p. 54).
Here it is particularly Pentecostalism which appears to inspire its
membership with the security and confidence necessary for the
taking of entrepreneurial risks. The individualism and freedom inherent in commitment to Christ allows Pentecostalist farmers 'to
break through traditional patterns and make changes in agricultural
methods' (Gerlach and Hine, p. 102; Read, 1965; McGavran, 1963).
Similar to Mormon Maoris in New Zealand (Mol, 1966, p. 13) the
Latin-American Pentecostalists impress their employers by their
sobriety, reliability, and capacity for hard work (Gerlach and Hine,
p. 108; Erasmus, 1961). The increasing competition of a sectarian
Pentecostalist identity with a Catholic sacralization of a local identity
tends to also make the economic (or manipulative) subsystem to
become more independent from the religious (or integrative) sub-
system. Again, dialectic takes over from legitimation.

POLITY

One of the major threads running through our analysis is the idea
that variety in religiosity relates to variety of identity fragilities (on
the functional level) and to variety of adaptive changes (on the
structural level). Western Christianity more than any other religion
had to continually integrate and consolidate a redoubtable parade of
changes produced by forces (such as marginality and rationality)
stronger than the religious ones. This made for greater abstraction
and versatility, we have said, and in the sixteenth century a sectarian
spirit of individualism, inner-worldly ascetism, and austerity
appeared to provide the fit for the emerging rational capitalism.
Although this fit endangered the heart of the religious function
(secularism is closer related to Calvinism and related sectarian move-

ments than any other form of Christianity), it still provided the security necessary for further differentiation and technological progress.

This major thread will also be used as our basis of analysis for the religious legitimation of the polity.

Up till fairly recently religious forces were used to legitimate the polity, whatever its form. The universal religions were particularly useful to legitimate or sacralize the larger as over against the smaller units of identity. Buddhism was enthusiastically adopted by the great Indian empire-builder Asoka. Mohammed and his immediate successors used Islam to eliminate tribal rivalries and to unify Arabian society (Wach, 1944, Chap. VII; Scharf, pp. 127–30). In eleventh-century Europe the ecclesiastical and feudal hierarchy were closely integrated. The relationship between God, Christ, the saints, the pope, and the believers sacralized the existing political structure (Weiler, p. 38). Later in Spain, Isabella and Ferdinand made Catholicism the effective foundation of a powerful monarchy straddling differences of custom, language, and law (Almerich, p. 459). Similarly in Norway and Denmark (Dawson, 1958, p. 95; O'Dea, 1966, p. 65). Indeed Scharf (p. 124) makes the valuable point that the rise of universal religion was conditioned by these specific political requirements.

It is not accidental that the legitimating link with political institutions first began to wane at the time of the Renaissance and Reformation. The spirit of rational individualism now unencumbered by powerful ecclesiastical controls would press forward to safeguard the sacred rights of the individual in independent political institutions. The sects or religious protest movements have generally inclined towards democracy (Weber (1969, p. 320) speaks about an elective affinity between sect and democracy) because survival dictated a sharing of power rather than the impossible overthrow of the status quo defending religious monopolies. At the time of the Renaissance democracy was hardly more than opposition to feudal privileges and a reassertion of 'a new bourgeois principle of selection according to purely individual criteria and not according to birth and rank' (von Martin, p. 4). Democracy could only develop after the Reformation had sanctified individualism sufficiently to relativize the hierarchical setting in terms of which both upper and lower classes placed themselves. The Reformation also emphasized the priesthood of all believers in spiritual and ecclesiastical matters and this principle found its way via the Puritan Revolution in England in the secular democratic theory of John Locke (Bellah, 1970, p. 68). A combination of implicit opposition to the status quo and explicit congregational principles makes present-day Pentecostalism in Brazil and Chile a force towards greater participation in democratic institutional structures (Willems, 1964, p. 104; 1966; 1967, p. 255).

It is particularly Alexis de Tocqueville who saw the connection between the decline of legitimating links and the rise of democracy. 'In proportion as a nation assumes a democratic condition of society and as communities display democratic propensities, it becomes more and more dangerous to connect religion with political institutions.... Agitation and mutability are inherent in the nature of democratic republics' (Vol. I, pp. 322–3). On the other hand, de Tocqueville felt that particularly in Protestant America unchangeable religious authority could optimize its function through restricting itself to its own resources.

It is particularly in Calvinism and the sects influenced by it that scholars have often looked for the legitimating source of democratic institutions. Yet neither Calvin whose personal point of view was as undemocratic and authoritarian as possible, nor the Genevan Constitution which went more in the direction of an oligarchy than a democracy (Troeltsch, Vol. II, p. 628) were directly responsible for this development. Indirectly, however, through Calvin's constant appeal to public opinion in his sermons (p. 628) and through his emphasis on the independence of the secular authority (p. 627), but even more important through the emphasis on the freedom of individual conscience in spiritual matters (Calvin, Book IV, Chap. X, Section 5), democracy was advanced.

Jellinek, who provided Max Weber with the crucial stimulus to investigate the impact of religion in the economic area, concluded that 'the idea of legally establishing inalienable, inherent and sacred rights to the individual [was] not of political but religious origin' (Jellinek, p. 77; Bendix and Roth, pp. 308–9). Not in England or France, but in New England congregationalism he found the principle of inherent, natural rights, institutionalized both in religion and politics.

Yet American historians maintain that it was the ever-receding western frontier rather than New England which fostered this combination of individualism cum religious and political democracy. 'Frontier individualism', says F. J. Turner (p. 300), 'has from the beginning promoted democracy.' On the other hand 'in each colony this (frontier) region was in conflict with the dominant classes of the coast' (p. 248). Essential to the institutionalization of democracy was the free land available to the frontiersmen. 'These free lands promoted individualism, economic equality, freedom to rise, democracy' (p. 259). On the other hand in the East social conditions had begun to crystallize and that meant to be moulded in hierarchical forms of unequal power. On the frontier, however, power was often uniquely concentrated in scarce, manual labour, thereby compelling those who needed assistance to treat both their labourers and co-operating neighbours with equal respect. This unique situation of newly settled lands appears more propitious to the institutionalization of democracy than for instance the preaching of populist values of Mencius in China in the fourth century B.C. (Browne, 1956, pp. 265 ff.) or the overthrow of the aristocracy by the proletariat (French and Russian revolutions).

It is in the U.S.A. then that the differentiation between religious and political functions and individualistic democratic modes of organizations of each became most clearly institutionalized.

The dialectic between religion and polity is characterized by both support and antithesis. The support lies in common adherence to sacred values of democracy. The antithesis lies in the religious adherence to values of integration, stability, Christian love, and equality before God, on the one hand, and in the political adherence to values of power, aggressive pursuit of political ends, and often opportunism on the other.

Still, neither individualism nor democracy can be taken for granted. The institutionalization and even sacralization of these values and patterns are therefore also obvious in such countries as the U.S. Speaking about the latter, de Tocqueville (Vol. I, p. 318) suggested that a society could not escape destruction unless the moral tie was strengthened in proportion to the relaxation of the political tie. Bellah (1970, pp. 137, 141) thinks that the maintenance of a really democratic value system requires a transcendental reference in terms of which the political process itself can be judged. This point of reference does not have to be located in traditional Christianity alone. Actually one can find people such as J. Paul Williams favouring 'teaching democracy as a religious ultimate' (Williams, 1962; Marty, 1972, p. 11).

There are, however, generally two problems with a sub-system (in our case: the polity) sacralizing its own patterns. The sacralization may well become dysfunctional for the adaptive requirements. A political party may sacralize specific planks in its platform and gradually lose vital support from a changing constituency. Secondly: the inner sacralization of the political subsystem (e.g. democracy) cannot very easily, elegantly, and comprehensively deal with other personal and social identity fragilities: anxiety, death, disaster, injustice, etc.

Or to say the same differently: the religious subsystem of a society can much more comfortably absorb such items as democracy in its sacred matrix than a political subsystem can absorb elements extraneous to its function.

SCIENCE AND EDUCATION

An important assumption in our analysis has been that the take-off vitality of new adaptations depends on the quality of integration (and therefore security) of previous adaptations. The new religious movements of the Reformation had the advantage of a close fit on the integrative level with emerging instrumental values necessary for economic, political, and technological differentiation.

Both Calvinism and Lutheranism exalted man's marginality in the sight of God. This had been done before, notably by St. Paul and St. Augustine, but now this emphasis could become one of the motivating forces for the achievement of secular goals. The fit between religious movements and emerging instrumental values consisted not so much in the legitimation of individual rationalism as such, but in the marginality and relativization which produced the former. Christianity in general and sectarian orthodoxy in particular anchored man's marginality in the emotions and thereby freed him to pursue his secular ends in a purposive fashion. It goes without saying that this was almost as far as any religious movement could go without betraying its own essential function. It was partly the fervency of these new religious movements which prevented the betrayal, but the easy transition in subsequent centuries from Puritanism to Unitarianism in New England communities shows what can happen when initial fervency dies out.

The Baconian religion of science in the seventeenth century is another example of an easy transition from religious to secular mar-

ginality and objectivity. It is also a good example of the affinity or
congruence between essentially contrasting functions. Francis Bacon
'replaced the name of "God" by the name "Nature"; but almost
everything else he left unchanged ... the laws of God were replaced
by the science of Nature; and at a later date, God's design and God's
judgements were replaced by natural selection. Theological deter-
mination was replaced by scientific determinism ... God's omnipotence and omniscience were replaced by the omnipotence of
nature and by the virtual omniscience of natural science' (Popper,
1963, p. 961). At the back of this seemingly facile and facetious transition was the spirit of rational inquiry and individualism common
to both. Merton suggests that the Puritan ethos may not have
directly influenced the method of science, but he thinks that there
is evidence 'that through the psychological compulsion toward certain modes of thought and conduct [the Puritan] value-complex
made an empirically-founded science commendable rather than, as
in the medieval period, reprehensible or at best acceptable on
sufferance' (p. 579). Grant (1969, p. 22) makes a similar point when
he says that 'Calvinist Christianity did not provide a public brake
upon the dissemination of the new ideas (expressed by the new
physical and moral sciences) as did Catholicism and even sometimes
Anglicanism.' Although this facilitated the dissemination, Grant
also perceptively points out that this happened 'almost without [the
Calvinists] knowing the [disadvantageous] results for their faith'
(ibid.). Puritanism provided the sanction or legitimation for an
emerging scientific ethos. The original members of the Royal Society
in England (patterned on Baconian teachings) who were disproportionately Puritan, felt that they were glorifying God by the study of
His handiwork (Merton, pp. 576, 577). This increased the take-off
vitality, and consequent independence, of a new adaptation all the
more so because it promised to lead 'to the domination of Nature
by technological invention' (ibid.). It is this confluence of legitimations, values, and needs which I presume has led at least some
scholars to suggest 'that seventeenth-century England was the turning point in the history of science and that the Puritans were its
chief agents' (Barbour, p. 48).

However, the deepest, and almost invariably misunderstood,
source of confluence lay in the illusionless view of man and nature.
Man as an abject sinner in an environment which could not boast
of any inherent sacred merit could only be redeemed by God's

mercy. Man's marginality was decreed and welded in his emotions by a fiery God who also miraculously loved him so much that he made the ultimate sacrifice on the cross. Exactly the same marginal view of man and his environment stripped this time from its cosmic, archetypal, setting was a prerequisite for the kind of science developed since the seventeenth century. All that was necessary was to upstage the instrumental and rational (science) and to downstage the integrating and emotional (religion), but the fundamental marginality (or capacity for standing outside one's structures) remained.

It goes without saying that the essential functional divergence of religion and science remained and has been clearly noted both before, during and after the Puritan episode when science first began to develop into a separate subsystem. Augustine, whom Calvin so often quotes approvingly, had a profound interest in science before his conversion but afterwards looked upon all his knowledge as vain. To him, happiness lay in a much superior knowledge of God (1945, p. 66; Polanyi, p. 26).

To Calvin reason is a most excellent blessing of the Divine Spirit and 'one of the essential properties of our nature'. God will punish those lazy believers who do not make use of the works of the ungodly in physics, dialectics, mathematics, and other similar sciences (Book II, Chap. III, pp. 16, 17). There is no trace here in Calvin of anything inherently wrong with reason as such. He is here very much a child of the Renaissance, using both Greek and Latin classical sources, adopting Cicero's style of pleading. And yet after all this has been said Calvin goes happily on to say that the reasoning about God by philosophers 'invariably savours somewhat of giddy imagination'. Some of them are blinder than moles, he says, and if there is any light in what they say, it is as rare and useless as a single flash of lightning in a dark night. All their efforts and power of intellect are 'fleeting and vain whenever it is not based on a solid foundation of truth'. And the only source of truth is God's grace, without which man's natural gifts are downright corrupt (ibid.).

Similarly, Pascal, after his brilliant work in mathematics and science, went so far as calling the sciences 'vain' (Pensée 67) and reason 'corrupt' (Pensée 440), even though reason constituted man's being (Pensée 439). To him, all virtue and all happiness was in Jesus Christ. 'Apart from Him there is but vice, misery, darkness, death and despair' (Pensée 545) and reason should recognize its own limitations (Pensée 267).

In the nineteenth century the Danish thinker Kierkegaard similarly stressed the limitations of reason and objective observation. 'The objective tendency, which proposes to make everyone an observer ... refuses to know or listen to anything except what stands in relation to itself' (Kierkegaard, p. 118). On the other hand the positive leap of the Chrstian faith more effectively leads to man's true destiny: utter self-denial and God-affirmation.

In the twentieth century the major theologians have expressed almost identical views. To Karl Barth a rationalistic *a priori* could never be a substitute for God's grace and God's freedom (Barth, 1947, p. 370). Emil Brunner recognized the autonomy of reason, but in the same breath stressed its limitations and relativity. To him, the Word of God was primary (Brunner, p. 473). Reinhold Niebuhr flatly stated: 'Every effort to identify meaning with rationality implies the deification of reason ... religious faith cannot be simply subordinated to reason or made to stand under its judgment' (Niebuhr, 1949, Vol. I, pp. 176–7).

From a more sociological angle all these theological views of science and reason share a common belief that only the religious orientation can provide a comprehensive, commitment-inducing set of meanings and that when science and reason are ultimate ends, a culture, a society, and person are likely to suffer the consequences of meaninglessness.

This is precisely what implicitly or explicitly many scientists, philosophers, and other scholars deny. The assumption that science and/or its core value, reason, was the master principle in relation to traditional religious commitments, can be traced as far back as Plato's Republic. It ran unobtrusively but nevertheless strongly in the philosophies of Descartes and Spinoza (Goldmann, p. 37) and culminated in the Enlightenment and the actual worship of Reason during the French revolution.

To Durkheim, scientific thought was 'a more perfect form of religious thought' (1954, p. 429). To some psychologists, such as B. F. Skinner, behavioural science is obviously superior to belief in God as a means of making sense of one's world. To Toffler, the turning away from rationality to religion is a 'sick nostalgia ... dangerously maladaptive' (p. 451). The list could be multiplied many times over.

Sociologically one can say about all these scholars that to them, the scientific sub-system can do without much transcendental assistance and that it can develop its own internal legitimating (or as we would say 'sacralizing') mechanism.

However, within the world of scholarship this is by no means the accepted or even majority position. There are many who, while in favour of the independence and freedom of the sub-system and strongly against a return to a previous situation of religious tutelage, also harbour a sense of alarm reminiscent of the sorcerer's apprentice who could cast the spell of the self-sweeping broom but could not stop it.

The Canadian philosopher, George Grant, deplores the present-day 'unalloyed drive to technological mastery for its own sake' and the 'self-propelling will to technology' (p. 27). The sociologist C. Wright Mills, tempers the optimism of both Marx and Freud about the goodness of rational awareness by observing that 'science, it turns out, is not a technological Second Coming' (1959). Habermas (p. 305) adopts Husserl's criticism of the 'objectivist illusion' and notes its potential perversion as a scientific profession of faith (p. 315). Earlier Pareto had pointed out that a society based on reason never did and could exist (Parsons, 1949, p. 420). Lorenz (1970, p. 213) similarly implies that reason is a singularly poor motivator when he compares it with 'a wonderful system of wheels without a motor to make them go round'.

The psychologist Wilhelm Reich found latent schizophrenia in standing aside and in observing one's own inner functioning (Reich, p. 119; Rieff, 1968, p. 154). To Carl Jung a culture founded on science was by definition neurotic (Rieff, 1968, p. 136). Klapp sees a correlation between the twentieth-century knowledge explosion and the increase in identity problems: ' . . as with Faust, when man knows the most, he begins to suffer an identity problem' (p. 21). To him the incredible revolution of youth against the idols of success and the Puritan virtues 'is also a challenge to rationalism (planning, technology, science, logic); it rejects the intellect as a sole valid method (the premise of Socrates, Descartes, J. S. Mill) . . . rejects progress as the eighteenth and nineteenth centuries conceived it' (p. 69). Michael Crozier regards student unrest as essentially a rebellion against the new hyper-rationalist world (Greeley, 1969, p. 57). A few decades earlier a fellow-countryman (Bergson, p. 112) noted the same 'dissolvent power of intelligence', against which he regarded religion as a defensive reaction.

The Eastern religions which could maintain their pre-spell, undifferentiated, stance seem to be very up to date all of a sudden when they speak about reason being safest 'when it is content to take the profound truths and experiences of the spiritual being...just as they are given...' (Aurobindo in Gandhi, p. 49) or when they look upon 'logic as a whore serving anyone who can pay the price' (Needleman, p. 15). In the Vedanta reason is seen as 'truth-empty' (Arapura, 1970, p. 163).

The entire field of education is similarly in full retreat from the exuberant nineteenth-century convictions that more knowledge would solve man's problems. The strong confidence in educational techniques appears to be subdued by an equal confusion about wider educational goals. Only a minority of schools and colleges affiliated with religious denominations appears less afflicted by problems of wider goals than by problems of staffing and finance. However, the secular educational institutions financed by the State in Anglo-Saxon countries are intrinsically baffled by their pupils' search for identity. They provide counselling services and often even start the school day with decreasingly meaningful flag-saluting rituals. However the learning process is never conceived or justified in an integrated transcendental frame of reference. Religion is vaguely revered as occupying itself with these kinds of questions, but the sub-system can never surrender its neutrality and therefore can hardly go beyond the boundary of observing and analysing religious orientations. It can hardly sacralize the identity of its clients and societies through demanding ultimate commitments, engaging in full-blown rituals and preaching particularistic theologies. It is probably because he covertly expected this from a good education system that Malcolm Muggeridge could write so bitingly:

> Education, the great mumbo-jumbo and fraud of the age, purports to equip us to live, and is prescribed as a universal remedy for everything from juvenile delinquency to premature senility. For the most part, it only serves to enlarge stupidity, inflate conceit, enhance credulity...(Muggeridge, 1969, p. 52.)

The vigorous success of science and education as sub-systems in Western societies has depended on numerous factors such as a congenial matrix of economic, political and religious forces. The knowledge explosion and better mastery of the environment have been the result. Other important factors for the success have been the relative independence of science and education within this congenial matrix. It facilitated both the optimization of its function and the maximization of rationality and reason as the main value component of this sub-system.

It seems that the success of science and rationality for mastery and instrumental action is balanced by an equal failure to integrate and stabilize man's world. Objective observation and strict cannons of rationality and scepticism appear to be dysfunctional for individual and social identity. They appear to avow change and by implication disavow continuity. The effort to maximize the autonomy of the sub-system by also developing internally integrating or sacralizing mechanisms, through for instance sacralization of the scientific ethos, has been unsuccessful, largely because this mechanism gnaws at the heart of the system. The insignificance of the militancy of Humanistic Associations and Rationalist Societies as compared with the impressive contribution of science and technology to the mastery of man's world is a case in point.

Another major reason for the signal failure of internal sacralizing mechanisms within the sub-system of science is its demonstrable incapacity to anchor a comprehensive system of meaning emotionally. Personal struggles, losses, frustrations, successes and failures, social conflicts, achievements, norms, beliefs, and values and views of reality can only be inadequately accounted for, and even less remedied, by the scientific ethos as a system of meaning.

The religious sub-system seems to operate the other way round. Its function is reconciliation and integration. It reinforces personal and social identity and heals the numerous fragilities through the emotional anchoring of a system of meaning. By implication it avows continuity and disavows mastery for its own sake.

The relation between both sub-systems has changed from super-ordinate legitimation to dialectical equality. It is possible to interpret present-day theological laments about the idolatry of reason as nostalgia for the irrevocable past. It is indeed highly unlikely that theological systems of meaning in Western society will ever again legitimate the economy, polity, or science.

On the other hand it is equally possible, and indeed plausible, to interpret the same lament as an exploitation of advantages in the skirmish of fundamentally equal opponents. For the discomfort of economists, politicians, and scientists with overarching problems of meaning and undergirding directions of purpose is inevitable given the segmental function of each sub-system. It is also an opportunity for scoring by the practitioners and apologists of traditional religions whose primary function it has always been to address themselves to the first question of the Westminster Confession: 'What is the chief end of man?'

SUMMARY

In Chapter III we proposed marginality as a major source for breaking encrusted habits and petrified beliefs. The segmentalization of Western society in relatively independent economic, political, and scientific sub-systems over the last 500 years came about partly because the integrative core values of the religious institutions had never been allowed to completely overrun the values of instrumentality, rationality, and individual autonomy. Other reasons for their emergence were the new inventions (printing), discoveries (America), culture contacts (trade and commerce), and behind these and their consequences for increased marginality, the human instinct for mastery. These new forces of breakthrough were strong and cumulative enough to allow the sub-systems to find their own level of independence and optimal functioning. The corollary of this chain of events was a changeover from religious legitimation to a dialectic with the religious sub-system.

The differentiation, we have maintained, was facilitated by the sectarian movements of the Reformation which on the religious, emotional level upstaged the same marginality which on the non-religious rational level was fundamental for the core values of instrumentality, efficiency, egalitarianism, and objectivity, around which the economy, polity, science, and education became structured. Important in this connection were the psychic energies released through the illusionless acceptance of man's basic depravity (i.e. non-sacredness) and the motivating power accompanying the emotional denudations of mundane securities. The emotional freedom of marginal man provided additional impetus for his instrumental endeavours. This liberty and these psychic energies were all the greater the more firmly the believer was immersed in the cosmic drama of sinful, fallen man redeemed by the astonishing grace of God.

Each sub-system attempts to maximize its function by independence, but by introducing self-legitimating sacralizing elements to achieve this goal it begins to march in the opposite direction from where its core value leads it. It is for this reason and also deficiency of comprehension that the religious sub-system of any Western society has maintained and consolidated its function. The internal sacralization of the other sub-systems (making a fetish out of 'private enterprise', 'democracy', 'scientific ethos') has been rather unsuccessful as measured against the more specific religious forces concretized in sects, cults, and churches. The intricate dialectic between the religious sub-system on the one hand and the economic, political, and scientific sub-system on the other hand, appears to be determined by 'armed peace', each jealous of its own independence, each optimizing its own specialist function, each held in check by the other's suspicions, each fully dependent on the other for supplementing society with the appropriate sanity, economic viability, political order, and scientific mastery.

Chapter X

Legitimation: Class and Family

CLASS

Inequality rather than equality appears to be the rule in human relations. Over the last few decades zoologists and ethologists have made the same observation in the animal world. They have discovered that a dominance relationship can have evolutionary advantages. It may enable a species to survive. The weaker animals die out when, at times of shortages and droughts, the stronger ones keep them away from food. If under the same conditions all animals have equal access to the limited supply (as is the case with some deer and bison) an entire herd may die out (Etkin, p. 21; for the same phenomenon among birds, Chance, p. 152). In many animal species the dominant males also have better sexual access to the females. Thus, the highly endowed ones contribute disproportionately to the gene pool (Ardrey, 1970, p. 130).

Advantages also arise from the institutionalization of these inequalities, in that a dominance relationship comes to be taken for granted. This institutionalization of inequalities is often called ranking order, and some ethologists say that without it, 'a more advanced social life cannot develop in higher vertebrates' (Lorenz, p. 34). There is general agreement that rank is a decided 'evolutionary success' (Ardrey, 1970, p. 171).

Why would this be? Particularly among highly aggressive animals an unquestioned rank-order minimizes lethal, intra-species fighting (Etkin, p. 20; Eibl-Eibesfeldt, p. 83). Where there is agreement about rank it is less necessary to waste valuable energy on the unremitting assertion of physical prowess. Aggression is channelled in a much more profitable direction, such as effective defence of the herd. The cohesion and, by implication, survival of the herd are strongly advanced, if the authority of the shrewdest animal is blindly accepted. An entire band of baboons has been observed to cope with the dangerous presence of a lion by following the instructions of an almost toothless old creature who was excellent at scouting (Lorenz, pp. 37–8; Washburn and de Vore, 1961).

All this has repercussions for identity. It is to the advantage of the individual animal to have a stable rather than a constantly embattled niche in the hierarchy of his herd, band, pack, or flock. On the group level the cohesive pack, strongly defending its identity, is thereby less vulnerable *vis-à-vis* other groups of animals. It is for reasons such as these that one can agree with Ardrey (1970, p. 361) when he says that 'rank satisfies identity'.

Would all this apply to human societies? It is not difficult to imagine the average primitive tribe similarly benefiting from dominance ranking. Improvement of the gene pool, instinctual following of the smartest savage, minimization of internal friction, intricate collaboration in the attack or hunt, all seem to augment the chances for survival of primitive man.

Yet, when social scientists discuss the origins and causes of inequality in human relations or of the formation of strata and classes, they do so without assuming that primeval identity-needs are imprinted in man's emotions. Instead they invoke private property, economic exploitation, lust for power, social reward, value hierarchy, or technology, as explanations for inequality. Some of them, living in cultures with strong egalitarian traditions, assume equality to be normal and inequality to be a regrettable aberration. Bergel (pp. 59–60), for instance, condemns the Indian caste system, because 'all systems of hierarchical stratification . . . threaten solidarity by creating resentment and antagonism with the ensuing danger of intergroup conflicts and possible disintegration'.

Yet others find that the Western negation of hierarchy has been the principal obstacle to understanding non-Western modes of social organization, such as caste systems (Dumont, pp. 35, 315). Like Parsons (1953 and 1954, pp. 69–70), Dumont feels that a hierarchy of values, ideas, and people is indispensable for social life (Dumont, p. 34). Of modern sociologists, Lenski (1970) probably takes primate evolutionary history most seriously. He links social inequality to the very existence of social organization, which in turn is a prerequisite for technological progress. Within the context of modern industrial society, he sides both with the conservatives, when they locate the inevitability of inequality in the nature of man, and with the radicals, when they locate inequality in the power struggles of society (Lenski, 1966, p. 441).

Earlier scholars pursued a different approach. In the eighteenth century, Rousseau, and Marx following him, in the nineteenth century, saw the emergence of property as the reason for social inequality (Dahrendorf, 1968, p. 158). This argument has proved to be rather unsound. In the Soviet Union, private property has been largely abolished, but social inequality is, if anything, greater than in countries in which private property continues (Inkeles, 1953). In the Soviet Union, as in the West, inequality seems to have more to do with desire for reward and privilege than with property. A young imprisoned mechanic, Ruska Doronin, in Solzhenitsyn's novel *The First Circle* (p. 269) says:

> If a man can buy things in a store other than the store that everyone uses, he will never buy anywhere else. If a person can be treated in a special clinic, he will never be treated anywhere else. If a person can ride in a personally assigned car, he won't think of riding any other way. And if there's some particular privileged place to go where people are admitted only with passes, then people will do anything to get that pass.

And yet, to explain inequality in terms of rewards and privileges has its own disadvantages. Some of the modern functionalists approach inequality and stratification in this way. For instance, Davis and Moore say that the universality of stratification rests on differential rewards for essential or less essential services (Davis and Moore, 1957; Davis, 1948). To Davis the importance and scarcity of personnel can therefore explain why, in India, sweepers have low, and Brahmins have high, status (1948, p. 370). These theories have been justifiably criticized, because they take equality as the norm (Dumont, p. 315), or because they fail to explain why class and caste maintain themselves (Buckley) or because the stratification itself prevents, rather than contributes, to efficient distribution of personnel resources (Tumin, p. 423).

None of these accounts of inequality and stratification is comprehensive, and most of them are culture-bound and time-bound.

Davis and Moore assume a society in which achievement is the criterion for hierarchy. It is true that without a strong achievement motivation a modern nation could hardly optimize the combined potential of its citizens. Yet there are and were societies in which birth is the major criterion or where (similar to primate bands) sheer power of the dominant group or class determines the order of rank. Even in modern industrial societies this power may be more important than one thinks, particularly if its referents are not confined to brute strength, wealth, position, and shrewdness, but also include knowledge, specialist skills, or even congenial relationships. Michels' (1949) 'iron law of oligarchy' shows that there is an inherent tendency towards self-perpetuation amongst the leadership to whom a group has delegated certain tasks and powers. Thus at the heart of even the most democratic of governments hierarchies tend to develop on the basis of administrative skills, the visibility of performance, or congenial relationships.

Yet, irrespective of the uniqueness of the mixture of the various criteria in specific societies and at specific times, the tenacity of a pattern of dominance can be more comprehensively explained when we turn from the differentiation/instrumental side of our basic dichotomy to consider the integration/identity one. The maintenance of an order of rank or a stratification system results partly from its congeniality to situational factors, partly from the direct consequence of a conservative need for 'sameness'—which, at the personal level, expresses itself as a 'like-seek-like' motivation. The assumption of Bergel, that the lowest echelons favour protest over sameness, or the assumption of Davis and Moore, that an instrumental allocation of resources is not counterbalanced by integrative mechanisms, contains all the biases of American egalitarian and pragmatic traditions. It is this point (that dominance patterns also provide for identity needs) which is missing from the sociological analysis of stratification systems, although Suzanne Keller (p. 68) at least hints that social core-groups are the integrative, or centripetal response to the centrifugal challenge of differentiation created by the occupational divisions of modern societies.

More relevant for our purposes, however, is the question: have these hierarchical divisions been important enough to become sacralized, thereby further stabilizing social groups and individual positions within it? There is ample evidence that they have. Many Australian aborigines classify themselves in terms of hierarchical divisions between tribes, phratries, and clans. These divisions are reinforced by each clan identifying itself with different sacred animals (Durkheim, 1954, pp. 141–8). Durkheim postulates that these classifications help to avoid territorial collisions: '. . . it is necessary that space in general be divided, differentiated, arranged and that these divisions and arrangements be known to everybody' (ibid., p. 443).

Polynesian religions sacralized hierarchy and rank in intricate detail. A system of taboos was a major mechanism for accentuating rank, thereby confirming Horton's observation (p. 165) that 'in nearly every case of taboo reaction the events and actions involved are ones which seriously defy the established lines of classification in the culture where they occur'. And so in Tonga, the remains of a superior's meal could be touched only at the risk of a sore throat. In New Zealand, the discarded cloak of a Maori chief 'could not with safety be donned by an attendant' (Lowie, p. 79). In Hawaii, a person 'whose shadow fell upon the king's house or back or who climbed over the royal stockade was doomed' (ibid.). On other islands the dominance of the upper caste was reinforced by the rule that 'anything touched by a superior became taboo, hence . . . the canoe or house entered by the chief became his property' (ibid., pp. 80–1). In Tikopia, the rank of elders was reinforced by the order in which they were served on ritual occasions, and elementary structures of society, such as filial respect and paternal authority, were objectified in spirits (Firth, 1970, pp. 54, 111).

The classic example for the sacralization of an order of dominance is the caste system of India. Here, the territorial boundaries of tribal societies have been replaced by occupational and other, more salient, divisions of less primitive cultures (Weber, 1958, p. 31). The lines of demarcation between caste and sub-castes are reinforced by elaborate rules and taboos stipulating who can do what work, who can marry what spouse, who can eat what food. These rules are held together by a sacred system of rewards and punishments promising higher or lower positions in the round of rebirth according to one's actions in this life. Inequalities of birth and endowment are thereby legitimated. Obviously these sacred legitimations make the change to achievement criteria rather difficult (Hutton, p. 124). Gandhi's campaign against the untouchability of the lowest caste (Zaehner, pp. 173–4), the Harijans (children of God), as he called them, was inevitable, granted the goal of elevating Indian independent nationhood at the necessary expense of caste identity, and granted the need of a modern nation for emphasizing criteria of achievement more than status by birth. The disruption of the sacred system of taboos that had been used to delineate concrete loci of identity, created its own consequent anguish.

In contrast with Hinduism, Christianity has been much more ambiguous about a particular order of dominance. In the New Testament, Jesus both advocates submission to Caesar (Matthew 22 : 15–22), and preaches God's reversal of man's status hierarchies (Luke 16 : 19–31). The result is that both inequality (Luther siding with the princes in the Peasant war of 1525) and equality (American Protestantism) have been ardently defended as legitimated by religion.

Christianity originated in a protest movement that was compelled to compromise with the status quo, and this development intimates the relative ease with which in subsequent history, achievement criteria have broken through the sacralizations of the system of dominance based on birth, heredity, or power. Thus, in the nineteenth century Marx and Engels could condemn the Christian churches for exploiting the working classes (Marx and Engels, 1964, pp. 126–9), while Friedrich Nietzsche complained about Christianity sacralizing the values of the underprivileged (Nietzsche, pp. 168–9).

In spite of its ambiguity, however, Christianity has time and again functioned effectively as the sacralizer of a specific system of dominance or a specific class identity. In the Middle Ages, it sanctified serfdom and feudalism (Marx and Engels, p. 99). In societies where class distinctions became major demarcations of identity, the established religious organizations reinforced the class in power, whereas Christian sectarianism reinforced proletarian systems of meaning. If established monopolies made sectarianism impossible, or if there was direct access to political power, sacred legitimations began to develop from within political movements (Labour Churches, Marxism). In most Western countries, the lower classes of the nineteenth century became estranged from established religion in accordance with the strength of the boundaries dividing the classes, and the extent to which Christianity sacralized upper class status. (There are exceptions, such as Ireland, Poland, and Quebec (Rioux, p. 50), where a threatened national identity transcended internal class divisions.) In Protestant more than in Catholic countries, sectarian movements vied with labour movements for the integration of lower-class identity. It is therefore no accident that even now the largest communist parties in Europe are to be found in Catholic countries where sectarian movements were more effectively blocked.

However, as the extent to which class became a major identity focus diminished, as in the Anglo-Saxon colonies, the more Christianity could avoid identification with a particular class, and the less typical-lower-class political movements could function to sacralize stratified identities. The U.S.A. is a good example. Here Marxism and Socialism have been singularly unsuccessful as agencies sacralizing identity for the disprivileged classes. On the other hand, the lack of established religious organizations enabled the Christian churches and sects to contribute to the integration of a variety of life-styles, social strata and classes (Demerath, 1965, p. 203). Generally one finds in specific localities certain churches (such as the Episcopalian) to be predominantly upper class and others (for instance the Church of God) to be predominantly lower class (Pope, 1942; Niebuhr, 1957; Lazerwitz, 1964). But here, as in Australia, class is not as sharply delineated as in some older countries, and the correlation with religious variables is therefore less marked (Mol, 1971a, p. 119).

The same point might be stated in terms of boundaries: when boundary divisions between classes are more salient for identity formation than other boundary divisions (between nations, tribes, interest groups, etc.), they are more likely to become sacralized than when they are less salient. For our purposes, class is no different from other identity foci. It may have a more venerable history, going as far back as vertebrate social organization, but nowadays in modern societies social class has to compete with other systems of meaning, life-styles, etc. A pattern of dominance has in common with other identity foci a variety of what we have called 'girders of identity frames'. In this chapter we have talked more in terms of a variety of criteria (such as birth, wealth, achievement, power, etc.) that would be more or less prominent according to time and place. Girders and criteria have much in common: they prop up an identity. Class and other identity foci have often been legitimated in ultimate terms, not only by the traditional religious organizations, but also by Marxism, 'which died as reason, but lived as dogma' (Wheelis, p. 134). This was never more true than when Marxism waxed enthusiastic about the messianic function of the proletariat.

THE FAMILY

Like the dominance order, kinship finds its origin and elaboration in evolutionary success. The very supremacy of man over his environment depended on his ability to use symbols, and this in turn depended on a prolonged period of learning and socialization. Yet protecting and guiding the helpless infant was only one of a variety of functions crystallized in the family. The regulation of sexuality and procreation were others. 'Marriage, by preserving exclusive or preferential rights of specified adult males over certain women, reduces the incidence of sexual competition among men and is thus a force of social order' (Pitts, 1964, p. 66). In many societies, the family also acquired economic functions. It would be inaccurate to claim, as some scholars do, that the marriage contract is *essentially* economic. Yet, as Malinowski (1962, pp. 13–14) points out, economic co-operation is certainly 'one of the obligations of marriage'.

Often in the past, the responsibilities of the extended family have included vocational, educational, and welfare duties. In modern industrial societies most of these functions have been lost. The nuclear family (one set of parents and their unmarried children) has to be mobile in order to meet the requirements of a highly complex division of labour, and therefore can ill afford to carry out the kinds of duties requiring permanent location.

Yet this curtailment of functions does not mean that therefore a 'decline of the family' has begun. The trend seems to go in the direction of a new type of family, performing, even more exclusively than before, certain vital functions for society (Parsons and Bales, 1955, p. 10). For modern adults 'the family is a refuge from the macro-world; it is the place to which they can retreat from the latter's tensions, frustrations and anxieties . . . the locale of highly significant expectations for self-fulfilment and emotional satisfaction' (Berger and Berger, 1972, p. 78).

This does not mean that the family fulfilled this function only in lesser extent in the rural communities of the past. It means that the anomie and anonymity in urbanized societies or the emphasis on rational, efficient calculation in the occupational spheres are more in need of the counterbalance of the integrative, emotionally anchored relationship in the family. This function of the family is as old as primate history. Harlow and Harlow found that emotional disturbance and permanent social and sexual inadequacy were the consequence of raising monkeys in isolation. They compared the monkeys with children reared in impersonal institutions or in homes with indifferent mothers or nurses. They say that from the first six months of life the emotional damage is progressive and cumulative, and that 'by two years many children have reached the point of no return' (Harlow and Harlow, p. 10).

A parental relationship therefore is crucial for the identity formation of an individual. How to view reality, how to decide which values have priority, what emotional reactions are legitimate, what beliefs should be entertained—are all questions answered in the course of the child's upbringing. By 'knowing' or 'living' the answers the child learns to occupy the niche in his environment prepared for him by his parents. The parents in turn act on behalf of the larger group or society which has its own stake in the survival of specific conceptions of reality. The success of the transmission and internalization of these beliefs, conceptions, and values depends on the ability of the parents to surround the learning of new roles and identities with emotional support (McCall and Simmons, pp. 203–220). In terms of our conceptual frame of reference: the provision of emotional security during the various stages of change, permits further change to be more confidently adopted.

To sum up our argument so far: in evolutionary history the family has fulfilled various functions at various times in various cultures: it has socialized the offspring, it has been crucial for the construction of the identity of the young, it has regulated sexuality and procreation, it has performed economic, educational, vocational, and welfare tasks, and through all these functions it has advanced and reinforced social order.

Have these functions also been sacralized? There is abundant evidence that they have. Contrary to economy or science, the family and religious institutions have converging functions: both are vitally engaged in integration and emotional anchorage. The family constructs identity, and religion sacralizes it.

In China the family has traditionally been the crucial focus of identity. What caste is to the Hindu, the family is to the Chinese. 'The Confucian tradition was the theoretical expression and the rational justification of the Chinese family-centered worldview, which may be characterized as the religion of "Familyism"' (Kitagawa, p. 78). This world-view legitimated and sacralized the widest possible range of values and norms of behaviour. '... Buddhism in China became to all intents and purposes a family religion' (ibid.). Religion was an all-pervasive influence in traditional Chinese homes. Paper door gods protected the house against evil spirits. The earth god had his altar on the floor and looked after family behaviour. In the hall or the main room were altars for the wealth gods, who helped a family to prosper, and the ancestral shrine with its many wooden spirit tablets, and the ever-burning lamp in front of them (Yang, pp. 28–9). Elaborate family sacrifices (burning of incense, candles, paper money) and mortuary rites articulated the role of the dead amongst the living. The scrupulous maintenance of rank-order during these performances simultaneously reinforced the existing family organization (Yang, p. 39).

There is similar evidence for the sacralization of Japanese family patterns (Morioka and Shimpo, p. 192), and for India, where the orthodox enhance their 'dharma by fulfilling family obligations' (Kitagawa, p. 129). In ancient Rome, Vesta, the guardian goddess of the household, was honoured 'by a short silence and/or the throwing of sacred salt cake into the fire' (King, p. 157). Family activities and estate boundaries were sacralized through honouring the Penates (guardians of the household storehouse) and the Lares (boundary gods, guardians of the property—ibid.).

Ancestor worship occurs in a wide variety of cultures, and can be seen as the reassertion of identity in the face of the fragility and temporality of a specific family. In some cultures the 'excessively powerful will of the dead dominates the whole life' (Van der Leeuw, 1964, p. 130). This 'will of the dead' often keeps an elaborate reward/punishment system of values intact from one generation to another. Ancestors in these cultures are 'images of authority and communication' (Firth, 1970, p. 77), occasionally visibly present with their skulls 'hanging censoriously in the rafters' (Geertz, 1966, p. 9). Ancestor worship so much impressed many observers (from Euhemerus in the third century B.C. to Herbert Spencer, 1897, p. 422) that they wrongly saw the origin of all religion in a glorification of the deeds of great ancestors.

Christianity furnishes many similar examples of family sacralization. Miner (p. 66) found that the attitudes towards God, Jesus, Mary, and Joseph reflected the actual attitudes towards persons in similar family roles: the authority of God and the compassionate entreating of Mary were congruent with a parental division of labour in Catholic households. William Christian in his study of a Spanish valley found a close correspondence between shrines and actual local and regional identities. Yet, the family, he says, does not have such a shrine. It has 'pictures and little images in the home', but no 'tutelary deities' (p. 81). The absence of a shrine is rather irrelevant for our frame of reference, as long as other mechanisms of sacralization are present, and in the Spanish households which Christian describes there are many other binding forces, such as common family devotions, attendance at church where family values are reinforced, etc. In another study (Johnson, 1973, p. 150) it was found that religious students had more respect for parental values than non-religious students, suggesting that for the first group family values had become more sacralized than for the second.

The need to perpetuate values, constantly to restore personal, group, and social identity, to buttress the boundaries of social order is also evident in the sacralization of internal family relationships. The duty to love parents, wife, husband, children, and—the opposite side of the coin—to refrain from establishing strong competitive ties with outsiders, for example through an adulterous relationship, is written down in many sacred codes. It safeguards the family as a transmission agency. And so the Qur'ān posits that God has instituted love and tenderness between men and women and that therefore husband and wife should act to one another lovingly and tenderly. It also strongly condemns adultery (Chan *et al.*, pp. 362–363).

It comes therefore as no surprise that when, through birth, marriage, or death, important alterations take place in the family structure, these changes (or identity fragilities) are in all cultures legitimated through religious ritual. Or as Bellah (1965, p. 173) expresses it:

> At the moment of marriage, when one leaves father and mother to cleave to another, or of death, when one on whom one depends is taken away, there are religious ceremonies, weddings and funerals, that operate to reinforce or redefine threatened identity.

Marriage ceremonies are radically different from one culture to another according to the variety of functions of the family in each specific culture. Yet religious sacralization accompanies them all, irrespective of whether for instance the marriage is arranged by the parents (as is usual in Hinduism) or whether romantic love is a prime ingredient as in modern industrial societies. Romantic love can also be seen as a good example of how the transition from one focus of identity (the family of orientation, in which one is born) is transferred to another (the family of procreation, which one establishes *de novo*), and how this is facilitated by strong emotional detachments from the original family through peer group loyalties, and by the forging subsequently of strong emotional attachment to the new unit. Love as the core-value in human relations has, also for this reason, been strongly stressed by modern Christianity.

The continued popularity of the rites of passage in even the most secularized of countries in the West is related to their salient function for changes in family identity. In Australia, only a minority of the population goes to church at all regularly, but the percentage of those not married or buried in a religious ceremony is very small (Mol, 1971a, pp. 226–7). In a communist country, such as Bulgaria, marriages, baptisms, and funerals 'are the most enduring aspects of religion' (Ochavkov, p. 87). In Denmark, less than 3 per cent of the population goes to church weekly, but 'almost all Danes have a church funeral' (Thorgaard, p. 137). Similar findings for other countries can be found in *Western Religion* (Mol, Hetherton and Henty). The lower divorce rates amongst religious people in the West also reflect the conserving role of religious orientations for family structures (Mol, 1971a, pp. 259–63).

SUMMARY

Contrary to the economy and science, class and family have always been major constructors of identity. Consequently, religious organizations have often legitimated and sacralized these identity foci. Close alliance rather than armed peace has been characteristic for the relationship.

Yet 'close alliance' with the castes, classes, and hierarchies of specific societies has also been a predicament for religious organizations, especially when specific hierarchical relations became questionable. What is sacralized is by definition impervious to change, and congenial to the status quo. Hinduism could and can hardly sacralize achievement criteria at the expense of ascriptive criteria without disrupting its pivotal doctrine of karma. Christianity has been more flexible, but even so, it has often been identified with the ruling classes in those countries where class was a salient focus of identity. Where this was not the case (such as in newly settled countries) it suffered less from the predicament of 'concretization'. Yet in these countries, too, a local division of labour between the various denominations often followed the dominance order. Both the denominational and sectarian competitive forms of organizations contributed to the flexibility of Christianity. The sects, in particular, have been very successful in sacralizing systems of meaning typical for the disprivileged. Another reason for the flexibility of Christianity has been its historical suspicions (anchored in sacred scriptures) of status criteria of birth, power, and wealth, and even achievement (good works).

No such embarrassment existed in the relation between the family and religious organizations. Family patterns have generally been unequivocally sacralized (exception: Luke 14:26, 'If anyone comes to me and does not hate his own father and mother and wife and children and brothers and sisters, yes, and even his own life, he cannot be my disciple'). This incontrovertible sanction occurred because the family was a crucial focus of identity and an irreplaceable transmitter of beliefs and values. In the West its functions have shrunk, but those that remained, such as the provision of an emotional matrix for confidence and security, have also been at the heart of the religious enterprise. The rites of passage, such as birth, marriage, and death ceremonies, have maintained themselves strongly even in those countries where other ecclesiastical activities have become eroded or discouraged.

Chapter XI

Self and Sexuality

We turn from the analysis of identity (its meaning, its relevance, its legitimation) to the actual *foci* of identity. Apart from such important foci as class, or family, which we have already discussed there is a variety of other primary sources of identity crucial enough to become sacralized. The identity of a man, his group, or his society in more primitive societies can usually be described easily, and so can the systemic linkages of that identity and the bases or primary foci that hold it all together.

In modern societies, it is much more difficult to see the unity of which one is a part. Most people would find it hard to detect a focus of their own identity, or as William James (1902, p. 193) calls it, 'the hot place in a man's consciousness', or 'the habitual centre of his personal energy'. The individual generally takes his personal and social identity for granted, just as, provided it functions properly, he takes his liver for granted. Yet it is not always difficult to detect a unifying focus of identity in other individuals, or in groups different from one's own: individual converts, or an ethnic association or a sect, are ready examples. If one cannot discern it in oneself or in one's own group, the reason is usually that one cannot step out of one's tradition, values, and beliefs, which seem so plausible that they do not need to be defended or even articulated. Albert Einstein put the dilemma in the form of a question: 'What does a fish know about the water in which he swims all his life?' (Watson, p. 121).

A more important analytical difficulty arises from the loosely woven character of modern societies. Marginality, diversity, and complexity have augmented the autonomy of the self and have proliferated the foci of identity to include the most concrete and the most abstract items. If, then, there is so much variety, how can we concretely classify these foci? What criterion can we introduce to describe this field of 'sacralized identities' and to analyse their composite set of advantages and disadvantages?

For a sociologist, the most obvious criterion is the distinction of the social and the individual, which we adopt because it also allows us to rectify the over-simplification of previous chapters, where we mixed personal, group, and social identity. This over-simplification was necessary in order to stress the structural sameness of identity and the sacralizing tendency operating on all these levels. Now we have a chance to point out that there are also important differences with important consequences for social interaction.

All our various identity foci can be put on a continuum running from personal identity on the left, through group identity in the middle, to social identity on the right. On the extreme left are those (for instance, the older psychoanalysts) for whom self-realization is the hub of existence and who ignore the independence of group and social identity. Towards the middle, are such movements as those formed by the ardent ecologists, followers of Women's Liberation, or Alcoholics Anonymous. They consist of relatively small numbers of individuals drawn together in a common purpose. In the middle of our continuum are also tightly knit religious sectarian groups: definite, distinguishable islands of group identity in a stormy cultural ocean, separate from the others through their cosmic interpretations. On the right-hand side are the foci of social identity often sacralized by universal religions which (even if their manifest stress seems to be mainly on personal control, morality, and experiences) are nevertheless latently involved in social integration. Marxism in the communist countries also falls in this section. Furthest to the right are some of the archaic and primitive religions sacralizing a social whole in which there is little room for personal, or at any rate separate, identity.

It should be clear that when we use 'social identity' in this context, we do *not* mean 'whatever in the social environment provides the individual members of a society with his or her identity' (McCall, p. 64), but 'whatever provides a society, tribe, or nation with its own unique wholeness'. Again, although both the basic outlines of personal, group, and social identity (all three deal with order, interpretation of reality, legitimation, rules, etc.) and the mechanisms leading to their sacralization, are structurally the same, none the less the units to which they refer can, and often are, at loggerheads with one another. The elaborate means that are employed by the universal religions to reinforce expected attitudes and interpretative patterns, and that are used constantly to repair the breaches of misconduct and misinterpretation, are evidence of the dangers which the Id, the aggressive individual instincts, represent for the social fabric. Social identity is always in the process of careful construction and restoration, and sacralization potential is an asset in this effort. The enemy, very often, is the individual.

Yet it is also clear that a person's identity is very much constricted by his living in a social environment. For that reason he cannot give free rein to his basic impulses, around which his personal identity might otherwise crystallize. Creativity, freedom, and innovation are often limited by strong social pressures. This is an important qualification of our continuum which otherwise might have conjured up images of harmonious development. There are constant boundary conflicts between personal, group, and social identity in all societies, because there is an inherent tendency in each to maximize allegiance. Some of the epics and tragedies symbolize and sublimate conflicts of this kind. In the Greek tragedies, loyalty to one's family is often contrasted with loyalty to a deeply felt personal or social duty (Homer's *Odyssey*; Aeschylus's *Agamemnon*; Sophocles's *Antigone* and *Oedipus Tyrannus*; also Shakespeare's *Romeo and Juliet* and *Hamlet*).

One might also place societies on a continuum according to which forces might dictate most of the clauses in an uneasy armistice. Societies where social conformity reigns supreme tend to be older and non-industrial, and therefore closer to the right-hand side of our continuum. Societies where individualism has been sacralized tend to be modern and urbanized, and so are put on the left-hand side of our continuum. But in all instances, we must acknowledge tensions that constantly pull in one direction or another. In the U.S.S.R., the tension between individualism and collectivism seems to be no less strong than in the U.S.A., where, on the one hand, Marcuse bitterly complains about the bureaucratic empires alienating the individual, and, on the other, Toffler (p. 301) warns of the danger of over-individualization, and Slater says that 'We seek more and more privacy, and feel more and more alienated and lonely when we get it' (p. 7). This is also true for the individualistic philosophies of the Enlightenment which were sharply criticized by Joseph de Maistre and Louis de Bonald (Maus, p. 10). They maintained that society was a *sui generis* reality, had a life of its own, and enforced the individual to respect authority and tradition. Their influence on Durkheim (1964b, p. 338) via Saint Simon and Comte proved to be substantial. Since then, sociologists have remarked on the continual battle of the corporate self against individuals (Coleman, 1973, p. 14; Zablocki, 1971) and have opposed the 'basic rugged individualism which underlies all of existential thought' (Tiryakian, p. 154; Monica Wilson, 1973).

Yet the interdependence of the items on our continuum is as obvious as their conflict. Sociologists who make it their life's work to describe and analyse social identity pay respectful attention to the socialization of individuals, whom they regard as both vehicles and innovators of social values and beliefs. Psychologists generally use personal identity as their prime referent, but many pay respectful attention to the 'looking-glass self' (Cooley, 1956b, p. 184) or the 'generalized other' (G. H. Mead, 1950, p. 154).

SELF AND SELF-REALIZATION

The emphatic emergence of selfhood is a rather recent phenomenon. Self-orientation existed in other societies, but seldom was it sacralized to the extent that it became the taken-for-granted linch-pin of systems of thought or of the mundane motivations of the man in the street. Self-realization is central to psychoanalysis, existentialism, humanism, and many other psychologies, philosophies, and theologies. Self-realization, for our purpose, may be taken to mean an emphasis on the integration of self with a corresponding reduction of emphasis on the integration of groups or society. Usually, self-realization is implied to be good and whatever restricts it is bad. The Self-Realization Fellowship (a Christian/Hindu sect with various congregations in California) emphasizes peace within, 'not in a society which disappoints' (Klapp, pp. 166–7). In this instance self-realization has manifestly sacred overtones. Generally however, devotees may be appalled to think that their vital concerns are in any way 'sacred', yet this is the usual case. Thomas Luckmann was certainly justified in calling the themes of autonomous individual self-expression and self-realization, 'the central topics of the modern sacred cosmos' (1967, pp. 109–10). Others, such as Carl Jung, have similarly spoken about the experience of the self 'as an experience of God', or about the discovery of the self as having 'the status of a religious experience' (Goldbrunner, pp. 160, 172).

In psychology and psychoanalysis, this 'faith'-like concern with the self is well developed. To Freud the Ego was central. Its successful adjustment depended on the way it handled the Id (representing one's biological endowment) and on the other hand the Superego (representing one's social and cultural tradition). Regrettably, either of these two forces might get out of hand. To Freud, the innate self was contra-social in character. Yet the damage the contra-social self could inflict on the larger social whole and, indirectly by repercussion, on himself, hardly concerned Freud. Sporadically he referred to it (Freud, 1972), but generally he took the social so much for granted that LaPiere (p. 92) is justified in calling the permissive milieu in which conflicts are minimized by allowing the individual complete opportunity for self-expression, 'the Freudian idea'.

The theme of harmonious self-realization as a *summum bonum* has guided psychoanalysis and psychology ever since, however much various protagonists may have otherwise differed. To Wilhelm Reich, the unafraid individual who 'satisfies his strong libidinal needs' is the ideal (Rieff, 1968, p. 168). To Abraham Maslow (p. 340; McConnell, p. 77) good is whatever actualizes man's inner nature, and 'anything that disturbs or frustrates or twists the course of self-actualization' is psycho-pathological. To R. D. Laing (1971a), the integration of the individual is the centre of analysis. Other, competing, kinds of identity, such as the family, are analysed in terms of their failure to contribute to this central goal. To Rollo May (1953, pp. 139, 188), striving for the creative consciousness of self is as worthy of praise as conforming to accepted norms is unworthy.

There are some exceptions to this psychological treatment of self-realization as an unmitigated *summum bonum*. Carl Jung (1958, p. 292) mentions 'the lurking danger of chaotic individualism'. Gordon Allport recognizes the problem of balance between personality growth and social cohesion (1960, p. 161; McConnell, p. 28), but then sees religion only in personal terms: 'A man's religion... is his ultimate attempt to enlarge and to complete his own personality by finding the supreme context in which he rightly belongs' (1957, p. 142). Erich Fromm believes that the normal person may be less healthy, in terms of human values, than the neurotic (McConnell, p. 41), but then continues to stress man's self-determination and self-sufficiency. To him, self-realization, not obedience, is virtue (1957, pp. 36, 37). Authoritarian religion (which to us is primarily sacralization of group or social identity) is vehemently rejected as leading to bondage. Yet humanistic religion (which to us is primarily sacralization of personal identity) is good, because it is centred around man and his strength (ibid.; also 1965, p. 283).

The psychiatrists, psychoanalysts, and psychologists have not been alone in stressing self-realization. They were long anticipated by a tradition which went back as far as Protagoras (480–411 B.C.), who regarded man as the measure of all things. The Renaissance repeated this theme even more strongly (Nisbet, 1973, pp. 193–6). To Reinhold Niebuhr (1949, Vol. I, p. 64), the Renaissance was, even more than classic thought, the real cradle for what he judges to be 'that very unchristian concept and reality: the autonomous individual'. To Descartes, the thinking self was at the centre of reality: individualism worked only for the good of others. It is often forgotten that he qualified that observation by adding '[if one lives] in a society where moral customs are not currupt' (p. 320).

Certainly, Feuerbach appeared to live in the fool's paradise where the maintenance of social order and morality could be taken for granted. To him man's existence was determined by his consciousness and this in turn consisted of 'self-verification, self-affirmation, self-love, joy in one's perfection' (p. 6). Inevitably therefore God was 'the manifested inward nature, the expressed self of a man' (p. 13), 'the highest subjectivity of man' (p. 31), 'nothing else than the projected personality of man' (p. 226), 'nothing else than man's highest feeling of self' (p. 284). However, when God becomes objectified (or as we would say, also reflects group or social identity), man becomes alienated from his true self. 'Only he who thinks is free and independent' (p. 39).

To Marx, man was also essentially bent on his self-realization and labour was the means towards this (Marx and Engels, 1964, pp. 42 and 50; Luijpen, p. 109; Bottomore, 1966, p. 134). However—and here Marx was a decided advance on Feuerbach—this self-realization was thwarted by the kind of society in which man lived. The mode of production (rather than the inherent boundary conflict between personal and social identity, as we would say) was to Marx the source of man's estrangement and he visualized a socialist society in which self-fulfilment and social integration would go hand in hand harmoniously.

Nietzsche stressed the centrality of the self. Tradition and authority poisoned man's nobility: man's will to power was not to be restrained. 'Reverence for oneself; love of oneself; unconditional freedom before oneself' (1954b, pp. 569–70) was to be the guideline. Yet he was less utopian than Marx in that he (dimly?) perceived the dysfunctional consequences of self-affirmation and realization for any system of morality in any society. God, to Nietzsche, represented the moral and social good, and when God was demolished, man would suffer the consequences. Man's freedom and the murder of God were intricately intertwined as seems clear from the following famous passage in the *Gay Science*:

> 'Whither is God', (the Madman) cried. 'I shall tell you. We have murdered him—you and I. All of us are his murderers . . . God is dead. God remains dead. . . . How shall we, the murderers of all murderers, comfort ourselves? What was holiest and most power-ful of all that the world has yet owned has bled to death under our knives. Who will wipe his blood off us? . . . Is not the greatness of this deed too great for us? Must not we ourselves become gods simply to seem worthy of it? There has never been a greater deed; and whoever will be born after us—for the sake of this deed he will be part of a higher history than all history hitherto.' (Nietzsche, 1954a, pp. 95–6.)

The same stress on self-affirmation and subjectivity characterizes twentieth-century existentialism. In Jean-Paul Sartre's *The Devil and the Good Lord*, the hero Goetz (very reminiscent of Nietzsche's madman) kills God in order to be free. He used to wonder, he says, what he could be in the eyes of God. But,

> 'now I know the answer: nothing. God does not see me, God does not hear me, God does not know me. You see this emptiness over our heads? That is God. You see this gap in the door? It is God. You see that hole in the ground? That is God again. Silence is God. Absence is God. God is the loneliness of man. There was no one but myself; I alone decided on Evil; and I alone invented Good. . . . If God exists, man is nothing.' (1960, p. 141.)

To Sartre, the restraining Other is best represented by the idea of God, the 'unstared stare', the source of man's alienation (Luijpen, 1964, p. 287; Sartre, 1956, p. 290).

The 'Death of God' theologians echo essentially the same theme: man's present-day self-determination and the corresponding loss of importance of a system of social integration herald the death of God. These theologians assume that God is represented by a transcendental system of meaning exerting social control over the personality.

The existentialist thinker, Martin Heidegger, regards the meaning assigned to the world as derived from the self. The self is realized in the world. Authentic existence, to Heidegger, is to create one's own norm. In becoming himself, man is a law unto himself. 'The authentic man is conscious of the vanity of Existence' and accepts existence in absolute solitude (Spier, p. 36). Transcendental projections of order, meaning, and morality fabricated to minimize Angst (the anxiety of meaninglessness), are unauthentic to Heidegger. Unauthentic existence is voluntarily to abandon one's freedom, to lose oneself in society and the masses, to fall away from one's true being (Heidegger, p. 220).

The idea of the sanctity of the self and its unimpeded development is obviously not confined to psychoanalysis and existential philosophy. The success of these interpretations lies in their congruence with similar ideas at the grass-root level. Humanism has always stressed the primacy of individual freedom, and has always taken the side of self-determination whenever the question of social conformity arose. In Australian research, those closest to a humanist interpretation of life were also much more likely to leave the choice of conduct to the individual. On the other hand, the orthodox believers had much more definite views of what they regarded as socially approved and socially unacceptable modes of behaviour (Mol, 1971a, p. 54).

All this does not mean that Christian theologians have abandoned the sacralization of self to the psychoanalyst, the existential philosopher, the humanist, and the man in the street who both loses and integrates himself in his job, his sexuality, his alcohol, his drugs, his astrology, his sport, his status, or his money (to some of which we shall return). Christianity, supremely well represented on the further (group and social) stages of our continuum, has also traditionally stressed the importance of individual salvation, individual conversion experiences, and individual union with God or Jesus. Indeed, Christianity has been so well represented in all the categories of our continuum that we might convert Troeltsch's three categories of mysticism, sect, and church into the personal, group, and social classification that we have employed. This conversion has the additional advantages of fitting better into sociological and psychological modes of thinking, *and* of better potential for cross-cultural comparisons. Troeltsch's categories are also less than comprehensive: they do not allow analysis, for example, of the modern sacralization of self-hood.

To Troeltsch mysticism was closely bound to the personal (Vol. II, p. 993). Mystics 'care solely for the individual and his eternal welfare' (p. 800) and are indifferent towards all social problems (p. 801). The Christian mystics, such as Meister Eckhart and Thomas à Kempis, stressed losing the self in the divine or personal identification with God. The gap between personal mystical commitment and institutional religious commitment is documented in a recent study (Hood, 1973, p. 34). There are equivalents in Islam. In place of the Islamic Confession of Faith the semi-secret mystic cult of Ilmu Sedjati has, 'I believe God is in myself and my breath is His representative (Prophet)' (Geertz, 1969, p. 316). In Hinduism, the Upanishads mention the entrance of the self into Nirvana or the complete absorption into Brahman as a 'feeling of unity approaching ecstasy' (Noss, 1963, p. 143). In Zen Buddhism mystic union with the Buddha-nature is the supreme way of self-integration.

Yet there are other non-mystical emphases on self-realization in traditional religions which, like mysticism, implicitly downgrade group or social identity. However very unlike mysticism these self-orientations stress, not withdrawal from the world but, on the contrary, involvement. For example, in Christianity, from the very beginning there has always been a general expression of a certain independence of each individual creature. It existed, for instance, in Thomas Aquinas (Niebuhr, H. Richard, 1956, p. 157). The Reformation gave a special impetus to what David Riesmann calls 'inner-direction' or the provision of a 'psychological gyroscope' to the individual which allowed him to operate fairly independently of the primary group and to maintain 'a delicate balance between the demands upon him of his life goal and the buffetings of his external environment' (1955, pp. 31–2). Since World War II and particularly since Vatican II, some Catholic theologians and scholars have also stressed the theme of self-awareness and self-realization. Teilhard de Chardin saw evolution moving beyond the collective towards the 'hyper-personal' and towards the increasing awareness of the self. The latter would naturally converge towards the centre around Omegapoint (p. 259) which to Teilhard is an autonomous focus, 'a distinct Centre radiating at the core of a system of centres' (p. 262) or more plainly 'God' (p. 294).

Gregory Baum interprets faith to mean 'acknowledgement of God's gift of himself to us in a new consciousness of ourselves and the world' (1969, p. 38) and Christians are those people to whom 'the Gospel of Christ explains, purifies and multiplies their depth-experiences' (p. 68). 'While there may at times be tensions between fulfilment and the requirements of community, we must never make the mistake of realizing the human person in principle as vis-à-vis society' (1967, p. 164). Leslie Dewart, like Baum a Catholic theologian at the University of Toronto, also emphasizes the everyday experience of contemporary man. The purpose of his book *The Future of Belief* is to integrate Christian theistic belief (in which the supernatural has lost all usefulness—p. 209) with those experiences—(p. 7).

In all three studies (as in many modern Protestant equivalents) the collective or social identity is minimized in order to put the full weight on personal identity. This is precisely what they have in common with the mystics and world rejectors of the Eastern religions, whom Bellah (1965, p. 181) accuses of having 'given little positive basis for a sense of social as against purely personal identity', although (as we shall see later) the social effect of mysticism may be too easily ignored.

Descending from the Olympic heights of intellectual systems to the more mundane foci of personal identity of the man in the street, we see that these have little to do with abstraction, awareness, consciousness, logical elegance, and consistency. What these orientations have in common is that the centre of integration is ultimately the self, even, or particularly, when every effort is made to deny or transcend the self. Losing the self is often a sophisticated way to integrate the self, irrespective of whether the means is psychoanalysis, existentialism, football, or alcohol.

The vernacular sometimes uses the word 'religion' to indicate the object around which a person's life revolves. There are some interesting and witty observations on this score by journalists. One of them had the following to say about the religion of football:

Ten years from now football ... may have replaced religion.... Sex is losing its mysterious authority to football, which is now overtaking it as an object of emotional attachment. Increasingly the writings of the football correspondents become hieratic, liturgical and poetic; those same writers become more and more a priestly corps. The footballers who score goals are accorded a semi-divine status. Football will become the ruling faith of the future. The ecumenical progress of football advances. In all the continents of the world, with the exception of North America—a pagan land whose denizens still prostrate themselves before the primitive shrines of baseball, American football, hockey and basketball—the heathens have been converted. Football knows no iron curtain. (Adapted from Taylor, p. 8.)

In the 'pagan' land of Canada, William Kilbourn, a professor of Humanities at York University, made very similar observations:

If I were asked by some stranger to North American culture to show him the most important religious building in Canada, I would take him to Toronto's Maple Leaf Gardens. Unlike most religious buildings, it is not dedicated to the worship of one sect or church, but with marvellous openjawed gluttony and Hindu profusion it engulfs the myriad rites and servants of many gods .... [Here] is the religious cult that celebrates the Garden's reason for being—Hockey Night in Canada. (Kilbourn, p. 6.)

Like football and hockey, the car has to many in the West become an object for self-identification, as the following adapted humorous parody shows:

Once upon a time there was a country that was ruled by a god named Car. In the beginning it did not amount to much. Then it came to pass that out of Dearborn, Michigan, there came a man who took Car and said, 'Let there be mass production', and slowly Car took over the country. Car temples were built, car stables were put up and special stores sprang up where people could go and buy gifts for Car.

Weekends became ritualistic: on Saturday the people would wash Car gently with soap and on Sunday they would pet it with a soft rag to remove any stray dust and ride around the country-side.

Car ruled the country for many years, demanding annual sacrifices of several thousand people and keeping most of the people in a downtrodden state as the people tried to meet financial pledges they had made to Car.

Astrology has similarly afforded man opportunities to lose himself in a larger enterprise. And, like magic, it has thereby strengthened the individual's confidence and sense of security. To the Chaldean astronomers, the fixed stars and the planets were 'the authors of all the phenomena of the universe and nothing here below [was] produced save in virtue of their combined activities' (Cumont, p. 72). Destiny and order are affirmed, arbitrariness and chaos denied. Even in the face of death, injustice, and pain, the individual can accept his fate. Twenty-five hundred years after the Chaldean heavenly calculations were first made, man still derives meaning for the past and guidance for the future from the horoscopes in his daily newspapers.

The upswing in anything occult in modern societies is well documented by increased sales of books on the topic, the library borrowings, the growth of witches' covens and satanic cults. University students show an increased interest in such things as sorcery, witchcraft, and mysticism. One may explain this as the search for pockets of meaning and commitment by those who lives are decentralized, dissipated, and impoverished by the technical age.

The 'unifying vision that bridges the distance between alienated man and his world' (Kerr, p. 136) seems to motivate many of those who follow their horoscope. The recurring themes in literature about the occult are the primordial belief in self-fulfilment, self-culture, self-realization (Taimi, 1967), a considerable amount of sexual symbolism and practice (Kenneth Grant, 1972), and a strong emphasis on order (Lyall Watson, 1973). These observations are consistent with an Australian survey where the need for guidance by one's stars appeared to be greatest amongst the insecure and frightened and where, to at least some of the respondents, the horoscope appeared to take the place of Christianity (Mol, 1971a, p. 43).

Drugs are reported to have the same centring effect on the personality as a profound religious experience. Timothy Leary: 'I have repeated this biochemical and (to me) sacramental ritual (of drug-taking) several hundred times, and almost every time I have been awed by religious revelations as shattering as the first experiences' (p. 14). To Leary, the experience is very individual: 'Drop out—detach yourself from the external social drama which is as dehydrated and ersatz as TV' (p. 223). 'You must start your own religion. You are God—but only you can discover and nurture your divinity. No one can start your religion for you' (p. 227). 'Turn on —find a sacrament (LSD) which returns you to the temple of God, your own body' (p. 223). Consciousness-expanding substances, says Leary, are 'part of the search for the meaning of life' (p. 228). Yet individual isolation is not altogether desirable. One should select a few spiritual companions and write down a common plan including rituals, vocabulary, costumes (anything—'robes, gray flannel suits, amulets or tatoos'—p. 230), shrines (one for each room in the house) and self-selected myths (p. 231).

Drugs appear to produce ecstasy which, in turn, lead to personality integration. Walter Houston Clark regards the hunger for a religious commitment to give meaning to life as 'the most pervasive and poignant urge of man' (p. 95). Psychedelics serve as keys which unlock the doors to man's religious self through ecstasy (pp. 96, 158). Although Clark is impressed with the potential of ecstasy and mystical religious erperiences for all of life and society, he also points to their besetting weakness of creating confusion or chaos (p. 161). The function of some kinds of ecstasy for the self may be counterbalanced by a corresponding social dysfunction, and perhaps for such reasons cautious scholars such as Huston Smith conclude that 'chemicals can aid the religious life, but only where set within the context of faith ... and discipline ...' (p. 166). Whatever the consequences of the psychedelic threat to social order, there can be no doubt that hallucigenic drugs are sometimes successful for structuring and reinforcing self-identity, and even more so because they generally require the total commitment of the devotee (Klapp, p. 176).

Yet this function should not be exaggerated. There is a variety of other foci of identity operating in the same way. One could actually defend the thesis that cohesive, generally small, sectarian groups have often managed to be strongly competitive with self-oriented, loosely organized psychedelic movements. The structure of the sect has often proved to be a superior vehicle for a consistent and stable reinforcement of self-identity, even when it minimized and restricted free and easy, unstructured self-realization. On the other hand, the heterogeneity and optionality of the larger, cultural, and social systems in the West have proved to be less than competitive for the identity formation of the very individuals, intellectuals, and professionals who were in its mainstream. Psychedelia can therefore also be diagnosed as an escape and withdrawal from a society the sheer amorphousness of which has made it an unattractive and uncompelling focus for self-identity.

SEXUALITY

It is not accidental that sex is now so widely regarded as a primary source of personality integration. The props of larger social structures have weakened, and the structuring of meaning around one of man's basic impulses may be both a necessary consequence and a new opportunity. In any age and culture, man's sexuality has been a potent form of self-affirmation and self-expression, all the more so when the social forces that were supposed to channel the instinct had become ineffective. Here, more than anywhere else, we have good evidence that the relation between personal, group, and social identity is not only one of harmonious interdependence and mutual reinforcement (which is the sacred assumption in much anthropological, psychological, and sociological literature) but also one of competition. The maximization of one *also* tends to minimize or atrophy the other.

Freud viewed civilization as the product of man's sacrifice of his primitive impulses in general and of the sublimation of his sexuality in particular. Culture and whatever was socially valuable, usurped some of man's sexual energy and trapped portions of his libido (Freud, 1972, pp. 45–6). Freud's ideas have been echoed and elaborated rather than challenged by scholars from a variety of fields. Unwin (p. 428) surveyed eighty societies over the last 4,000 years and came to the similar conclusion that the limitation of sexual opportunity has a positive effect on what he calls productive social energy. The anthropologist, Service (p. 38), made the point that sub-humans differ so notably from humans because the latter have learned to suppress their sex urges for the sake of cultural advance. The sociologist, Sorokin, saw a parallel between the sexual anarchy of Greece from the third century B.C. onwards and the rapid decline of Greek creative genius (1956, p. 124). The same parallel he observes for other cultures, such as the twentieth-century West. Yet he also finds many examples of creative minorities exercising sexual restraint during these periods of decadence (p. 128).

If we turn to the other side of this issue—the self—we can see that the relationship between self and society is not one-directional. The more amorphous the social order and the less effective social control, the more likely man's self-realization may crystallize around his sexual impulses. Logically, this leads us to speculate that the more religions are concerned with sacralizing social or group identity, the more they will advocate sexual restraint. On the other hand, the more they stress personal identity, the more they will stress the sacredness of sexual fulfilment. True as this may be, harmonious interaction is not to be ignored for the sake of emphasizing boundary conflicts. After all, many religions use extensive sexual symbolism in rituals that reinforce the group or the society. The sexual act symbolizes commitment, self-giving, and the union of opposites—elements crucial for the cohesion and survival of any social unit. In the Urbanna tribe of Central Australia, successful business negotiations or vendetta reconciliations are sealed by sexual intercourse. After the negotiating visitors have discussed their business, they and their accompanying woman or women depart to a short distance from the camp. If the hosts accept the negotiations, the males among them all have sexual intercourse with the women; if not, they do not go out to join them. Similarly, the use of women is offered to a party of men intent on vengeance. 'If they be accepted, then the quarrel is at an end, as the acceptance of this favour is a sign of friendship' (Spencer and Gillen, 1938, p. 98).

Another example of sexuality symbolizing the unity of opposites are the androgynous and hermaphroditic myths. The actual impossibility of uni-sexuality is minor compared with the unity it represents. Because of its relevant symbolism, Eliade (1967, p. 175) relates androgyne to 'a general formula signifying autonomy, strength, wholeness; to say of a divinity that it is androgyne is as much as to say that it is the ultimate being, the ultimate reality' (see also Norman O. Brown, 1959, p. 132).

The strongly unifying character of sexuality makes it an appropriate source of integrative symbolism on any level, whether social, group, or personal. Mysticism, the most self-oriented expression of religiousness, often describes religious experience (of knowing the ultimate *rasa*—meeting the real self—Geertz, p. 318) in sexual terms. Mysticism fuses 'the erotic with the ethical and religious element' (Troeltsch, 1931, Vol. II, p. 801). If there are sometimes also 'misgivings about the erotic completion of feeling' (ibid.) in mysticism, the reason may be that certain forms of mysticism have latent social functions, as when, for instance, restraint (not-grasping and not-coveting in Hinduism) is stressed.

Positive codes, as well as negative taboos, operate in most societies, and make plain the importance of the harmonious interaction between the sacralization of self (and often sexual fulfilment) and sacralization of social identity (and often sexual restraint). Regulation does not mean prohibition. This combination of positive codes and negative taboos in particular societies is usually a very good indication as to where the sensitive division between personal and social identity is drawn.

Yet all these qualifications should not obscure the waning capacity of Western culture to prescribe strong and clear regulation of sexual conduct. The more homogeneous sub-groups, such as certain churches, sects, cults, or communes, appear to have a much stronger effect, reminiscent of Sorokin's minority restraint. Those not under the sway of these groups are more likely to use their freedom to maximize the self-integrating potential of sexual fulfilment and to minimize the effect of social or group restrictions.

This freedom to decide one's own sexual destiny runs closely parallel to the advocacy of self-realization and individualism. The Renaissance is a good example (Savramis, 1969, p. 50) and in the nineteenth century, Feuerbach (p. xii) stressed the relation between sensuousness and integration (or better the cessation of 'doubt and conflict'). To him, the root meaning of alienation was sexual—the whole thinking of alienated man was determined by his repression of sexuality (Feuerbach, 1963, p. 130). To Freud and the Freudians, sexual fulfilment is closely bound to personal wholeness. In many surveys a positive correlation is found between self-orientation and sexual permissiveness, or between religious involvement (presumably having a stronger group or social reference) and sexual restraint (Mol, 1971a, pp. 162–3; de Neuter, p. 385).

Nor have these concerns left untouched those theologians in the West who are worried about the relevance of Christianity. Harvey Cox (1965, p. 213) wants to protect sexuality against all the principalities and powers (such as cultural conventions and social pressures) that seek to dehumanize it. Savramis (1972, pp. 201–2) calls sexual ethics 'Christian' only when it has a wholesome effect on the individual and when it liberates him. Cole too blames Christianity 'for preserving, if not for creating, the negative fear of sex in western civilization' (p. 277), and thinks that the individual should cultivate inner integrity and emotional sincerity by regarding sex as a divine gift (p. 322).

This position is more unique in the history of religions than appears at first sight. Societies and cohesive groups within them have always channelled and patterned the sexual behaviour of their members. To relativize the social context of these patterns and to centre them on personal decision is a rather modern phenomenon.

In Christianity it was hardly relativized: Paul preached moderation and preferred celibacy to marriage. To Augustine, permanent abstinence became a supreme good. Thomas Aquinas thought that sexual desire and sexual experience interfered with (man's) high calling (Cole, p. 91). To Luther, the power of sex was the result of sin (Ibid., p. 118), and Calvin believed strongly that it should be harnessed and controlled. More important, however, than these theological views *per se* was their representation and actualization in the mundane world and the ecclesiastical organization.

However much celibacy, for instance, created tension for individual priests, monks, and nuns, there is a good reason to believe that it had a beneficial effect on the spiritual and organizational strength of the Catholic Church. The celibacy of Methodist circuit riders on the frontier strengthened Methodist organization (S. D. Clark, 1948, p. 149). For the many utopias in American history, sexual abstinence was an important mechanism of sacrifice augmenting allegiance to the group, and therefore its cohesion. In these utopian communities, the ban on sexual relations was often enunciated at the very times when energy and attention had to be devoted to group tasks (Kanter, p. 78). The controversy around celibacy in modern Catholicism (see Schreuder, p. 178) reflects the predicament of amorphous societies and Catholic structures, and the escape to the last stronghold of personal identity.

Some of these observations can also be made for other societies and other religions (Weber, 1964, p. 241). Islam is rightfully regarded as a religion with little sexual asceticism. Yet Ibn Khaldun observed in the fourteenth century, that abstinence from pleasures led to greater religiosity (Vol. 1, pp. 179–80); the pilgrims to Mecca may not have sexual relations until after the sacrifice at Minā (Gibb, p. 57); and the Sufis think that their best and most distinguished members are 'the unmarried, if their hearts are unstained and their minds free from sin and lust' (ibid., p. 106). In Hinduism the control of sexual energy is often regarded as having a beneficial effect on spiritual knowledge and higher loyalties (Gandhi, pp. 29–32; Erikson, 1969, p. 120). Reichel-Dolmatoff (p. 145) mentions how the Amazonian tribe he studied thought that one could only be successful in the hunt 'in a state of abstinence'. On Java, Geertz found the belief in the relationship between instinctual deprivation and spiritual power 'almost universal' (1969, p. 323).

Thus, in sum, emphasis on sexual fulfilment appears to occur in periods of history when social and group amorphousness upgraded the significance of the self as the centre for sacralization. On the other hand sexual restraint seems to accompany strong social and group cohesion, and sacralized group and social identities. World-denying mysticism appears to be a significant exception, as it is both immensely personal and often sex-restraining. However, in this instance, one could argue that the divine unity that the mystic seeks is, in the last resort, union with a point of reference in which are reflected the socially desirable values, such as humility, consideration, and predictability, rather than values such as self-assertion, aggressiveness, and ambition.

FUNCTIONS AND DYSFUNCTIONS OF SELF-ORIENTATION

There is no doubt that the technological and scientific advance of the West would have been impossible without extensive innovation, which itself depended on the cake of custom being systematically and consistently relativized. The rational individualism of the last 400 years has proved to be an appropriate vehicle of change, in the same way as the sacralization of social conformity has proved to be the vehicle of stability. The stress on selfhood advanced the flexibility of societies. And if ripe old age is the goal of an individual, psychological studies (*Time*, 12 Nov. 1973, p. 60) have shown that aggressiveness, narcissism, authoritarianism, ambition, distrust of others, disregard for others' viewpoint, a tendency to blame others, and a resistance to blaming oneself are much more functional than the contrary, socially more desirable values.

The dysfunction follows logically from the function: the more flexible a society becomes, the more precarious its sacred, taken-for-granted, systems of meaning will be. Such systems of meaning infuse society with stability, and by definition they inhibit innovation. Even so, the precariousness of social identity also implies that social expectations, values, and beliefs can no longer be taken for granted. They lose their plausibility, and the ensuing freedom of the self is thus irremediably tied to social volatility and alienation. The neglect and diminution of group and social identity that result from an overemphasis on the self worries even some present-day psychiatrists and psychologists despite their professional emphasis on personality, rather than social, integration.

Wheelis, for instance, is seriously concerned about the weakening of the superego and the corresponding weakening capacity of the ego to control impulse (p. 99). He sees reciprocity between the strength of the superego and the strength of the ego (p. 164), and accuses his fellow psychiatrists of working 'with a nineteenth-century conception of social character, assuming that values persist unchanged and that the only significant variable is individual psychodynamics' (p. 172). Erikson (1963, p. 282) is similarly critical of the exclusive focus of early psychoanalysis 'on one single endeavour—introspective honesty in the service of self-enlightenment and its incapacity to say much about 'the way in which the ego's synthesis grows—or fails to grow—out of the world of social organization'. Psychoanalysis is seized upon by patients as a faith (p. 417) and a refuge because of the 'discontinuities of existence' (p. 279). Elsewhere, Erikson (1962, p. 254) contrasts an optimum ego synthesis, to which the individual aspires, and an optimum societal metabolism for which societies and cultures strive.

Frankl, however much he remains within a subjectivist frame of mind, is highly critical of self-actualization as an end it itself. Man can only find his (personal) identity 'to the extent to which he commits himself to something beyond himself, to a cause greater than himself' (p. 9; McConnell, p. 56). And of course, many of the values and the meaning systems, on which Frankl feels a person's self-actualization depend, are constructed and reinforced by what we have called 'group' and 'social' identities, as Desmonde suggests (p. 139) when saying that 'only by devoting himself to a higher cause . . . can (an individual) integrate his personality and attain complete emotional fulfilment'.

From here it is only a relatively short step to those who are either frightened by, acquiesce in, or approve of, the animal in man. After all, it is not unbecoming to assume with Hobbes (p. 95) that the unbridled or animalistic self is the ultimate consequence of a powerless social order. There is certainly a connection between Nietzsche's adulation of self-sufficient manhood and his subsequent judgement that man is the most bungled and sickliest of animals because he 'has strayed more dangerously from (his) instincts' (1954b, p. 580).

It is also no accident that precisely when modern man escapes from his tottering structures into the last bastion of self-affirmation, that in his theatrical successes he has the baby stoned to death (Edward Bond's *Saved*), or has the hero say, on hearing that his wife is pregnant, 'I don't care if it has two heads' (John Osborne's *Look Back in Anger*). The cruelties of Edward Albee's *Who's Afraid of Virginia Woolf* are symptomatic of a culture where social standards are rapidly losing their taken-for-grantedness (see, on this theme, Duncan Williams's *Trousered Apes*).

Avant-garde plays do not necessarily represent popular taste or popular values, of course. Before he met condemnation for his dubious private values, Vice-President Agnew (p. 8) could still with relative impunity voice the vehemence of popular reaction to the erosion of social values, when he condemned the atrocities of campus radicals as the offspring of 'affluent, permissive, upper-middle-class parents who learned their Dr. Spock and threw discipline out of the window—when they should have done the opposite'. These children, from homes where the construction of individual selfhood is the exclusive criterion for upbringing, Agnew characterized as 'dropped off by their parents at Sunday School to hear the "modern" gospel from a "progressive" preacher more interested in fighting pollution than fighting evil—one of those pleasant clergymen who lifts his weekly sermons out of old newsletters from a National Council of Churches'.

A substantial amount of permissiveness; overemphasis on self-affirmation; rebellion against society; or literary exultation of bestiality, arises because modern Western societies are now segmentalized and privatized. Paradoxically it may also happen because social order and social values are still strongly defended by, for example, Agnew's former constituents. In other words, the precarious balance between the self and the social is constantly broken, but not irreparably, and not without the backlash of the maligned party.

Some authors have written rather eloquently about the fundamental paradox between self-affirmation and social responsibility. For instance, Steinbeck seems to be engaged, in at least some of his novels, with the agonizing question of why it is that the people one admires because of their generosity, kindness, honesty, and understanding are often failures in American society, and why the people one detests because of their acquisitiveness, ruthlessness, and sharpness become the symbols of success. The first set of values obviously advances group or social cohesion, and is presumably admired for that reason. The second set of values obviously does the reverse and is therefore detested, but strengthens ego boundaries and leads to economic success in those industrialized Western societies where competition and entrepreneurship are at a premium.

Scholars have expressed the same in more formal language. The historian Teggart (p. 196) writes that the breakdown of customary modes of action and of thought leads to 'an individual's release in aggressive self-assertion'. Charles Cooley (1956b, pp. 147–8) observed that the individual, 'without cogent and abiding allegiance to a whole, and without the larger principles of conduct that flow from such allegiance . . . is likely (to be thrown) back upon sensuality and other primitive impulses'.

In Sorokin's sensate cultures, such as present-day European culture, in which 'the true, ultimate reality-value is sensory' (Sorokin, 1966, pp. 23–5), the self is characteristically 'corporeal', ready 'to fight for physical integrity and the interest of self', intent on 'uninhibited satisfaction of individual lust' (1937, Vol. I, pp. 83, 88). This contrasts sharply with ideational cultures, where social and practical values are built on the principle of sacrifice (p. 99).

Ellul criticizes existentialist subjectivism because of the absence of the social dimension. He contrasts modern concepts of freedom which always tend 'in the direction of a greater mastery of self, of individual autonomy', with the biblical ones where obedience is prior and where the 'Christian life is an ever deeper belonging to God' (1969, pp. 282, 284).

Slater (p. 7) says: 'When a value is as strongly held as is individualism in America, the illnesses it produces tend to be treated by increasing the dosage, in the same way an alcoholic treats a hangover or a drug addict his withdrawal symptoms.' He therefore feels that, as a matter of first priority, individualism should be assigned a subordinate place in the American value system as this value 'is not a viable foundation for any society in a nuclear age' (p. 118).

The critics of self-orientation in modern society seem to feel in their bones that a person's sense of security or authenticity depends on the continuity of values, such as honesty, reciprocity, trust, capacity for give and take, commitment to specific forms of social order and justice, reliability, social responsibility. All these values and the beliefs that undergird them, they demand, must be socially reinforced. A stable, or even sacralized, system of social values and beliefs is thought to be necessary for the long-run maintenance of personal integrity, however much, in the short run, the individual may take refuge in his own buttressed world.

The criticism is well taken. The assumption of conflict and of shifting boundaries between personal and social identity demands a second look at the conceptual apparatus of those social psychologists and social philosophers who espouse various forms of phenomenology and existentialism. I allude to Natanson's journeying self; Goffman's performing self; Berger and Luckmann's role-playing self; Lifton's protean man; Orr and Nichelson's self as process. All these concepts direct the attention to the façade—rather than to the niche—constructing self. This in turn leads to an underestimation of the boundary construction of social, group, and personal identity and a corresponding emphasis on culture-bound socialization processes at the expense of conflict and maintenance. It also leads to a diminished emphasis on the sacralizing potential of the various forms of identity, and by implication a restricted usefulness for the analysis of religious phenomena.

The scholarly critics appear to have the average citizen of modern societies on their side. In an inarticulated way the public seems to feel the personal danger of living in a society where trust is openly accepted to be a façade for the power-hungry, and where appearance of honesty is more useful than being intrinsically honest. The argument of usefulness is never a very strong one with the man in the street. The cleavage between individual and social need cannot be naïvely abridged by the rational argument that men should surrender ego-enhancing and id-expressing satisfactions for the sake of the social good. This is particularly so when advancing the social good carries only feeble social rewards. The man in the street is vaguely aware that in the past the norms of goodness, honesty, reliability, etc., were implemented not because their social necessity could be demonstrated, but because they could be dinned into the recalcitrant through lifelong socialization processes, reinforced by sacred forces which would compensate on the infallible level of omniscience and omnipotence for what a fallible society could only feebly strengthen.

The conceptual advantage of linking religion closely to the need for stable selfhood or a stable order can be demonstrated by addressing ourselves to situations where other classifications have run into difficulties. In his large sample of primitive societies, Swanson successfully relates the belief in the immanence of a soul (in our scheme an instance of the sacralization of personal identity) to the relative freedom of the individual from involvement in a society in which there are persistent, structurally unresolvable, conflicts (1966, pp. 126–36, 176). However, with his conceptual frame of reference (sharply distinguishing between magic and religion or *mana* and spirits—p. 29) he finds this difficult to relate to two other phenomena: (a) that there is also a significant correlation between belief in the immanence of a soul and societies with important debt relationships (p. 135); and (b) that there is also an identification of spirits with sovereign groups (p. 176) (in our schema an instance of the sacralization of group identity). All this makes sense in terms of our conceptual apparatus, as one may expect personal identity to be relatively more important (and therefore sacralized) when the social order leaves conflicting expectations of reference groups or debt relations unlegitimated, meaningless, and unresolved. Our conceptual distinction between various forms of identity but similar sacralization processes, also allows us to avoid falling victim to a classification that defines spirits exclusively in terms of one form of identity (the social). Instead of being puzzled by finding a spirit (or a soul) also on the personal level, as Swanson was, our conceptual apparatus leads us to expect it. Yet this does not mean that the distinction between *mana* and spirit cannot be very useful for other purposes. All that we are saying, is that sacralization of personal identity can be achieved in a variety of ways.

SUMMARY

To bring order among a great variety of identity foci we have plotted the latter on a continuum ranging from those primarily serving self-integration, through those advancing group-integration, to those mainly dealing with social identity.

In keeping with the rational individualism that has been so propitious for modern technological development, the sacralization of selfhood has progressed at the expense of the cohesion of social identity. Although Christianity and the other universal religions have traditionally allowed ample scope for personality integration, they have always tempered this effort by stressing those values that would advance rather than impede the integration of society. This is well exemplified by Reinhold Niebuhr's statement that the autonomous individual is an unChristian concept.

Yet Western intellectual movements and mundane sources of motivation and meaning have tended to a much more exclusive stress on self-realization and on those values that strengthen the ego. The implication of this tendency has often been a further erosion of social stability and a weakening of the superego. Drugs, astrology, the occult, money-making, status-seeking, and sexual fulfilment are all widely used as mechanisms, or foci, for private meaning-systems, which have rather tenuous bonds to a larger, social, frame of reference.

The dysfunctions of this stress on self-realization are likely to make the pendulum swing further towards the social side of the continuum. There are already clear indications of this happening when the younger generation shows a preference for socially integrative, expressive values over against the personality integrating values of self-affirmation, aggressiveness, and instrumental achievements.

Chapter XII

Cults and Sects

Groups, too, have a wide variety of foci around which identity can crystallize. Witchcraft is the focus around which covens are structured. The relief of drug problems is the goal of former addicts who formed Synanon, now a full-fledged, tightly knit, commune in the U.S.A. The miraculous arrival of Western opulence from heaven is the centre of attention in native cargo cults. Salvation is the focus of most sects. Causes (such as ecology) have been and are the focus of strongly dedicated action groups. Both radical left- and radical right-wing political goals have become foci for group identity. 'The John Birch Society has become (the members') church, accepted as God's vessel of salvation, as God present with them for guidance, for comfort and for strength. Welch has become the revealer of God's eternal truth. . . .' (Broyles, p. 122; Klapp, p. 356).

All these groups have a specific identity in common. All of them are clearly delineated within a larger, usually more heterogeneous, social whole which is luke-warm, noncommittal, or downright suspicious about sectarian goals. They are all vocal about the inadequacies of the society in which they find themselves. They create sharper boundaries between in-group and out-group and thereby consolidate in-group identity.

These groups are commonly hostile to individual expressions that deviate from group norms and goals. They delineate themselves just as strongly from self-orientations as from noncommittal society. Too much diversity within a group leads to heterogeneity, and this endangers whatever the group stands for. On the other hand by structural minimization of private ties, the cohesion of the total group is maximized (Kanter, p. 87). Consequently these groups often develop a variety of mechanisms to anchor a sense of individual self-fulfilment in group goals, and to trap a considerable portion of a person's libido for sectarian purposes.

These kinds of groups are vulnerable on two fronts: society at large tends to be sensitive and defensive about alleged inadequacies and individuals tend to resent restrictions. Yet in modern societies their vigour is more conspicuous than their vulnerability. The amorphousness of the larger social whole and the anomy of self-orientations give them a competitive advantage.

Group identity is a buffer between personal and social identity. It often channels, sublimates, and thereby extenuates individual protests. It sometimes protects society by encysting the protest or by goading it towards reform. Group identity is often strengthened by sacralizations. Yet groups do not necessarily have to persist for long to acquire a sacralized identity. Some social action groups or cargo cults disintegrate because their goals may be accomplished or become irrelevant. Others may be wiped out by fearful governments: in some African states the Jehovah Witnesses have been decimated or driven underground. Sometimes groups change their goals. Festinger and Riecken give examples of doomsday cults that persisted after their prophecy had failed. In our frame of reference this suggests that the latent provision of identity was more important than the overt focus of the group.

The conflict between personal, group, and social identity must not obscure their interdependence. Groups *both* provide individuals with possibilities for self-fulfilment, *and* constrict individual autonomy for the sake of group cohesion. Groups *both* reinforce many of the goals and values of a society, *and* weaken societal cohesion by protest against society and the provision of conflicting systems of meaning.

There is an awesome diversity among groups that sacralize identity. A sect is obviously such a group. But so is the local chapter of the Women's Liberation Movement which would be called 'religious' only in the vernacular. Some of these groups are organized around rather traditional religious ends; others have very mundane goals. Because our interest is in a general theory, the particular foci (whether manifestly or only latently 'religious') are, for the moment, less important than the groups that crystallize around them. This does not mean that the variety of foci is irrelevant. On the contrary. Important conclusions about the character of a particular society can be drawn from the kinds of foci around which group identities are formed. They are usually astute indicators of basic problems of the societies in which they occur. Both witchcraft and drug addiction are symptoms of the incapacity of modern societies to impose a viable, uniform system of meaning and morals. Cargo cults are a response to a breakdown of primitive cultures and the emergence of new sets of expectations. Sects are enclaves of disenchantment and alienation in Western civilization.

Within this broadly conceived frame of reference, are we able to account sociologically for the emergence and persistence of these groups?

SECTS

The sociology of religion has occupied itself with the church-sect typology from its inception, and sects are typical for the kinds of groups we have in minds. The problem is that they are also typically *Western* forms of religious organization and we want our theory to be large enough to be relevant for non-Western societies as well. We therefore want to look at them as *one* kind of group rather than as *the* kind of group that sacralizes identity.

Troeltsch, who utilized the church/sect distinction, fell into the trap of classifying religious phenomena in terms of Western, culture-bound, organizational (rather than functional) categories, and this limited the value of his typology. After all, Christianity is the exception rather than the rule in that it developed complex forms of religious organization to safeguard sacralizing functions from the effect of instrumental functions. Yet, this very organizational structure hindered the monopolization of those sacralizing tendencies that were spontaneously emerging elsewhere in the same societies. Troeltsch's Christianity-bound categories did not provide the tools to analyse these tendencies that have now become so prominent in the modern West. As a result, the sociology of religion has ever since been unable to provide a good analysis of the inter-dependence and conflict between religious organization and religious functioning. Yet this dialectic is the crux of Western ecclesiastical dilemmas. Religiosity is a reality prior to and independent of religious organization (Simmel, 1959, p. 24; Levine, 1959, p. 28; Wilson, 1973, p. 13).

Troeltsch's church/sect distinction (Vol. I, p. 331–43) may be regarded as just one instance of a more general set of phenomena and generalizations, however. Sects may be said to sacralize the identity of groups that flourish precisely because the social whole of which they are part is uncongenial or inadequate as a system of meaning for some people. On the other hand, churches sacralize identities that are essentially congruous with and congenial to the social whole.

On the basis of this distinction one can expect the less powerful lower classes to be over-represented in the sects, and the more powerful middle and upper classes, who defend the social status quo, to be over-represented in the churches. One can also expect the sects to have stronger group boundaries than the churches. After all, to them the environment is less congenial and more hostile. Thirdly, as a consequence of the greater group cohesion, one can expect the sect members to have stronger mutual bonds, to be more prepared to sacrifice for the group (ascetic behaviour; commitment), and to be more involved (greater individual participation in the ritual). On the other hand, the membership of the churches take their churches much more for granted. One is born into them in the same way as one is born in one's congenial social milieu.

Within the roomy context of Christian religious beliefs, one can also expect those items to be stressed which are more congruous with, and more meaningful to, the specific group or social identity. The sects, therefore, tend to emphasize the radicality of the Gospel, the rejection of the present age, and the all-pervasive change to be brought about by a future event (millennium, parousia). The status quo is *not* congenial. The churches, on the other hand, tend to emphasize tradition (e.g. the apostolic succession), the holiness of the sacerdotal office, the evolution of a better social order. The status quo is a relatively adequate context.

This rough retranslation of Troeltsch needs much painstaking and detailed refinement, but the major components are all there, and are all organically derived from, or related to, the one sociological parent component which one scholar correctly observes to be 'the extent to which a religious body accepts the culture of the social environment in which it exists' (B. Johnson, 1971, p. 128; also Burch, p. 284).

Since Troeltsch, the church-sect typology has been refined and elaborated in many directions (H. R. Niebuhr, 1957; H. Becker, 1950, pp. 114–17; Pope, 1942; Muelder, 1957; Dynes, 1955; Yinger, 1970, pp. 256–81; Bryan Wilson, 1967a). Lately, it has been severely criticized as having 'no power to explain or elucidate' and as 'a dead concept, obsolete, sterile and archaic' (E. Goode, 1967, p. 77); 'culture-bound', 'institution-bound and institution-binding'; an example of the sociology of religion tying 'itself to a decrepit theoretical wagon and (choking) on the dust in its tracks' (Demerath, 1967, pp. 82, 83); and 'unreliable', blocking 'more vigorous and impressive development of a sociology of religious phenomena' (Eister, 1967, p. 85); 'badly wanting on all three criteria' of a good typology, namely, generality, analytical clarity, and formal theory (B. Johnson, 1971, p. 125). The problem for those who utter these justified criticisms is their inability to provide better alternatives.

If our assumption of a fundamental need for identity (order, interpretation of reality, system of meaning, integration) is correct, then we should also find that sects (among other groups) will thrive when that other fundamental, but conflicting, need—for mastery (instrumental action, control of environment, adaptation, rational efficiency)—has overextended itself and has created meaninglessness and disorder. Why in particular should it be sects that fulfil this function, and why should it be fulfilled at the level of the group? After all, the need for identity is also expressed on personal and social levels? It may be that in differentiated, modern societies, groups such as sects can function more strategically as antibodies in the bloodstream of the social order, counterbalancing the destructive potential of the forces of adaptation. It may be that in these societies, groups such as sects, can function more strategically as protective shields against the powerlessness, anomy, and victimization of individuals.

The bi-facial character of group identity (one face towards the individual, the other towards the social) is not unimportant. Theories explaining sectarianism in terms of social protest only, have foundered because the other face was ignored. They always had difficulty in explaining why sectarianism was such a viable form of religious organization even when there was no strong social order to protest against, for example, on the American frontier. H. Richard Niebuhr and the historians whom he uses (1957, pp. 141–2, p. 290, footnote 7) account for sectarianism on the frontier by maintaining that all these poor frontiersmen were deprived in their lack of effective inhibitions of emotional expression cultivated by formal education, and by lack of the security of settled communities where the awesome manifestations of nature could be accepted with greater confidence and better shelter. The elitist bias of this explanation is as curious as the capacity for comparative analysis is wanting. After all, the same sectarian phenomena occurred in urban settled areas.

More pertinent for the emergence of sectarianism on the North American frontier was the anomie created by the operation of rugged individualism which lacked a sustaining social context. The most independent individualists had a predilection for the frontier. S. D. Clark (1948, p. 30) links the individualism on the Nova Scotia frontier to the settlers there originating 'from those elements of the New England population which were least stable, least a part of the New England cultural system'. All frontier areas tended to attract the misfits, the restless, the thriftless, and the irresponsible. Drinking and gambling often made the labour force unreliable and families unstable (Clark, 1968, pp. 152–3). W. W. Sweet (p. 4) says: 'The pioneer is always an independent individualist, determined to go his own way in religion as well as in politics, and therefore the frontier was fruitful in the multiplication of new sects.' Yet this does not in any way explain why frontier religion was so often sectarian, in the sense of being revivalistic, enthusiastic, rather than church-like, reserved, and dignified. H. Richard Niebuhr (p. 141) attempts to account for frontier sectarianism also through the pathology of loneliness. 'The isolation of frontier life fostered the craving for companionship, suppressed the gregarious tendency and so subjected the lonely settler to the temptations of crowd suggestion to an unusual degree.' Apart from the bias implicit in this pathological explanation, again it fails to acknowledge that sectarian religiosity also emerged in situations where loneliness was not a factor. We are probably somewhat closer to the truth when we hypothesize that the anomic tendencies of the kind of individualism flourishing on the frontiers of North America (the references to intemperance, profanity, gambling, and licentiousness are numerous—Sweet, (p. 231) were uncongenial to the social and kinship responsibilities emerging from a more enduring kind of settlement. The frontier necessitated the creation of a new identity and it is for that reason that the new settlers so often rejected (as was the case in the Maritime Provinces of Canada—S. D. Clark, 1948, p. 83) the respectable Anglican and Presbyterian churches which served as agents of English and Scottish cultural preservation. Charismatic movements are eminently equipped for this task through their capacity for emotional stripping and welding. The charismatic sects contributed strongly to the formation of this new identity. As Clark (1948, p. 88) points out: 'the evangelical movements were essentially movements of social reorganization or social unification'. We may add that it was no accident that frontier sectarianism, as well as sectarianism elsewhere, made such a sharp distinction between the sin of selfishness and self-indulgence and redemption through surrender to Christ.

On the other hand, once the creation of this new identity had taken place it also seems inevitable that these sects should turn into denominations intent upon maintaining the status quo. The metamorphosis of sects into denominations which has understandably drawn so much attention on the North American continent, where it was, and is, a recurring phenomenon, is, in the final resort, typical only for changing, mobile societies. It is in those societies that one can most clearly observe the relevance of sects for the forging of a new identity, and the relevance of denominations and churches for maintaining this identity, once it was formed.

We have described sectarianism on the frontier as bi-facial. Its emergence and strength are related to the change from a contra-social individualism to responsible community formation (the individual face). Yet it is also related to the carving of order and identity from the non-order of the surrounding wilderness (the social face).

Underlying our argument has been a guarded scepticism about the deprivation hypothesis of sect formation, or as it is sometimes put, sectarianism as the religious response of the disinherited. When we now turn to the most recent and modern sect in Christianity, the Jesus Freaks, the deprivation thesis again seems less than adequate. Certainly it is difficult to think about them as economically, politically, or intellectually poor.

The Jesus Freaks, or Jesus People movement, began in California, where most modern, off-beat and esoteric religions have their origin. Its membership consists primarily of the very young, drop-outs from high school, college, and the drug culture, who come mainly from middle- to upper-class homes with histories of permissiveness and lack of authority in which tensions are often high. (Enroth, Ericson and Peters, pp. 44, 212; Peterson and Mauss, pp. 264, 274). Their commitment to Jesus is total. They accept the literal truth of the Bible (King James Version). They are both against the Establishment and against institutional religion. They engage in friendly, loving proselyting, and many have severed all ties with families and peers. They usually live in communes or Christian homes with strict taboos on sex and drug-taking. The movement has now spread over the whole of North America and to overseas countries as well. The circulation of their underground papers runs into the hundreds of thousands. Even from this very short account, it seems clear that the group provides the individual with a completely changed new identity. It provides an enclave of meaning, love, and sincerity in a society which is rejected because of its meaninglessness, tension, and hypocrisy.

To account for the success of the sect, Peterson and Mauss lean rather heavily on Glock's deprivation theories of religion. They maintain that the Jesus People suffer from ethical deprivation (discrepancies between ideals and social realities); from psychic deprivation (search for new values, a new faith, a quest for meaning and purpose); and from social deprivation (lack of social acceptance, search for social belonging). As these theories also predominate among scholars studying cargo cults, we will postpone a more extensive discussion until the end of this chapter. Here it suffices to say that if deprivation or, as Glock more correctly, has it 'felt-deprivation' (1973, p. 210) means 'whatever is non-order, non-meaning, non-identity' we are actually talking about the same thing. However, one would have to stretch the meaning of deprivation far beyond common-sense notions to infuse the concept with these connotations.

The Jesus Freaks themselves regard any kind of theorizing about their beliefs with great contempt. They call it 'head-tripping'. When a freak was asked how he could say he was free in Christ and then talk about leaving it up to Christ to guide his life in predetermined paths, he fixed a straight and intense glare and replied with a mixture of disdain and surprise:

> Man, you're a head-tripper! If you want to head-trip, do it some place else. We could sit here from now until doomsday rapping about head-trips. If you want to know about Christ, the Savior, that's cool. But I'm not going to sit here and get into asinine head-trips. They don't go anywhere (Peterson and Mauss, p. 273).

Given the temptations of immoderate, competitive, claims of scientific explanations, and given the goal of identity reinforcement where logical, rational counter-arguments tend to be dysfunctional, the interviewee scored an interesting point!

ETHNIC GROUPS

Like sects, ethnic groups also tend to sacralize group identity. Yet, in contrast to sects, they do not generally forge a new identity but preserve an old one. This may explain why their fervour is less pronounced, although the maintenance of any strong boundary (whether old or new) requires emotional commitment.

Ethnic groups are very appropriate examples of the buffer function that we mentioned earlier. They protect individual immigrants from the acculturation demands of the host society. By creating a home away from home they preserve an old world identity in the new country. In doing so they contribute to the looser weave or the lesser integration of the receiving culture. To put this in somewhat stronger terms: by the very fact that they are functional for personal identity, they are dysfunctional for social identity.

An interesting example of formal prayers being used for consolidating the ethnic group comes from eighteenth-century U.S.A. The German Lutheran pastor Helmuth, who was of the opinion that 'English and Lutheranism were no more compatible than were English and the agrarian virtues' (Glatfelter, p. 219), together with a colleague, Schmidt, had the following prayer inserted in the Lutheran liturgy of 1786:

> And since it has pleased Thee chiefly by means of the Germans, to transform this state (of Pennsylvania) into a blooming garden and this wilderness into an airy pasture-land, help us not to deny our nation, but rather to educate our beloved youth, so that German churches and schools will not only be maintained, but might attain a still more flourishing condition. (Mol, 1961, p. 46.)

In the countries of immigration, migrant churches have always been the most effective bastions of ethnic preservation. More often than not they were and are at the centre of the organized social activities of immigrant groups. 'Without the influence of the Ukrainian churches it is unlikely that much of this (Ukrainian) culture would exist (in Canada) today' (Millett, p. 52). This also applies to non-Christian religions. Speaking about a Lebanese community in Alberta, Barclay says: 'To some extent the strictest Muslims are those who are least assimilated to Canadian Society' (p. 78) and 'From the point of view of the iman at Lac La Biche, it is those

Lebanese who are most assimilated who are the poorest Muslims and from the point of view of the local school superintendent, it turns out to be the children of the poorest Muslims who are best integrated into Lac La Biche society' (pp. 82–3).

By implication ethnic minorities tend to shun the churches of the host society since these represent *par excellence* the foreign ways of acting and reacting, or, as we should say, they sacralize the social order which is uncongenial to the unassimilated immigrant or racial group. In New Zealand, a Maori expressed his lack of interest in the European (or Pakeha) church services as follows:

> I have to go to school with Pakehas, go to the pictures with them, share the same pub, work with them and even see the kids have Pakeha wives. But I don't have to worship with them, and I won't. (Mol, 1966, p. 17.)

There is good evidence that in all countries migrants go to church less (Mol, 1970b and 1971b), particularly when the churches do not represent the desired ethnic identity. In Britain there is a massive defection of migrants who used to regularly attend the Anglican churches in the West Indies (Clifford Hill, pp. 22–3) to the Pentecostalist sect which 'forms a buffer between the immigrant group and society' (Calley, p. 145).

Just as religious organization and religious functioning both interact and conflict in Western civilization, so ethnic groups provide similar evidence. It would be wrong to leave the impression that the viability of religious organizations depends on whether or not they sacralize specific identities. Particularly in modern, differentiated societies religious organizations have become identities in their own right. Scholars such as Gibson Winter (1968) actually use (religious) identity only in the sense of (religious) organization. Certainly, the Catholic Church has furnished bountiful examples of independent, internal, organizational strengthening without being subservient to specific national, group, or individual identities. Organization and function should be kept separate in our analysis. The ethnic group example which makes this distinction necessary is provided by the research undertaken by Lloyd Warner and his staff in Yankee City. They noticed that the Protestant Northern Irish could no longer be distinguished from the native American population. Yet the Southern Irishmen 'through their Catholic Church structures, present themselves in a highly organized community system with the

Yankee City social system' (Warner and Srole, p. 218). Even fourth-generation Southern Irish were still not completely absorbed in Yankee City. There was no Catholic Church in the town before the Irish arrived in the nineteenth century, and the newly established church became an Irish institution. On the other hand the Northern Irish Presbyterian found a climate congenial to their own beliefs and readily adjusted to the existing church structure. The integration of the Irish in Yankee City was not determined by ethnic, but by religious differences (Mol, 1961, p. 29).

CARGO CULTS

Cargo cults are millenarian movements in which the native followers have strong, almost frenzied, beliefs in the miraculous arrival of plentiful 'cargo', desirable Western goods such as tinned food, tractors, radios, rifles, etc. Often dead ancestors are the putative purveyors of this opulence. Warehouses are built, jetties and docks constructed, and airstrips prepared to receive these goods. Sometimes all existing valuables are destroyed, pigs are slaughtered, and all foodstuffs are consumed during the period of preparation for the great event (Worsley, 1957, p. 53). The movements have occurred in the South Pacific (primarily Melanesia) ever since contacts with white Europeans became sustained, particularly since the beginning of the twentieth century.

Anthropologists have given various explanations for the emergence of cargo cults. Lucy Mair, the first anthropologist to use the term 'cargo cult' (originally coined by white settlers, officials, and missionaries), explained the movement as the product of native envy (Mair, p. 67; Christiansen, pp. 19, 84). Firth (1963, p. 113) thinks that the peculiar fantasies and projections of the cult are the outcome of native incapacity to bridge the gulf between wants and the means to satisfy those wants. Worsley emphasizes the cult's reaction against oppression by another class or nationality (p. 227), and the political effect of welding 'previously hostile and separate groups together into a new unity' (p. 228). Like Worsley, Talmon regards this and other millenarian movements as 'the religion of deprived groups' (p. 530) and as forerunners of political action (p. 534). In addition she stresses their radical rejection of the present (p. 526) and their special efficacy in bridging the future and the past. To her, they are a breakthrough to the future *and* an infusion of the old with new meanings (p. 533).

In terms of our frame of reference, cargo cults are examples of transitions to a new identity made necessary by the forceful presentation of new cultural elements. The cult, guided by its charismatic leaders, strips from its followers the old patterns (destruction of valuables and means of sustenance, inversion of standards and beliefs), and welds them to new ones, in which both certain ancestral traditions and the culture-destroying products of Western technical superiority are intermingled. The commitment (frenzied anti-Westernism, sacrifice), the ritual of the working parties, the objectification of the apocalypse, the symbols and myths surrounding the cargo and the ancestors are, to us, so many mechanisms of sacralization of the new group identity.

Theories of deprivation and envy suffer from Western perspectives of rationality and are thus in difficulty in reconciling the destruction of valuables with the belief in their miraculous arrival at a later stage. Theories which explain cargo cults as primitive pre-political action programmes suffer from Western perspectives of pragmatism and achievement orientation. They overestimate the need for power and material goals (instrumentalism), correspondingly underestimate the need for a system of meaning and an interpretation of existence (integration). The strength of millenarian movements in Western societies where men may participate in political processes is an embarrassment to theories of this kind.

DISCUSSION

One way to evaluate the validity of theories about religious phenomena is to see whether their predictions have come true. Worsley's neo-marxist orientation leads him to predict that cargo cults are 'destined to disappear' (p. 255). To him they are pre-political expressions of backward native movements. Peter Berger's humanist orientation leads him to predict the inexorable progress of secularization (1967b). In the meantime cargo cults still emerge in Papua-New Guinea at the very time that elections are institutionalized, and national censuses in the West show that sects grow not only faster than the respectable denominations and churches, but faster than the population at large.

From the 1961 to the 1971 Census, the Canadian population increased by 18 per cent (from 18,238,247 to 21,568,310). The major Protestant denominations grew by less: the Anglican Church increased from 2,409,068 to 2,543,180 (6 per cent), the United Church from 3,664,008 to 3,768,800 (3 per cent). The Catholic Church increased slightly more than the population, from 8,342,826 to 9,974,895 (20 per cent). Yet the Pentecostalists increased their number from 143,877, 220,390 (53 per cent), and the Jehovah Witnesses grew from 68,018 to 174,810 (157 per cent). The same pattern prevails in earlier periods of Canadian history. In the 1951 Census report of Canada (Vol. X, p. 160), it was observed that from 1871 to 1951 the smaller sects increased approximately fifteen times, as compared with the growth three to four times of the principal religious denominations. (See also Fallding, 1972, p. 109). This also applied to other Western nations.

In the U.S.A., the Church of God and the Assemblies of God have increased their number tenfold between 1925 and 1958 (Davies, 1967, p. 85; also Wolf, 1959). The 1974 *Yearbook of American and Canadian Churches* published by the National Council of Churches shows that the substantial membership gains were largely among conservative, missionary-minded congregations. Over the last decade, the seminaries and journals catering for evangelicals in the U.S.A. have flourished to the same extent that the liberal seminaries and journals have weakened. Dean Kelley has argued that the liberal churches, in contrast with the growth of the conservative churches, are suffering because of their dilute and undemanding form of meaning (Kelley, 1972).

These data appear to contradict Stark and Glock's finding (1970, p. 189) based on a sample of San Francisco area laymen, that the liberal denominations gain at the expense of the more conservative churches. Bibby and Brinkerhoff, using a Canadian urban sample (1973, p. 281), solve this descrepancy by suggesting that conservative churches and sects generally have greater holding power over their membership than the liberals, even though they lose more adherents to them than they gain from them. Yet the increase of sectarian membership in all parts of the world, even in Latin America, is much in excess of the population, to such an extent that holding power or a higher birthrate could hardly begin to explain the variance. Glock and Stark as well as Bibby and Brinkerhoff appear to have worked with unrepresentative data and samples.

There is nothing in Troeltsch's church/sect typology which could have led to the prediction of the growth of evangelical sectarianism in general or of sects in particular. Nor do any of the current theories of religious behaviour contain much predictive power, or for that matter, show much interest in the comparative viability of sects in modern societies. A major reason for this absence or failure of predictions and the lack of explanations for the flourishing state of sects, is the built-in bias towards instrumentalism inherent in the scientific study of religion, together with an overemphasis on differentiation in the analysis of modern societies.

There are occasional exceptions, explanations to sectarian behaviour that stress the corporate need for meaning, integration, and identity. Bryan Wilson, for instance, closely follows Durkheim in his analysis of the Exclusive Brethren. He says. '... their worship of God is worship of the community ... deity is the community objectified' (1967b, p. 336). Like Durkheim, Wilson goes somewhat further than we would want to go. It is particularly the objectification mechanism of the sacralization process which to us makes the identity of the group so different from the concrete, factual, and actual group. True, the enclave character of the concrete group is reflected in the kinds of symbols that are stressed. Yet the Exclusive Brethren are unlikely to perpetuate themselves as a group without the fundamental, transcendental interpretation of what they stand for. In other words, we place the accent not on worship as being somehow less real, as a reflection of something more basic, as an escapist projection and compensation for an uncongenial, mundane existence, but on worship as *one* element in the sacralization process of identity which somehow makes a basic difference to that very social existence. It is this function which makes sects and other forms of Christianity often therapeutic rather than pathological, and therefore more viable than they are often supposed to be. This point will become clearer when we now turn to the more instrumentalist theories regarding the emergence of sects, which, we suggest, have hindered more accurate predictions of sect growth.

What has been the traditional answer to the question: why do sects emerge? Compensation, deprivation, and resentment are the terms most commonly used to explain sectarian behaviour. Weber writes that the privileged classes require of religion that it legitimates their position (1964, p. 107), but that the underprivileged handle the frustrations of their life by projecting compensations into a future existence (ibid., p. 108). Weber follows Nietzsche by postulating that the poor resent the unequal distribution of mundane goods, and blame the privileged, whom they therefore wish to see punished by God's wrath (ibid., p. 110). Bernard Barber (1965, p. 509) finds messianic movements comprehensible 'only as a response to wide-spread deprivation'. Yonina Talmon (1965, p. 530) says that radical millenarianism is essentially 'a religion of the deprived groups', although she also thinks of millenarianism as 'often born out of the search for a tolerably coherent system of values, a new cultural identity and regained sense of dignity and self-respect' (ibid., p. 531).

More recently the concept of deprivation has been expanded by Charles Glock (1973). He detects five types. *Economic* deprivation or limited access to consumer goods generally leads to sectarian religious movements (p. 213). Yet, where the nature of the depriva-tion is correctly assessed, secular means (such as political power) are used to eliminate the causes; in consequence, Glock implies, reli-gious resolutions, compensating for feelings of deprivation, are unnecessary. *Social* deprivation, or unequal distribution of social rewards, such as prestige, power, status, opportunities, is much more likely to evoke a church-like religious response, and therefore the churches 'tend to gain their greatest commitment from individuals who are most deprived of the rewards of the larger society' (p. 218). *Organismic* deprivation refers to physical deformity or mental ill-health, such as neurosis or psychosis. *Ethical* deprivation refers to the incompatibilities in the values of a society or to discrepancies between ideals and realities. Finally, *psychic* deprivation occurs 'when persons find themselves without a meaningful system of values by which to interpret and organize their lives' (p. 212). In the case of ethical and psychic deprivation, Glock says, 'a religious resolution may be as efficacious as a secular one in overcoming the deprivation directly' (p. 213).

The crudity of the deprivation theories lies partly in their deroga-tion of the maintenance function of the church-type religion, but primarily in their assumption that in an undeprived state man would not need religion, or even more fundamentally, that religion is a way to help smooth man's road to mastery. But looking at religion in terms of technological progress, social differentiation, or the contribution it makes to man mastering his environment is to choose a conceptual apparatus which by implication neglects an essential function and precludes a comprehensive answer to such questions as, why sectarian religious forms arise on the frontier (revivalism), or in the modern urban wilderness (Jesus Freaks) or in primitive societies (cargo cults). Other criticisms of the deprivation theories have focused on their incapacity to account for negative cases; their reductionist tendency (Thrupp, 1970); their implicit denial that the structures of social organization are crucial (Swanson, 1966, p. 177); and their explanatory poverty as compared with socialization, accommodation, and cognition variables (Bibby and Brinkerhoff, 1974).

As we see it, religion deals with the interpretation of any reality— not just with a reality which can be reduced to a form of deprivation. Our objection to deprivation theories is essentially the same as Geertz's objection to Malinowsky's 'thoroughgoing instrumentalist view' of religious phenomena and the world 'as consisting of techniques for coping with life rather than as consisting of a way, one way, of conceiving it' (Geertz, 1968, pp. 92–3).

Sectarian religiosity is *not* just a means for better coping with existence, but more fundamentally, a relevant way of conceiving that existence. The millennium of the Jesus Freaks, or the cargo of a primitive society, are *not* just compensations for the relative deprivations of this world, but more fundamentally, a relevant way of interpreting present disorder in the light of a future event. The actual theological form of that future event is obviously informed by one's particular cultural and religious heritage. What we have called 'identity fragilities' in the mundane situation of a minority or disprivileged group are obviously accounted for in theological beliefs, religious rituals, sacred objectifications, and sectarian commitments. But this does not mean that the latter were concocted solely to produce the consequences of these sacralizing mechanisms.

The instrumentalist approach of the deprivation theories; the Marxist stress on compensation; the Feuerbachian and subsequently Freudian projection theories of religion; the Durkheimian 'society worship'; the Wilsonian 'group worship'; even our own identity approach—are, in fact, competitive ways of perceiving the world. These competitive ways are not so very far removed from theologizing, since these competing interpretations can hardly avoid a biased understanding of let us say, revivalism, the Jesus Freaks or the cargo cults. In this instance, scientific fairness may have the unintended consequence of scientific humility and a lesser inclination to summarily dismiss the Jesus Freak's head-tripping accusation.

After all, the Jesus Freak could have turned the scales by pointing embarrassingly to the religious elements in sociological interpretations.

The legitimating consequence for a marginal group of theological beliefs, religious rituals, sacred objectifications, and sectarian commitments is a function of reality interpretation and not necessarily the other way round. It is not true, as the Marxists and others would have it, that reality interpretations are nothing but a function of the need for legitimating the existing economic, political, and other arrangements of specific societies. To say all this more simply: the enhanced capacity for coping with deprivations or anxiety is to us not the *goal* of sacralizing specific group identities, but the *by-product*. It is tempting to cite only one cause in relating the obvious saliency of the deprivation factor in the formation of these groups to the obvious enhanced capacity of the same groups to cope with this deprivation. And yet, one's vision of the world is interdependent with one's position in that world. If the group's position in that world is marginal *vis-à-vis* other groups in an established society, or if it has undergone drastic changes (such as occur through Western influence on primitive tribes), or confronts the massive uncertainties and excessive individualism of the virgin frontier, then the boundaries of that group are likely to be firmly drawn, all the sacralization mechanisms are likely to operate, and specific visions of the past and the future are likely to be firmly established.

The line of demarcation between our kind of theorizing about the emergence of sects and the deprivation explanations should not be drawn too sharply, particularly when deprivation is used in the wide sense in which Glock uses it (comparative lack of access to goods, power, prestige, rewards; comparative lack of satisfaction with prevailing systems of meaning) when it becomes almost synonymous with the term we prefer—marginality. Etymologically there is justification for calling groups for whom existing interpretation of reality lack plausibility 'marginal' rather than 'deprived'. Yet deprivation, alienation (which to Werner Stark, Vol. II, p. 5 is the 'last root of all sectarianism'), and marginality all point in the same direction: something in the environment or social system has broken through a taken-for-granted system of meaning, and has thereby rendered it inadequate. Groups arise to create new islands of meaning or a new identity, and to counterbalance the very disrupting influence of marginality.

SUMMARY

The identity formation of closely knit groups can be regarded as an astute response to the erosion of social, and the anomie of personal, identity. Groups are often the defenders of social values *vis-à-vis* the individual and the protectors of individuals against social alienation. They create miniature communities in a segmentalized, differentiated social whole. Through sacralizing their identities they counterbalance potential chaos with an emotionally anchored order.

Ethnic groups shield their members against the pressures of the host society enabling them to act, react, and speak in unaccustomed ways. Ethnic churches generally reinforce and sacralize ethnic, or old-world identity. Sects, too, shield their members by providing islands of order and meaning in an inhospitable, encroaching cultural sea. Like sects, cargo cults attempt to provide a new identity by intermingling new and old elements.

Sectarian behaviour has often been interpreted as the behaviour of (usually economically) deprived groups. To scholars who explain sects in this way the accent lies on unreachable mundane goals that are assumed to be primary for the membership. To their way of thinking, theologies, rituals, commitments, and objectifications compensate for the pain of failure to achieve. Yet this instrumental assumption is a bias, in that it regards the need to interpret the world as secondary to the need to master that world. Our view is that a systematic interpretation of reality, and a manipulation of man's world, are interdependent and stand in dialectical rather than causal relation to one another.

The emergence and persistence of sects and cults in modern affluent societies can be much better accounted for if one postulates the interdependence between basic needs for identity and mastery, than if one postulates the dependence of the one upon the other. If one assumes, with the Marxists, materialists, and assorted rationalists, that man's interpretation of reality is nothing but a function of his material wants, then, plainly, sects, cults, and forms of evangelical sectarianism should be in a state of miserable decadence.

Chapter XIII

Universal Religions

Religions sacralize ontological assumptions about man and society. When the assumptions about man are stressed at the expense of the assumptions about society, we have cases of deifications of the self. When both man and society are seen as juxtaposed to specific groups, we are usually dealing with sects. The universal religions, however, tend to see man and society as adapting to one another.

Buddhism, Christianity, Confucianism, Hinduism, and Islam sacralize a social identity, but *not* at the expense of man. Their survival very much depends on their capacity to mute, as well as to motivate, individuals, to constrain as well as to co-opt recalcitrant groups, to reform as well as to reinforce the social whole.

It is the last reinforcing or integrating function that has received most attention, but a strong case could be made out to show that the muting and motivating, the constraining and the co-opting, the reforming and reinforcing are necessary for the integration of any society. A relevant religion will reflect, reconcile, and sublimate the strains and stresses of the society in which it is embedded. A religion that strengthens social solidarity will thereby simultaneously reinforce the frame of reference for the reconciliation of personal and group divergences. It will channel personal motivation and group co-operation into directions advantageous for the larger social whole.

Similar points were first made by Durkheim in *The Elementary Forms of the Religious Life*. He interpreted the rites and ceremonies of the most primitive tribes (the central Australian aborigines) to be essentially directed to the preservation of tribal identity. Gods of ancient as well as modern societies represented to Durkheim the moral authority of those societies (1954, pp. 206–9). There is, as Talcott Parsons points out, a positivistic bias in Durkheim's treatment of religion, which he considers to be reducible to a social entity (1937, p. 427). Parsons finds the opposite idea, that society is a religious phenomena, more acceptable. Yet the difference between the two positions is not very great. A religious sub-system and a society will be conditioned by each other. Religious organizations are constantly under pressure to be relevant both in terms of their symbol-systems (relevance A) and action programmes (relevance B). Societies are constantly under pressure to sacralize a uniform and uniting interpretation of reality.

Durkheim's propositions have also been attacked from other quarters. Anthropologists have pointed to the shaky empirical base for his theory. They have shown that the central Australian tribes were by no means the most primitive. Even, if this were the case, they say, it would be inadmissible to generalize on the basis of only one case (Lowie, pp. 158 ff.; Seger, pp. 15 ff.). However warranted in themselves, neither these criticisms, nor that of Goldenweiser who maintains that the enrichment, elaboration, and refinement of religious experience by the spiritual contributions of individuals is a 'glaring refutation of Durkheim's theory' (p. 72), have invalidated Durkheim's major insights about the relations between religion and society. Goldenweiser might with more justification have pointed to Durkheim's underestimation of the fact that religious integration of personal and group identity is often actually, and always potentially, at odds with the integration of the social whole. As it stands Durkheim's theory can quite comfortably incorporate individual religious experiences of the kind to which Goldenweiser alludes. They rarely reinforce contra-social individualism, and are commonly in full accord with socially legitimated views of reality. Certainly, the very personal experiences of, and beliefs in, God of believing Christians ultimately strengthen the socially crucial values of humility, compassion, contentedness, and responsibility, and militate against the contra-social values of self-centredness and self-affirmation. Even if some of these individual religious experiences re-orient a universal religion, the ultimate effect is still a better congruence with the socially legitimated views of reality.

Criticism of Durkheim is justified when it is against the anti-religious bias of his positivism, or his unwarrantably simple, undifferentiated functionalism in which he underrates the amount of conflict between the parts of the social whole. Durkheim's theory does not allow for the potential divisiveness of religious organizations or for their separation from society (Bottomore, 1962, p. 223; Dobbelaere and Lauwers, p. 542). But criticism of his exciting perceptions of the latent functions of religion, is *not* justified. The sociology of religion needs more such perceptions, and must resist the outcry against sociological obscurantism and the clamouring for down-to-earth empiricism that have often aborted the systematization of latent functions, and compelled the premature surfacing of those sociologists skilled in digging below the obvious.

Durkheim's analysis has been profitably used and extended by several scholars, prominent among whom is Guy Swanson. In the *Birth of the Gods* (1966), Swanson linked the character of a god to the character of the social structure in which the god was worshipped. His unit of analysis was not 'society', but the more flexible and small 'sovereign group' (p. 20), which had an 'original and independent jurisdiction over some sphere of life' (p. 42), such as the family, village, or neighbourhood. In a sample of fifty societies, Swanson found that wherever a man was relatively free of involvement in such sovereign groups, the individual's soul was more likely to be conceived as co-essential with his body (p. 176). The sacralization of personal identity, as we suggested in Chapter XI, rises in importance according to the weakness of the social whole. The more 'sovereign' an individual is in his social context, the more will personal identity tend to become sacralized. Swanson also points to the correspondence in jurisdiction of certain kinds of spirits and sovereign groups (p. 175); and between beliefs in high gods ('who produce reality'—p. 56) and social diversity or complexity (p. 65). By complexity Swanson means the situation when there are more than four sovereign groups within the one society.

At times, Swanson comes close to the same positivistic assumptions that Durkheim entertained, namely that social organization is the primary reality which produces this variety of beliefs (e.g. p. 190). Yet the universal religions generally cover a variety of societies, and can hardly be said to be produced by each of them. On the contrary, these religions often form the strongest link between societies and can be shown to have their own independent effect on the social structure. In one respect, Swanson seems to regress from Durkheim: he suggests that disbelief will follow in the wake of man's knowledge and control of his social structures (pp. 188, 189). Durkheim, by contrast, thought that there was 'something eternal in religion' (p. 430), although he appears to be of two minds about the matter when, on the next page (p. 431), he expects the control of science over religion to become constantly 'more extended and efficient, while no limit can be assigned to its future influence'.

More than both Durkheim and Swanson, we have assumed that the sacralization of identity is an inevitable process in both ancient and modern societies, and that tendencies develop within the secular sub-systems of modern societies (economy, polity, science) towards the creation of independent, sacralizing mechanisms. We have cast a rather wide net by adding such categories as objectification and commitment to the sacralization mechanism. Swanson tends to confine himself to one (supernatural beliefs), and Durkheim to two (beliefs and ritual). Through this inclusiveness we think that we can gain the strategic advantage of seeing the similarities, rather than the discrepancies, between, for instance, ancient religious beliefs and modern nationalism instead of being mesmerized by such trivial differences as those between supernaturalism and scientific abstractions. A common commitment to a transcendent order appears to be functionally more salient than the different contents of specific systems of meaning.

How does this general frame of reference apply to the universal religions? In which ways are they imbedded in social structures, and social structures in them? In which way have they muted as well as motivated individuals, constrained as well as co-opted recalcitrant groups, reformed as well as reinforced the social whole? Unfortunately, we can here only begin to sketch the vaguest outlines of an answer to these questions.

ISLAM

Mecca at the time of Mohammed was characterized by a weakening solidarity of tribes, clans, and families. The rich merchants were more interested in augmenting their riches than in carrying out family or clan obligations (Watt, 1961, p. 7). This, in turn, was associated with a pervasive growth of individualism in the region (Watt, 1956, p. 387). Simultaneously, there had been a migration from the increasingly more barren desert to the adjacent Fertile Crescent (Leeuwen, pp. 252, 253).

The faith which Mohammed inspired in his followers had a pronounced effect on the situation. The new Islam community created an overarching solidarity, controlling and subduing internal divisions even when revolts and tribal wars continued to break out. Very soon after Mohammed's death in A.D. 632 Syria, Iraq, and Egypt became part of the Muslim Empire. Within a century the Arabs had reached both the Atlantic Ocean to the West and the Indus river to the East, rolling over the exhausted Byzantine and Persian Empires, paving the way for a new integration of the region. 'Islam emerged into the civilized outer world, not as the crude superstition of marauding hordes, but as a moral force that commanded respect and a coherent doctrine that could challenge on their own ground the Christianity of East Rome and the Zoroastrianism of Persia' (Gibb, p. 13). It managed to maximize its integrative potential, not by abolishing tribal solidarity within its own ranks or by directly challenging pagan religions, but by adding the monotheistic faith in Allah (Scharf, p. 41). It coalesced with the movement away from tribal solidarity towards a larger measure of individualism (the ethical prescriptions of the Qur'ān are fundamentally individualistic—Watt, 1961, p. 11) and yet restrain the potential chaos of diverging individual aspiration (Ibn Khaldun, Vol. I, p. 305) through the ardour of the common faith. All universal religions provide the larger context, the 'sacred canopy', for personal and group diversities. Individuals may believe that their universal religion functions primarily to sacralize their local identity; yet in actual fact, it binds local identity with cosmic bonds.

BUDDHISM

Change through addition and co-optation rather than through substitution also typifies the successful emergence of other universal religions. This change may be conditioned by the lack of vitality and of relevance of the existing religions and the insufficiency of the interlocking identity patterns, as in the case of Buddhism. The faith sprang from the teaching of Gautama Buddha, born in 557 B.C. in North India, where his father was the king of the city of Kapilavastu. He was a member of the Kshatriya or Warrior caste. In this period of history the priestly caste of Brahmins had begun to alienate the lower Kshatriya caste by claims of superior social and moral prestige. Gautama accepted the law of Karma (the law of deeds fixing one's future reincarnation) and the transmigration of the soul.

Yet he stressed the uselessness of the large variety of Hindu gods, and denied the sacredness of the Vedas in which worship and sacrifice to these gods were prescribed. For a localized system of meaning he substituted one that was more abstract, general, and universal. The close ties between an exclusive reality-interpretation and family and village loyalties were loosened. Instead these loyalties and individual experiences were now ordered and legitimated in a larger frame of reference. To the Buddha, suffering (the first noble truth) was the primary characteristic of existence. Suffering was caused by man's desire for pleasure, existence, and prosperity (the second noble truth). Suffering would be overcome by the destruction of desire (the third noble truth), and the way to achieve this destruction was to follow the holy eightfold path (the fourth noble truth): right belief; right aspiration; right speech; right conduct; right means of livelihood; right endeavour; right mindfulness; and right meditation.

In the ethics of Buddhism one finds the subtle outlines of the muting (e.g. non-indulgence), as well as the motivating, of the individual (e.g. being compassionate to others); the constraining (relativization of caste and family, and strict rules of poverty and abstinence of the Sangha monastic order) as well as the co-opting of groups (caste, family, and Sangha as vehicles of Buddhist teaching and practice); the reforming (the Nichiren sect in thirteenth-century Japan spoke boldly against political corruption) as well as the reinforcing (the sacred Sanskrit phrase 'Om mani padme hum' reinforced Tibetan national consciousness—Noss, p. 246) of the larger society.

The sociologically interesting consequence of this ethical system, together with the ascetic rules of the Buddhist Sanghas (religious orders), is their id-repressing self-denial, and the consequent facilitation of social solidarity. More positive motivations for solidarity so typical for Western and Oriental monotheism, as distinct from passive quiescence in solidarity, was relatively weak in Buddhism. The accent fell on the annihilation (muting) of individuality rather than on the positive commitment (motivation) of individuality to social solidarity. This in turn is related to the world-denying rather than the world-affirming kinds of asceticism which Max Weber regarded as the crucial difference between those cultures which did not, and those which did develop means of rational manipulation of the economy.

Even so, at the level of integration, Buddhism was quite success-ful. It spread throughout Asia, partly because it relativized the caste system to which Hinduism was shackled. In India, Gautama's large following was due partly to his attitude towards caste, partly to his charismatic personality. The Buddha personified through his living and preaching the new universalist vision, and provided the required leadership.

The spread of Buddhism outside India, several centuries after the death of Gautama, received a strong impetus from the emperor Asoka, who not only made Buddhism the religion of the state, but also strongly advanced its propagation in other regions (Bouquet, p. 85). In Asoka's empire, the economic changes (towards a more settled agrarian economy); the military changes (the conquests); the political changes (administering control over a variety of kingdoms and republics); and the social changes (opposition to the rigidity of caste system)—all required new integration. Asoka found this in a group of unifying principles, emphasizing social responsibility, con-sideration, generosity, toleration, and non-violence, exemplified by the emperor in his role as member of his Buddhist Order of monks, the Sangha (Thapar, p. 304). Actually, not only Buddhism, but all universal religions, can be regarded as sacralizers of new, larger, frames of identity, relativizing and yet also legitimating the boun-daries of smaller entities such as tribe, caste, and family. The establishment of these newer, larger, identities (a nation, an empire) are invariably preceded by conflicts and changes rendering previous integrative patterns obsolete (Nisbet, 1973, p. 173).

HINDUISM

Hinduism, which spawned Buddhism and then on the Indian sub-continent, managed to assimilate it again, may be regarded as an absorbing sponge. The Jainist principle of *ahimsa* (non-injury to living beings) became central to Hinduism's own beliefs, and the Buddhist attitudes towards desire and Nirvana (the goal of exis-tence, the 'ceasing to be re-born') were taken over. Hinduism became adjusted to the invading Muslims, in the tenth century A.D. even to the point of imposing the veil on women (Zaehner, p. 137) and accommodating the worship of Islamic saints (Weber, 1958, p. 20). In the nineteenth century the British variety of Christianity was accommodated, as Hindus found room for reform movements and abolished *suttee* (the burning of widows) (Parrinder, p. 34). Throughout this process of adjustment, Hinduism succumbed neither to its unresolved inconsistencies nor to its labyrinthine complexities.

Its viability has rested in this openness to local conditions and to the sponge-like absorption of identity needs. The exegesis of Upanishad reasoning; the monistic (monism = all being is one) approaches of Hindu philosophers; the universalism of Brahmin gurus—were all minor when compared with the importance which ordinary people attached to the thousands of deities and shrines. The personal devotion (Bhakti) to specific gods sustained and gave meaning to the experiences and hopes of everyday life.

The absorptiveness of Hinduism functions basically to safeguard and perpetuate an Indian identity, although one should not underestimate the effect of Hinduism in such countries as Indonesia. One is born a Hindu. The Western taste for exotic meaning systems has only recently, and then only in slight degree, changed this emphasis: now small select groups in the jaded West adopt Hindu religiosity to escape into the very tranquillity that Western culture long ago bartered away for industrial progress. Yet the Hindus themselves are increasingly acquiring the opposite taste for technology, which keeps starvation at bay and promises radios and motorbikes for everyone. At the very time that non-Hindus take a serious interest in Hindu religion, Hinduism itself struggles increasingly with attacks from within on the few central items (caste and the transmigration of souls) linking the polymorphous complexity.

The absorptiveness and the mystical relativity which make Hinduism so courteously and confidently hospitable to other religions stand in sharp contrast to the boundary maintenance of Judaism, Christianity, and Islam. The missionary thrust of the latter two is well attested by history and goes back essentially to their original vision of preserving a 'saving remnant' in the corrupt amorphousness of a dying empire. Judaism also saw itself as a saving remnant, but always as one nation over against others. Hinduism, on the other hand, represented a passive type of religiosity, with a pervasive capacity to sublimate, but without much outward thrust or militancy.

Absorptiveness is closely related to the flexibility of boundaries around the religious vision, whereas the clear delineation of boundaries and strong division between insiders and outsiders are closely related to the internal cohesion that is a prerequisite for external proselyting. The fascinating paradox is that the universalistic spirit of technology and science arose in conjunction with the particularistic, motivationally sharply focused religiosity of the West and *not* in conjunction with the relativistic and motivationally very diffuse religiosity of the East. The metaphysical thinking, the acute logical analysis, the rigorous ethical systems of discipline (Kraemer, p. 182), the aristocratic soteriologies of Indian religion seem to stand much closer to the world of scholarship than the thundering, vital Jahweh of Judaism and Christianity, or Allah who is 'white-hot Majesty, white-hot Omnipotence, white-hot Uniqueness' (Kraemer, p. 221).

One way of resolving this paradox is by postulating that the hovering closeness between Indian religion and Indian social/local identity (Hinduism unhesitatingly admits 'that gods are the projections of our human will, desires and thoughts'—Kraemer, p. 162) prevents the interdependence, the motivational fructification, and the leverage which became necessary for the emergence and the maintenance of the scientific, economic, and political enterprise of the West. In other words, although religion anywhere serves to sacralize social identity, both the product and the mechanism of the sacralization processes may differ radically, and with very different consequences, from one culture to another. This is so, quite apart from the fact that the identity that is to be sacralized may be subject to quakes of vastly differing magnitude and frequency. One might further suggest that in this respect Europe has traditionally occupied a much more quake-prone section of the globe than India or China.

With respect to the 'product' of the sacralization process, it may be said that a religious meaning system that is able to generate a significant degree of independent action and critical leverage is by implication more likely to legitimate social differentiation than one that is merely a pale, impotent, reflection of the identity it sacralizes.

This is closely related to the variety within the mechanism for sacralization: the objectification–commitment aspect of the mechanism may generate the ethos necessary for social differentiation, precisely because the first (objectification) widens the gap between heavenly and earthly spheres (thereby facilitating manipulation and division of labour) and the second (commitment) preserves the lifeline between those two spheres sufficiently to maintain motivation. The myth and ritual mechanisms on the other hand have much less leverage to manipulate the identity which religion sacralizes.

Hindu absorptiveness is an excellent illustration of our basic tenet that the universal religions sacralize a social identity. Yet, contrary to some prominent Western theologians, we maintain that religions other than Christianity in actual fact do the same. The best way to make this point is through a critical analysis of Tillich's typification of Buddhism (Nirvana) as dealing with the ontological principle of 'identity' in contrast with Christianity (the Kingdom of God), in which 'participation' is the item at issue (1961, pp. 68 ff.). Tillich says that with the migration of Buddhism from India, through China to Japan, the controlling attitude towards nature increased, 'but it never conquered the principle of identity', in the way in which Calvinist Christianity did. Similarly, with social relations—in Christianity, free individuals participate in, and if needs be transform, community, but in Buddhism individuals identify with the social whole (1961, pp. 70 ff.).

Tillich confuses a number of things. (1) More individual autonomy and greater social differentiation in no way diminish the search for identity or the desire to interpret action in terms of a system of meaning. Yet it is with these searches and desires that any religion is most closely associated. More individual autonomy and greater social differentiation may proliferate identity foci or diversify pockets of meaning. Yet in both Buddhism and Christianity conformity to the ethical requirements of the social whole, and repressions of the id, are regarded as prerequisities of meaningful communal existence. (2) Tillich appears to deny that there is close congruence between a sacralized system of meaning with individual actions in the West, although he affirms precisely this in the East. This is wrong. If, in the West, nature is looked upon as something to be controlled, and society as something to be transformed, then the justification for this control and transformation lies in taken-for-granted assumptions about what man and society are intrinsically. These assumptions may, in the final resort, rest on a belief in the Kingdom of God, or they may be more secular, but in either case the assumptions are essential for the control and transformation. In other words, there is congruence in both the West and the East. (3) The substantial differences between Buddhism and Christianity do not lie in the process of sacralization of identity as such, but (a) in the different assumptions as to the identity of man and society; and (b) the different saliencies within the sacralization mechanism (crudely put: objectification/commitment versus ritual/myth).

Arend T. van Leeuwen, a Dutch theologian and historian of religion, makes a similar distinction to that made by Tillich. To him, the uniqueness of Judaism, Christianity, and Islam lies in their theocracy; all the other universal religions are ontocracies, that is to say 'founded upon an apprehension of cosmic totality'. Only the Bible rejects this view in favour of an emphasis on the rule of a judging God (p. 287). We may suggest, however, that the really important item is not so much the agent of judgement, as in the fact that, whether Buddhist or Christian, the individual knows and feels himself judged in the light of a taken-for-granted social identity.

CONFUCIANISM AND MAOISM

In China, the integration of the social order has been no less the underlying goal of ancient and modern religious and ethical systems. In popular religion, the many gods were closely associated with the boundaries of their identity: the Hearth Gods sacralized the identity of the family. They were represented by coloured pictures above the hearth which were set on fire on New Year's Eve 'to take a report on the family to Heaven' (Parrinder, p. 73). Confucius (551–479 B.C.) contributed to the integration of the larger social order through his widely accepted teaching, rather than through an intensely devotional spirit. Man is born good and there is an essential oneness between nature and morality. In order for man to remain good, he ought to practise self-mastery, increase his knowledge, worship his ancestors, be supremely loyal to his parents and the rulers, and above all be just in his dealings with other man. The deep humanism of Confucius has pervaded Chinese culture ever since, but has also institutionalized age and sex differences, and has led to a thorough conservatism and resistance to change. Taoism (the teaching of Lao Tse, born 604 B.C.) was similarly philosophical; Tao is the moulding principle of the universe, sometimes translated as God, sometimes as Way or Path or Ultimate Reality. Yet Taoism has also been closely associated with the folk temples and images. Neither Confucianism nor Taoism has been particularly popular with the regime of Mao Tse-tung. Yet the present deification of Mao is intrinsically similar to the earlier deification of the Emperor. Both have had a unifying effect on China. Mao personifies, or is the focus for, Chinese identity. All four elements of the sacralization process are present in Maoism:

objectification (the future society to be built); commitment (the fervour surrounding the exegesis of Mao's thought surpasses much of Western religiosity); ritual (the witnessing and confessing at the meetings in which the Red Book is studied); beliefs and myths (the ethics of the Red Book, the sacred story of the Long March). Yet there are also interesting differences, which have the effect of bringing present China in line with the requirements of a technological society: Maoism directs Chinese interests away from the family as a source of identity towards national goals of industrial advance.

MARXISM AND NATIONALISM

Observers have found similar sacralizing characteristics in Marxism in general, which has frequently been compared with a religion. The Soviet poet, Evgeny Evtushenko, writes about communism as his religion (p. 42; Lenski, 1970, p. 412); Stephen Spender talks about communists living 'in a state of historical-materialist grace' (Koestler, p. 256); and Raymond Aron compares Catholicism and communism in France and Italy as rival churches (Aron, 1955, pp. 139–40; Koenker, p. 7).

As a minority in Western democracies, communist parties display all the characteristics that are typical of sectarian behaviour: the surrender of the individual to the group cause; the emphasis on sharp boundaries between outside and inside; a strong, almost eschatological, faith in a future event; the ritualization and reinforcement of the common faith in party meetings.

When communism becomes the ruling party it maintains most of these characteristics. Yet the 'outsider' is now further removed: he is the American capitalist in an overseas country rather than the exploiter of workers around the corner. National policies and programmes now become interwoven with the party programme, and have to be defended as part of a set of assumptions which if not entirely sacred, are none the less handled with care. Sometimes national policies gain precedence over party doctrines, because friendly relations with another nation prove to be more important than rapport with the persecuted sister party in that same country. The incapacity of Marxism to continue to sacralize the rather weak base of an international identity, and the increasing tendency of these parties to sacralize a national identity, is well illustrated by the deep suspicion and hostility between the Russian and the Chinese variety of Marxism. The Chinese in their long history have always been threatened, invaded, and attacked through their north-west border, and the Russian communist party has, ever since World War II, extolled the virtues of Russian nationalism (Baron, p. 203).

In all the communist countries, other forms of religious commitment are treated as essentially hostile incursions. The German Democratic Republic has instituted a Youth Consecration Ceremony (*Jugendweihe*) to compete with Christian confirmation, and those who undergo confirmation incur great educational and occupational disadvantages (Wilhelm, p. 222). These ceremonies have the same function as, for instance, the Birth Festival of Nazism or the Socialist wedding ceremonies and burial services (Koenker, pp. 104 ff.): they sacralize a social identity and tie the individual and his family to the social whole at the very moment that kinship solidarity is structurally precarious.

Ceremonies to sacralize a national identity can be found in all countries, irrespective of their degree of industrialization or primitiveness, irrespective of their form of government. In cases where national identity is weak, as compared with regional identity, ceremonies are sometimes used to strengthen the former. Yet there is a limit to this kind of conscious manipulation: if national identity scarcely exists, sacralization alone will hardly shape and reinforce it.

In the West, nationalism has often been strengthened by either Christianity, or what Jean Jacques Rousseau called 'civil religion' (pp. 115 ff.). According to Rousseau a purely civil profession of faith is necessary to produce the 'sentiments of sociability without which it is impossible to be either a good citizen or a faithful subject' (pp. 123–4). Further, subjects must be intolerant about the essentials of this civil religion, otherwise the sanctity of the laws will be undermined. In Australia, national identity is sacralized, for instance, through the solemn marches and religious services on Anzac Day that commemorate the heroic and ill-fated landing of Australian soldiers at Gallipoli on the 25th April 1915. An entire myth has been woven around this event culminating in the essence of Australian manhood: independence, matter-of-fact sincerity, and 'mateship'. May Day in Moscow or Memorial Day in the United States (Warner, 1962, pp. 8–9) have essentially the same effect. The contents of the myths, the wordings of the national anthems, the goals for the future, and the foci of commitment may differ, but the function (to sacralize a national identity) is the same. Bellah, who discusses the American variety of civil religion, has detected biblical archetypes at every point: 'Exodus, Chosen People, Promised Land, New Jerusalem, and Sacrificial Death and Rebirth' (1970, p. 186). These archetypes are also clearly present in the thoroughly 'atheistic' celebrations in the Soviet Union, which is not surprising if one recalls the measure in which Karl Marx represented a Biblical prophetic tradition. Van Leeuwen calls Marx's new order in which man can fully recover his identity 'a secularized eschatology in which the proletariat has assumed the broad features of the Servant of the Lord, whose vicarious suffering for the whole creation inaugurates the new age' (p. 336).

The strengthening of nationalism has often been seen as the exclusive prerogative of Christianity, at least in those countries where it is, or was, the dominant state religion. Yet, the civil religions discussed above are often entirely separate from denominational or church organizations. This is so, mainly because the organizational disunity of Christianity in such countries as Australia, Canada, New Zealand, the U.S.A., etc., is felt to clash with the unifying national function of a civil religion. Even so, the churches in these countries, contribute each in its own way, to the sacralization of a national value system. Herberg (pp. 88 ff.) finds the spiritual structure of the American Way of Life underlying the factual preaching not only in Protestant churches, but also in Catholic churches and in Jewish synagogues. The individualism, the dynamism, the pragmatism, the beliefs in equality and democracy of the American ethos are all there at the heart of the religious message.

CHRISTIANITY

Christianity too fits our general frame of reference. In all of its various forms, it encourages the values that strengthen the social whole, and discourages those that enhance the id. Self-denial, loving thy neighbour, being balanced, meeting expectations, being charitable, just, and kind are all values which build a stronger society, and are therefore encouraged; self-deification, egocentricity, harshness, cruelty are all values which weaken it, and are therefore discouraged.

Yet encouragement in the abstract is not enough. Ritualization and articulation of values and beliefs must be counterbalanced by a minimization of deviance. Penance and confession have been the traditional means for bringing sinners back into the fold. Deviance is punished by rejection; conformity is rewarded by acceptance.

The problem facing a universal religion, such as Christianity, in a modern society is that it becomes more and more difficult to exert this kind of influence, which requires sustained and intimate relations between individuals. Yet the very complexity of role structures in a modern society, the invisibility of much social behaviour, and the consequent inability to judge it, and the evaluation of individuals in terms of their contribution to instrumental goals only, all work towards less intimate relations. Christianity has fought the battle against these opposing forces through the intimacy of local churches and congregations. Part of its early heritage was to stress the closely knit community of believers. During long periods of history, the parish did indeed sacralize local identity, and under existing conditions the scrutiny of individuals could be generally fair and just. With the disappearance of local identity as a viable unit, both the churches and the sects have often attempted to substitute an organizational identity of common allegiance to the same articles of faith or to the same church. Yet this substitution jeopardized the comprehensive congruence with the identity patterns of specific societies. Thus, of necessity, Christianity in highly industrialized societies, tended towards both ecclecticism and voluntarism.

Christian sects have been able to take advantage of the situation created by industrialization and urbanization. Quite apart from their general congruence with the life-styles of a particular, lower class constituency, and their natural proclivity to establish firm boundaries, they have also maximized that part of the sacralization mechanism (commitment) which seems to stand up best to the differentiating/alienating forces of modern societies.

This commitment—the faith relationship with Jesus or God—has its own social advantages. It allows for a remarkable degree of individual independence without jeopardizing the interiorization of social values. Yet the ideal of the self-directed (or inner-directed) personality, so typical for Protestant and sectarian Christianity, has found its own nemesis. There is a limit to the amount of freedom a viable society can safely delegate to the individual. The unchecked, unsupported, unritualized relationship with God that is a not altogether foreign corollary to the stress of individual salvation could so easily be eroded, leaving little for the individual but his private values, beliefs, perceptions, and projections. In other words, the considerable amount of individualism legitimated by Christianity is both its glory and its predicament.

The goodwill that Christian beliefs and Christian functionaries continue to enjoy from the population at large, is the result of a dim but correct realization that Christianity and the value integration of Western societies belong together. In the *Religion in Australia* survey, respondents associated belief in God with moral responsibility. The question: 'Without belief in God we would have no morals, would we?' seems to sum up the position of many who hardly ever attended church. Respondents who believed in God were much more likely to have a clearly delineated view of acceptable and unacceptable conduct. The unbeliever on the other hand was more guided by a 'live and let live' philosophy (Mol, 1971a, p. 54). He was also disliked, partly because his moral and social responsibility was suspect.

Both Christianity and society in the 'democratic' West (in contrast with the 'communist' West) have considerably loosened their hold on non-conforming groups. The segmentalization of society involves a greater independence of the segments with a corresponding decrease of the cohesion of the social whole. Specific groups obtain the freedom to deviate from the values sustaining the culture. The Gay Liberation movements and homosexual organizations in the West represent attitudes and values obnoxious to the large majority, yet they successfully defend their right to function freely. The tolerance that they enjoy further relativizes whatever little consensus remained regarding sexual ethics.

Segmentation has reduced the position of Christianity from that of being the supreme sacralizer to that of competitor with alternate foci of identity. The repercussions of this change in status are still reverberating through the Christian churches, and have led to an excessive defeatism particularly in those quarters which continue to think in the wide terms of society at large. Yet on all levels of institutional loyalty, identity formation, and ideology, Christianity is in no way a losing proposition (for an elaboration, see Mol, 1972b).

Another feature of modern societies that has had a profound effect on Christianity is the elaboration of organizational techniques by which to maintain external independence and internal, efficient use of resources. The institutionalization of Christianity has led to a number of dilemmas. It has pressed Christianity, more forcefully than would have been the case otherwise into the defence of the status quo. Any organization tends to lose more from change than it gains, and this is even more the case when the organization sacralized a stable identity. 'The class structure, the political preferences, the racial prejudices, the cultural values of (church) membership, stamp the image and therefore the effective mission of a church' (Mol, 1969, p. 79). The Christian Church has also been embedded in the hierarchical power structures of its own personnel: '. . . irrespective of the system of checks and balances within the organization, the routinization of the charisma of the early leaders deflected the original goal of fervent faith and spontaneous missionary zeal' (ibid., p. 82).

Christianity is no exception to a general observation which Bellah made (1969, p. 196): 'Every religion seeks to remake the world in its own image, but is always to some extent remade in the image of the world. This is the tragedy of religion. It seeks to transcend the human, but is human, all too human. Every religion seeks to proclaim a truth which transcends the world, but is enmeshed in the very world it desires to transcend.'

SUMMARY

Universal religions always reinforce the society-strengthening, and denounce the society-destroying, values and beliefs. They condemn contra-social individualism, but encourage a measure of individualism that is beneficial to the social whole. They respond in similar ways to groups or sub-systems within a particular society: their consonance or dissonance with the culture in which they are embedded is a decisive criterion for the support they receive from universal religions.

The complexity of modern industrial societies has necessitated an increasingly greater independence of individuals and groups, which has made difficulties for the achievement of social integration and for the maintenance of comprehensive systems of meaning. The problems of Western civilization at large are fittingly reflected in the anguish of those Christian and Jewish organizations that primarily sacralize a social as over against a group identity. The problems are more successfully resolved in those Christian groups and sects that see themselves as saving remnants. The missionary zeal and the commitment associated with the image of a saving remnant or a chosen people have made Judaism, Christianity, and Islam unique amongst the universal religions. The other traditional religions are more reflexive, and provide closer congruence, and less dialectic, with the identities which they sacralize. Yet all religions, including 'secular' religions such as Marxism, Maoism, and Nationalism, establish the order of a common viewpoint and a system of meaning. They all attempt to sacralize a specific interpretation of reality, and thereby unify with varying degrees of success the societies in which they find themselves.

Chapter XIV

Objectification

SACRALIZATION

In the first chapter of this book sacralization was identified as the process of safeguarding and reinforcing a complex of orderly interpretations of reality, rules, and legitimations. This process we defined as a counterbalance to unchecked, infinite adaptations in symbol-systems. The sacralization process, we said, goes beyond mere institutionalization of patterns since it encourages qualities of untouchability and awe, and wraps systems of meaning and motivation in 'don't touch' sentiments.

It is this quality of the separateness of the holy, the sacred, or the numinous that has received so much attention from scholars. To Rudolph Otto the numinous is 'perfectly *sui generis* and irreducible to any other (state of mind)' (1950, p. 7). Emile Durkheim (1954, p. 38) puts it even more strongly:

> In all the history of human thought there exists no other example of two categories of things so profoundly differentiated or so radically opposed to another. The traditional opposition of good and bad is nothing beside this . . . the sacred and the profane have always and everywhere been conceived as two distinct classes, as two worlds between which there is nothing in common. (1954, pp. 38–9.)

Roger Caillois observes that there is no definition of religion in which the opposition between the sacred and the profane is not involved (1959, p. 19). To van der Leeuw, the sacred is 'what has been placed within boundaries' . . ., 'the completely different, the absolutely distinct' (1964, pp. 47–8). Eliade follows Otto's description of the numinous as the wholly other, as reality of a wholly different order (1959a, pp. 9–10). To Weber (1964, p. 9) the sacred 'is the uniquely unalterable'

The sacred can dwell in a large variety of objects and ideas: stones, trees, buildings, persons, spirits, space, and time. In all instances, it lends an extraordinary quality to the object or idea. It evokes awe or dread. In its presence, one must tread with circumspection. Rites are often required to approach the sacred, and these rites invariably accentuate its separation from the profane.

There are no societies in which the sacred is not manifest in some form or other. In some primitive societies, the totemic animal is treated with great circumspection and is eaten only under specified conditions (Durkheim, 1954, pp. 128–9). In ancient Rome, the identity of one's family was sacred: a *gens* had its own secret cults. In Western societies, Christianity is often the sacralizer of particular systems of meaning. Yet the vernacular wisely and justifiably uses both the terms religion ('his work is his religion') and sacred ('nationalization is the sacred cow of the Labour Party') in a sense which has little if anything to do with organized Christianity.

Even in our most modern scientific communities and efficient bureaucracies certain areas of analysis and observation (particularly those going to the heart of a 'taken-for-granted' order) are treated gingerly or discussed in whispers. The pet theory of the head of a university department is sometimes in this category. So is loyalty to one's firm or the established hierarchy of command. 'Bureaucracy not only, like religion, integrates society-at-large in a functional way, it also creates, again like religion, systems of domination and subordination throughout all of society' (Zijderveld, p. 136).

How are we to think about the distinction between the sacred and sacralization? The quality of separateness in the sacred has been so obvious, and has therefore so much occupied the mind of scholars, that the much less obvious, much more latent, sacralization process has often been ignored. When the opposition between the profane and the sacred is so manifestly visible, the thought that either might be profoundly shaped and effected by the other has perhaps appeared like a contradiction in terms. And yet the opposition, or conflict, between the two is not more significant than their complementarity. Their dialectical relationship corresponds to that which exists between the integrative/emotional and the differentiating/rational processes: both conflict and complement, both differ profoundly and yet are very relevant for one another, both grow in reaction to one another, and even undermine one another. The point where the function of each is maximized is never equilibrated, and is always under strain. The more that one maximizes its function at the expense of the other, the greater the likelihood of movement in the opposite direction towards restoring the impossible, hypothetical, balance—always provided that there are the appropriate external or internal cultural resources for the balancing act!

A culture in which the sacred overwhelms the profane to the point of no return, is just as doomed as the society in which the profane erodes the sacred. In contrast with some of the American religions and cultures before the Spanish conquest, Western civilization has never allowed this to happen: the Greek, or predominantly rational/ instrumental strain never eliminated its opposite, the Hebrew/ Christian religious/integrative strain, but was always forced to retreat to lesser maximization and lesser consistency of its pre- dominant mode in the face of surging, freshly reactivated, religious movements. Conversely, religious movements in the West had re- peatedly to seek reintegration following the onslaught of rational and technological pressures. The West has always had ample cultural resources for restoring the balance on either side.

All this appears to confirm Durkheim's insistence on the opposi- tion between the sacred and the profane. Opposition there certainly is and this opposition is undoubtedly functional, as our discussion of objectification will demonstrate. We dissent from Evans- Pritchard's comment in his criticism of Durkheim, that the sacred and the profane, 'are so closely intermingled as to be inseparable' and that the dichotomy was not much use (Evans-Pritchard, 1965, p. 65; Goody, p. 143). Durkheim may have underrated the inter- mingling of sacred and profane somewhat, but their interdependence was very much implied in his assertion that God was society, and in his discussion of mana.

It is this conflicting, but also complementary, relationship between the sacred and the profane that we wish to bring out by using 'sacralization' (becoming, or making sacred) rather than 'the sacred' (being sacred). It is the process of sacralization rather than the state of sacredness which more readily conveys the dialectical emergence of the integrative complement. Neither Durkheim nor Evans- Pritchard is clear on this point, and that is why their conceptual frame of reference is inadequate to account *both* for the emergence of sacrednesses in our time, *and* for the objectifying, separating characteristics of these forms of sacredness, once they have emerged. Both thought primarily in terms of primitive cultures, where sacralization patterns were fully developed rather than embryonic. Because scholars dealing with past and primitive societies have been most prominent in the analysis of the sacred, their definitions, in terms of its ideal type, or fully developed form, have been accepted rather uncritically. The uncritical acceptance of their definitions has been reinforced because it goes against the grain of the evolutionary biases and assumptions of scientific superiority in the West to suppose that something can be mature in primitive cultures but only embryonic in modern society. It is for these reasons that the widespread conclusion has been drawn that the sacred is in decline. We dissent from this judgement. Sacralization processes seem to be interrupted and prevented from maturing, but they are not disappearing, and appear to be as viable as ever.

Another reason for stressing the sacralization process, rather than the separateness of the sacred, is that 'change' or 'process' language is more appropriate for analysing 'changing' situations. A sociological theory that seeks to develop generalizations which account for past and present, primitive and modern, must have a conceptual apparatus that encompasses both stability and change; similarities and differences. Treating the sacred as a fossil of the primitive past emphasizes the differences rather than the similarities between societies and cultures.

How is sacralization related to institutionalization? It has been suggested by ethologists that the former is an extension of the latter. Lorenz says:

. . . customs and taboos may acquire the power to motivate behaviour in a way comparable to that of autonomous instincts. Not only highly developed rites or ceremonies but also simpler and less conspicuous norms of social behaviour may attain, after a number of generations, the character of sacred customs which are loved and considered as values whose infringement is severely frowned upon by public opinion. (Lorenz, 1970, pp. 222–3).

This fits in with our previous suggestion that the sacralization process wraps systems of meaning and motivation in 'don't touch' sentiments. Fallding (1974, p. 14) similarly uses sacralization as 'the full flowering of the process of institutionalization', but, like Cazeneuve (p. 440), he thinks of sacralization as the bridge between the real and the ideal, wrongly assuming that there can be an uninterpreted reality. In a similar vein, van der Leeuw suggests that the religious dimension of custom consists in its capacity to instil fear and awe 'before superior Power' (1964, p. 454). But the religious dimension also includes 'a sense of distance' (ibid.), what I have alluded to as the objectification dimension.

OBJECTIFICATION

Objectification is the tendency to sum up the variegated elements of mundane existence in a transcendental frame of reference where they can appear in a more orderly, more consistent, and more time-less way.

This tendency towards objectification and the process by which it is realized, are closely linked with man's progressive capacity for abstract thinking and his ability to use symbols. The elaboration of symbol systems arose from the advantage that they had for *both* the manipulation of the environment (instrumental mastery), *and* the security man needed within that environment (integrative under-standing). From the hovering closeness of the world of myth, man progressed to objectification of mythical beings and gods and to worship and sacrifice as a means of communication (Bellah, 1970, pp. 27–9). The awe of the sacred guaranteed common loyalty to socially crucial values and beliefs. The more removed or objecti-fied the system of meaning became, the more a potentially divisive chaotic division of labour could be left on its own, since in this case the vicissitudes of the mundane order could not exercise any essentially disruptive effects on objectified and transcendental con-ception of order in which people believed. The separateness of the sacred was a prerequisite for order and security, all the more so because in the transcendental point of reference, the major, relevant archetypes and features on the mundane world were emotionally anchored. Neither moth nor rust could corrupt these essential characteristics. Yet, in spite of their remoteness, these characteristics had a significant effect on the mundane order because men were committed to them: commitment was the pivot of articulation between the transcendent and the mundane. In this transcendental point of reference order could appear less arbitrary, less vulnerable to contradictions, exceptions, and contingencies. Thus, the arbitrary, the unexpected, the frustrations and contingencies could be absorbed and 'digested' as not altogether meaningless, but as part and parcel of an orderly world. The potential for differentiation increased according to the believed-in guarantees of the transcendental order.

There were 'degrees' of objectification, or remoteness, according to the complexity of a particular culture: the greater the complexity, the more elaborate the systems of abstract thought and belief became. *Mana*, supernatural power concretized in persons and things, seems to be only one step removed from the mundane. It hardly distinguishes between the transcendent and the immanent (Tillich, 1959, p. 63). It fills vacua of meaninglessness, and guarantees the security of common, taken-for-granted feelings towards something that is beyond potentially disruptive events and social relations. But it does so in ways which leave the sacred little leverage of its own.

Further removed is *Maya* which originally (in the Rigveda) also meant supernatural power, but which in later Indian thinking, came to mean 'cosmic illusion'. The mundane world and the experiences it provides are regarded as 'more or less direct products of Maya' (Eliade, 1967, p. 238). Maya is the 'utmost universalization of mythic being, . . . the unbounded frame and structure of all individual myths, unified into a single interpretive system' (Arapura, 1973, p. 117). In Maya (or rather Brahman-atman, the one cosmic identity to which it points) order is summed up and projected. It is a timeless realm, where the profane is relativized. This relativization has a balancing effect on the mundane. Through a progressive derogation of the significance of the mundane, the individual feels liberated from its clutches. Yet this kind of objectification has a weak potential for active motivation, however much it maximizes consolation and tranquillity. The world-view it encourages is essentially negative towards the mundane, however much is succeeds in providing the appropriate serenity to encounter the mundane.

The objectification process advances a further stage in Judaism, with Jahweh, Christianity, in God, and Islam, with Allah. Here, too, as in Hinduism, the consoling, relativizing, adjusting element is maximized. Jahweh forgives the recalcitrant nation; God reconciles man through Christ; Allah's mercy and compassion are boundless. Death and failure are not the end. Yet, in addition, the complex relationship of mundane rewards and punishments, salvation and judgement, is now also objectively dramatized in the person of God, who actively governs history and who judges man with respect to his active co-operation in this government.

About the beginning of the sixteenth century in Europe, a further change occurred. Until then the transcendental frame of reference of Christianity was primarily conceived in terms of its social or group relevance. On the mundane, social level the church represented the transcendental drama of sin and salvation. The church concretized a subtle and sensitive system of meaning. Its verdicts and judgements coincided with the basic structures of the identities it reflected, whether of nation, region, or group. Conversion was usually social conversion, or to a group rather than to a new personal identity, although these forms were closely intertwined.

The change that slowly emerged at that time made the individual personal relationship with the divine more significant and reduced the significance of the institutional concretizations of that relationship. Further objectification and further abstraction began to loosen institutional and, behind it, social control. This change was not altogether foreign to the requirements of the newly arising commercial classes, whose trade had a relativizing effect on ideas about social cohesion, and who tended to move towards more individualistic, competitive positions. Nor was the change foreign to the existing sacralized system of meaning: the personal commitment to the divine had always been prominent. By this time, the institutional supports were weakened and the social control function became stressed in much more abstract terms, through the divine scheme of salvation. This change also meant a relatively greater emphasis on the basic unchangeability (predestination) of existence. Only an increased and constant projection of awe on to the divine attributes of initiative, wrath, and mercy, could counterbalance the loosening consequences of increased individualism.

It is this articulated stress on the constancy and unchangeability of God which Weber (1952) uses in the analysis of the effect of Calvinism on newly emerging economic structures. To Weber, this provision of the Archimedean point facilitated and even encouraged economic change in the direction of rational capitalism. To us, any religion provides a transcendental point of reference (the Vedanta too has its Archimedean point—Arapura, 1970, p. 162), but the fulcrum, or point of leverage, may be too close to the mundane and thereby prevent further differentiation or instrumental manipulation. It may have a tranquillizing rather than an activating effect. It may be too weak to counterbalance for the potential anomie of the mundane world. The fulcrum may also have to carry too heavy a burden in relation to the corresponding institutional support on earth. As a result, commitment, or the link of faith, may break.

This possibility seems to be the perpetual predicament of Protestantism. Warner (1961, pp. 75, 199) wrote of the anaemic liturgical apparatus, the devitalized spiritual imagery, and the visual poverty of Protestantism as major reasons why the West was unable to carry or cope with a rationality founded on technological empiricism. Carl Jung (1972, p. 59) regards Protestantism as both a great risk and a great opportunity—the opportunity being that of greater potential for self-criticism, the risk being the inability effectively to deflect destructive forces through confession and absolution. If Warner and Jung mean that the relativization of ecclesiastical safeguards left too little support for the link of faith or commitment, we agree with them.

Although the commitment link between the Christian Archimedean point of reference and the mundane world seems for many to have snapped, what has remained, and even flourished, is the inspired confidence in abstract, independent, thinking. That so often solid traditions of learning grew up together within the Calvinist tradition is surely not just a historical accident.

It is clear from our analysis so far, that if the objectified point of reference is to sacralize at all, it must be different from and yet reflect the profane. As we have said earlier: it both opposes and complements the mundane. It transcends, but it is also congruent. How can this difficult feat be accomplished? There is no problem in respect to the transcendent. Millennia of symbol growth have increased the capacity for objectification and abstraction. But how can it also remain relevant and how can it continue sensitively to reflect the profane with its conflict, turmoil, frustration? We have already mentioned that certain objectified qualities of the divine (such as initiative, wrath, and mercy) can be crucial in a specific cultural situation. The conceptual apparatus of successful and surviving religions has generally demanded a strong sense of awe and commitment even though it has retained a deliberate vagueness. Bellah mentions this not only of T'ien and Tao in Chinese religion (1970, p. 87), but also of the concept of God in American civil religion. 'God (is) . . . a word that almost all Americans can accept but that means so many different things to so many different people that it is almost an empty sign' (1970, p. 170). Richardson thinks that the conceptual openness and vagueness of trans-historical symbolism prevents 'man from expecting any absolute fulfilment in time' (1967, p. 24; Bellah, 1970, p. 202). Thanks to the openness and vagueness of the Judaeo-Christian terminology, Bacon and Spinoza could continue to use it while filling it with a different content (Goldmann, p. 296). Doctrine, says Demerath (1965, p. 68), 'can be a *tabula rasa* which the parishioner can turn to his own liking'. Islam institutionalized flexibility and vagueness (Soddy, p. 166). Lack of content is also a prerequisite for the comprehension and validity of abstract, general laws (Weber, 1949, p. 80). Secular ideologies are often like 'large metal filing cabinets with vacant drawers or slots waiting to accept new data' (Toffler, p. 337), Toffler continues to explain this in terms of man's tardiness to accept new sets of stimuli. To us, it rather points to the function of any sacralized frame of reference to provide the stability necessary for the acceptance of change.

The built-in strain towards unification of identity therefore pushes *both* towards externalization or objectification, outside the immediate and the conditioned, *and* towards a vagueness which allows absorption of a large variety of experiences without jeopardizing the essential stability of the framework.

The need for vagueness of the objectified frame of reference also applies to the time component. The time element is not without significance in any developed system of meaning. In societies with only embryonic symbol-systems the future is hardly discerned, nor are future events anticipated. Yet as soon as social organization and solidarity develop, and patterns are transmitted to the next generation, birth and death begin to need interpretation. The past becomes significant as the receptacle of meaning. An increasingly more objectified past becomes increasingly more independent of the present, and removed from the arbitrariness of the present. In some of the higher religions, revelation (or the objectified, independent past) is therefore a necessary and well-fitting element.

The future, too, is affected. As soon as pattern-maintenance becomes a social prerequisite the future can no longer be arbitrary. Perhaps for this reason wrong action for a Hindu is not so much related to living in time, but to the belief that nothing exists outside time (Eliade, 1967, p. 242). Motivation for action requires goals and rationales. Goals which tend to contrast rather than harmonize with the id, especially need explicit objectification and transcendental reinforcement. Yet safeguarding the status quo is by no means the only function of the explicit future orientation. Particularly in

Judaeo-Christian-Islam religion, the future is objectified in order that it might also serve as a receptacle and even as a leverage for change. Thus, it must be abstract and vague enough for this change to be suitably incorporated, whilst remaining relevant for the interpretations of the signs of time.

The belief in the coming of the Messiah in Judaism illustrates these functions. It provided the present with purpose and legitimation, while simultaneously articulating the imperfections and the predicament of the present. The actual arrival of the Messiah, of course, would relinquish the very social function that the expectation provided. It would concretize the expectation, and thereby negate the function of its vagueness and unfulfilment. Similarly in Christianity, the arrival of the Messiah soon became the supreme event in the past around which the meaning of the present became crystallized. Yet the parousia, the returning of Christ, or the millennial dreams, the concept of the fulfilment of time, and the hope of heaven, were elements without which Christianity could hardly have survived as a viable religion. An objectified structured future is closely linked with a structured outline of the present. The fact that Christian sects rather than Christian churches strongly hold on to this future orientation may be an additional reason for their growth and expansion (Mol, 1969, pp. 45–6).

The idea that individualism, and an increasing amount of independence and freedom of the self have occurred hand in hand with the extent of quality of objectification has been implicit in the foregoing analysis. Through objectification, order could become more fully sacralized, and the further this process advanced the more the tight control of the individual could be relaxed. Consequently the risks of potential disorder through more individualism, rationalism, and differentiation could be taken with greater confidence. In the final resort, a cosmic and relevant system of meaning and order was assumed to be invulnerable to this possible danger.

This assumption proved to be wrong, in that history from the Reformation onwards has taught us that one cannot take a specific, individualistic, faith commitment for granted in the same way that an ecclesiastical institution might be taken for granted. This point we have already discussed. What is significant now is the consequence of the snapping of the commitment link. The severance emancipated abstract thought from emotionally anchored, transcendental, Christian orientations. Abstract thought moved much more decidedly and independently into the instrumental/adaptive sphere towards which, from the Greek heritage, it was already disposed. The transcendental Christian frame of reference remained a viable orientation only for those Protestants who were sheltered in cohesive communities. For the others, it was spun off and 'lost in space'. Yet when commitment to a Christian Archimedean point broke down, it did not simply atrophy: it became channelled into much more horizontal, closer-at-hand ideologies and causes.

This re-channelling of commitment seems to have escaped observers of religion from Comte and Hegel to the modern secular theologians. Instead they have continued to stare into space, where they have continued to discern the 'spun off' Christian system of meaning. They firmly concluded that they saw, with their own eyes, the disappearance of the sacred. Yet, as we have maintained, the counterbalancing integrative needs of modern societies, groups, and persons are not necessarily succumbing to instrumental ones. The desacralization of abstractions does not mean desacralization of *all* abstractions. On the contrary, awe-surrounding tendencies, or as we would rather say, strong commitments of reverence, keep emerging from modern systems of meaning, order, and identity. Abstract notions about existence are in no way exempt from this tendency. Motivation towards consistency and unity of interpretation guarantee the very sacralization of abstract forms of order. What may start out as an instrumental/rational form of inquiry may end up as a framework of sacralized assumptions.

Simmel (1911, pp. 245 ff.; also Aron, 1969, p. 207) saw the process of objectification (*Vergegenständlichung* or *Obejektivierung*) as part and parcel of the evolution of man and society, associated with what we have called differentiation, in which the emotional component is insignificant. The inevitable tragic consequences of the objectification process in history, according to Simmel, was man's increasing difficulty with the pursuance of integrity and unity in the face of an inevitable plurality. Cassirer, on the other hand, saw objectification as orderly projection with a significant commitment component. He says that language objectifies sense-perceptions and that all men's cultural activities (myth, poetry, art, religion, etc.) 'fulfil one and the same task: the task of objectification' (1946, p. 27). Whether or not objectification is seen as a cultural liability or an asset depends, I submit, on whether or not the commitment component is prominent in the definition and use of the term. Reification is used on the other hand for the kind of objectification in which a specific commitment component is present, but the commitment is thought of as completely wrong or at least as a cultural liability.

Our analysis is in no small way enhanced by Peter Berger's (1967a, p. 202), yet he, and most nineteenth-century philosophers, including Feuerbach and Marx, regarded a certain area of objectification (or *Versachlichung*) as wrong because it meant commitment to something which conflicted with their own sacred, individualistic, humanistis ideology. This area they called reification (or *Verdinglichung*) which meant those objectifications which desacralized full individual self-determination in that they treated things as external to the mind. The majesty and hegemony of the personality were injured, so it was thought, if these things were perceived as independent from, rather than dependent upon, man the constructor of symbols. Dehumanization and alienation were thought to be the direct consequence of reification (or as Marx called it, false consciousness) in that man the creator became subject to his own creations. Commitment to, and acceptance of, reifications was bad, in that they took man's independence away from him. Similarly, Tillich (1959, p. 212) calls these objectifications 'demonic'. Objectifications on the other hand that were nothing more than innocent abstractions would pass the muster. The bias of those who use, and have used, the reification concept, unfailingly consists in their assumption that their perception of reality is the only 'real' one, whereas the reifiers make the unreal 'real'. The uselessness of this distinction for scientific analysis should be clear, yet the result of this influential theorizing has been the view that alienation erodes self-realization (as a *summum bonum*), rather than that alienation is the severance of the individual from any sacralized identity. The latter view we think is more honest: it does not hide in an unstated system of meaning for which the distinction is implicitly missionary. And it is more useful for sociological analysis (it treats the sacred as a category rather than a specific instance of ideological condemnation).

There are other interesting examples of sacralized assumptions emerging right at the heart of scholarly work. In this age of ecology nature begins occasionally to take the place which self-realization has for those who work with the reification concept. Theodore Roszak (1973) speaks about the sacramental approach to nature as one of the ways out of the devastating dilemmas which science and rationality have hurled the world into. Zijderveld (1971) rejects this kind of emotional romanticism and replaces it with his own intellectual asceticism or sociological stoicism as a panacea so that man may 'survive in a human way' (pp. 168–9). Yet Zijderveld does not sacralize his own assumptions to such an extent that he remains close-minded for man's intrinsic tendency to .deify human realities, to idolize his own progress, his own being, his own psyche (p. 174).

It has become clear in this chapter that objectification has always been impotent to sacralize unless it was accompanied by emotional commitment. The 'separateness' of the sacred had to be embedded in feelings of awe and loyalty, if it was to have any sacralizing effect. We shall turn in the next chapter to the issue of commitment.

SUMMARY

Objectification is the projection of meaning and order into a transcendent point of reference where the essences and archetypes of the mundane can be made to appear more orderly, consistent, and timeless. The contradictions, the exceptions, the contingencies of the mundane can consequently be understood as less arbitrary than they appear to those involved in the immediate situation. In the history of the human race both the degree of objectification (how remote and independent is the transcendent from its concrete base?) and its quality (how relevant is it for a comprehensive range of social and psychological phenomena?) have proved to be crucial factors for technological, economic, and scientific progress. It would be an oversimplification to attribute the rise and complexity of scientific/ rational abstractions only to the kinds of objectifications viable in Western religion. An important element in their emergence has been the marginality and comparison-compelling culture contacts that we described in Chapter III.

Yet without the religious sanctioning of abstract forms of thought, these forms of thought would never have grown to the point where they appear to be completely independent from this sanction. This observation may be interpreted as redoubtable evidence for the desacralization or secularization of modern society, if it were not for the fact that, at the very heart of technology and scholarship, sacred islands have begun to emerge where commitment to unified inter-pretations is assumed. They seem to suggest that however strongly cognitions and emotions are opposed to one another, they are also complementary in human existence.

Chapter XV

Commitment

Commitment is the second of the four closely linked mechanisms of the sacralization process. It can be defined as focused emotion or emotional attachment to a specific focus of identity. It is an anchoring of the emotions in a salient system of meaning, social, group, or personal, whether abstract or concrete. When committed Christians proclaim Jesus to be their Saviour, they identify with a person whose biography and activities are concretely described, but who also represents such abstract principles as sacrificial love and moral judgement.

Yet the deepest commitment can also be to a political party. The American Communist Party was to its members the source of such deep commitment, that party lines and Marxist interpretations could shift substantially without risk of apostasy (Howe and Coser, p. 521; Becker 1960, p. 33). A person's strong commitment to money-making or to his work may account for many of his attitudes, behaviour patterns, and priorities.

CONSISTENCY AND MOTIVATION

The point of these illustrations is not to elaborate again the variety of identity foci, but to articulate the close relationships that exist between commitment and consistency of behaviour. An emotional anchorage in a specific central point of reference can say a great deal about a large variety of ethical choices, thought patterns, and actions. Knowing the wherewithal of the commitment of a person, a group, or a society, makes the person, the group, or the society predictable. The predictability in turn improves security and stability. Hypocrisy is therefore despised in any culture: the commitment to the actual system of meaning is kept hidden behind an ostensible, usually more acceptable one. This lessens predictability because the actual frame of reference is generally *both* less integrative (money-making as against Christian charity) *and* more hidden, thereby confusing evaluation.

The last two sentences of the previous paragraph implicitly qualify the first one. It is too simple to say that there is a close relationship between commitment and consistency of behaviour. It is an entire system of meaning, strengthened by objectification, ritual, and myth as well as by commitment, which provides consistency and predictability. Often the short-cut from commitment to consistency is made without protest and correction because in modern societies the other mechanisms of sacralization, and the identity that it reinforces, seem to be less relevant. Yet we could not possibly analyse other societies without paying attention to these other factors. We want to keep our theoretical options open. Our frame of reference should be big enough to cover the enormous diversity among cultures and evolutionary stages. Nor do all instances of deeply felt commitment in modern societies have equal effects on consistency, on group cohesion or social integration. A specific identity, a specific definition of reality, and all the other mechanisms of sacralization remain fully relevant in modern societies.

All this has important implications for motivations. What one does, or what one thinks one ought to do, depends on the way in which one interprets situations. The system of meaning which one accepts has a built-in, hierarchical arrangement of priorities. The choices that one makes amongst many alternatives are decisively influenced by one's assumptions about, and commitments to one's own, one's group's, or one's social identity. Here, too, we should distinguish between the actual and the façade. For the sake of the façade, the hypocrite may behave in one way, but when unseen he will act in accordance with his actual system of meaning. A deep rift may exist between actual and merely professed beliefs. Weber made the astute observation that spectator religion has little influence on behaviour because it provides 'no inner motivation' (1964, p. 102), although he paid little attention to commitment as the critical factor in the explanation of motivation. He thought of rationalization, the spirit of efficiency, and rationality of modernity, as comprising 'a conception of motivational commitment . . . (both in the sense of) commitment to the cognitive validity of the ideas and practical commitment . . . readiness to put one's own interests at stake in the service of the ideas' (Parsons, 1964b, p. xxxiii). The basic antithesis between rationalism and commitment, however, remains peripheral in Weber's work.

Parsons is more careful at this point. In *The Structure of Social Action* he locates the source for social action in expressive rather than cognitive symbol systems (1949, pp. 732 ff.). Again in *The Social System* (1951, pp. 367-9) he considers that religious commitments contain directives for action.

Because of its effect on motivation and predictability, commitment is looked upon as desirable in any society. Commitment to a social or group identity strongly contributes to the formation of consensus and this makes a society, or a group, more viable. In pluralistic societies, one may often criticize what from certain perspectives are the wrong kinds of commitment, and yet one prefers a wrong commitment to no commitment at all. Uncommitted or alienated youth are a continual source of suspicion in these societies, if only because they implicitly deny the security and stability of the status quo. Understandably, the uncommitted are regarded as allies by all those who favour change, whether constructive or destructive.

OTHER EFFECTS

In a very general way, as we have seen, commitment reinforces identities, systems of meaning, or definitions of reality. More specifically the effect of this reinforcing process is consistency, predictability, and motivation. Bellah observes that commitment 'operates to enhance the definiteness with which I know who I am or my group knows what it is' 1965, p. 173). Carrier uses commitment more or less as a synonym for 'integration, religious practice and sense of belonging' (p. 228) suggesting that it unifies churches and believers. Klapp says that commitment 'redeems identity' (pp. 68, 257), but generally uses 'centring' to describe the integration of self and personality (e.g. p. 151). This process of centring with its resulting psychological benefit he finds pre-eminently illustrated by the dedication to a *summum bonum* (p. 152), by enthusiastic, militant, crusades which carry 'both a cross and a sword' and are 'a prime route of identity transformation (p. 257).

Virginia H. Hine (1970, pp. 63, 65) makes the same doubtful point about the identity-altering and bridge-burning aspect of commitment. It is inconsistent to regard commitment—as Hine does when she uses commitment in Heberle's sense of 'devotion which claims the entire man' (1949, p. 356) or in James's sense of 'surrender to a higher, eternal power' (1902, p. 108)—as both integrative and alterative. The confusion arises because the different processes involved remain unspecified. In the case of identity-alteration, what occurs is emotional detachment from one identity and emotional attachment to another, a process that we have called conversion. In the case of identity integration, only the element of emotional attachment is involved. We use 'conversion' and 'charisma' for identity change, and 'commitment' for identity consolidation: Certainly, lifelong commitment to a sect or party can hardly be described as altering identity. Hine is led astray because commitment is particularly obvious in a new movement. Yet the characteristics she describes of highly committed people—unshakeable strength of conviction, conceptual clarity concerning the ideological system of the movement, the capacity to interpret all incoming data or events in terms of movement ideology, . . . a tendency to categorize people as either 'for us or against', the willingness to sacrifice kinship ties, social status, sometimes economic security, the capacity to influence others and to inspire a devoted following (Hine, 1970, p. 62)—are typical of all members in cohesive groups and not only of new converts. Personality or group integration goes together with clarification and the accentuation of priorities and boundary lines, but this is true for both existing and changing systems.

Thus, it is clear that if commitment is to have any of these sacralizing, integrating, and centring effects, it has to be strong commitment. For Tillich, total surrender (1958, p. 3) is necessary for ultimate concern, and to Erikson (1969, p. 169), an unhesitating commitment delineates identity more clearly. Durkheim used the strength of a person's commitment to explain suicide rates. If a person's commitment (for instance to the army or his country) is very strong, Durkheim argued, he is more likely to sacrifice his life for the cause (1951, p. 225). In other words, his very personal existence becomes subservient to the existence of the source of his identity. This Durkheim called altruistic suicide. The opposite case was that of anomic suicide, which occurred when life had lost its meaning through the absence of social supports; a person was more likely to destroy himself when his identity was weak, and he had no strong commitment of any kind. Gerlach and Hine (p. 102) also made a number of observations about the strength of commitment, which might lead to such singlemindedness that 'all conversational roads lead to one ideological Rome'. Its strength increases, they say, with the cost (p. 104).

A variety of other concepts is used to describe the same phenomenon of sacralization through strong feeling states. *Awe and reverence* are often used in the sense of strong sentiments which make the focus of identity more sacred. A sense of awe and reverence aids the objectifying process, but the process feeds on itself and therefore, as Geertz observes, the holy also 'enforces emotional commitment' (1959, p. 421). Although awe and commitment can often be used interchangeably, there is a difference in that awe is more appropriately used for the feeling state in a full-blown sacred system of stable, mainly non-Western societies; commitment is the sentiment generally used in relation to the emerging, embryonic, proliferating, sacred systems of modern industrial societies. Yet, given time, commitment usually grows into awe.

Another term often used to describe strong sentiments towards the sacred is *ecstasy*. It originally meant 'stepping outside oneself' in Greek, but then interestingly enough became translated as *alienatio* in Latin (Spoerri, p. 1). Laski, in her classic book on the subject, points to the synthesizing effect ecstasy has on mental organization. She describes how some ecstatic experiences provide a sense of purification, renewal, and union (pp. 396–71). This union with a cosmic reality or with a personal absolute, 'whereby the person concerned not just dissolves as salt in water, but also undergoes radical changes as iron in a fire', has also been noted by Frei (p. 24). In Hinduism, ecstasy (*samādhi*) has been regarded as 'the generic means of returning fortuitous existence to ultimate reality' (Arapura, 1972, p. 90). Klapp (p. 182) detects cultic trends and searches for identity in what Alan Watts calls, 'the new ecstatics'—the emerging quest for ecstasy through such things as pop art, psychedelics, sexual mysticism, mantra chanting, and folk rock. A different concept for rather similar phenomena on the social level was used by Durkheim (1954), when he observed that '*collective effervescence*' and group frenzy was certainly effective for impressing collective representation or social solidarity on social groups.

Maslow uses the term '*peak-experiences*' in a very similar way to our 'strong commitment', to indicate a kind of elation which moves 'towards the perception of unity and integration in the world' (p. 66). It 'is felt as a self-validating, self-justifying moment . . . it justifies not only itself, but even living itself' (p. 62). It is an intrinsic core-experience, which is a meeting ground 'for Christians and Jews and Mohammedans, but also for priests and atheists, for communists, for conservatives and liberals, for artists and scientists... for thinkers and for doers' (p. 28). There are some problems with Maslow's conceptualization: it is perhaps too elitist, for instance, when he refers to the concretization of symbols by the uneducated as idolatrous (p. 24). It is too narrow, as for instance when he excludes rituals, dogmas, and ceremonials as being of doubtful value to the 'peaker' (p. 28). Consequently a comprehensive general theory of human behaviour in which peak experiences can be seen as contributing to a stable, persisting, identity is altogether absent. Yet, Maslow's main observations on the integrating and reconciling (p. 65) effect of peak experiences are well taken.

Faith is often the theological synonym for what is here called commitment. It is the link of sentiment between the ordering focus and the actual identity. Christians think characteristically in terms of personal faith, although they also talk about the 'faith of the Church', or the traditions to which the religious organization is committed. It is in this personal sense that Marx (p. 51) used the word when he coined the striking phrase: 'Luther shattered faith in authority because he restored the authority of faith.'

All these terms, and the description of their effects, come close to commitment and its effects, but, the concept 'commitment' has also been used in different and less relevant ways. Glock and Stark use it in the rather inclusive sense of any dimension of religiosity (belief, practice, experience, knowledge, and consequence). From our point of view this vague use of the term diminishes its utility, although Glock and Stark think of commitment as therapeutic, rather than as pathological (Stark, 1971, p. 175). Kiesler, whose approach to commitment in psychology is as empirical as Glock and Stark's in sociology, thinks of commitment in terms of the pledging or binding of oneself to a course of action (1971, p. 26), and stresses its relative resistance to change. He links commitment to what Leon Festinger called 'cognitive dissonance' (the tendency to reject or deny information that challenges preconceptions) and suggests that the one varies with the other (1969, p. 234).

If commitment then integrates, strengthens, or sacralizes systems of meaning, definitions of reality and identities, can the opposite also be maintained, namely that lack of commitment weakens a specific identity? Undercommitment is often observed amongst migrants and others who are highly mobile. What is more, the anomie or alienation of these groups can be seen as the direct result of the weakness of their identity and their lack of commitment to whatever identity remains.

Toffler directly links loss of commitment and the subsequent sense of having lost one's roots to both the high rate of mobility (pp. 89, 148) and to 'the full crushing burden of overchoice' (p. 315) in modern Western societies. Mrs. Gouldner links undercommitment and lack of commitment to multiple memberships in a variety of organizations (Gouldner, 1960, p. 482; Hickman, p. 176). Lack of commitment can also be fostered by permissiveness. The lack of solidarity of one's group or one's society can be the outcome of too much permissiveness (Kanter, 1972, p. 185).

Yet undercommitment should in no way be confused with negative commitment, which has also often had an integrating consequence. Weber noticed how much Jewish religion was a religion of retribution: in no religion 'do we find a universal deity possessing the unparalleled desire for vengeance manifested by Yahweh' (Weber, 1964, p. 112). The influence of Nietzsche and his own rationalistic bias push Weber mistakenly into the direction of a 'compensation' kind of explanation: what is unattainable on earth is projected as available in heaven. Yet it is much more appropriate to regard Yahweh's characteristics as consonant with the very antagonism that the Jews felt for the conquering Babylonian and Assyrian armies. This antagonism was an effective rallying point for Israel. A common commitment against a threat has often strengthened group or social identity. Jung, too (1958, p. 430), missed the social significance of Yahweh's vindictiveness and irreconcilability when he utterly condemned these attributes.

In Hinduism, this negative commitment is sometimes no less closely associated with salvation than positive commitment. Sisupala, King of Chedi, attained salvation through his all-consuming hatred for Krishna and 'sometimes, to be an enemy of one's god and to arouse his jealous anger (mana) is a shorter cut to him than devotion by acts of faith, love and formal worship' (Walker, 1968, Vol. I, pp. 51, 52). Van der Leeuw (1964, p. 36) observes how sometimes sentiments of hate and fear, rather than respect and love, exist between the sacred and an individual. As we have remarked earlier, in modern societies the commitment of the young against the establishment has many integrating functions, in contrast with a lack of commitment that leads to identity crisis and alienation. Keniston tends to overlook both this sharp difference between negative commitment and lack of commitment, and the potential dysfunctions of openness, creativity, and flexibility (1964, pp. 102, 103; 1968, p. 276).

Liberal Christianity has recently echoed the plight of the uncommitted in recognizing a mystical Christian presence that avoids any strong doctrinal position or strong commitment. In a recent book the idea has been put forward that one should aim at commitment without ideology, not commitment to a system of meaning, but to a growth process (Batson, Beker, Clark, p. 184). This seems like sacralizing a pathological condition. After all, the problem of modern technological societies is the lack of viable systems of meaning and identities to which moderns can commit themselves. Feeling without focus presents the same dilemma that a taxi-driver found himself in, when an absentminded fare forgot to give him the address, but urged him to drive fast. While being raced through many unfamiliar streets, the passenger asked whether the driver knew where he was going, upon which the latter replied: 'No, but I am driving fast.'

REASON

Commitment is often regarded as dysfunctional by rationalists.

Thus, William Warren Bartley argues that no initial commitment is necessary, because everything can be subjected to criticism and continued testing. 'The position may then be held rationally without needing justification at all, provided it can be and is held open to criticism and survives severe testing' (1963, pp. 147–8). It is on these grounds that Bartley rejects Christians' initial leap of faith, and even the view of fellow rationalists, such as A. J. Ayer, who argues that rationality cannot itself be a subject of justification because it is itself the standard for justifying beliefs. For the same reason he also rejects Popper who wrote:

> ... whoever adopts the rationalist attitude does so because he has adopted, consciously or unconsciously some proposal, or decision, or belief, or behaviour, an adoption which may be called 'irrational' ... (and which) we may describe ... as an irrational faith in reason. (Popper, 1962, p. 231.)

Trigg (p. 120) also judges any basic commitment as totally blind and haphazard, unless an all-ambracing rationality acts as the supreme adjudicator. To Trigg, objectivity has to be absolutized or sacralized (p. 43), and he therefore rejects Wittgenstein's view (1967, p. 59) that commitment precedes and generates its own standards (Trigg, pp. 30, 49).

Presumably philosophers such as Bartley and Trigg would deny Nietzsche's view (1956, p. 288) that there is no such thing as a science without assumptions, and that 'a faith is always needed to give science a direction, a limit, a *raison d'être*'. They would also berate Durkheim and Mauss (1969, p. 86) for saying that it is 'the emotional value of notions which plays the preponderant part in the manner in which ideas are connected or separated', and Habermas (1971, p. 311) for saying that objectivity is conditioned by fundamental interests, not essentially different from the pressures and seductions of particular interests against which it arraigns itself.

This rejection is actually inevitable if rationality and objectivity have become wrapped in 'don't touch sentiments' by those for whom it is the linch-pin of a way of life. Generally the shoe has been on the other foot. In the nineteenth century, the three great demystifiers, Marx, Nietzsche, and Freud (Ricoeur, 1973, p. 206), unwrapped the 'don't touch sentiments' of Christianity, and showed convincingly that context and commitment were interdependent. Their successors have now equally justifiably unwrapped the 'don't touch sentiments' of the cardinal creeds of objectivity and rationality, and have shown equally convincingly that context and commitment are crucial for the maintenance of these views of scientific order.

It is not accidental that, in this debate of reason versus commitment, representatives of the religious traditions have tended to relativize reason rather than commitment. Their concern is with unifying faith rather than bisecting analysis. And so Kierkegaard (1941, p. 279) talks about abstract thought nullifying reality, and in Zen Buddhism (Noss, pp. 235–6) disciples are admonished to cease analytic and discursive reasoning, since it distracts their attention from the Oneness of Nirvana.

In Britain, the very rationalist circles who spawn these arguments support our contrary set of assumptions on the existential level. They have channelled a great deal of their emotional commitment into 'Ban the Bomb', 'Improved Sex Ethics' and 'Racial Equality' movements thereby illustrating our point that there is a dialectic between emotional anchorage and technical reason, between expressive and instrumental action, between identity/integration and alienation/differentiation. These actions and programmes of the British rationalists almost always find their justification in strongly held sacralized philosophical positions. As Parsons correctly observes: '. . . a philosophical belief becomes religious in so far as it is made the basis of a commitment in action' (1951, p. 367). Awareness of the religious element is usually repressed by the rationalists, but occasionally it surfaces, as in the July 1963 editorial of *The Humanist* (journal of the British Rationalist Association), in which the social need for emotive symbolism was recognized, but in which the problems that the Rationalist Association would have in providing for it were also mentioned.

Those philosophers who stress the dysfunction of commitment are usually right within their cognitive, rational frame of reference. After all, commitment modifies scepticism, the linch-pin of a rationalist system of meaning. Yet they are equally wrong in their assumption that this system of meaning is self-sustaining, and that it can be taken for granted. Motivations, beliefs, and values are necessary for its maintenance, and these in turn are always emotionally anchored. The narrowness of the rationalist argument is a direct consequence of a failure to think in terms of the larger dialectic, or of the social and psychological prerequisites for a cognitive system of meaning.

Arguing for the dysfunction of commitment the rationalists illustrate the opposite. In the autobiography of the Australian author, Donald Horne, he describes a long meeting with Freethinkers who were 'such zealots in its cause that after I had spent my first afternoon with them I felt not only stripped but skinned' (1967, p. 212). The efficacy of the rationalists lies as much in their missionary zeal as in the coherence of their argument. Their commitment is often a prerequisite for the very acceptance of the argument. They deceive themselves when they think that the power of their argument is solely cognitive and not emotive/contagious.

The function of commitment, that is its capacity for integration and emotional anchorage, is the weakness of reason which 'is an inherently dynamic force subject to continual change . . . (with) a strong tendency not to permit the development of settled routines and symbolic associations which would minimize psychological strain' (Parsons, 1964c, p. 71). And obviously the function of technical reason (its capacity for efficiency, change, and innovation) is the weakness of commitment.

It would be wrong to leave the impression that only philosophers deny or underrate the significance of commitment. In anthropology, Lévy-Bruhl (e.g. 1922, p. 426) tended to think that the further back one went on the evolutionary path of man, the more prominently man was determined by his affections and emotions. Modern man on the other hand was much more governed by the laws of logic and reason. But, although man has become more capable of dealing in abstractions, the need for integration, emotional anchorage has in no way diminished. Lévi-Strauss has refused to regard the primitives as in anyway less rational, believing that both moderns and primitives interpreted reality in essentially similar, structural, forms. Yet Lévi-Strauss, too, underrates the saliency of commitment (e.g. 1963, p. 71), and pays therefore little attention to its integrative potential. His 'extreme intellectualism' (Geertz 1968a, p. 405) has a negative effect on his capacity to deal with the kind of question which occupies us: 'What does commitment do for a given individual, group or society?'

The ethologist, Lorenz, on the other hand, in no way underrates the importance of commitment and militant enthusiasm, which he regards as 'a true autonomous instinct' (1970, p. 234), 'evolved out of a communal defence response of our pre-human ancestors' (p. 232), 'indispensable to the functioning of the compound system' (p. 231). Even so, this militant enthusiasm is also 'prone to miscarry most tragically if not strictly controlled by rational responsibility based on causal insight' (ibid.). Eibl-Eibesfeldt (p. 163) echoes the same sentiment when he says that it will depend on man's reason whether the capacity for enthusiastic commitment brings him benefit or harm. The internal contradiction of these (very popular) approaches lies in the assumption of a universal, taken for granted, *summum bonum* in which sceptical, divisive reason determines its dialectical opposite: a unifying commitment.

SACRIFICE

Sacrifice is a form of commitment that reinforces a system of meaning or an identity by clarifying priorities. On the social or group level, sacrifice enhances those beliefs and values—expressed, for instance, in the favouring or reconciling the gods—which strengthen the society or group. On the other hand, the sacrifice itself (property, a scapegoat) and its symbol (sin), are by implication given less emphasis to enhance the sacred.

Referring to the variety of theories that attempt to account for sacrifice Leach says (1968, p. 523), 'Some argue that the victim is identified with God and then sacramentally eaten; others that the victim stands in substitution for the giver of the sacrifice; others that the victim is a symbolic representation of sin, and so on.' He then ventures that these theories 'cannot all be true at once, and none of them reach into the heart of the problem which is "why should the killing of an animal be endowed with sacramental quality at all?"' Yet, all these theories and questions fit into the frame of reference mentioned in the first paragraph. Whether through the eating of the victim, through the mediation of sacrifice, or through the sacrifice representing competing orientations or value-threatening actions, in all instances the sacramental quality of the sacrifice consists in the reinforcement of a group or social identity.

The classic work on the meaning and function of sacrifice by Hubert and Mauss at first sight appears to differ from this interpretation. The authors ask themselves the question: what is the common function which provides the unity beneath the diverse forms of sacrifice? They answer their own question by saying: '. . establishing a means of communication between the sacred and the profane worlds . . .' (p. 97). And why does the profane enter into a relationship with the divine? Answer: ' . . . because it sees in it the very source of life' (p. 98). Yet sacrifice also involves an act of abnegation and submission by the sacrificer (p. 100). Hubert and Mauss suggest that personal renunciation nourishes social forces and redresses equilibria that have been upset (pp. 102–3).

The actual difference of this position and our frame of reference is slight. After all, communication between the profane and the sacred strengthens the relationship, and, in due course, the values and beliefs for which the sacred stands are reinforced at the expense of those that weaken its existence. In other words: sacrifice clarifies priorities and strengthens certain commitments. By acting out the relationship between the profane and the sacred, the point of view of the gods or supernatural forces is strengthened and specific interpretations of reality maintained. Our difference with Hubert and Mauss is that we would like to put more stress on the latent, specific purpose rather than simply on the fact of the communication.

Self-sacrifice has often been a problem in theories about sacrifice. Martyrdom severs, rather than strengthens, the communication of the individual and the sacred, but martyrdom also exemplifies the clarification of priorities: the system of meaning is professed to be even more important than one of the most precious possessions of the individual—his own life. It is therefore understandable that those sects such as the Anabaptists (Littell, p. 237) immeasurably strengthened the cohesion of their group through their readiness and willingness to suffer martyrdom.

In such a group, sacrifice is usually a deliberate act, but this is not always the case. When Jesus was crucified it was at first seen as the unfortunate outcome of a power struggle within the Jewish nation or between the Roman conquerors and the Jews. Later the sacrificial interpretation (Christ dying to reconcile man to God) gained ground, and the event came to be seen as a crucial vehicle for reinforcing the relation between God and man. This was true, too, for the assassination of Abraham Lincoln in 1865. Bellah (1970, p. 178) regards Lincoln as the Christian archetype whose sacrificial death 'was indelibly written into the civil religion'.

Changes in priorities are often accompanied by changes in sacrificial customs. To delineate the new priorities, which often result from new culture contacts, the sacrifices take on such sombre forms as annihilation. In the nineteenth century, thousands of Southern Bantus died after they had killed their cattle and destroyed their crops in response to a prophet's appeal. A group of four hundred Guiana Indians massacred one another in order to be reborn in white skins (Worsley, 1957, p. 225). Christiansen explains the mass destruction of valuables, which often accompanies the rise of cargo cults, by the need to turn over a new leaf. 'Everything is discarded that is reminiscent of the old unsatisfactory existence . . .' (p. 113).

Our discussion of sacrifice has so far centred only on societies or groups within a society. Yet there are examples of individuals who have found their self-identity through such self-denying acts as self-starvation and even self-mutilation (Lowie, 1965, p. 195). Jung (1958, pp. 256–7) makes the point that true sacrifice is giving without receiving something in return. In the last resort, he says, the giving of oneself proves that one possesses oneself. Strauss makes a similar observation: '. . . any long-standing commitment means an agreement to sacrifice' (1959, p. 42). 'Self-sacrifice signifies often the firmest of identities and the most total of commitment' (ibid.).

Asceticism is usually a way of clarifying personal priorities and purifying one's loyalties. To St. Francis, poverty was the avenue for closer union with God. To such diverse personages as Ho Chi Minh, Mao Tse-tung, and Malcolm X, strict morality and rigid self-discipline were essentially means for maintaining and improving devotion to the sacred cause (Gerlach and Hine, p. 109). On any level, then, whether social, group, or personal, sacrifice clarifies priorities and strengthens the commitment to whatever is at the apex of a hierarchical system of meaning. Sacrifice sacralizes the focus of identity. It makes a cause more sacred and inviolable (Kanter, p. 76).

PLURALISM

In modern pluralistic societies peculiar problems have arisen for commitment. Individuals occupy a variety of roles, and their commitment to any of them may be weakened by the demands of the others, since there is competition between groups for the loyalty and commitment of members. Nor are cultural forces altogether neutral in this battle for allegiance. In certain periods, the commitment to differentiating/instrumental foci of identity seems to be in the upswing: at others (as in the 1970s) the opposite values of integration and expression are emphasized. Let us take each of the personal and group levels of commitment separately, particularly in so far as they concern religious organizations.

Since commitment, reliability, and responsibility go together, there is pressure on the individual to maximize his commitment to the most important of these roles. He resolves this dilemma in a variety of ways, one of which is to use the segregation of role performances, for example, home roles are separated from office roles. Another device is the establishment of a hierarchy of commitments, by which conflicts can be resolved through prior decisions as to the significance of one role relative to another. A very common example is the husband's strong commitment to the instrumental values of his occupation at the expense of the expressive values of the family. These instrumental values are well expressed in the following quotations from Duerr (1971): 'Competition and conflict are the heart of any effective economic systems . . . If you don't want to

compete, don't hope to be happy and successful in management ...
The only kind of people I am comfortable around are those who are
operating out of enlightened, long-term self-interest ... They are
predictable ... I am uneasy with someone who claims to be working
for a cause, or for the benefit of humanity. Even if he is consciously
sincere, it is impossible to figure out in advance what his decision is
going to be ...'

Yet, if these values are carried over in the family situation they
disrupt rather than integrate. Or the other way round: if a man's
dedication to his family is greater than to his business, his career
prospects tend to suffer through the relativization of his business
or professional loyalties. In this jostling for positions on the commitment hierarchy, religious organizations are never partial: they
favour commitment to expressive values, even when the organization is under pressure to adhere to principles of rational efficiency
in its own operations.

The successful maximization of one role at the expense of all
others is illustrated by celibacy in the Catholic Church. By insisting
on celibacy for its professionals the church concretely exemplified
the quality of wholehearted commitment it had in mind for its
entire membership. It also maximized the priestly role through disallowance of any competition with others, such as parental roles.
The priest could now focus fully on his commitment to the
expressive expectations of the Church, and thereby strengthen the
organizational cohesion of Catholicism. The strength of the Catholic
Church has in no small way been the result of its capacity to sublimate the sex instinct of its professionals into spiritual channels (see
Simmel, 1955, pp. 143–6).

Today, celibacy is the subject of intense scrutiny, research, and
discussion (see, e.g., Schreuder, 1970 or Greeley, 1972), and it is not
accidental that this is happening just as the cohesion of Catholicism
is weakening. There is a strong correlation between the perceived
cost of celibacy and the commitment to the church (Schoenherr and
Greeley, p. 422). In the U.S.A., Catholic churchgoing dropped from
a weekly average of 74 per cent in 1958 to 63 per cent in 1969
(Gallup Polls). In the Netherlands, where the celibacy issue is even
more the subject of heated debate, Catholics vote decreasingly for
their own party (Katholieke Volks Partij) with the result that this
party (the biggest only a decade ago) has now dropped to third place.
It is not only on the personal level that competition for commit-

ment has sometimes negatively affected the integration or sacralization of identity. It is also true for group identity. As in Catholicism,
Protestants too have often identified commitment to an ultimate
system of meaning with commitment to the ecclesiastical organization in which it was embedded. Yet, because for Protestants, the
ultimate system of meaning was often directed to individualistic
convictions, and because the dedication of its married professionals
could never be as exemplarily 'total', the Protestant churches have,
as a general rule, been much less cohesive than the Catholic. The
difference in church attendance between Protestant and Catholic
countries can be closely linked to differences in organizational cohesion (Mol, 1970c and 1972a). There is, however, an even greater
difference between religiously homogeneous and heterogeneous
countries. In the latter, where the population is mixed Protestant
and Catholic, church attendance is uniformly higher. This suggests
that in pluralistic societies those religious organizations which had
to compete with one another for membership allegiance were more
successful than the religious monopolies or state churches which
had to compete only with more invisible foci of identity. In pluralistic societies with multiple religious organizations, religious organizations as such (rather than what they embedded) appear to become
sources of identity. Having to compete meant clearer identity
boundaries, and stronger membership loyalties.

Weber never understood the importance of religious competition
in these countries and was rightly criticized by Richard Niebuhr for
suggesting that the vitality of the American churches was to be
found in the fact that economic sanctions had been substituted for
the political sanctions of church adherence in Europe. Niebuhr
(1957, p. 206) suggests that the source of vitality is rather 'the inten-
sive cultivation of . . . loyalty by the denominations'. Harrison
stresses the same variable when he says, 'The divine presence among
the people was sometimes interpreted to signify the possession of
God by the community, so that the will of the congregation was
equated with the will of God' (1959, p. 54).

The point of this discussion is that the constantly changing
patterns of shallow and strong commitments in modern differentiated societies are significant factors in the search for meaning,
identity, and stability. This search favours the formation of a hierarchy of commitments, whereby the strongest overrules the weakest
and provides the necessary emotional anchorage for others. In this

complex of identity foci, ultimate systems of meaning, and the more concrete reference to religious organizations have to compete with hosts of others. The necessity for competition in pluralistic societies may have a negative effect in that certain foci of identity lose out in the battle, but they may also have a positive effect, in that those foci of identity which survive become stronger through their capacity to elicit strong commitment.

SUMMARY

Commitment anchors a system of meaning in the emotions and, given time, develops into awe which provides the system with insulatory sentiments. Yet the holy also engenders commitment. This mutual enforcement could easily lead to petrifaction, if it were not for the differentiating and instrumental forces which encourage competition, scepticism, and rationality.

Commitment is of necessity closely linked with consistency and predictability. This is so because the motivation for action resides in expressive orientations with strong commitment as a salient element, and not in cognitive orientation (in which rationality and technical reason are crucial). It is for this reason that the very popular rationalistic assumption of a universal, taken-for-granted, *summum bonum*, in which sceptical, divisive reason determines its dialectical opposite (a unifying commitment), is both naïve and Quixotic.

Sacrifice is a form of commitment that clarifies priorities in a hierarchy of potentially competing meanings. In pluralistic societies the actual competition between a large variety of identity foci has created dilemmas of commitment. Certain foci of identity fail in the competitive battle, but those which survive tend to become stronger through successful boundary defence. Lack of commitment, lack of identity, meaninglessness, anomie, and alienation are all very much related symptoms of societies in which definitions of reality are no longer taken for granted because competition has relativized them all.

Chapter XVI

Ritual

Rites articulate and reiterate a system of meaning, and prevent it being lost from sight. They act out and sacralize sameness. They restore, reinforce, or redirect identity. They maximize order by strengthening the place of the individual in the group, or society, and vice versa by strengthening the bonds of a society *vis-à-vis* the individual. They unify, integrate, and sacralize. With this short summary of what we think ritual is and does, we hope to account for both primitive and modern rites.

Some approaches to ritual are much narrower, and question whether the secular urbanized world needs rituals to the same extent as primitive societies (Gluckman, 1962, p. 37), but rituals are not confined to religious organizations; they include the Sunday afternoon car-ride of a family. Other definitions of ritual are even wider than this, and refer to the repetition of any non-rational action. Ethologists, for instance, speak about rites when they observe seagulls, wolves, and other animals making certain repeated head movements or baring vulnerable sections of their body for no ostensible purpose. Konrad Lorenz has shown convincingly that nature ritualizes and inhibits actual fighting, so that the aggressive drive is checked 'without really weakening it or hindering its species-preserving function' (1970, p. 72). We use the term 'ritual' in the more restricted sense of the repetitive enactment of human systems of meaning. Yet the embryonic ritual of the animal world is likely to be part of the origin of the more complex human variety, which appears to have become elaborated and expanded in religion, and this, according to Bergson (1935, pp. 111 ff.), similarly replaces dangerous instincts with social customs. Anthropological theories generally agree that ritual contributes to the cohesion, and therefore to the survival capacity, of primitive culture. Energy or libido is diverted from potentially group-weakening activities to group-strengthening activities. In ritual, Turner says, 'the raw energies of conflict are domesticated into the service of social order' (1970, p. 172). 'Ritual adapts and periodically re-adapts the bio-psychical individual to the basic conditions and axiomatic values of human social life' (p. 177). Rites cleanse or purify, and, in the process, reinforce social expectations and superimpose constraint. Durkheim called them piacular (1954, pp. 434, 455). Ritual does more than just repair or 'remake individuals and groups morally' (1954, p. 414): it strengthens the existing links with the past and the future of one's culture. It thereby *represents* society (ibid., p. 415).

ANXIETY

Many psychologists and anthropologists have stressed the anxiety-relieving function of ritual. The hunter or fisherman who is faced with the uncertain outcome of his efforts gains confidence from ritual performance (Wallace, pp. 174–7). Cazeneuve (pp. 6–8) regards rites as the actual consequence of human anxiety, which, he thinks, is produced by social constraint as it affects man's conscience. Rites mitigate this anxiety.

Malinowski saw that the Tobriand Islanders had two modes of fishing: relatively easy fishing within the lagoon; and the much more dangerous, anxiety-rendering activity in the open seas. Only with the latter was 'extensive magical ritual to secure safety and good results' (1954, p. 31) associated.

Radcliffe-Brown (1939, pp. 35, 39; Homans, 1951, p. 325) attacked Malinowski's anxiety theory of ritual by saying that if it were not for rites the individual would feel no anxiety, and that rather than anxiety being resolved by rites, it was produced by them. When we realize that the two anthropologists wrote of different things, the controversy disappears. Malinowski was thinking about the individual's enhanced confidence, or about ritual as a reinforcement of personal identity; Radcliffe-Brown was concerned with ritual as an agency which sacralized social identity, and this type of ritual inevitably exercises restraint upon the individual, and may therefore produce anxiety for him (see also Homans, 1951, p. 330; 1962, pp. 192–201).

The anthropologists' observation that there is a correlation between anxiety and religion is important. We must not let this observation slide into another deprivation theory of religion, however, and thus it is perhaps preferable to think of anxiety, as well as of alienation and of anomie, as produced by an entire cluster of forces (including instrumentality, rationality, scepticism, differentiation, and so on). Ritual is, after all, 'one of the fundamental defence mechanisms of society against the tendency to anomie' (Parsons, 1949, p. 713). Our dominant and most general assumption has been that this cluster creates the necessity for its own counterbalance in emotionally anchored meaning, integration, and identity. Ritual together with other sacralization mechanisms is thus part of this balancing act.

PERSONAL IDENTITY

Ritual integrates personal identity. Just as change (any change—travel, a win in the lottery, the death of a close relation, a new job, career promotion, marriage, etc.) usually affects personal identity negatively, so does the re-enactment of sameness (daily routines, the stereotyped forms of social intercourse, the Sunday trip to church, the coffee-break, the persistent reminders of one's fit in an hierarchical order at home or at work, the recurrence of seasonal activities for the farmer, etc.) affect it positively. Some of these changes, such as birth, puberty, marriage, and death, have such impact that rites have developed to blunt their negative effect, which we discuss in a separate section on rites of passage. These rites are not the only ones sacralizing a specific personal identity. Sometimes personal habits have become so ingrained that to break them is regarded as sacrilege. Freud observed some very peculiar ingrained habits in his practice, such as the ritual rinsing of wash-basins after use, sitting in one particular chair only, leaving the best of one's meal on the plate, etc. (Freud, 1959, p. 120). Yet Freud's indomitable rational/scientific bias made him interpret these habits as pathological rather than as therapeutic. Similarly, religious rites and ceremonials are to Freud illustrations of obsessional neuroses (ibid., pp. 126–7). And yet in the same pages of his article on obsessive actions and religious practices, Freud declares obsessive neuroses and religious ceremonials to be necessary prerequisites for the development of human civilization, because both demand the renunciation and the sacrifice of socially harmful instincts and the re-establishment of the original balance of values. Freud's intellectual arrogance consisted in his belief that enlightened man might do without these neuroses and rituals, and that reason was adequate to determine which habits were worth maintaining.

Jung believed that ritual restored wholeness (1959, p. 188), which in turn was the most important of archetypes, the irrepresentable models, primordial images, and invisible core meanings that held sway over the unconscious (1958, p. 469; 1959, p. 5; 1960, p. 214). Like Freud, Jung thought primarily of the individual, and therefore he discussed such religious rites as the Catholic Mass with respect to its contribution to individuation (1958, p. 273); the psychological process that made a human being into a 'whole man' (1940, p. 3), and which promoted selfhood and self-realization (1959a, p. 143). In the rite of the Mass, 'the Eucharist transforms the soul of empirical man, who is only a part of himself, into his totality, symbolically expressed by Christ' (1958, p. 273). Christ represented the union of opposites (1958, p. 430) and this was expressed in the Mass by the androgynous nature of the mystical Christ—his blood being the masculine wine, and his body the feminine bread (1958, p. 221). Jung made other observations about ritual. It was a 'method of mental hygiene' (1958, p. 76). It provided 'a feeling of security', particularly useful when risky decisions had to be made (1964, p. 260). It diverted 'the libido from its natural river-bed of everyday habit into some unaccustomed activity' (1960, p. 44). It secured 'the co-operation of the unconscious' in the battle against the caprice of a rootless consciousness (1964, p. 346). Yet it also consolidated consciousness, and built dams and walls 'to keep back the dangers of the unconscious' (1959, p. 22). Jung's persistent use of the conscious/ unconscious distinction is confusing. *Both* the rootlessness accompanying mobility in modern society, *and* the disrupting potential of man's unharnessed, aggressive instincts are counterbalanced and checked by ritual and by the other mechanisms of sacralization. To introduce the unconscious and conscious distinction into the analysis goes against the grain of scientific parsimony at this point, and dims its clarity. Jung had other related biases, such as his romantic eulogy of man's conscious, reflective knowledge of the hidden processes of order in existence (1958, p. 294). Yet Jung's stock in the religious and theological world is remarkably high. His disgust for reductionist explanations of divine mystery (1958, pp. 251, 296); his reverence for the independence of sacred manifestations; and the importance he attached to religious belief and practice—have much to do with this popularity. It is for reasons such as these that a critical sociolo-

gist such as Nagendra praises Jung's 'sound ontological presuppositions' (p. 129).

The integrative function of ritual for the individual has been
observed by other scholars. Faith can serve, as Erikson (1968, p. 106)
rightly said, as a 'ritual restoration of a sense of trust'. Roszak
(1973, p. 74) makes the point that dreams are fundamentally re-enact-
ments of the mythical identity of man.

SOCIAL IDENTITY

What is true for personal habits in relation to personal identity is
equally true for social customs in relation to social identity. Here
too the formation of customs can be viewed as an early stage of the
sacralization process. Procedural customs in a bureaucracy can
acquire a 'don't touch' quality. Weber uses 'ritualism' to indicate
how customs had become crystallized around such diverse items as
military methods and archery, etiquette and literary forms, in China
(1964, pp. 108 ff.); or around caste duty in India (1958, p. 24). In
the modern West sociologists of the family, such as Bossard and
Boll, think that 'sherry before dinner may become as much a family
ritual as family prayer before going to bed; and listening to a Sunday
night program may be the center of a ritual complex just as much
as the reading of the Bible' (p. 465). To them these rituals are a
'relatively reliable index of family integration' (p. 467).

However, rituals consolidate beliefs as well as customs. Strong
beliefs about the rights of workers in industry were consolidated
through the rituals of the early trade-union movement. Songs, regular meetings, witnessing to the beliefs and goals, all these advanced
solidarity. In a variety of countries these rituals became elaborated
in the so-called labour churches (Scharf, p. 169; Allen, p. 81 ff.).

In the meantime the ritual of religious institutions, everywhere
in the West, continued to sacralize those beliefs and values which
society at large regarded as crucial for its existence: the prayers of
confession, thanksgiving, and intercession, hymns about faith and
commitment, sermons, and masses or communion celebrations, all
in diverse ways interpreted reality, and reconciled men to the
environment in which they were embedded. Outside the religious
institutions in the West competing ritualizing was also going on.
The trade-union movement; the service clubs; masonic lodges; and

even school assemblies, and national anthems at public gatherings, have tended to sacralize sentiments and group identities, both now and in the past.

Klapp provides an interesting account of these lesser known kinds of ritual such as passing the 'joint' among marijuana smokers (Powell, 1962; Klapp, pp. 160, 175), which he regards as a counterbalance to the alienating, rationalistic forces in American society. In contrast to British positivists, such as A. J. Ayer for whom the domain of ritual and religion is 'beyond the range of serious enquiry' (p. 125), Klapp maintains that if a society supports 'only rational consensus (science, information, legislation, and practical reform)' (p. 122), its supply of non-rational consensus will become disastrously weak. Suitable ritual, on the other hand, provided man with a sense of identity and belonging (pp. 125, 137).

It seems characteristic for modern societies, however, that pockets of meaning, or strongly defended group identities, put up a healthier resistance to the anomic perils of the social whole than the wider, more amorphous social systems of meaning. Thus, tightly organized, cohesive, competitive groups have an advantage, because they are under no necessity to compromise their beliefs. Groups such as Mormons, Jehovah Witnesses, etc., also effectively use the mode of ritual suited to situations of competition: witnessing. Every act of witnessing anchors the belief system deeply in the emotions of the believer, since faith has to be proclaimed against the non-believer. The boundaries around the belief system are thus firmly drawn, and provide an alluring picture of order and discipline to those who feel betrayed by the flaccid and faceless forces of freedom and meaninglessness.

RITES OF PASSAGE

Ritual is particularly relevant at times of crisis, or when a change of identity takes place (Bellah, 1965, p. 173; Berger and Luckman, p. 156). Van Gennep named the rituals that dealt with transitions from one stage in a life-cycle, season, year to another stage, 'rites of passage'.

The 'ceremonies of birth, childhood, social puberty, betrothal, marriage, pregnancy, fatherhood, initiation into religious societies, and funerals' (p. 3) all have in common a passing from one status to another. Van Gennep (p. 11) subdivided these rites in preliminal (*limen* is threshold—thus *preliminal* means to face the status from which one will be separated), liminal (transitional) and postliminal (incorporative) rites. Van Gennep chose the 'threshold' imagery because the door and the threshold provided 'the boundary between the foreign and domestic worlds in the case of an ordinary dwelling, between the profane and sacred worlds in the case of a temple' (p. 20). A Roman arch of triumph represented the separation between the foreign, enemy world, and the familiar territory. The victor became incorporated again through sacrifice to Jupiter Capitoline, and to the deities protecting the city (p. 21). Rites of passage accentuate the permanent quality of the change. The Haida cut a special opening in the wall of the house for the coffin, in order to prevent a return of the deceased (p. 157). The Western habit of carrying the bride across the threshold also signifies the irrevocable transition from one world to another. Until the publication of van Gennep's book in 1908, lines of classification were drawn differently (initiation, purification, etc.), but since his theories have found acceptance, the emphasis has been on the similarity of patterns of rites of passage, the 'spatial separation of distinct groups as an aspect of social organization' (p. 192), and particularly on the ever-present threshold or transition phase between the old and new status.

Van Gennep's three stages coincide closely with what we have called (a) the emotional detachment; (b) phase of meaninglessness; and (c) emotional attachment to a new focus of identity. Differing from van Gennep, we have put more attention, in discussing charisma and conversion, on the emotional stripping and welding, since the new identity was more voluntarily espoused, and less embedded in existing cultural expectations. The transition accomplished by conversion and charisma was, for that reason, emotionally more salient, painful, and dramatic. There is, then, a difference of structured versus relatively unstructured change, but in both instances the transition remains, and is from one identity, or unified system of meaningful behaviour to another. In both instances there is a desacralization of old identity and the sacralization of a new identity.

Eliade ignores van Gennep's idea that rites of passage were primarily social devices for changing status positions, since he regards ritual as primarily a re-enactment of sacred prototypes, and therefore, the function of initiation is primarily to reveal a transcendental world (Eliade, 1965, p. 132). Our reinterpretation of van Gennep in terms of identity rather than status changes is an implied critique of both van Gennep and Eliade. Van Gennep's theory might be integrated with a more general theory of religious behaviour, in which both reinforcement and change of systems of meaning, identities, and definitions of reality were central variables. In such a theory, the rites of passage would become instances of one of the sacralization mechanisms that dealt with change in structured identities. Our criticism of Eliade, on the other hand, is directed to his disinclination to generalize sociologically on the basis of his extensive data, or to regard the sacred as anything but 'given'. We look upon sacralization as a sociologically meaningful, important, and analysable process, however much we stress that our view is only one perspective amongst many.

LIMINALITY

Recently, van Gennep's theories have drawn renewed anthropological interest. Gluckman (1962), Meyer Fortes (1962), and Leach (1968) all pay tribute to the significance of *the Rites of Passage*. Victor Turner (1969) similarly uses the vocabulary of van Gennep, while infusing it with new meaning. To Turner the transitional, liminal stage has its own pregnant function going far beyond the inevitable instability and confusion of the in-between stage observed by van Gennep, and noted in our analysis of conversion and charisma (Chapter IV). Turner uses the term 'permanent liminality' (1969, p. 145), a stage in which *communitas* can come to optimum fruition (ibid.). *Communitas* to Turner is a modality of social relationship (p. 96) which stresses the opposite of structure, namely 'the sentiment for humanity' (p. 111). The best way of putting this difficult concept into words, he says, is to use Martin Buber's 'das Zwischenmenschliche', the spontaneous, immediate, dynamic facing of others, a flowing from I to Thou (p. 127). 'Communitas has an existential quality; it involves the whole man in his relation to other whole men' (ibid.). 'Communitas breaks in through the interstices of structure, in liminality; at the edges of structure, in marginality; and from beneath structure, in inferiority' (p. 128). It is not just the product of liberated instinctual energies, released from cultural constraint, but includes rationality, volition and memory (ibid.). The boundaries of *communitas* are 'ideally coterminous with those of the human species' (p. 132). *Communitas* 'is to solidarity as Henri Bergson's open morality is to his closed morality' (ibid.).

Turner illustrates the *communitas*, or the meta-structural aspects of social relations, from a variety of historical sources. The Franciscan order attempted to preserve *communitas* through insisting on poverty for its members, and by resisting structural and economic bondage. Like Francis of Assissi, Caitanya (1486–1533) inspired his disciples of the Vaisnavite movement in Bengal through a deep personal love relationship. The Buddha, Gandhi, Tolstoy, and the hippy community of San Francisco—all have in common the practice and preaching of human kindness, humility, and status reversal.

The reader who is sensitized to modern problems of alienation and meaninglessness will readily recognize their affinity with liminality and *communitas*. In both instances there is a relativization of past structures and a search for new forms of identity. This may be clearly set out, as in the rites of passage of primitive societies, or it may be preliminary and tentative, as in modern societies men face an over-choice of identity foci. Turner's emphasis on openness, rationality, and universality have important links with a climate of alienation, anomie, and anxiety.

The principal conditions for the atrophy of sacralized systems of meaning should not be confused with the feeling states that accompany the vision of a new identity, and here we disagree with Turner. Those who launch unconventional, new interpretations of reality can spread *agape* around precisely because they speak with their followers on a common wavelength. This common understanding is the beginning of structure, even if the new, vaguely perceived, identity is as yet negative (we, the lost, as over against you, the squares). In addition, even if competition for identity foci prolongs the tentative search, there is still a hidden, taken-for-granted system of values and routines which frames and guides the transition to new forms. The new prophets proclaim *agape* because they already move within the security of the new vision. By implication, little is left for liminality, as the conditions for the breakdown of the old identity lie in the preliminary sphere, and the emotional balance and integration (characterized by I–Thou relationships, humanitarian sentiments, etc.) lie in the postliminary one. Turner's attempt to find liminal and *communitas* characteristics in apocalyptic, millenarian movements is also rather fruitless because these movements focus and inform the new, postliminary, identity. Obviously any new vision, new interpretation of reality, or new identity is relatively unstructured. Yet the unstructuredness of a new movement is radically different from the unstructuredness of liminality, when the old has been rejected and the new is yet unborn.

Turner is also unaware of structure in the I–Thou relationship. The like-seek-like motivation inevitably consolidates and structures the I–Thou. Buber's primary distinction between I–Thou (a concern with the other's wholeness, subjectivity) and I–It (divisiveness, manipulation, objectivity) is reminiscent of the integration/differentiation dialectic of our frame of reference (Buber, 1950, pp. vii, 3, 23, 46, 62, 93). The binding, unity-seeking sentiment of I–Thou strongly reacts to, transcends, and thereby modifies, meaninglessness of any kind, including the one so obvious in the liminal phase.

Nor can we accept Turner's tendency to identify liminality with *communitas*, the undifferentiated (p. 96) and affection (p. 139), as though these elements are not equally present in the preliminal and postliminal stages; indeed, as though these elements are not basic for the entire stabilizing and sacralizing function of religious movements. To us, the forces of identity consolidate, unify, and anchor emotionally, whereas the forces of instrumentality differentiate and divide. Nor do they do this only in the rather restricted liminal phase. It is precisely because of the emotional attachment to the identity in the preliminal and postliminal phases, that transitional rites become so salient. They strip and weld emotionally. The saliency of rites at periods of transition is all the more evident because of the basic threat which transition presents to identity and integration. Transition, or the necessity for a new identity, for whatever reason, makes the existing system of meaning more fragile. It is particularly at the fragile points of existence that sacralization mechanisms do their work.

This rather fundamental critique of Turner's conceptual scheme may be more relevant for pre-industrial societies than for modern ones. If, in modern cultures, the old has been rejected, without viable alternatives being found for the crystallization of new identities (however urgent the search), the holding, neutral, liminal stage must gain importance. There is, then, a similarity between the sublimation of experiences of meaninglessness offered by the theatre of the absurd, and the basic sympathy one feels for liminars (the Turner language for 'threshold'—'in-between' people), as one recognizes their experiences as one's own. But to regard this phase as in any way 'permanent' flies in the face of built-in mechanisms of order and integration.

RITES OF REBELLION

The articulation and sublimation of meaninglessness in modern art forms provide us also with a useful analogy for yet a different kind of ritual. This category of rites, which Gluckman (1954, p. 1) called 'rituals of rebellion', does not at first sight easily fall within our frame of reference. Instead of reinforcing the major beliefs and values of society, these rites thwart them. They blatantly subvert the moral and sexual conventions. Caillois describes the ritual debauchery and extravagance of St. Sylvester's eve in Europe, which to him is a time 'in which the order of the universe is suspended' (1959, p. 14). Like Eliade (1959a, p. 187), Caillois guesses that these rites recapitulate the mythical past and exuberantly anticipate the abundance of the coming spring. Gluckman thinks that they are cathartic release mechanisms which by allowing the expression of tension minimize actual conflicts (Gluckman, 1954, pp. 20 ff.).

These rites seem to have something in common with what we have called 'negative commitment'. The ritual expression of commonly felt hostilities and frustrations has integrating consequences. In the same way as in a dream, repressions are re-enacted and rendered less libido-absorbing and more harmless, so rites of rebellion may restore social equilibrium by taking the pressure off social repressions and restraints. The articulation and enactment of meaninglessness in modern art forms appears similarly to take the pressure off the instinctive discomfort that human beings feel when faced with chaos and disorder. Rites of rebellion, like sublimations provided by modern art, take some of the sting out of reality. The function of rites of rebellion may be thought of as a counterbalance to the ever-present dysfunctional, rigidifying potential of prevailing sacralization patterns. They may be regarded as self-correcting rites that enhance the survival of a particular system of meaning through greater flexibility and through absorption of harmful elements before the latter can become institutionalized. One may compare rites of rebellion with charisma in that both provide channels of transition, but with the significant difference that charisma is involved in an actual transition, whereas rites of rebellion only potentially pave the way to transition.

RELATION WITH THE OTHER DIMENSIONS OF SACRALIZATION

There is a long, but rather fruitless debate as to whether myths were prior to rites (Kluckhohn 1965; Leach, 1968, pp. 521, 524), but this is more a matter of definition than a 'chicken and egg' controversy as Kluckhohn thinks. When the definition is wide (as e.g. the ethological one), obviously rites are prior to myths. When the definition is narrow (enacting a belief) the opposite is the case. Yet rites in either definition have in common a repetitive function of arousing sentiments and unifying activity that is ostensibly engaged in for its own sake. This repetitive activity is the independent contribution of ritual to the sacralization process. It does most of the actual work of anxiety release or conflict resolution (Wallace, p. 199). It achieves this only by heavy reliance on commitment, through emotional detachment and attachment. This commitment factor is ever present in ritual, but the opposite (that a ritual factor is ever present in commitment) seems somewhat less defensible. Ritual action therefore differs fundamentally from rational action. The first stabilizes through emotional anchorage, the other facilitates change precisely because it avoids emotional commitment. The difference between them is the same as the one between Pareto's non-logical and logical action. 'Indeed so prominent is ritual in (Pareto's) treatment that it is quite safe to say that one of the principal empirical bases for this thesis of the importance of non-logical action is the prevalence of ritual' (Parsons, 1949, p. 208, also p. 675). Myths retain some of these emotive elements. Yet in contrast with ritual they possess an internal, verbal, logic of their own. To this topic we turn in the next chapter.

SUMMARY

Rites represent sameness in action and thereby consolidate the sameness of a system of meaning. They restore, reinforce, or redirect identity. They restore, through recommitting to memory, a system of meaning, through reabsorbing individuals in the common fabric, and through confessions of sins of omission and commission. They reinforce through superimposing the constraint of social expectations, through linking the past to the present, through filling the emotional voids of instrumental, rational existence. They redirect through surrounding stressful situations with emotional support, through desacralizing an old identity, and through sacralizing a new one.

Chapter XVII

Myths, Theology, and Dreams

Myths, not only interpret reality and provide a shorthand for basic personal and social experiences, but they also sacralize them (Eliade, 1964, p. xviii; Schorer, 1960, p. 355). They provide the fitting contour for existence. They hold arbitrariness and chaos at bay, and they reinforce identity. The variety of myths is so great that one scholar calls the search for unitary theories of mythical function 'largely a waste of time' (Kirk, p. 252). Yet irrespective of whether a particular myth is primarily a narrative, an iterative tale, or a speculation about existence (Kirk's categories), it is always an implicit or explicit statement about man's place in his environment. And this universal function of making statements about man's place is the common character of myths.

They are narratives, tales, or speculations not just for their own sake but with the added function of sacralizing meaning and identity. However much details vary, their basic structure is therefore more durable than other narratives or tales, and they differ in basic function in that they outline and anchor the definition of what life and its relationships are about. Their durable structure and their sacralizing function often give them considerable autonomy. Myths, therefore, not only are conditioned by specific cultures and subcultures, but also condition them in turn (Otto, 1967, p. 271; Bruner, 1960, p. 283).

How are the other three dimensions of the sacralization process related to myths? Very often objectification, commitment, and ritual are also evident in myth. A sacred narrative usually contributes to the resolution of basic conflicts through objectification. 'Mythical symbolism leads to an objectification of feelings' (Cassirer, 1946, p. 43). It is usually anchored in the emotions and the securities of the people. It is often enacted and dramatized ritually, or as Thomas Mann (1960, p. 374) has it: it is 'a renewal of the past in the present'.

Yet not all dimensions have to be simultaneously present for the process to be 'sacralizing'. True, they seem to be almost indissolubly connected the further back in evolutionary history one goes. In modern societies, however, they appear to operate much more independently. Already in ancient Greece, myth and ritual only occasionally coincided (Ringgren and Ström, Vol. II, p. 65; Burket, p. 41). It is an error to assume that myth *must* be expressed ritually, as do some of the narrower functionalist theorists (Preusz, 1933; de Vries, 1967, pp. 210–11), however much it may be true for a specific primitive culture. And even there, myth and ritual are sometimes separated (Kluckhohn, 1965, pp. 145 ff.). Commitment, too, seems sometimes to be independent of myth.

THE EVOLUTION AND STRUCTURE OF SYMBOLS AND MYTHS

One of the elementary assumptions of this book has been that the adaptations and consolidations of genetic materials have their counterpart in the adaptive (rational, instrumental) and consolidating (affective, integrative) spheres of symbol-systems. There is *both* a division of labour *and* a dialectic between these adaptations and consolidations. Signs, symbols, language, and myths (in that order) emerged because of their contributions to the survival of *homo sapiens*. The differentiation and dialectic between symbols of adaptation and the symbols of consolidation also emerged because of their contribution to man's growing independence from nature. Dialectic is a prerequisite for the further consolidation of man's freedom from nature.

Thus, we cannot follow Parsons (e.g. 1937, pp. 417, 676) and Schneider (1970, p. 31) when they equate symbols in general with religious symbols, although in later work (1961, p. 970) Parsons distinguishes between cognitive and expressive symbols (see also Bellah, 1970, pp. 241–2). Van der Leeuw (1964, p. 448) too defines symbol as 'the encounter between secular and sacred' and as the 'participation of the sacred in its veritable, actual, form'.

Suzanne Langer's distinction between discursive symbols (in our terms, the concepts dealing with purposive ends, rationality, and instrumentality) and non-discursive symbols (in our terms, the concepts dealing with integration and expressiveness) is more useful. Langer, from whom we also accept the definition of symbol as an instrument of conception (1972, p. 289), suggests that the non-discursive symbols are the domain of music, art, and religion (1951, p. 113). There are historical precedents for related distinctions. Even before Confucius, Chinese philosophers categorized the natural world in two inter-acting elements: yang and yin. Yang is roughly present in such disparate items as change, motion, life, activity, procreation, fire, masculinity, summer, and the sun. Yin, on the other hand, predominates in stability, quiescence, death, rest, harmony, darkness, femininity, winter, and the moon (Watts, 1963, pp. 54 ff.; Toynbee, 1946, pp. 51, 63, 65). Toynbee finds the yang–yin or differentiation–integration, or challenge–response, dialectic in such diverse sources as the Biblical stories of the Fall, Job, Goethe's Faust, etc. Each of this primordial pair both conflicts with, and is complementary to, the other. Lévi-Strauss (1963, p. 89) also regards the principles of yang and yin, united in the totality of *Tao*, the most general model of Totemism, which turns opposition from an obstructor of integration into a constructor. Yang and yin have also been seen as the basic model for the opposition between war and peace (Heraclitean Ionism); striving and loving (Empedocles); and even the sickness and well-being of acupuncture (Durkheim and Mauss, p. 80; Lyall Watson, p. 148).

Plato often contrasts *logos*, containing more rational, sceptical elements, with *mythos* containing more expressive elements. (Aall, p. 71, Gorgias 523A, Protagoras 320C, Phaedo 61B). William James (1902, pp. 365 ff.) describes the conflicting and complementary characteristics of aggressive strength and gentle saintliness. Hegel contrasts *Begriff* (philosophical, rational understanding, and abstract differentiation) with *Vorstellung* (representation and religious expression)—(Coreth, p. 988). Weber (1958, p. 332) opposes restlessness to peace; Arapura (1972) anxiety to tranquility. Husserl contrasts objectivity and scientific rationalism with subjectivity and human expressivity (Poole, pp. 69, 84). Ian Barbour (1971, pp. 219–22) applies the concepts of linguistic analysis to the language *about* religion ('spectator language'), such as the sociology and psychology of religion) and the language *of* religion ('actor language', in which a centre of loyalty and commitment to religion is assumed).

There is considerable difference between these dichotomies, but they have one thing in common: one of the pair fits in the instrumental/rational/scientific sphere, the other in the integrative/expressive/religious sphere.

The dialectic relation between these two spheres is characterized by both conflict and complementarity. Complementarity is usually clearly noted, but the references to conflict are relatively few. Yet the conflict between, for instance, observing and practising religion should be articulated. The difference is rather similar to the one between talking about love and being in love, analysing a piece of art and creating it. Protagonists of specific religious positions have often resented the aloof and neutral bisecting of their faith. The greater the commitment, the greater the resentment generally is. Christian sectarians provide abundant examples. But so does for instance the Indian sage, Aurobindo, when he scathingly remarks:

> [The attempts of the rational mind] to explain religion have resulted in the compilation of an immense mass of amazingly ingenious perversions, such as certain pseudo-scientific attempts to form a comparative Science of Religion. It has built up in the approved modern style immense facades of theory with stray bricks of misunderstood facts for their material. (Gandhi, 1950, p. 44).

A modern religious movement, such as Transcendental Meditation, compares the discussion of one's mantra (slogan-like prayer formula) with pulling the seed out to see how it is growing, and Needleman makes the same point rather forcefully when he says that hearing about one's religion, rather than practising it, is to be compared with millions of people suffering from a painful disease and gathering together to hear someone read a textbook of medical treatment . . . without undergoing the treatment (Needleman, 1970, p. 138, pp. 16–17).

Atheists and scholars make very similar observations. Aldous Huxley (1964, p. 33) heartily agrees with the Wordsworth statement about the meddling intellect which takes the mystery out of Reality, mis-shapes the beauteous forms of things, and murders to dissect. Mary Douglas (1969, p. 63) accuses the structural anthropologists of doing so much semantic chopping of myth that 'much of its meaning gets lost'. Werner Sombart compares the nations who analyse their myths with the little girl who took her doll apart to see what it was like inside, thereby for ever destroying its usefulness (van der Leeuw, 1948, p. 22). The psychiatrist, Wheelis, muses that insight is only a sorry substitute for absolute value, that extended awareness is both cause and effect of the loss of identity, and that the examination of mores makes them relative (p. 163, 21, 101). The philosopher

Heidegger denies that there is much redemptive value in accepting or even believing his theorizing (Spier, p. 37).

Obviously all these remarks also apply to our social scientific approach of religion. There is an inevitable bias and partiality in the very fact of observation. Analysing religious phenomena means that one observes them from a specific point of view always distinct from other points of view, including the 'insider' or 'believer's' perspective. Apart from the fact that the observer's stance is necessarily partial through the very aloofness inherent in the method, there is always the danger, in scientific enterprise, of making one's perspective into a world-view in which the researcher has invested a great deal of his emotions.

The reductionism, such as reducing of religious phenomena to sociological variables, of which social scientists are so often accused is generally nothing but a sacralized perspective, but with the maturation of the social sciences, the necessity to believe strongly in the perspective may be less urgent. The hostility which the sociologist of religion sometimes encounters from the religious practitioners basically represents the clash of competing, sacralized perspectives. It is impossible completely to resolve this competition. The social scientist can only minimize it by avoiding the sacralization of his own perspective.

And yet our very definition is a bias, in that it draws the attention to identity as a basic need. A religious practitioner would turn it all around and would start from the opposite point of view: his identity is shaped, interpreted by his religion. He is what he is because of his religious beliefs. Identity is secondary and a by-product. Both the social scientific approach of this study, and the theological approach are biased perspectives. Even our emphasis on dialectic and interdependence will only partly modify the contrast of perspectives.

However, the advance of the scientific scholars of religion in the 1970s, over their precursors in the nineteenth century, lies in their greater care with the ever-present potentiality of perspectives being sacralized. This care is evident in the writings of some of the British scholars who contributed to Bryan R. Wilson's book *Rationality* (1970). It is also evident in Evans-Pritchard's discussion of Nuer religion where he writes that one's own beliefs have an inevitable effect on the way one feels, thinks, and writes about the beliefs of others (1956, p. vii; also 1965, p. 109). Another British scholar,

Ninian Smart (1973, p. 7), even grants that being a saint is more important than studying religion.

By contrast the great demystifiers of the nineteenth century (see for this characterization Ricoeur, 1973) roguishly and blunderingly sacralized the perspective of selfhood (Feuerbach), of the economic variable (Marx), of the will to power (Nietzsche), of sexuality (Freud)—all in the name of a greatly superior science, and to the detriment of a correspondingly inferior religion. These somewhat naïve approaches are not likely to persist once the basic dialectic between instrumental and integrative symbols is taken seriously and the intricate workings of the dialectic are diagnosed.

How is myth related to symbol? One can take myth, as Ricoeur (1972, p. 316) does, as a symbol developed into narrative form, but we prefer to regard it as a new synthesis of the thesis of integrative, and the antithesis of instrumental, symbols. Precisely because of this synthesis, it reconciles, anchors emotionally, and dramatically enacts a basic cultural conflict. Its function is therefore very similar to that of integrative symbols and dissimilar to the one of instrumental symbols, however much it absorbs and digests these in the structure of its narrative.

A good example of the synthesizing function of myth is the story of the irrational adventures of a mighty Indian sage, Mārkandeya (Zimmer, pp. 35 ff.). At the beginning of the myth, cosmic order deteriorates. Lust and evil have won from enlightenment. But Vishnu devoures the sterile chaos. Inside Vishnu wanders a holy man, Mārkandeya. He is many thousand years old. In the course of his aimless, unending, wandering he slips out of Vishnu's mouth, falls in the dark ocean, and despairs of life. But then he becomes aware of the sleeping god who swallows him, and restores him to the harmonious world within. The essence of the myth lies in the union of the incompatibles of chaos and order, creation and destruction, evolution and dissolution, divine vision and terror of the void, through Māyā, the energy wielded by Vishnu.

The persistence of a myth depends on the kind of meaning that has been attributed to the figures and objects it comprises. Tobacco smoke (Lévi-Strauss, 1966) can be nothing but a name of an observable phenomenon, but it can also, in addition, become the carrier of a fundamental cultural notion. We use 'symbol' therefore in two different senses: (a) the carrier of the fundamental notion; and (b) the notion itself, lying both latently and loosely behind the object.

We use the word 'loosely' advisedly, as the notion may jump from one carrier to another, or in advanced societies, may even stand independently in its naked abstractness. It was in this second sense that we discussed symbols dealing with notions of integration and notions of instrumentality.

This capacity of the fundamental notion loosely to jump from one carrier to another is, I think, what Lévi-Strauss means when he uses the word *bricolage* (1962, p. 26). Bricolage is the improvisation of the mythical message out of handy materials that happened to be lying around. The message made from these improvised materials is logically constructed out of binary oppositions (Lévi-Strauss, 1967, p. 226), or to say it in our terms—the dialectic between notions of integration and instrumentality follows a pattern, however much the carriers or concretizations of these notions seem to be randomly distributed. A myth, then, is the synthesis, or crystallization, as Lévi-Strauss (ibid.) calls it, of diverse cultural elements around a suitable symbolic core.

In this crystallization process, Lévi-Strauss underrates the expressive/emotive element. Myth may arouse strong aesthetic emotion he says (Jakobson and Lévi-Strauss, p. 202), and forms the bridge between emotive experience and rational thought (1967, pp. 192–3). Yet, in his analysis, he disregards emotions, as consequences that can explain nothing, or as results of the impotence of the mind. He accuses Durkheim of reducing totemism to a sentimental basis (1963, p. 71). He scoffs at attempts to reduce intellectual processes to inarticulate emotional drives, and underestimates commitment in relation to myth (1958, p. 50; 1966a, p. xlviii). Of course, to reduce emotional drives to intellectual processes, as Lévi-Strauss appears to be doing, will not do either. A dialectical, rather than a reductive, relationship between these two appears better to reflect and describe the social reality of myth.

The very durability of a myth depends on its capacity to arouse a common commitment, and emotionally to anchor a system of meaning. Myths relativize discordance through emotional sublimation and provide objectification of basic experiences through emotional displacements. These experiences rather than the pleasure of playing a game of cerebral gymnastics motivate the emergence of myth.

The salience of emotion for the formation and existence of myth has been brought out by a number of scholars. Wundt (1967) writes of myth as an expression of social consciousness readily accessible to the changing influence of emotions and affections. Cassirer (1955, p. 69) expressly points to its non-intellectual, intuitive character: myth is 'an intuitive unity preceding and underlying all the explanations contributed by discursive thought'—a point that he makes more strongly in later works. In *An Essay on Man* (1954, p. 102) myths are described as 'impregnated with emotional qualities', and in the posthumously published *The Myth of the State* (1946, p. 27) he described myths as sprouting forth from deep human emotion of which they were the expression. Klapp takes a similar position and severely criticizes the positivistic fallacy to reduce symbols of the type found in myths to discursive reference (p. 325). Ellul (1971, p. 86) notes the capacity of myths to evoke feelings instinctively, and to arouse intuitive identification.

MYTH AND SOCIAL IDENTITY

Interwoven with the above account of the construction of myth has been a variety of remarks touching on the issue of what myth does for a society, which we now pursue in greater detail.

Since myths provide the fitting contour for existence, and so hold arbitrariness and meaninglessness at bay, they contribute to the integration of a society. The anthropologist Radcliffe-Brown regards the need for conformity in order to safeguard the cohesion of society as the major utility of myth. Myths, he says,

> serve to express certain ways of thinking and feeling about the society and its relation to the world of nature, and thereby to maintain these ways of thought and feeling and pass them on to succeeding generations. (1948, p. 405.)

Malinowski denies that myths are idle tales to satisfy intellectual curiosity: they are a hard-worked active force, a narrative resurrection of a primeval reality, and a pragmatic charter of primitive faith and moral wisdom (1954, p. 101). They are the dogmatic backbone of primitive civilization, determining the present life, fates, and activities of mankind, supplying man with the motive for ritual and moral actons (1954, p. 108).

Lévi-Strauss is often credited with an altogether new approach to the study of myth. He criticized the idea that mythology reflected social structure and social relations, and that it provided an outlet for repressed feelings. These interpretations were 'too easy' . . . 'a clever dialectic will always find a way to pretend that a meaning has been unravelled' (1958, p. 51). Instead, he proposed the structuralist method, which entailed breaking up a myth into constituent units, arranged in lines or columns, to decode the hidden message. He maintained that each level of meaning always refers to some other level, whichever way the myth is read (1970, p. 340).

Mythical thought to him portrays the nature of reality, simplifies and organizes 'the diversity of empirical experience in accordance with the principle that no factor of diversity can be allowed to operate for its own purposes in the collective undertaking of signification' (1970, p. 341). Mythical thought always progressed according to the Hegelian logic of thesis, antithesis, and synthesis. It mediated, reconciled, and resolved binary oppositions. Thus, Lévi-Strauss used the word 'dialectical' to describe the relationship between myth and empirical facts (1969, p. 29).

In fact, the approach of Lévi-Strauss hardly differs from the wider functional approaches to religion and myth. The basic premise regarding the integrating function of myth is implicitly reinforced in all Lévi-Strauss's work. The difference between functionalists and structuralists consists primarily in that they answer different questions: 'What does myth do for society?' and 'What are the universals in the composition of myth?' respectively. As soon as they move into one another's area they tend to agree.

Not only does Lévi-Strauss underestimate the emotional factor in the emergence and acceptance of myth, but his frame of reference is not large enough to see myth as one amongst several other possible ways of sacralizing definitions of reality. His thinking is not applied to modern religious phenomena, nor does he pay much attention to the growing capacity of increasingly better-educated people to think in abstract terms. One might plausibly argue that the theoretical advance in the sociology of religion lies in the direction of the analysis of sacralizing processes, or of the emergence of religious phenomena, rather than by the more static analysis of structure.

THEOLOGY

Are these observations of myth relevant for present-day theological elaborations?

Throughout this volume we have struggled to answer the question: 'Why are sects and sectarian/evangelical forms of Christianity
in modern society so viable?' By looking at some fundamental theological themes of these groups, we may adduce reasons for their
relative success.

Compared with the more liberal sections of the theological spectrum the orthodox sectarians continue to occupy themselves with the
traditional concepts. In contrast to liberalism, the binary oppositions
in all the theologizing and preaching of these groups revolve around
the themes of sin and salvation. Altogether different terminology
may be used. Very concretely Adam, the Fall, Pharaoh, Goliath, the
scapegoat, any moral aberration, pork, the tower of Babel, or the
crucifixion, may represent sin. Or more abstractly, sin may be
represented under the guise of man's disobedience, self-sufficiency,
anxiety, predicament, confusion, arrogance, hell, etc. Vice versa,
paradise, exodus, Boaz, the Messiah, Moses, God, Mary, the millennium, the resurrection, righteousness, grace, or angels, may represent salvation.

In the manner of Lévi-Strauss we may similarly postulate with
good reason that in this theologizing and preaching there is often
a hierarchical build-up, for example, from Ruth, the stranger, and
Boaz, the native, to the danger of rejection and the desirability of
acceptance, to the idea that God's work of salvation from man's
predicament and sin finds its climax in Jesus Christ, who became sin
so that man could be saved. Similar patterns can be detected in most
sectarian/evangelical sermons with God or Christ at the synthesizing
apex of the argument, or God as the *coincidentia oppositorum* (Simmel, 1959, p. 17).

There are, of course, differences from the primitive myths we
discussed earlier. There is a much more abstract level of discourse.
Concrete, modern, situations, or concretizations of symbols, may be
convenient points of departure, but the elaborations can much earlier
and much longer take place on a plateau of vague images and
thought alone.

Another difference is that the basic underlying theme of sin and
salvation deals less with the antithesis of nature (disorder) and culture (order), as Lévi-Strauss (incorrectly?) has it for his myths, than
with the theme of order and disorder within culture itself. After all,
man's autonomy, arrogance, sin, etc., is a threat to the social and
cultural, rather than to the natural, order. It is not nature which is

by definition disorderly and chaotic, and culture which is by definition orderly and systematic. Lévi-Strauss's intellectualistic bias may show up in his underestimation of the integrating, orderly elements of physical nature and evolution, and his overestimation of its disintegrating, threatening characteristics. We believe that there is a dialectic between adaptation and integration or instrumentality and identity both in the evolution of genetic and symbolic materials.

Sectarian sermons may be as effective as they are because they deal essentially with these basic themes of sin and salvation, disorder and order, rational autonomy and faith (integration). Their effectiveness may also lie in their capacity to anchor this theology in the emotions of its adherents through the note of contagious conviction in praying and preaching. As in mythical narratives, the familiar view of man's place in existence is reinforced in a kaleidoscopic variety of ways and with an impressive array of theological subtleties.

It is through the kaleidoscopic diversity, and yet the underlying similarity, of the dialectical theme, that sectarian preaching differs from its liberal counterpart and even more radically from, for example, the scientific analysis of religion. In a simple-minded, direct, parsimonious, fashion, scientific analysis regards its job as done, once the basic truth has been clarified and presented. The distinctiveness of myth and of sectarian preaching lies in their constant reiteration of a basic truth with whatever variations of the narration. Myth in particular, and religious activities in general, always reinforce definitions of reality. The scientific analysis of religion does the opposite: it hesitatingly builds up an argument, ready to surrender or qualify the 'tentative' truth at any time.

MYTH AND MODERN STRUCTURES

In science too, emotions are invested in specific conceptions and notions. Specific theories, for instance about genetic mutations or psychoanalysis, are defended with great ardour and corresponding lack of appreciation for counter-arguments. Perhaps this narrating and sacralizing of scientific positions has caused some scholars to speak of the myth of science. Plato recognized the indispensability of myth to science, and Tillich (1966, p. 25) elaborates this observation by saying that myth is 'an essential element of everything in the intellectual and cultural sphere'. Tillich goes even further by calling science myth-creative, because 'concepts like evolution, will to power, life, etc., have a mythical character. They no longer serve only for the construction of the empirical order, but rather indicate the transcendent presuppositions of this order' (1966, p. 24). Tillich uses the concept of myth too widely for our taste. Yet he is correct, if he means to say that there is a tendency towards self-sacralization ('myth-creation' in his language) in the assumptions of science. Warner (1961, p. 103) and more specifically Ellul detect all-embracing, motivating mythical foundations in history and science. The role of myth is 'to make a fact meaningful', says Ellul (1970, p. 18): as we should say, the role of myth is to sacralize perceptions or definitions of reality.

The mythical character of science is taken for granted by other scholars who condemn it as 'self-contradictory and unempirical' and insist that 'the destiny of even the scientific world can be thematized in terms of religious symbols' (Gilkey, pp. 96–7).

The mythical character of Marxism has also been successfully unearthed. Eliade thinks that Karl Marx carried on 'one of the great eschatological myths of the middle Eastern and Mediterranean world' (1967, p. 25). The proletariat, representing the elect, redeems society. As in the Judaeo-Christian eschatology history has an absolute goal: a classless society and a Golden Age without tension (p. 26).

The myth of progress with its basic and optimistic confidence in the goodness of history is discerned 'as the most dominant and characteristic article in the creed of modernity' (Reinhold Niebuhr, 1948, p. 171). History is fulfilment according to this myth, in contrast with traditional Christian theology which designates the end of history as 'both judgment and fulfilment' (ibid., p. 173). Progress is also often called a faith, a provider of meaning beyond the reach of discursive understanding, a creator of gods (Wagar, p. 7).

The fundamental myth of rebirth and reconciliation has been discerned in virtually all of Shakespeare's plays (Weisinger, p. 133), while McLuhan (p. 290) speaks about the myths of Hollywood, Madison Avenue, and the mass media. Ingmar Bergman's films represent, for Progoff (p. 195), encompassing images of life, living myths, 'true beyond all statements of truth'. Others have found resemblances between art, play, and myth. Huizinga thinks of myths as rooted in the primeval soil of play (p. 23). Cassirer (1955, pp. 260–1) says that art attempts to reconcile image and meaning, and is actually more successfuly than religion in doing so. Lévi-Strauss (1970, pp. 15–16) thinks that music overcomes the contradiction between historical, enacted time, and a permanent constant, and likens the structure of music to the structure of myth.

It is not accidental that so many have seen links between myth and art, or between myth and taken-for-granted ideologies. All have an essentially integrative, sublimating or reinforcing function. The distinction between art and myth lies generally in the medium they employ to achieve this integration. Myth sacralizes, insulates basic notions and sentiments in 'don't touch sentiments', whereas art and play enact and engage. Yet this distinction too is somewhat doubtful. The elements of acting out (ritual) and reiteration (myth) are prominent in art and play as well.

DREAMS AND PERSONAL IDENTITY

What myth does for social identity, the dream does for personal identity. Campbell (1949, p. 19) puts it as follows: 'Dream is the personalized myth, myth the depersonalized dream . . . in the dream the forms are quirked by the peculiar troubles of the dreamer, whereas in myth the problems and solutions shown are directly valid for all mankind.' In dreams, as in myths, the reliving (or rather re-ordering) of experiences has integrating consequences; '. . . dreams help a person assimilate the events of the day by re-running some of them and comparing them with previous experience before filing the lot away in the memory banks' (Watson, pp. 234–235).

As in myths, in dreams also, seemingly unrelated materials are brought into a common structure. In dreams, too, fundamental notions loosely jump from one carrier to another. The saliency of hidden factors is brought to the surface in dreams as in myths. Likewise, they lend themselves readily to the analysis of latent functions. Non-rational, emotional forces are deeply involved in their composition. This functional similarity between myth and dream is probably a major reason why, in primitive societies, religious meaning was attached to dreams, and why sometimes dreams were associated with the flight of the soul or the essence of personality.

Unlike myths, dreams sometimes initiate and legitimate a specific mundane decision. Thus a dream might prompt an individual's decision to go on an expedition in North American primitive societies. Yet, dreams like myths legitimate traditions, legality, and patterns of authority in the same Indan tribes (Müller, p. 171).

Psychologists in particular have stressed the link between dream and myth. Jung (1917, p. 23; 1972, p. 63) relates myth to 'dream thinking' which to him is the reliving of original observation. He takes over Abraham's remark that myth is a remnant of the infantile mind of a people, and that dream is the myth of the individual (1912, p. 26). This was of course also Freud's position (Freud, 1938, p. 954; de Waal, p. 175). The thesis that myth does for social identity what the dream does for personal identity is well illustrated by Jung's analysis of a dream of one of his patients.

The patient (an intellectual and scientist) dreamed that he was entering a solemn house 'of inner composure of self-collection'. In this house he heard the same voice that he had heard in many other dreams. The voice said: 'What thou art doing is dangerous. Religion is not a tax which thou payest in order to get rid of the woman's image, for this image is indispensable. Woe to those who use religion as a substitute for the other side of the soul's life . . . (religion is) the ultimate accomplishment added to every other activity of the soul. . . .' When the patient left the house he had a vision of a flaming mountain and an unquenchable sacred fire (Jung, 1972, pp. 42, 43).

Jung then explained the dream by saying that the suppression of the woman's image (we would say the expressive, integrative side of personality) reflected the patient's persistent avoidance of his emotional needs. The patient was afraid that these needs would get him into trouble and into 'responsibilities, such as love, devotion, loyalty, confidence, emotional dependence and general submission to the soul's needs'. These things had 'nothing to do with science or an academic career; and, moreover, the word "soul" was nothing but an intellectual obscenity, not to be touched with a barge pole' (pp. 50–1). If we interpret Jung freely, we might say that by suppressing this integrating element, the individual might create the very divisiveness and neuroses which would cause him to consult a psychoanalyst in the first place. To Jung, the denial of the voice or the unquenchable fire was the very cause of the neurotic condition, and the acceptance of the sacredness of the unquenchable fire, 'the *conditio sine qua non* of his cure' (p. 52).

Generally the psychoanalysts tend to think about dreams as resolving the conflict between unconscious, or latent, forces, and conscious or manifest forces. This has often led some to assert the dubious proposition that awareness integrates. It is safer, and closer to the facts, to assume that conflict occurs between the aggressive/rational side of personality and the integrative/emotional side, and that the *anima* (or female/emotional figure) in male dreams and the *animus* (or male/aggressive figure) in female dreams, are *par excellence* compensating mechanisms for greater wholeness. It is probably this reconciling, compensating, unifying function of the dream that has led some analysts of dreams to claim that they have found basic religious processes in them, and to even call dreams 'the language of God' (Sanford, p. 212).

Yet the tendency of some psychologists to equate dream and myth is much too simple. If the basic function of myth is to integrate a culture it must of necessity constrain personality. Dreams mitigate the very problems of constraint that myth exacerbates. Myths reconcile social tensions, dreams the personal ones. Yet in reconciling tensions, myths, by implication, often articulate and clarify social expectations. In reconciling individual tensions, dreams bring to the surface the very repressions necessary for the value structure of a society, even if it be conceded that the function of myth called 'impulse repression' did not altogether escape the psychoanalysts (Kluckhohn, 1968, p. 138).

Dreams have also been seen as similar in intention to ritual. Both serve 'a double and contradictory function: they release and communicate dangerous thoughts and emotions; but at the same time they disguise and transform them so that the element of danger is contained and to some extent dealt with. An effective ceremony protects society from destructive forms of conflict; an effective dream protects the sleeper from anxiety' (Bott, p. 206).

SUMMARY

Myth sacralizes by recurrent narration. The further back in evolutionary history one goes, the more the narration consists of concrete elements. Yet behind these elements, even in primitive culture, are fundamental notions of integration/identity and instrumentality/ adaptation. Myths sacralize through the emotional anchorage of integrative reconciliations, but they can do so only through the presentation of the binary opposition with instrumental symbolism. It is in the repetitive presentations and representations that the reconciling function of myth resides.

Sectarian and evangelical theology also revolves around the analogous theme of sin and salvation, alienation and integration, or disorder and order. The effectiveness of this branch of Christianity may very well reside in its loyalty to this theme, and the kaleidoscopic diversity with which the theme is dramatized over and over again.

What myths do for social identity, dreams do for personal identity. Here too fundamental notions may jump loosely from one concrete carrier to another. Here, too, disconnected experiences are re-ordered into an emotionally anchored unit.

Chapter XVIII

Conclusion

Concentrating as heavily as we have done on the sacralization process contains the risk of a conservative bias. One cannot help but be impressed by the intricate sophistication of the process even if one has to extrapolate and speculate to complement one's partial understanding. Yet change is the order of the day. Change has again and again clumsily trampled underfoot the refined web of sacralizations woven around peoples and societies. To account for change and to check the conservative bias we have adopted a framework of countervailing processes: an inexorable tendency towards conservation and integration is cross-cut by a similar inexorable tendency towards change and differentiation. These basic inexorable processes are conditioned by a whole variety of forces. Change is facilitated by culture contact, military conquests, trade, death, scepticism, and man's feverish search for independence from, and mastery of, his physical environment, etc. Stability is facilitated by social control, daily routines, customs, habits, like-seek-like motivation, play, art, sacralization, etc.

There is nothing eternal about the dialectic between these 'inexorable' processes. Both too much stability, and too much change, can wreck a system. The dialectic as such seems to be a prerequisite for the viability and survival of personal, group, or social identity. Too much oscillation in either direction can jolt everything out of kilter.

Religion, or whatever sacralizes identity, has been put squarely on the stabilizing side of the dialectic. It operates similarly to the white blood corpuscle which consumes the intruding germ, so stabilizing the system. But in the complex world of the psyche or of culture, change can never be completely stilled. The versatility and adaptability of man's symbolic inventions make that apparent. The past is both irrevocable and unique. Religion therefore operates more as the oyster that adjusts itself to the intruding grain of sand by coating it with nacre, rather than as the white blood corpuscle that demolishes the germ. Conversion, charisma, and the rites of birth, initiation, marriage, and death are all essentially mechanisms for incorporating, rather than for annihilating, change. All of them desacralize (or emotionally strip) a previous identity, and sacralize (or emotionally weld) a new one. Conversion does this for personal identity in the relatively unstructured situation, in the same way that charisma does it for social identity. The rites of passage, on the other hand, do it in more structured settings where change is both predictable and inevitable.

Yet religion is not just reactive, as Marx would have it, or as is implied in the more modern deprivation theories of religion. The naïvety and arrogance of these perspectives on religion consist in the assumption that change need not be embedded in order; that change occurs without its dialectic with stability. Not only does the oyster have to incorporate the grain of sand for the sake of survival, but it also contributes to the ecological system of which it is part. This, we think, was Weber's point.

In spite of his own cluster of biases, Weber saw that change was also conditioned by the sacralized perspectives on the world in which one exists. Without a specific kind of religious ethic at specific points of history, Weber appeared to say, a specific kind of change was highly unlikely, if not impossible. His life's work consisted in proving this one, major, point. Weber perhaps overstressed the role of the Calvinistic doctrine of calling as the single, most powerful contributing factor to the development of rational capitalism. We think, rather, that the relativization of the mediating, ecclesiastical structures not only freed the forces of individualism, but also facilitated the spirit of competition between individuals. Man's reliance on social rewards was reduced in significance by the illusionless view of man. This devaluation was made possible by overloading the transcendental point of reference with personal control functions, and this concentration, in turn, facilitated the sacralization of marginality, with profound consequences for the development of modern economic, political, and scientific sub-systems. Yet in overloading, and in sacralizing marginality, the commitment link to the transcendental frame of reference inevitably snapped for large proportions of the Western population, thereby letting the forces of differentiation, alienation, anomie, and meaninglessness ostensibly run amuck.

We purposely say 'ostensibly'. Society appears to be no different from the ant-heap disturbed by the horse's hoofs. In both the ant-heap and society, feverish reconstruction and reintegration begin as soon as destruction has taken place. The difference between the ant-heap and society is that in the latter both the forces of destruction and reconstruction are much more latent, complex, and invisible. Therefore, 'ostensibly' the forces of differentiation, alienation, anomie, and meaninglessness run amuck, whereas actually at the very heart of technocratic empires, or the societies in which they are embedded, reintegration has already begun. The problem is that our tools for discerning these latent processes are still inadequate. Guessing and speculating complement inadequate knowledge.

Yet, without the daily routines, stable hierarchies, the personal loyalties, and the emotional satisfactions of speaking on a similar wavelength, our technocratic empires would have succumbed long ago to the forces of rationality and efficiency that originally produced them. Semi-sacred formulas such as 'free enterprise', 'democracy', 'rational scepticism' and 'objectivity' have emerged at the heart of some of the sub-systems of modern societies, such as the economy, polity, and science. It is obvious, too, that in modern Western societies, a great deal of anomic potential has been siphoned off and absorbed by the family, sects, churches, fraternal, service, sports, and mutual interest groups, etc. Particularly when these groups are closely knit, they become buffers between individual and society. They are often the defenders of social values *vis-à-vis* the individual, and the protectors of individuals against social alienation.

It is at this point that Durkheim's theory of the integrative function of religion for society has to be both revised and elaborated. The correction is necessary because the integration/sacralization at the level of self or group may have a disintegrating/desacralizing effect on the wider social whole. As a result of his focus on primitive society, Durkheim operated too exclusively on the social level without paying the necessary attention to the dialectical conflicts between the parts and the whole in modern complex societies. Sacralization takes place at a variety of potentially, if not actually, conflicting levels. The survival of universal religions, therefore, does not only depend on the viability of the cultural identity which they sacralize, but also on their capacity to mute, as well as to motivate, individuals; to constrain, as well as to co-opt, recalcitrant groups; to reform, as well as to reinforce, the social whole.

This elaboration of Durkheim is, however, too simple. Modern societies consist of a cross-stitching network of pockets of meaning, definitions of reality, of identities not easily reduced to a simple self-group-society continuum. There is a continual shifting and changing of boundaries, even within the loosely grouped categories of the continuum. And this is not altogether without significance for the patterns of sacralization that are available. It is for this reason, that the modern world sometimes has the appearance of a cemetery of discarded and stunted forms of sacredness. The identity to be sacralized has often prove to be too slippery an entity to be an appropriate vehicle of stability.

The continued and increasing strength of evangelicalism, sectarianism, and verticalism in the predominantly Christian West is not foreign to this development. It seems to represent an age-old interpretation of existence that modernity has in no way rendered less viable, if only because the themes of sin and salvation, alienation and integration, and disorder and order, are still pertinent to man's most basic experiences.

These age-old themes seem to be extremely tenacious, however often generations of rationalists have attempted to bury them contemptuously and prematurely. The cemetery of discarded forms of sacredness may contain the graves of numerous causes, liberalisms, rationalisms, but not that of orthodox sectarianism. In those newer Western nations where a tertiary education has increasingly come within the reach of the general public, the differences between the educated and non-educated on indicators of traditional, Christian, religiosity, are remarkably small. This suggests that theological cognitions have much less to do with the viability of Western religion than most nineteenth-century and many twentieth-century scholars thought. The well-educated do not appear to be particularly upset by the scientific crudity of Biblical religion, if only because, for them, the meaning of biblical stories and theologies lies on the wider plain of emotionally anchored expressions of existence.

This observation is less true for those older European countries where both the intelligentsia and the proletariat have evolved a cocoon of separate accents and life-styles in comparison with the older bourgeoisie who felt that they had a monopoly of Christianity. The humanistic rationalism of European intelligentsia, or the socialist fervour of the European proletariat, often became competing faiths, in a way that was much less true for the U.S.A. and Canada. There Christianity always remained a much more viable option, because class was never salient enough as a separate focus of identity to become separately sacralized.

This finally brings us to the subject of relevance. We have maintained that from the sociological point of view, the relevance of the sacralization process lies in extending institutionalization. Religion, we have said, stabilizes a system of meaning, reinforces a definition of reality, sacralizes identity. Its relevance therefore lies *both* in the interpretation of existence, for example, in the dramatization of the dialectic of sin and salvation, *and* in the healing or reconciling of a fragile identity—for example, social action among the disprivileged. This relevance for order seems to be essential for the viability of any religion, whether ancient or modern. And yet the order that is summed up in a religious frame of reference, and to which ultimate commitment is a prerequisite, may be relevant precisely because it is altogether different from mundane complexities and frustrations. An increasing degree of otherness seems to go together with the increasing economic and cultural complexity necessary for man's more complete mastery over nature. If the relevance of the Christian kind of 'otherness' is presently regarded as problematic in the modern West, both consequence and cause of this state of affairs may lie in present-day social anomie and personal alienation. Yet the search for identity on all the levels discussed in this study is a significant and forceful attempt to escape the predicament. The future therefore seems to lie with those religious commitments to order and identity that intricately and sensitively re-establish the social authority necessary for the safeguarding of pivotal social values (such as responsibility, charity, reliability, etc.) and yet involve sufficient individualism and personal motivation to keep the motor of human existence humming with a minimum of friction.

Bibliography

Editions cited are those available to the author.

AALL, Anathon, *Geschichte der Logosidee*, Frankfurt: Minerva, 1968.

ADORNO, T. W.; Frenkel-Brunswik, Else; Levinson, D. J.; Sandford, R. N., *The Authoritarian Personality*, New York: Harper, 1950.

AGNEW, Spiro, 'Agnew Advises Yale to Fire Its President', *The Milwaukee Journal*, 29 April 1970, p. 8.

ALLEN, Richard, *The Social Passion: Religion and Social Reform in Canada 1914-28*, Toronto: University of Toronto Press, 1971.

ALLPORT, Gordon W., *The Nature of Prejudice*, Garden City, New York: Doubleday, 1954.

—, *The Individual and His Religion*, New York: Macmillan, 1957.

—, *Personality and Social Encounter*, Boston: Beacon Press, 1960.

—, 'Behavioral Science, Religion and Mental Health', *Journal of Religion and Health*, Vol. 2, No. 3, April 1963, pp. 187–97.

ALMERICH, Paulina, 'Spain', in Mol, Hetherton and Henty (eds.), *Western Religion*, The Hague: Mouton, 1972, pp. 459–77.

AQUINAS, Thomas, *Summa Theologica*, New York: Random House, 1945.

ARAPURA, John G., 'Language and Knowledge: A Vedantic Examination of a Barthian Issue', in *Union Seminary Quarterly Review*, Vol. XXV, No. 2, Winter 1970, pp. 151–68.

—, *Religion as Anxiety and Tranquillity*, The Hague: Mouton, 1972.

—, 'Maya and the Discourse About Brahman', in Sprung, M. (ed.), *Two Truths in Buddhism and Vedanta*, Dordrecht, Holland: Reidel, 1973, pp. 109–21.

—, 'Some Special Characteristics of the Problem of *Sat* in Advaita Vedanta' (Unpublished paper), Hamilton, Ontario: McMaster University, 1974.

ARDREY, Robert, *The Territorial Imperative*, London: Collins, 1969.

—, *The Social Contract*, New York: Athenaeum, 1970.

ARÈS, Richard, 'Le Fait Religieux au Canada', in *Relations*, Issue 265, January 1963, pp. 11–13.

ARON, Raymond, *The Century of Total War*, Boston: Beacon Press, 1955.

—, *La Philosophie Critique de l'Histoire*, Paris: Vrin, 1969.

AUGUSTINE, *The Confessions*, London: Sheed and Ward, 1945 (first written in A.D. 399).

BAAL, J. van, *Symbols for Communication*, Assen: van Gorcum, 1971.

BABBAGE, S. Barton, *Hau Hauism: An Episode in the Maori Wars*, Wellington: Reed, 1937.

BARBER, Bernard, 'Acculturation and Messianic Movements', in Lessa, William, A. and Vogt, Evon Z. (eds.), *Reader in Comparative Religion*, New York: Harper, 1965 (originally published in 1941), pp. 506–9.

BARBOUR, Ian G., *Issues in Science and Religion*, New York: Harper, 1971.

BARCLAY, Harold B., 'A Lebanese Community in Lac La Biche, Alberta', in Elliott, Jean Leonard (ed.), *Immigrant Groups* (Vol. II of *Minority Canadians*), Scarborough, Ontario: Prentice-Hall, 1971, pp. 66–83.

BARON, Salo Wittmayer, *Modern Nationalism and Religion*, New York: Meridian, 1960 (first published in 1947).

BARTH, Karl and Thurneysen, Eduard, *Komm, Schöpfer Geist*, Munich: Kaiser Verlag, 1932.

BARTH, Karl, *The Doctrine of the Word of God* (*Church Dogmatics*, Vol. I, Part I), Edinburgh: Clark, 1936.

—, *Der Römerbrief*, Zürich: Zollikon, 1947.

BARTLEY, William Warren, *The Retreat to Commitment*, New York: Knopf, 1963.

—, *Morality and Religion*, London: Macmillan, 1971.

BATSON, C. Daniel; Beker, J. Christiaan; Clark, W. Malcolm, *Commitment Without Ideology*, Philadelphia: United Church Press, 1973.

BAUM, Gregory, 'Man in History: The Anthropology of Vatican II', in Dunphy, William (ed.), *The New Morality*, New York: Herder and Herder, 1967, pp. 157–73.

—, *Faith and Doctrine*, Paramus, N.J.: Newman Press, 1969.

BECKER, Ernest, *The Birth and Death of Meaning*, Glencoe, Illinois: The Free Press, 1962.

BECKER, Howard, *Through Values to Social Interpretation*, Durham, N.C.: Duke University Press, 1950.

BECKER, Howard and Barnes, Harry Elmer, *Social Thought from Lore to Science*, Washington: Harren Press, 1952.

BECKER, Howard, 'Notes on the Concept of Commitment', *American Journal of Sociology*, Vol. LXVI, July 1960, pp. 32–40.

BELLAH, Robert N., 'Durkheim and History', *American Sociological Review*, Vol. 24, 1959.

—, 'Religious Evolution', *American Sociological Review*, Vol. 29, 1964, pp. 358–74.

—, 'Epilogue: Religion and Progress in Modern Asia', in Bellah, Robert N. (ed.), *Religion and Progress in Modern Asia*, New York: Free Press, 1965, pp. 168–229.

—, 'The Sociology of Religion', in *International Encyclopaedia of the Social Sciences*, New York: Macmillan, 1968, Vol. 13, pp. 406–14.

—, *Tokugawa Religion*, New York: Free Press, 1969.

—, *Beyond Belief*, New York: Harper, 1970.

BEN-DAVID, Joseph, *The Scientist's Role in Society*, Englewood Cliffs, N.J.: Prentice-Hall, 1971.

BENDIX, Reinhard and Roth, Guenther, *Scholarship and Partisanship* (Essays on Max Weber), Berkeley, California: University of California Press, 1971.

BENNETT, John C., 'The Reformation of the Church', *Union Seminary Quarterly Review*, Vol. 19, No. 2, January 1964, pp. 99–105.

—, 'A Missing Dimension', *Christianity and Crisis*, Vol. 29, No. 16, 29 September 1969, pp. 241–2.

BENVENISTE, Emile, *Indo-European Language and Society*, London: Faber and Faber, 1973.

BERGEL, Egon Ernest, *Social Stratification*, New York: McGraw-Hill, 1962.

BERGER, Peter L., 'Charisma and Religious Innovation: The Social Location of Israelite Prophecy', *American Sociological Review*, Vol. 28, No. 5, December 1963, pp. 940–50.

—, *The Sacred Canopy*, Garden City, New York: Doubleday, 1967a.

—, 'A Sociological View of the Secularisation of Theology', *Journal for the Scientific Study of Religion*, Vol. VI, No.1, Spring 1967b, pp. 3–16.

—, *A Rumor of Angels*, Garden City, New York: Doubleday, 1969.

BERGER, Peter L. and Berger, Brigitte, *Sociology*, New York: Basic Books, 1972.

BERGER, Peter L. and Luckmann, Thomas, *The Social Construction of Reality*, London: Allen Lane The Penguin Press, 1967.

BERGSON, Henri, *The Two Sources of Morality and Religion*, New York: Holt, 1935.

BIBBY, Reginald W. and Brinkerhoff, Merlin B., 'The Circulation of the Saints: A Study of People Who Join Conservative Churches', *Journal for the Scientific Study of Religion*, Vol. 12, No. 3, September 1973, pp. 273–83.

—, 'Sources of Religious Involvement: Issues for Future Empirical Investigation', *Review of Religious Research*, Vol. 15, No. 2, Winter 1974, pp. 71–9.

BIRNBAUM, Norman, 'Conflicting Interpretations of the Rise of

Capitalism: Marx and Weber', *British Journal of Sociology*, Vol. IV, No. 2, June 1953, pp. 125–41.
—, *The Crisis of Industrial Society*, Oxford: Oxford University Press, 1969.
BOISEN, Anton T., *The Exploration of the Inner World*, New York: Harper, 1936.
BORKENAU, Franz, 'The New Morality and the New Theology', in Birnbaum, Norman and Lenzer, Gertrud (eds.), *Sociology and Religion*, Englewood Cliffs, N.J.: Prentice-Hall, 1969, pp. 282–92.
BOSSARD, James A. S., and Boll, Eleanor S., 'Ritual in Family Living', *American Sociological Review*, Vol. 14, August 1949, pp. 463–9.
BOTT, Elizabeth, 'Psychoanalysis and Ceremony', in Fontaine, J. S. La (ed.), *The Interpretation of Ritual*, London: Tavistock, 1972, pp. 205–37.
BOTTOMORE, T. B., *Sociology*, London: Unwin, 1962.
—, *Elites and Society*, Harmondsworth: Penguin, 1966.
BOUQUET, A. C., *Comparative Religion*, London: Penguin, 1954 (first published in 1942).
BRINTON, Crane, *The Shaping of the Modern Mind*, New York: New American Library of World Literature, 1958.
BRONOWSKI, J., *The Identity of Man*, Garden City, New York: Natural History Press, 1965.
BROWN, Norman O., *Life Against Death*, London: Routledge and Kegan Paul, 1959.
BROWNE, Lewis, *The World's Great Scriptures*, New York: Macmillan, 1956.
BROYLES, J. Allen, *The John Birch Society*, Boston, Massachusetts: Beacon Press, 1964.
BRUNER, Jerome S., 'Myth and Identity', in Murray, Henry A. (ed.), *Myth and Mythmaking*, New York: Braziller, 1960, pp. 276–87.
BRUNNER, Emil, *Das Gebot und die Ordnungen*, Zürich: Zwingli, 1939.
BRYCE, James, *Studies in History and Jurisprudence*, New York: Oxford University Press, 1901.
BUBER, Martin, *I and Thou*, Edinburgh: Clark, 1950.
BUCKLEY, Walter, 'Social Stratification and Social Differentiation', in *American Sociological Review*, Vol. 23, No. 4, August 1958, pp. 369–375.
BURCH, William R. Jr., 'Sectarian Rhetoric and the Survival of Uniqueness', in Webb, Stephen D. and Collette, John (eds.), *New Zealand Society* (Contemporary Perspectives), Sydney: Wiley, 1973, pp. 283–94.
BURCKHARDT, Jacob, *The Civilization of the Renaissance in Italy*, New York: Random House, 1954 (first published in 1860).

BURKE, Kenneth, *Permanence and Change*, Los Altos: Hermes, 1955.

BURKERT, Walter, *Homo Necans*, Berlin: de Gruyter, 1972.

BURRIDGE, K. O., 'Lévi-Strauss and Myth', in Leach, Edmund (ed.), *The Structural Study of Myth and Totemism*, London: Tavistock, 1969, pp. 91–115.

CAILLOIS, Roger, *L'Homme et le Sacré*, Paris: Gallimard, 1950.

—, *Man and the Sacred*, Glencoe, Illinois: Free Press, 1959.

CALLEY, Malcolm J., *God's People* (West Indian Pentecostal Sects in England), London: Oxford University Press, 1965.

CALVIN, John, *Institutes of the Christian Religion*, Vols. I–III, Edinburgh: Calvin Translation Society, 1845 (first published in 1536).

CAMPBELL, Joseph, *The Hero With a Thousand Faces*, New York: Pantheon, 1949.

CAMPBELL, Thomas C. and Fukuyama, Yoshio, *The Fragmented Layman*, Philadelphia: United Church Press, 1970.

CANNEGIETER, J. E., 'De geestelijke Structuur van Deventer', *Sociologisch Bulletin*, Vol. 12, 1958, No. 3, pp. 126–32.

CARRIER, Hervé, *The Sociology of Religious Belonging*, London: Darton, Longman and Todd, 1965.

CASSIRER, Ernst, *The Myth of the State*, New Haven: Yale University Press, 1946.

—, *An Essay on Man*, Garden City, New York: Doubleday, 1954 (first published in 1944).

—, *The Philosophy of Symbolic Forms*, Vol. II: *Mythical Thought*, New Haven: Yale University Press, 1955 (originally published in 1925).

CASTANEDA, Carlos, *Journey to Ixtlan* (the Lessons of Don Juan), New York: Simon and Schuster, 1972.

CAZENEUVE, Jean, *Les Rites et la Condition Humaine*, Paris: Presses Universitaires de France, 1958.

CHAN, Wing-tsit; Fārūqī, Isma'īl Rāgī al; Kitagawa, Joseph M.; Raju, P. T., *The Great Asian Religions*, New York: Macmillan, 1969.

CHANCE, Michael R. A. and Jolly, Clifford J., *Social Groups of Monkeys, Apes and Men*, New York: Dutton, 1970.

CHRISTIAN, William A. Jr., *Person and God in a Spanish Valley*, New York: Seminar Press, 1972.

CHRISTIANSEN, Palle, *The Melanesian Cargo Cult* (Millenarianism as a Factor in Cultural Change), Copenhagen: Akademisk Forlag, 1969.

CLARK, Elmer T., *The Small Sects in America*, Nashville: Cokesbury Press, 1937.

CLARK, S. D., *Church and Sect in Canada*, Toronto: University of Toronto Press, 1948.

—, *The Developing Canadian Community*, Toronto: University of Toronto Press, 1968.

CLARK, Walter Houston, *Chemical Ecstasy* (Psychedelic Drugs and Religion), New York: Sheed and Ward, 1969.

COHEN, Percy S., 'Theories of Myth', *Man*, Vol. 4, No. 3, September 1969, pp. 337–53.

COLE, William Graham, *Sex in Christianity and Psychoanalysis*, New York: Oxford University Press, 1955.

COLEMAN, James S., 'Loss of Power', *American Sociological Review*, Vol. 38, No. 1, February 1973, pp. 1–17.

COMTE, Auguste, *The Positive Philosophy*, New York: Blanchard, 1858.

COOLEY, Charles H., *Human Nature and the Social Order*, Glencoe, Illinois: Free Press, 1956a (first published in 1902).

—, *Social Organization*, Glencoe, Illinois: Free Press, 1956b (first published in 1909).

CORETH, E., 'Hegel, Georg Wilhelm Friedrich', in *New Catholic Encylopaedia*, Vol. VI, New York: McGraw-Hill, 1967, pp. 987–90.

COX, Harvey E., *The Secular City*, London: S.C.M. Press, 1965.

—, *The Feast of Fools*, Cambridge, Massachusetts: Harvard University Press, 1969.

—, 'The Ungodly City: A Theological Response to Jacques Ellul', *Commonweal*, 9 July 1971, pp. 354–5.

CREUZER, Friedrich, 'Der Mythos in seinem Verhältnis zum Symbol', in Kerényi, Karl (ed.), *Die Eröffnung des Zugangs zum Mythos*, Darmstadt: Wissenschaftliche Buchgesellschaft, 1967, pp. 44–58.

CRYSDALE, Stewart, *The Changing Church in Canada*, Toronto: United Church Publishing House, 1965.

CUMONT, Francois V. M., *Astrology and Religion Among the Greeks and Romans*, New York: Dover, 1960 (first published in 1912).

DAHRENDORF, Ralph, *Essays in the Theory of Society*, Stanford, California: Stanford University Press, 1968.

DAVIES, H., *Christian Deviations: The Challenge of the Sects*, London: S.C.M. Press, 1961.

DAVIS, Kingsley, *Human Society*, New York: Macmillan, 1948.

DAVIS, Kingsley, and Moore, Wilbert E., 'Some Principles of Stratification', in Coser, Lewis A. and Rosenberg, Bernard (eds.), *Sociological Theory*, New York: Macmillan, 1957, pp. 408–20.

DAWSON, Christopher, *Religion and Culture*, London: Sheed and Ward, 1949.

—, *Religion and the Rise of Western Culture*, Garden City, New York: Doubleday, 1958.

DE LEVITA, David J., *The Concept of Identity*, New York: Basic Books, 1965.

DEMERATH, N. J., *Social Class in American Protestantism*, Chicago: Rand McNally, 1965.

—, 'In a Sow's Ear: A Reply to Goode', *Journal for the Scientific Study of Religion*, No. 6, 1967, pp. 77–84.

DEMERATH, N. J. and Hammond, Phillip E., *Religion in Social Context*, New York: Random House, 1969.

DESCARTES, René, *Correspondance*, Tome VI, Paris: Presses Universitaires de France, 1956.

DESMONDE, William H., *Magic, Myth and Money*, Glencoe, Illinois: The Free Press, 1962.

DEWART, Leslie, *The Future of Belief*, New York: Herder and Herder, 1966.

DILISTONE, F. W. (ed.), *Myth and Symbol*, London: S.P.C.K., 1966.

DITTES, James E., 'Typing the Typologies. Some Parallels in the Career of Church–Sect and Extrinsic–Intrinsic', *Journal for the Scientific Study of Religion*, Vol. 10, No. 4, Winter 1971, pp. 375–83.

DOBBELAERE, Karel and Lauwers, Jan, 'Definition of Religion—A Sociological Critique', *Social Compass*, Vol. XX, No. 4, 1973, pp. 533–51.

DOUGLAS, Mary, *Purity and Danger*, New York: Praeger, 1966.

—, 'The Meaning of Myth, with special reference to "La Geste d'Asdiwa" ', in Leach, Edmund (ed.), *The Structural Study of Myth and Totemism*, London: Tavistock, 1969, pp. 49–68.

DUERR, Carl, *Management Kinetics*, New York: McGraw-Hill, 1971. (Excerpts are from *National Times*, 5–10 July 1971, pp. 23 and 26.)

DUMONT, Louis, *Homo Hierarchicus* (essai sur le système des castes), Paris: Gallimard, 1966.

DUNCAN, Hugh Dalziel, *Symbols and Social Theory*, New York: Oxford University Press, 1969.

DURKHEIM, Emile, *Suicide*, Glencoe, Illinois: Free Press, 1951 (first published in 1897).

—, *Elementary Forms of Religious Life*, Glencoe, Illinois: Free Press, 1954 (first published in 1912).

—, *The Division of Labor in Society*, Glencoe, Illinois: Free Press, 1964 (first published in 1893).

—, *The Rules of Sociological Method*, Glencoe, Illinois: Free Press, 1964a (first published in 1895).

—, 'The Dualism of Human Nature and its Social Conditions', in Wolff, Kurt (ed.), *Essays on Sociology and Philosophy*, New York: Harper, 1964b (first published in 1914), pp. 325–40.

DURKHEIM, Emile and Mauss, Marcel, *Primitive Classifications*, Chicago: University of Chicago Press, 1969 (first published in 1905).

DUTT, Nalinaksha, *Early Monastic Buddhism*, Calcutta: Oriental Book Agency, 1960.

DYNES, R. R., 'Church–Sect Typology and Socioeconomic Status', *American Sociology Review*, No. 20, 1955, pp. 555–60.

EIBL-EIBESFELDT, Irenäus, *Love and Hate*, London: Methuen, 1971.

EISENSTADT, S. N. (ed.), *The Protestant Ethic and Modernization*, New York: Basic Books, 1968.

EISTER, Alan W., 'Toward a Radical Critique of Church–Sect Typologizing', *Journal for the Scientific Study of Religion*, Vol. 6, No. 1, Spring 1967, pp. 85–90.

ELIADE, Mircea, *Patterns in Comparative Religion*, New York: Sheed and Ward, 1958.

—, 'Methodological Remarks on the Study of Religious Symbolism', in Eliade, Mircea (ed.) and Kitagawa, Joseph M. *The History of Religions* (Essays in Methodology), Chicago: University of Chicago Press, 1959, pp. 86–107.

—, *The Sacred and the Profane*, New York: Harcourt, Brace and World, 1959a.

—, *Shamanism*, New York: Pantheon, 1964 (first published in 1951).

—, *Rites and Symbols of Initiation*, New York: Harper, 1965.

—, *Myths, Dreams and Mysteries*, New York: Harper, 1967 (first published in 1957).

ELLUL, Jacques, *The Technological Society*, New York: Knopf, 1965.

—, *To Will and to Do*, Boston: Pilgrim Press, 1969.

—, *The Meaning of the City*, Grand Rapids, Michigan: Eerdmans, 1970.

—, *Autopsy of Revolution*, New York: Knopf, 1971.

ENROTH, Ronald; Ericson, Edward E.; Peters, C. Breckinridge, *The Jesus People* (old-time religion in the age of Aquarius), Grand Rapids, Michigan: Eerdmans, 1972.

ERASMUS, Charles J., *Man Takes Control*, Minneapolis: University of Minnesota Press, 1961.

ERIKSON, Erik H., 'The Problem of Ego Identity', in Stein, Maurice R.; Vidich, Arthur J.; White, David Manning (eds.), *Identity and Anxiety*, Glencoe, Illinois: Free Press, 1960, pp. 37–87.

—, *Young Man Luther*, New York: Norton, 1962.

—, *Childhood and Society*, New York, Norton, 1963 (first published in 1950).

—, *Insight and Responsibility*, New York: Norton, 1964.

—, *Identity—Youth and Crisis*, New York: Norton, 1968.

—, 'Identity, Psychosocial', in *International Encyclopaedia of the Social Sciences*, New York: Macmillan, 1968a, Vol. 7, pp. 61–5.

—, *Gandhi's Truth*, New York: Norton, 1969.

ERIKSON, Kai T., *Wayward Puritans*, New York: Wiley, 1966.

ESSIEN-UDOM, E. U., *Black Nationalism* (The Rise of the Muslims in the U.S.A.), Harmondsworth: Penguin, 1966.

ETKIN, William, *Social Behavior from Fish to Man*, Chicago: University of Chicago Press, 1967.

ETZIONI, Amitai, *The Active Society*, New York: Free Press, 1971.

EVANS-PRITCHARD, E. E., *Nuer Religion*, Oxford: Clarendon, 1956.

—, *Theories of Primitive Religion*, Oxford: Clarendon, 1965.

EVTUSHENKO, Evgeny, *A Precocious Autobiography*, New York: Dutton, 1963.

FALLDING, Harold, *The Sociological Task*, Englewood Cliffs, New Jersey: Prentice-Hall, 1968.

—, 'Canada', in Mol, Hetherton and Henty (eds.), *Western Religion, a Country by Country Sociological Enquiry*, The Hague: Mouton, 1972, pp. 101–15.

—, *The Sociology of Religion*, Toronto: McGraw-Hill Ryerson, 1974.

FANFANI, Amintore, *Catholicism, Protestantism and Capitalism*, London: Sheed and Ward, 1935.

FENN, Richard K., 'Toward a New Sociology of Religion', in *Journal for the Scientific Study of Religion*, Vol. 11, No. 1, March 1972, pp. 16–32.

FESTINGER, Leon and Riecken, Henry, *When Prophecy Fails*, Minneapolis, Minnesota: University of Minnesota Press, 1956.

FEUER, Lewis S., 'What is Alienation? The Career of a Concept', in Stein, Maurice and Vidich, Arthur (eds.), *Sociology on Trial*, Englewood Cliffs, New Jersey: Prentice-Hall, 1963, pp. 127–47.

FEUER, Lewis S. and Perrine, Mervyn W., 'Religion in a Northern Vermont Town: A Cross-Country Comparative Study', *Journal for the Scientific Study of Religion*, Vol. 5, No. 3, Fall 1966, pp. 367–382.

FEUERBACH, Ludwig, *The Essence of Christianity*, New York: Harper, 1957.

FINDLAY, J. N., *Hegel, A Re-examination*, London: Allen and Unwin, 1958.

FIRTH, Raymond, *Elements of Social Organization*, Boston: Beacon Press, 1963.

—, *Essays in Social Organization and Values*, London: Athlone, 1964.

—, *Rank and Religion in Tikopia*, London: Allen and Unwin, 1970.

FISCHOFF, Ephraim, 'The Protestant Ethic and the Spirit of Capitalism. The History of a Controversy', *Social Research*, Vol. XI, 1944, pp. 53–77.

FLETCHER, Joseph, *Situation Ethics: The New Morality*, Philadelphia: Westminster Press, 1966.

—, *Moral Responsibility: Situation Ethics at Work*, Philadelphia: Westminster Press, 1967.

FORTES, Meyer, 'Ritual and Office in Tribal Society', in Gluckman, Max (ed.), *Essays on the Ritual of Social Relations*, Manchester: University Press, 1962, pp. 53–88.

FOX, Robin, 'Totem and Taboo Reconsidered', in Leach, Edmund (ed.), *The Structural Study of Myth and Totemism*, London: Tavistock, 1969, pp. 161–78.

FRANK, Jerome D., *Persuasion and Healing*, Baltimore: Johns Hopkins Press, 1961.

FRANKL, Viktor, *Psychotherapy and Existentialism*, New York: Washington Square Press, 1967.

FRAZER, James G., *The Golden Bough*, New York: Macmillan, 1922.

FREI, G., 'Ekstase in Katholischer Schau', in Spoerri, Th. (ed.), *Beitrage zur Ekstase*, Basel: Karger, 1968, pp. 11–29.

FRENCH, Harold W., *The Ramakrishna Movement and the West*, Unpublished Ph.D. Thesis, McMaster University, Hamilton, 1972.

FREUD, Sigmund, *Totem and Taboo*, New York: Moffat, 1918.

—, *Basic Writings*, New York: Random House, 1938.

—, 'Obsessive Actions and Religious Practices', in *The Standard Edition of the Complete Psychological Works of Sigmund Freud*, London: Hogarth, 1959, Vol. IX (first published in 1907), pp. 117–27.

—, *The Future of an Illusion*, Garden City, New York: Doubleday, 1964.

—, *Civilization and Its Discontents*, London: Hogarth, 1972.

FRIJDA, N. H., *Emigranten, niet-emigranten*, The Hague: Staatsdrukkerij, 1960.

FROMM, Erich, *Psychoanalysis and Religion*, New York: Bantam Books, 1957.

—, *Escape from Freedom*, New York: Avon Books, 1965.

FUSTEL DE COULANGES, *The Ancient City*, Boston: Lee and Shepard, 1882.

GANDHI, Kishor, *Lights on Life-Problems* (Sri Aurobindo's views on important life-problems compiled and arranged from his writings), Bombay: Sri Aurobindo Circle, 1950.

GAUTHIER, Philippe, 'Notes sur l'étranger et l'hospitalité en Grèce et à Rome', *Ancient Society*, Vol. 4, 1973, pp. 1–21.

GEERTZ, Clifford, 'Ethos, World-View and the Analysis of Sacred Symbols', *The Antioch Review*, Vol. XVII, No. 4, December 1959, pp. 421–37.

—, 'Religion as a Cultural System', in Banton, Michael (ed.), *Anthropological Approaches to the Study of Religion*, London: Tavistock, 1966, pp. 1–46.

—, *Islam Observed*, New Haven: Yale University Press, 1968.

—, 'Religion: Anthropological Study', in *International Encyclopaedia of the Social Sciences*, New York: Macmillan, 1968a, Vol. 13, pp. 398–406.

—, *The Religion of Java*, New York: Free Press, 1969 (first published in 1960).

GELLNER, Ernest, 'Concepts and Society', in Wilson, Bryan R. (ed.), *Rationality*, New York: Harper, 1971, pp. 18–49.

GENNEP, Arnold van, *The Rites of Passage*, London: Routledge and Kegan Paul, 1960 (first published in 1908).

GEORGES, Robert A. (ed.), *Studies on Mythology*, Homewood, Illinois: Dorsey Press, 1968.

GERLACH, Luther P. and Hine, Virginia H., *People Power Change*, Indianopolis: Bobbs-Merrill, 1970.

GERTH, Hans H. and Martindale, Don, 'Preface', in Weber, Max, *Ancient Judaism*, Glencoe, Illinois: Free Press, 1952, pp. ix–xxvii.

GIBB, H. A. R., *Mohammedanism*, New York: Mentor Books, 1953.

GILKEY, Langdon, 'Biblical Symbols in a Scientific Culture', in Burhoe, Ralph Wendell (ed.), *Science and Human Values in the 21st Century*, Philadelphia: Westminster Press, 1971, pp. 72–98.

GILLISPIE, Charles Coulston, *The Edge of Objectivity*, Princeton: Princeton University Press, 1960.

GLATFELTER, Charles Henry, *The Colonial Pennsylvania German Lutheran and Reformed Clergymen*, Unpublished Ph.D. dissertation, Baltimore Md.: Johns Hopkins University, 1952.

GLOCK, Charles Y., 'Religion and the Integration of Society', *Review of Religious Research*, Fall 1960, pp. 49–62.

GLOCK, Charles Y. and Stark, Rodney, *Religion and Society in Tension*, Chicago: Rand McNally, 1965.

—, *Christian Beliefs and Anti-Semitism*, New York: Harper, 1966.

GLOCK, Charles Y.; Ringer, Benjamin B.; Babbie, Earl R., *To Comfort and to Challenge*, Berkeley, California: University of California Press, 1967.

GLOCK, Charles Y. (ed.), *Religion in Sociological Perspectives*, Belmont, California: Wardsworth, 1973, pp. 207–20.

GLUCKMAN, Max, *Rituals of Rebellion in South-East Africa*, Manchester: Manchester University Press, 1954.

—, 'Les Rites de Passage', in Gluckman, Max (ed.), *Essays on the Ritual of Social Relations*, Manchester: Manchester University Press, 1962, pp. 1–52.

GOFFMAN, Erving, *The Presentation of Self in Everyday Life*, Garden City, New York: Doubleday, 1959.

—, 'Characteristics in Total Institutions', in Stein, Maurice R., Vidich. Arthur J., White, David Manning (ed.), *Identity and Anxiety*, Glencoe, Illinois: Free Press, 1960, pp. 449–79.

GOLDBRUNNER, Josef, *Individuation* (A Study of the Depth Psychology of Carl Gustav Jung), New York: Pantheon, 1956.

GÖLDEL, R. W., *Die Lehre von der Identität in der deutschen Logik— Wissenschaft seit Lotze*, Leipzig, Hirzel, 1935.

GOLDENWEISER, Alexander, 'Religion and Society: A Critique of

Emile Durkheim's Theory of the Origin and Nature of Religion', in Lessa, William A. and Vogt, Evon Z. (eds.), *Reader in Comparative Religion*, New York: Harper, 1965, pp. 65–72.

GOLDMANN, Lucien, *The Hidden God*, London: Routledge and Kegan Paul, 1964.

GOODE, Erich, 'Some Critical Observations of the Church–Sect Dimension', *Journal for the Scientific Study of Religion*, No. 6, 1967, pp. 69–77.

GOODY, Jack, 'Religion and Ritual: The Definitional Problem', in *The British Journal of Sociology*, Vol. 12, 1961, pp. 142–64.

—, 'Evolution and Communication: "The Domestication of the Savage Mind",' *The British Journal of Sociology*, Vol. XXIV, No. 1, March 1973, pp. 1–12.

GOULDNER, Alvin W., *Enter Plato*, New York: Basic Books, 1965.

GOULDNER, H. P., 'Dimensions of Organizational Commitment', in *Administrative Science Quarterly*, 1960, No. 4, pp. 468–90.

GRAMONT, Sanche de, 'There are no superior societies', in Hayes, E. Nelson, and Hayes, Tanya (eds.), *Claude Lévi-Strauss: The Anthropologist as Hero*, Cambridge, Massachusetts: M.I.T. Press, 1970, pp. 3–21.

GRANT, George P., *Technology and Empire*, Toronto: House of Anansi, 1969.

GRANT, Kenneth, *The Magical Revival*, London: Frederick Muller, 1972.

GREELEY, Andrew M. and Rossi, Peter H., *The Education of Catholic Americans*, Chicago: Aldine, 1966.

GREELEY, Andrew M., *Religion in the Year 2000*, New York: Sheed and Ward, 1969.

—, *Priests in the United States*, Garden City, New York: Doubleday, 1972.

GREEN, Robert W. (ed.), *Protestantism and Capitalism: The Weber Thesis and Its Critics*, Boston: Heath, 1959.

GREGORY, W. Edgar, 'The Orthodoxy of the Authoritarian Personality', *Journal of Social Psychology*, Vol. 45, 1957, pp. 217–232.

GUSTAFSSON, Berndt, 'Sweden', in Mol, Hetherton and Henty (eds.), *Western Religion*, The Hague: Mouton, 1972, pp. 479–510.

HABERMAS, Jürgen, *Knowledge and Human Interests*, Boston: Beacon, 1971.

HAGEN, Everett E., *On the Theory of Social Change*, Homewood, Illinois: Dorsey Press, 1962.

HAILSTONE, Patrick, 'Is our world doomed?', *Hamilton Spectator*, 29 May 1972, p. 22.

HARDING, Thomas G., 'Adaptation and Stability', in Sahlins, Marshall

D. and Service, Elman, R. (ed.), *Evolution and Culture*, Ann Arbor: University of Michigan Press, 1960.

HARLOW, Harry F., and Harlow, Margaret K., 'Social Deprivation in Monkeys', in Goode, William J. (ed.), *Readings on the Family and Society*, Englewood Cliffs, New Jersey: Prentice-Hall, 1964, pp. 7–10.

HARRISON, P. M., *Authority and Power in the Free Church Tradition*, Princeton, New Jersey: Princeton University Press, 1959.

HAYES, E. Nelson and Hayes, Tanya (eds.), *Claude Lévi-Strauss: The Anthropologist as Hero*, Cambridge, Massachusetts: M.I.T. Press, 1970.

HEBERLE, Rudolph, 'Observations on the Sociology of Social Movements', *American Sociological Review*, Vol. 14, No. 3, June 1949, pp. 346–57.

HEIDEGGER, Martin, *Being and Time*, New York: Harper, 1962.

—, *Identity and Difference*, New York: Harper, 1969 (first published in 1957).

HEGEL, Georg W. F., *The Phenomenology of Mind*, New York: Harper, 1967 (originally published in 1807).

HENDERSON, J. McLeod, *Ratana, The Origins and the Story of the Movement*, Wellington: The Polynesian Society, 1963, Memoir, Vol. 36.

HENDERSON, Lawrence J., *Pareto's General Sociology*, New York: Russell and Russell, 1967 (first published in 1935).

HERBERG, Will, *Protestant-Catholic-Jew*, Garden City, New York: Doubleday, 1955.

HERBST, Peter, 'A Critique of the Materialist Identity Theory', in Presley, C. F. (ed.), *The Identity Theory of Mind*, St. Lucia: University of Queensland Press, 1967, pp. 38–64 and 154–61.

HERSKOVITS, Melville J., *The Human Factor in Changing Africa*, New York: Knopf, 1962.

HICKMAN, David Charles, *The Social Context of Religious Orientation*, unpublished Ph.D. dissertation, Canberra: Australian National University, 1969.

HILL, Clifford S., *West Indian Migrants and the London Churches*, London: Oxford University Press, 1963.

HILL, Michael, *A Sociology of Religion*, London: Heinemann, 1973.

HILLER, Harry H., *A Critical Analysis of the Role of Religion in a Canadian Populist Movement: The Emergence and Dominance of the Social Credit Party in Alberta*, Unpublished Ph.D. dissertation, Hamilton: McMaster University, 1972.

HINE, Virginia H., 'Bridge Burners: Commitment and Participation in a Religious Movement', *Sociological Analysis*, Vol. 31, No. 2, Summer 1970, pp. 61–6.

HOBBES, Thomas, *The Leviathan*, Oxford: Clarendon, 1909 (first published in 1651).

HOLMES, Robert Merrill, *The Academic Mysteryhouse*, Nashville, Tennessee: Abingdon, 1970.

HOLZNER, Burkart, *Reality Construction in Society*, Cambridge, Massachusetts: Schenkman, 1968.

HOMANS, George C., *The Human Group*, London: Routledge and Kegan Paul, 1951.

—, *Sentiments and Activities*, Glencoe, Illinois: Free Press, 1962.

HOOD, Ralph W. Jr., 'Forms of Religious Commitment and Intense Religious Experience', *Review of Religious Research*, Vol. 15, No. 1, Fall 1973, pp. 29–36.

HORNE, Donald, *The Education of Young Donald*, Sydney: Angus and Robertson, 1967.

HORTON, Robin, 'African Traditional Thought and Western Science', in Wilson, Bryan R. (ed.), *Rationality*, New York: Harper, 1970, pp. 131–71.

HOWE, Irving and Coser, Lewis, *The American Communist Party: A Critical History, 1919–1957*, Boston: Beacon, 1957.

HUBERT, Henri and Mauss, Marcel, *Sacrifice: Its Nature and Function*, London: Cohen and West, 1964 (first published in 1898).

HUDSON, Winthrop S., 'Puritanism and the Spirit of Capitalism', in Green, Robert W. (ed.), *Protestantism and Capitalism*, Boston: Heath, 1959, pp. 56–64.

HUGHES, H. Stuart, 'Structure and Society', in Hayes, E. Nelson and Hayes, Tanya (eds.), *Claude Lévi-Strauss: The Anthropologist as Hero*, Cambridge, Massachusetts: M.I.T. Press, 1970, pp. 22–46.

HUIZINGA, Johan, *Homo Ludens*, London: Temple Smith, 1970 (first published in 1938).

HUNT, Richard A. and King, Morton, 'The Intrinsic–Extrinsic Concept: A Review and Evaluation', *Journal for the Scientific Study of Religion*, Vol. 10, No. 4, Winter 1971, pp. 339–56.

HUTTON, J. H., *Caste in India*, London: Oxford University Press, 1969.

HUXLEY, Aldous, 'Culture and Individual', in Solomon, David (ed.), *L.S.D., The Consciousness-Expanding Drug*, New York: Putnam, 1964, pp. 29–39.

HYMA, A., 'Calvinism and Capitalism, 1555–1700', *Journal of Modern History*, Vol. X, 1938, pp. 321–43.

IBN KHALDUN, *The Muqaddimah* (3 vols.), Princeton: Princeton University Press, 1967 (completed in 1381).

INGLIS, Brian, *Private Conscience—Public Morality*, London: Deutsch, 1964.

INGLIS, K. S., *Churches and the Working Classes in Victorian England*, London: Routledge and Kegan Paul, 1963.

INKELES, Alex, 'Social Stratification and Mobility in the Soviet Union', in Bendix, Reinhard, and Lipset, Seymour Martin, *Class, Status and Power*, Glencoe, Illinois: Free Press, 1953, pp. 609-22.

JAKOBSON, Roman and Lévi-Strauss, Claude, 'Charles Baudelaire's "Les Chats" ', in Lane, Michael (ed.), *Structuralism*, London: Jonathan Cape, 1970, pp. 202-21.

JAMES, William, *Principles of Psychology* (2 vols.), New York: Holt, 1890.

—, *The Varieties of Religious Experience*, New York: Modern Library, 1902.

JASPERS, Karl, *General Psychopathology*, Chicago: University of Chicago Press, 1963.

JELLINEK, George, *The Declaration of the Rights of Man and of Citizens. A Contribution to Modern Constitutional History*, New York: Holt, 1901.

JOHNSON, Aubrey R., *The Cultic Prophet in Ancient Israel*, Cardiff: University of Wales Press, 1962.

JOHNSON, Benton, 'On Church and Sect', *American Sociological Review*, Vol. 28, 1963, pp. 539-49.

—, 'Church and Sect Revisited', *Journal for the Scientific Study of Religion*, Vol. 10, No. 2, Summer 1971, pp. 124-37.

JOHNSON, Martin A., 'Family Life and Religious Commitment', *Review of Religious Research*, Vol. 14, No. 3, Spring 1973, pp. 144-50.

JONG, O. J. de, 'De Kerken der Hervorming van 1517 tot 1813', in Weiler, A. G., Jong, O. J. de, Rogier, L. J. and Mönnich, C. W. (eds.), *Geschiedenis van de Kerk in Nederland*, Utrecht: Aula, 1962, pp. 83-167.

JUNG, Carl Gustav, *Wandlungen und Symbole der Libido*, Leipzig: Franz Deuticke Verlag, 1912.

—, *The Integration of the Personality*, London: Routledge and Kegan Paul, 1940.

—, *Psychology and Religion: East and West* (The Collected Works of C. G. Jung, Vol. 2), New York: Pantheon Books, 1958.

—, *The Archetypes and the Collective Unconscious* (The Collected Works of C. G. Jung, Vol. 9, Part 1), New York: Pantheon Books, 1959.

—, *Basic Writings*, New York: Random House, 1959a.

—, *The Structure and Dynamics of the Psyche* (The Collected Works of C. G. Jung, Vol. 8), New York: Pantheon Books, 1960.

—, *Civilization in Transition* (The Collected Works of C. G. Jung, Vol. 10), New York: Pantheon Books, 1964.

—, *Psychology and Religion*, New Haven: Yale University Press, 1972 (first published in 1938).

JUNG, C. G. and KÉRENYI, Karl, *Einfuhrung in das Wesen der Mythologie*, Zürich: Rhein Verlag, 1951.

KAILL, Robert C., 'Ecumenism, Clergy Influence and Liberalism: An Investigation into the Sources of Lay Support for Church Union', *Canadian Review of Sociology and Anthropology*, Vol. 8, No. 3, August 1971, pp. 142–62.

KAMENKA, Eugene, *The Ethical Foundations of Marxism*, London: Routledge and Kegan Paul, 1962.

—, *The Philosophy of Ludwig Feuerbach*, New York: Praeger, 1970.

KANT, Immanuel, *Critique of Pure Reason*, New York: St. Martin's Press, 1965 (first published in 1787).

KANTER, Rosabeth Moss, *Commitment and Community*, Cambridge, Massachusetts: Harvard University Press, 1972.

KAPLAN, Abraham (ed.), *Individuality and the New Society*, Seattle: University of Washington Press, 1970.

KAUFMANN, Walter, 'The Inevitability of Alienation', in Schacht, Richard, *Alienation*, Garden City, New York: Doubleday, 1970, pp. xiii–lxv.

KELLER, Suzanne, *Beyond the Ruling Class* (Strategic Elites in Modern Society), New York: Random House, 1963.

KELLEY, Dean, *Why Conservative Churches are Growing*, New York: Harper, 1972.

KENISTON, Kenneth, *The Uncommitted*, New York: Harcourt, Brace and World, 1964.

—, *Young Radicals* (Notes on Committed Youth), New York: Harcourt, Brace and World, 1968.

—, *Youth and Dissent* (The Rise of a New Opposition), New York: Harcourt, Brace, Jovanovich, 1971.

KERÉNYI, Karl, 'Was ist Mythologie?', in *Die Eröffnung des Zugangs zum Mythos*, Kerényi, Karl (ed.), Darmstadt: Wissenschaftliche Buchgesellschaft, 1967, pp. 213–33.

KERR, John Stevens, *The Mystery and Magic of the Occult*, Philadelphia: Fortress Press, 1971.

KIERKEGAARD, Søren, *Concluding Unscientific Postscript*, Princeton: Princeton University Press, 1941.

KIESLER, Charles A.; Collins, Barry E.; Miller, Norman, *Attitude Change*, New York: Wiley, 1969.

—, *The Psychology of Commitment*, New York: Academic Press, 1971.

KILBOURN, William, 'Prologue', in Kilbourn, William (ed.), *Religion in Canada*, Toronto: McClelland and Stewart, 1968, pp. 6–24.

KIMBALL, Solon T., 'Introduction', in Gennep, Arnold van, *The Rites of Passage*, London: Routledge and Kegan Paul, 1960, pp. v–xix.

KIMMEL, William and Clive, Geoffrey (Eds.), *Dimensions of Faith*, New York: Twayne, 1960.

KING, Winston L., *Introduction to Religion*, New York: Harper, 1954.

KIRK, G. S., *Myth*, Cambridge: University Press, 1970.

KITAGAWA, Joseph Mitsuo, *Religious of the East*, Philadelphia: Westminster Press, 1960.

KLAPP, Orrin E., *Collective Search for Identity*, New York: Holt, Rinehart and Winston, 1969.

KLUCKHOHN, Clyde, 'Myths and Rituals: A General Theory', in Lessa, William H., and Vogt, Evon Z. (eds.), *Reader in Comparative Religion*, New York: Harper, 1965, pp. 144–58.

KOENKER, Ernest B., *Secular Salvations*, Philadelphia: Fortress Press, 1965.

KOESTLER, Arthur, *The God that Failed*, London; Hamish Hamilton, 1951.

KÖRNER, S., *Kant*, Harmondsworth; Penguin, 1964.

KRAEMER, Hendrik, *The Christian Message in a Non-Christian World*, London: Edinburgh House Press, 1938.

KUHN, Thomas S., *The Structure of Scientific Revolutions*, Chicago: University of Chicago Press, 1970.

LAEYENDECKER, Leonardus, *Religie en Conflict*, Meppel, Netherlands: Boom, 1967.

LAING, R. D., *Self and Others*, Harmondsworth: Penguin, 1971.

—, *The Politics of the Family and Other Essays*, New York: Random, 1971a.

LANE, Michael, 'Introduction', in Lane, Michael (ed.), *Structuralism*, London: Jonathan Cape, 1970, pp. 11–39.

LANGER, Suzanne K., *Philosophy in a New Key*, New York: Mentor, 1951.

—, *Mind: An Essay on Human Feeling*, Vol. II, Baltimore: Johns Hopkins University Press, 1972.

LANTERNARI, Vittorio, *The Religions of the Oppressed*, New York: Knopf, 1963.

LAPIERE, Richard, *The Freudian Ethic*, New York: Duell, Sloan and Pearce, 1959.

LASKI, Margharita, *Ecstasy, A Study of Some Secular and Religious Experiences*, London: Cresset Press, 1961.

LAUWERS, Jan, 'Les théories sociologiques concernant la sécularisation—Typologie et critique', *Social Compass*, XX, 4, 1973, pp. 523–533.

LAZERWITZ, Bernard, 'Religion and Social Structure in the United States', in Schneider, Louis (ed.), *Religion, Culture and Society*, New York: Wiley, 1964, pp. 426–39.

LEACH, Edmund R., 'Genesis as Myth', in Middleton, John (ed.),

Myth and Cosmos, Garden City, New York: The Natural History Press, 1967, pp. 1–13.

—, 'Ritual', in *International Encyclopedia of the Social Sciences*, Vol. 13, New York: Macmillan, 1968, pp. 520–6.

—, 'Introduction', in Leach, Edmund (ed.), *The Structural Study of Myth and Totemism*, London: Tavistock, 1969a, pp. vii–xix.

—, (ed.), *The Structural Study of Myth and Totemism*, London: Tavistock, 1969.

—, 'Lévi-Strauss in the Garden of Eden', in Hayes, E. Nelson, and Hayes, Tanya (eds.), *Claude Lévi-Strauss: The Anthropologist as Hero*, Cambridge, Massachusetts: M.I.T. Press, 1970, pp. 47–60.

—, *Lévi-Strauss*, London: Fontana, 1970a.

—, 'The Legitimacy of Solomon: some Structural aspects of Old Testament History', in Lane, Michael (ed.), *Structuralism*, London: Jonathan Cape, 1970b, pp. 248–92.

LEARY, Timothy, *The Politics of Ecstasy*, New York: Putnam, 1968.

LEEUW, G. van der, *Inleiding tot de theologie*, Amsterdam: Paris, 1948.

—, *Religion in Essence and Manifestation*, London: Allen and Unwin, 1964 (first published in 1933).

LEEUWEN, Arend Th. van, *Christianity in World History*, London: Edinburgh House Press, 1964.

LEIBNIZ, Gottfried Wilhelm, *Neue Abhandlungen über den Menschlichen Verstand*, Vols. I and II, Frankfurt am Main: Insel Verlag, 1961 (written in 1704).

LENSKI, Gerhard, *The Religious Factor*, Garden City, New York: Doubleday, 1961.

—, *Power and Privilege*, New York: McGraw-Hill, 1966.

—, *Human Societies*, New York: McGraw-Hill, 1970.

LEVINE, Donald N., 'The Structure of Simmel's Social Thought, in Wolff, Kurt (ed.), *Georg Simmel*, Columbus, Ohio: Ohio State University Press, 1959, pp. 9–32.

LÉVI-STRAUSS, 'The Structural Study of Myth', in Sebeok, Thomas A. (ed.), *Myth: A Symposium*, Bloomington, Indiana: Indiana University Press, 1955, pp. 50–66.

—, *La Pensée Sauvage*, Paris: Plon, 1962.

—, *Totemism*, Boston: Beacon Press, 1963 (French edition 1962).

—, *Du Miel aux Cendres*, Paris: Plon, 1966.

—, 'Introduction a l'oeuvre de Marcel Mauss', in Mauss, Marcel, *Sociologie et Anthropologie*, Paris Presses Universitaires de France, 1966a, pp. ix–lii.

—, *Structural Anthropology*, Garden City, New York: Doubleday, 1967 (first published in 1958).

—, 'The Story of Asdiwal), in Leach, Edmund (ed.), *The Structural Study of Myth and Totemism*, London: Tavistock, 1969, pp. 1–47.

—, *The Raw and the Cooked*, London: Jonathan Cape, 1970 (first published 1964).

—, 'The Sex of the Heavenly Bodies', in Lane, Michael (ed.), *Structuralism*, London: Jonathan Cape, 1970b, pp. 330–9.

LÉVY-BRUHL, *Les Fonctions Mentales*, Paris: Felix Alcan, 1922.

LEWIS, C. S., *Letters to Malcolm: Chiefly on Prayer*, London: Bles, 1964.

LIFTON, Robert J., *Boundaries: Psychological Man in Revolution*, New York: Random, 1967.

LINCOLN, C. Eric, *The Black Muslims in America*, Boston: Beacon Press, 1961.

LIPSET, Seymour, Martin, 'Prejudice and Politics in the American Past and Present', in Kaplan, Abraham (ed.), *Individuality and the New Society*, Seattle: University of Washington Press, 1970, pp. 89–147.

LITTELL, Franklin Hamlin, 'The Social Background of the Anabaptist View of the Church', in Birnbaum, Norman and Lenzer, Gertrud (eds.), *Sociology of Religion* (a book of readings), Englewood Cliffs, New York: Prentice Hall, 1969, pp. 230–7.

LITTLE, David, *Religion, Order and Law*, New York: Harper, 1969.

LOCKE, John, Works (10 vols.), London: Johnson *et al.*, 1801.

LORENZ, Konrad, *On Aggression*, London: Methuen, 1970.

—, *Studies in Animal and Human Behaviour*, Vol. II, London: Methuen, 1971.

LOWIE, Robert H., *Primitive Religion*, New York: Grosset and Dunlap, 1952 (first published 1924).

—, 'The Vision Quest Among the North American Indians', in Lessa, William A. and Vogt, Evon Z. (eds.), *Reader in Comparative Religion*, New York: Harper, 1965, pp. 194–7.

LUCKMANN, Thomas, *The Invisible Religion*, New York: Macmillan, 1967.

LUIJPEN, William A., *Phenomenology and Atheism*, Pittsburgh, Pennsylvania: Duquesne University Press, 1964.

MACHIAVELLI, Nicolo, *The Prince*, London: Dent, 1948 (first published in 1513).

MacINTYRE, Alasdair, *Secularization and Moral Change*, London: Oxford University Press, 1967.

MAIR, Lucy P., *Australia in New Guinea*, London: Christophers, 1948.

MALINOWSKI, Bronislaw, *The Foundations of Faith and Morals*, London: Oxford University Press, 1936.

—, *Magic, Science and Religion, and Other Essays*, Garden City, New York: Doubleday, 1954.

—, *A Scientific Theory of Culture and Other Essays*, New York: Oxford University Press, 1960.

—, *Sex, Culture and Myth*, New York: Harcourt, Brace and World, 1962.

MALZBERG, B. and Lee, E. S., *Migration and Mental Disease*, New York: Social Science Research Council, 1956.

MANN, Thomas, 'Freud and the Future', in Murray, Henry A. (ed.), *Myth and Mythmaking*, New York: Braziller, 1960, pp. 371–5 (first published in 1936).

MANN, W. E., 'Sect and Cult in Western Canada', in Blishen, B. R. *et al.* (ed.), *Canadian Society*, Glencoe, Illinois: Free Press, 1961.

MARCUSE, Herbert, *One Dimensional Man*, London: Sphere Books, 1968.

—, *Negations*, Boston: Beacon Press, 1969.

MARIEL, Pierre, *Rituels des Sociétés Secrètes*, Paris: La Colombe, 1961.

MARTIN, Alfred von, *Sociology of the Renaissance*, New York: Harper, 1963 (first published in 1932).

MARTIN, David, 'Towards eliminating the concept of secularisation', in Gould, Julius (ed.), *Penguin Survey of the Social Sciences 1965*, Harmondsworth; Penguin, 1965, pp. 169–82.

—, *A Sociology of English Religion*, London: S.C.M., 1967.

—, 'England', in Mol, Hetherton and Henty (eds.), *Western Religion*, A Country by Country Sociological Inquiry, The Hague: Mouton. 1972, pp. 229–47.

—, 'An essay in conceptual and empirical synthesis', in *ACTS of the 12th C.I.S.R. Conference*, Lille, France: CISR, 1973, pp. 517–28.

MARTIN, H. V., *Kierkegaard, The Melancholy Dane*, London: Epworth, 1950.

MARTY, Martin E., 'Ethnicity', *Church History*, Vol. 41, No. 1, March 1972, pp. 5–21.

MARUYAMA, Magoroh, 'The Second Cybernetics: Deviation-Amplifying Mutual Causal Processes', *American Scientist*, Vol. 51, No. 2, June 1953, pp. 164–79.

MARX, Karl, *Early Writings*, London: Watts, 1963.

MARX, Karl and Engels, Friedrich, *On Religion*, New York: Schocken, 1964.

MASLOW, Abraham, *Motivation and Personality*, New York: Harper, 1954.

—, *Religions, Values and Peak-experiences*, Columbus: Ohio State University Press, 1964.

MAUS, Heinz, *A Short History of Sociology*, London: Routledge and Kegan Paul, 1962.

MAY, Rollo, *Man's Search for Himself*, New York: Norton, 1953.

MAYBURY-LEWIS, David, 'Science or Bricolage', in Hayes, E. Nelson and Hayes, Tanya (eds.), *Claude Lévi-Strauss: The Anthropologist as Hero*, Cambridge, Massachusetts: M.I.T. Press, 1970, pp. 150–63.

MAZUR, Allan, 'A cross-species comparison of status in small established groups', *American Sociological Review*, October 1973, Vol. 38, No. 5, pp. 513–30.

McCALL, George J. and Simmons, J. L., *Identities and Interactions*, New York: Free Press, 1966.

McCONNELL, Theodore A., *The Shattered Self* (The Psychological and Religious Search for Selfhood), Philadelphia: Pilgrim Press, 1971.

McGAVRAN, Donald, *Church Growth in Mexico*, Grand Rapids: Eerdmans, 1963.

McGUIRE, William J., 'Inducing Resistance to Persuasion', in Berkowitz, Leonard (ed.), *Advances in Experimental Social Psychology*, New York: Academic Press, 1964, pp. 192–229.

McLOUGHLIN, William G., 'Is there a third force in Christendom?', *Daedalus*, Winter 1967.

McLUHAN, Marshall, 'Myth and Mass Media', in Murray, Henry A. (ed.), *Myth and Mythmaking*, New York: Braziller, 1960, pp. 288–299.

—, *The Gutenberg Galaxy*, New York: New American Library, 1969.

MEAD, George Herbert, *Mind, Self and Society*, Chicago: University of Chicago Press, 1950 (first published in 1934).

MEAD, Margaret, *Culture and Commitment*, New York: Doubleday, 1970.

MENDELSON, E. Michael, 'The Uninvited Guest', in Leach, Edmund (ed.), *The Structural Study of Myth and Totemism*, London: Tavistock, 1969, pp. 119–39.

MERTON, Robert K., *Social Theory and Social Structure*, Glencoe, Illinois: Free Press, 1957.

MICHELS, Robert, *Political Parties: A Sociological Study of the Oligarchical Tendencies of Modern Democracy*, Glencoe, Illinois: Free Press, 1949 (first published in 1911).

MIDDLETON, John, 'Introduction', in Middleton, John (ed.), *Myth and Cosmos*, Garden City, New York: The Natural History Press, 1967, pp. viii–xi.

MIDDLETON, Russell, 'Do Christian Beliefs cause Anti-Semitism?', *American Sociological Review*, Vol. 38, No. 1, February 1973, pp. 33–52.

MILLETT, David, 'The Orthodox Church: Ukrainian, Greek and Syrian', in Elliott Jean Leonard (ed.), *Immigrant Groups* (Vol. II of *Minority Canadians*), Scarborough, Ontario: Prentice-Hall, 1971, pp. 47–65.

MILLS, C. Wright, *The Sociological Imagination*, Oxford: Oxford University Press, 1959.

MINER, Horace, *St. Denis—A French-Canadian Parish*, Chicago: University of Chicago Press, 1939.

MOBERG, David O., *The Church as a Social Institution*, Englewood Cliffs, New Jersey: Prentice-Hall, 1962.

—, *The Great Reversal*, Philadelphia: Lippincott, 1972.

MOL, Johannis (Hans) J., 'Theoretical Frame of Reference for the Interactional Patterns of Religion and the Adjustment of Immigrants', *R.E.M.P. Bulletin*, Vol. 7, No. 2, Spring 1959, pp. 21–43.

—, *Churches and Immigrants*, The Hague: Research Group for European Migration Problems, 1961.

—, *Church Attendance in Christchurch, New Zealand* (Project 4, Department of Psychology and Sociology, Canterbury University), Christchurch, New Zealand: Department of Psychology and Sociology, 1962.

—, 'The Function of Marginality', *International Migration*, Vol. 1, No. 3, 1963, pp. 175–7.

—, *Changes in Religious Behaviour of Dutch Immigrants*, The Hague: Research Group for European Migration Problems, 1965a.

—, 'Integration versus Segregation in the New Zealand Churches', *British Journal of Sociology*, Vol. 16, No. 2, June 1965b, pp. 140–9.

—, *Race and Religion in New Zealand*, Christchurch: The National Council of Churches in New Zealand, 1966.

—, 'A Collation of Data about Religion in Australia', *Social Compass*, Vol. 14, No. 2, 1967, pp. 120–5.

—, *The Breaking of Traditions*, Berkeley, California: Glendessary Press, 1968a.

—, 'Religion', in McLeod, A. L. (ed.), *The Pattern of New Zealand Culture*, Ithaca, New York: Cornell University Press, 1968b.

—, 'Sociology in Australia and New Zealand', *The American Sociologist*, Vol. 3, No. 2, May 1968c.

—, 'The Merger Attempts of the Australian Churches', *The Ecumenical Review*, January 1969a, pp. 23–31.

—, *Christianity in Chains*, Melbourne: Nelson. 1969.

—, 'The Social and Political Influence of Religion', in Osborne, Charles (ed.), *Australia, New Zealand and the South Pacific, A Handbook*, New York: Praeger, 1970a, pp. 268–72.

—, 'The Decline in Religious Participation of Migrants', in Ford, Thomas R. and Jong, Gordon F. de (eds.), *Social Demography*, Englewood Cliffs, New Jersey: Prentice-Hall, 1970b, pp. 255–60.

—, 'Secularization and Cohesion', *Review of Religious Research*, Vol. 11, No. 3, Spring 1970c.

—, *Religion in Australia*, Melbourne: Nelson, 1971a.

—, 'Immigrant Absorption and Religion: an attempt towards an explanatory model on the basis of socialization theory', *International Migration Review*, Vol. 5, No. 1, Spring 1971b, pp. 62–71.

—, 'The Dysfunctions of Sociological Knowledge', *The American Sociologist*, Vol. 6, No. 3, August 1971c, pp. 221–3.

—, 'Religion, Occupation and Education in Australia, an Analysis of the 1966 Census', *The Australian Quarterly*, Vol. 43, No. 4, 1971d.

MOL, Johannis (Hans) J.; Hetherton, Margaret; Henty, Margaret (eds.), *Western Religion (A Country by Country Sociological Investigation)*, The Hague: Mouton, 1972a.

MOL, Johannis (Hans) J., 'Religion and Competition', *Sociological Analysis*, Vol. 33, No. 2, Summer 1972b, pp. 67–73.

—, 'The Sacralization of Identity': in Archer, Margaret S. (ed.), *Current Research in Sociology*, The Hague, Mouton, 1974.

MÖNNICH, C. W., 'De Kerken der hervorming sinds 1813', in Weiler, A. G., Jong, O. J. de, Rogier, L. J. and Monnich, C. W. (eds.), *Geschiedenis van de Kerk in Nederland*, Utrecht, Aula, 1962, pp. 237–93.

MOONEY, James, *The Ghost-Dance Religion and the Sioux Outbreak of 1890*, Chicago: University of Chicago Press, 1970 (first published in 1896).

MORE, Thomas, *Utopia*, Harmondsworth: Penguin, 1965 (first published in 1516).

MORIOKA, Kiyomi and Shimpo, Mitsuru, 'The Impact of the Physical Movement of Population on Japanese Religions after the World War II', in Verscheure, Jacques (ed.), *Acts of the 11th Conference of the C.I.S.R.*, Lille, France, C.I.S.R., 1971, pp. 184–211.

MUELDER, Walter, 'From Sect to Church', in Yinger, J. Milton, *Religion, Society and the Individual*, New York: Macmillan, 1957, pp. 480–8.

MUGGERIDGE, Malcolm, *Jesus Rediscovered*, London: Collins, 1969.

MÜLLER, F. Max, *Anthropological Religion*, London: Longmans Green, 1892.

MULLER, Werner, 'North America', in Krickeberg, Walter, Trimborn, Hermann, Muller, Werner and Zerries, Otto, *Pre-Columbian American Religions*, London: Weidenfeld and Nicolson, 1968, pp. 147–229.

MURDOCK, George Peter, 'How culture changes', in Hollander, Edwin P. and Hunt, Raymond G. (eds.), *Current Perspectives in Social Psychology*, New York: Oxford University Press, 1970, pp. 90–99.

NADEL, S. F., 'Study of Shamanism in the Nuba Mountains', *Journal of the Royal Anthropological Institute*, Vol. LXXVI, 1946, pp. 25–37.

NAGENDRA, S. P., *The Concept of Ritual in Modern Sociological Theory*, New Delhi: The Academic Journals of India, 1971.

NASR, Seyyed Hossein, *Ideals and Realities of Islam*, New York: Praeger, 1967.

NATANSON, Maurice, *The Journeying Self*, Reading, Massachusetts: Addison-Wesley, 1970.

NEEDLEMAN, Jacob, *The New Religions*, Garden City, New York: Doubleday, 1970.

NEUTER, Patrick de, 'Amour, Sexualité et Religion: enquête par Questionnaire et par images d'aperception auprès d'un groupe de collégiens', *Social Compass*, Vol. XIX, No. 3, 1972, pp. 365–87.

NIEBUHR, Reinhold, *The Children of Light and the Children of Darkness*, London: Nisbet, 1945.

—, *The Nature and Destiny of Man*, Vol. II: *Human Destiny*, London: Nisbet, 1948.

NIEBUHR, H. Richard, *Christ and Culture*, New York: Harper, 1956.

—, *The Social Sources of Denominationalism*, New York: Meridian, 1957 (first published in 1929).

NIETZSCHE, Friedrich, 'The Gay Science', in Kaufmann, Walter (ed.), *The Portable Nietzsche*, New York: Viking, 1954a, pp. 93–102 (first published in 1887).

—, 'The Antichrist', in Kaufmann, Walter (ed.), *The Portable Nietzsche*, New York: Viking, 1954b, pp. 565–656 (first published in 1895).

—, *The Genealogy of Morals*, Garden City, New York: Doubleday, 1956 (first published in 1887).

NISBET, Robert A., *The Sociological Tradition*, London: Heinemann, 1967.

—, *Social Change and History*, New York: Oxford University Press, 1969.

—, *The Social Philosophers*, New York: Thomas Y. Crowell, 1973.

NOCK, A. D., *Conversion*, Oxford: Clarendon, 1933.

NOSS, John B., *Man's Religions*, New York: Macmillan, 1963.

NOTTINGHAM, Elizabeth K., *Religion and Society*, Garden City, New York: Doubleday, 1954.

NYGREN, Anders, *Meaning and Method*, London: Epworth Press, 1972.

OBAYASHI, Hiroshi, 'The World Come of Age: Cultural Fact or Faith's Demand', *Union Seminary Quarterly Review*, Vol. XXVI, No. 2, Winter 1971, pp. 99–116.

OCHAVKOV, Jivko, 'Bulgaria', in Mol, Hans, Hetherton, Margaret and Henty, Margaret (eds.), *Western Religion*, The Hague: Mouton, 1972, pp. 83–99.

O'DEA, Thomas F., *The Sociology of Religion*, Englewood Cliffs, New Jersey: Prentice-Hall, 1966.

O'FARRELL, Patrick, *The Catholic Church in Australia*, Melbourne: Nelson, 1968.

OMAN, John, *Grace and Personality*, Cambridge: University Press, 1925.

ORR, John B. and Nichelson, F. Patrick, *The Radical Suburb: Soundings in Changing American Character*, Philadelphia: Westminster, 1970.

OTTO, Rudolf, *The Idea of the Holy*, London: Oxford University Press, 1950 (first published in 1917).

OTTO, Walter F., 'Der ursprüngliches Mythos', in Kerényi, Karl (ed.), *Die Eröffnung des Zugangs zum Mythos*, Darmstadt: Wissenschaftliche Buchgesellschaft, 1967, pp. 271–8.

PARK, Robert E., 'Cultural Conflict and the Marginal Man', Introduction in Stonequist, Everett V., *The Marginal Man, A Study in Personality and Culture Conflict*, New York: Scribner, 1937, pp. xiii–xviii.

—, *Race and Culture*, Glencoe, Illinois: Free Press, 1964.

PARRINDER, Edward Geoffrey, *What World Religions Teach*, London: Harrap, 1963.

PARSONS, Talcott, *The Structure of Social Action*, Glencoe, Illinois: Free Press, 1949 (first published in 1937).

—, *The Social System*, Glencoe, Illinois: Free Press, 1951.

—, *Religious Perspectives of College Teaching*, New Haven, Connecticut: Hazen Foundation, 1952.

—, 'Revised analytical approach to the theory of social stratification', in Bendix, Reinhard and Lipset, Seymour Martin (eds.), *Class, Status and Power*, Glencoe, Illinois: Free Press, 1953, pp. 92–128.

—, *Essays in Sociological Theory*, Glencoe, Illinois: Free Press, 1954.

—, 'Christianity and Modern Industrial Society', in Tiryakian, Edward (ed.), *Sociological Theory, Values, and Sociocultural Change*, Glencoe, Illinois: Free Press, 1963.

—, 'Evolutionary Universals in Society', *American Sociological Review*, Vol. XXIX, 1964, pp. 339–74.

—, 'Durkheim: Contribution to the Theory of the Integration of Social Systems', in Wolff, Kurt H. (ed.), *Essays on Sociology and Philosophy*, New York: Harper, 1964a.

—, 'Introduction', in Weber, Max, *The Sociology of Religion*, Boston: Beacon, 1964b.

—, 'Introduction', in Weber, Max, *Theory of Social and Economic Organization*, Glencoe, Illinois: Free Press, 1964c, pp. 3–86.

—, *The System of Modern Societies*, Englewood Cliffs, New Jersey: Prentice-Hall, 1971.

PARSONS, Talcott and Bales, Robert F., *Family, Socialization and Interaction Process*, Glencoe, Illinois: Free Press, 1955.

PARSONS, Talcott; Shils, Edward; Naegele, Kaspar D.; Pitts, Jesse R. (eds.), *Theories of Society*, New York: Free Press, 1961.

PASCAL, Blaise, *Pensées*, London: Dent, 1932.

PETERSON, Donald W. and Mauss, Armand L., 'The Cross and the Commune: An Interpretation of the Jesus People', in Glock, Charles Y., *Religion in Sociological Perspective*, Belmont, California: Wadsworth, 1973, pp. 261–79.

PIAGET, Jean; Sinclair, Hermine; Bang, Vinh, *Épistémologie et Psychologie de l'identité*, Paris: Presses Universitaires de France, 1968.

PIRENNE, Henri, *Medieval Cities*, Princeton, New Jersey: Princeton University Press, 1970 (first printed in 1925).

PITTS, Jesse R., 'Introduction to Personality and the Social System', in Parsons, Talcott; Shils, Edward; Naegele, Kaspar D.; Pitts, Jesse R. (eds.), *Theories of Society*, Glencoe, Illinois: Free Press, 1961, pp. 685–716.

—, 'The Stuctural–Functional Approach', in Christensen, Harold T., *Handbook of Marriage and the Family*, Chicago: Rand McNally, 1964, pp. 51–124.

PLATO, *The Republic*, New York: Dutton, 1950.

POLANYI, Michael, *Science, Faith and Society*, Chicago: University of Chicago Press, 1966.

POLYBIUS, *The Histories* (2 vols.), Bloomington: Indiana University Press, 1962.

POOLE, Roger, *Towards Deep Subjectivity*, New York: Harper, 1972.

POPE, Liston, *Millhands and Preachers*, New Haven, Connecticut: Yale University Press, 1942.

POPPER, Karl R., *The Open Society and Its Enemies*, Vol. I: *Plato*, Vol. II: *Hegel and Marx*, London: Routledge and Kegan Paul, 1962.

—, 'Science: Problems, Aims, Responsibilities', in *Federation Proceedings*, Vol. XXII, Baltimore, Md.: The Federation of American Societies for Experimental Biology, 1963, pp. 961–72.

POWELL, Elwin H., 'Beyond Utopia: The Beat Generation', in Rose, Arnold M. (ed.), *Human Behaviour and Social Processes*, Boston: Houghton Mifflin, 1962, pp. 360–77.

PRESLEY, C. F. (ed.), *The Identity Theory of Mind*, St. Lucia: University of Queensland Press, 1967.

PREUSZ, K. T., *Der Religiöse Gehalt der Mythen*, Tübingen: Mohr, 1933.

PROGOFF, Ira, 'Waking Dream and Living Myth', in Campbell, Joseph (ed.), *Myths, Dreams and Religion*, New York: Dutton, 1970, pp. 176–95.

QUERIDO, Augusto, 'Portugal', in Mol, Hetherton and Henty (eds.), *Western Religion*, The Hague: Mouton, 1972, pp. 427–36.

RADCLIFFE-BROWN, Alfred Reginald, *Taboo*, Cambridge: University Press, 1939.

—, *The Andaman Islanders*, Glencoe, Illinois: Free Press, 1948 (first published in 1922).

RADHAKRISHNAN, S., *Religion and Society*, London: Allen and Unwin, 1947.

—, *An Idealist View of Life*, London: Allen and Unwin, 1951.

RADIN, Paul, *Primitive Religion*, New York: Dover, 1957 (first published in 1937).

RANGANATHANANDA, Swami, 'A Traveller Looks at the World', *Prabuddha Bharata*, Part III, September 1970.

READ, William R., *New Patterns of Church Growth in Brazil*, Grand Rapids, Michigan: Eerdmans, 1965.

READ, William R.; Monterroso, Victor M.; Johnson, Harmon A., *Latin American Church Growth*, Grand Rapids, Michigan: Eerdmans, 1969.

REICH, Wilhelm, *Cosmic Superimposition*, Rangeley Me: The Wilhelm Reich Foundation, 1951.

REICHEL-DOLMATOFF, Gerardo, *Amazonian Cosmos*, Chicago: University of Chicago Press, 1971.

RICHARDSON, Herbert W., *Toward an American Theology*, New York: Harper, 1967.

RICOEUR, Paul, 'The Symbol gives rise to thought', in Walter H. Capps (ed.), *Ways of Understanding Religion*, New York: Macmillan, 1972, pp. 309–17.

—, 'The Critique of Religion', *Union Seminary Quarterly Review*, Vol. XXVIII, No. 3, Spring 1973, pp. 205–12.

RIEFF, Philip, *Freud, the Mind of the Moralist*, Garden City, New York: Doubleday, 1961.

—, *The Triumph of the Therapeutic*, New York: Harper, 1968.

RIESMAN, David; Glazer, Nathan; Denney, Revel, *The Lonely Crowd*, Garden City, New York: Doubleday, 1955.

RINGGREN, Helmer and Ström, Åke V., *De Godsdiensten der Volken* (Vols. I and II), Utrecht: Spectrum, 1963.

RIOUX, Marcel, *Quebec in Question*, Toronto: James Lewis and Samuel, 1971.

RIVERS, W. H. R., 'The Sociological Significance of Myth', in Georges, Robert A. (ed.), *Studies on Mythology*, Homewood, Illinois: Dorsey Press, 1968, pp. 27–45 (originally published in 1912).

ROBERTSON, H. M., *Aspects of the Rise of Economic Individualism. A Criticism of Max Weber and His School*, Cambridge, England: Cambridge University Press, 1933.

ROBERTSON, John C., 'The "New Morality" Debate: An Analysis and Assessment', in Parekh, Bhikhu (ed.), *Dissent and Disorder: Essays in Social Theory*, Toronto: World University Service, 1968, pp. 60–71.

ROBERTSON, Roland, *The Sociological Interpretation of Religion*, Oxford: Blackwell, 1970.

ROBINSON, John A. T., *Honest to God*, London: S.C.M. Press, 1963.

ROBINSON, John A. T. and Edwards, David L., *The Honest to God Debate*, London: S.C.M. Press, 1963a.

ROHEIM, Géza, *Animism, Magic and the Divine King*, London: Kegan Paul, 1930.

ROKEACH, Milton, *The Open and Closed Mind*, New York: Basic Books, 1960.

ROSS, F. H., *The Meaning of Life in Hinduism and Buddhism*, London: Routledge and Kegan Paul, 1953.

ROSZAK, Theodore, *Where the Waste Land Ends*, Garden City, New York: Doubleday, 1973.

ROUBICZEK, Paul, *Existentialism for and against*, Cambridge: University Press, 1966.

ROUSSEAU, Jean Jacques, *The Social Contract*, New York. Hafner, 1954.

ROY, Gabrielle, *The Cashier*, Toronto: McLelland and Stewart, 1970.

RUITENBEEK, Hendrik M., *The Individual and the Crowd* (A Study of Identity in America), New York: Nelson, 1964.

RUSSELL, Bertrand, *Why I am not a Christian*, New York: Simon and Schuster, 1964 (first published in 1957).

SADDHATISSA, H., *Buddhist Ethics*, New York: Braziller, 1970.

SAMUELSSON, Kurt, *Religion and Economic Action: A Critique of Max Weber*, New York: Harper, 1964.

SANFORD, John A., *Dreams: God's Forgotten Language*, Philadelphia: Lippincott, 1968.

SARGANT, William, *Battle for the Mind*, London: Pan, 1963 (first published in 1957).

SARTRE, Jean-Paul, *Being and Nothingness*, New York: Philosophical Library, 1956.

—, *The Devil and the Good Lord*, New York: Vintage, 1960.

—, *Anti-Semite and Jew*, New York: Grove Press, 1960a.

SAVRAMIS, Demosthenes, *Entchristlichung und Sexualisierung*, Munich: Nymphenburger, 1969.

—, *Religion und Sexualität*, Munich: List, 1972.

SCHACHT, Richard, *Alienation*, Garden City, New York: Doubleday, 1970.

SCHARF, Betty R., *The Sociological Study of Religion*, London: Hutchinson University Library, 1970.

SCHEIN, Edgar H., *Coercive Persuasion*, New York: Norton, 1961.

SCHNEIDER, Louis, *Sociological Approach to Religion*, New York: Wiley, 1970.

SCHOENHERR, Richard A. and Greeley, Andrew M., 'Role Commitment Processes and the American Catholic Priesthood', *American Sociological Review*, Vol. 39, No. 3, June 1974, pp. 407–26.

SCHORER, Mark, 'The Necessity of Myth', in Murray, Henry A. (ed.), *Myth and Mythmaking*, New York: Braziller, 1960 (first published in 1946), pp. 354–8.

SCHREUDER, Osmund, *Der Alarmierende Trend*, Munich: Kaiser, 1970.

SCHUTZ, Alfred, 'The Stranger: an essay in social psychology', in Stein, Maurice R.; Vidich, Arthur J.; White, David Manning (eds.), *Identity and Anxiety*, Glencoe, Illinois: Free Press, 1960.

—, 'The Problem of Rationality in the Social World', in Emmet, Dorothy and MacIntyre, Alasdair, *Sociological Theory and Philosophical Analysis*, London: Macmillan, 1970 (originally published 1943), pp. 89–114.

SEEMAN, Melvin, 'On the meaning of alienation', *American Sociological Review*, Vol. XXIV, 1959, pp. 783–91.

—, 'The signals of '68: alienation in pre-crisis France', *American Sociological Review*, Vol. 37, No. 4, August 1972, pp. 385–402.

SEGER, Imogen, *Durkheim and his Critics on the Sociology of Religion*, New York: Columbia University, Bureau of Applied Social Research, 1957.

SEPPÄNEN, Paavo, 'Finland', in Mol, Hetherton and Henty (eds.), *Western Religion*, The Hague: Mouton, 1972, pp. 143–73.

SERVICE, Elman R., *Primitive Social Organization (an Evolutionary Perspective)*, New York: Random House, 1968.

SHIBUTANI, Tamotsu, *Society and Personality*, Englewood Cliffs, New Jersey: Prentice-Hall, 1961.

SHILS, Edward A., 'Authoritarianism: right and left', in Christie, R. and Jahoda, M. (eds.), *Studies in the scope and method of 'the Authoritarian Personality'*, Glencoe, Illinois: Free Press, 1954, pp. 24–49.

—, 'Charisma, order and status', *American Sociological Review*, Vol. 30, No. 2, April 1965, pp. 199–213.

SHINER, Larry, 'The Concept of Secularization', *Journal for the Scientific Study of Religion*, Vol. VI, Spring 1967.

SIMMEL, Georg, *Philosophische Kultur*, Leipzig: Werner Klinkhardt, 1911.

—, *Lebensanschauung*, Munich: Duncker and Humblot, 1922.

—, *Conflict and the Web of Group-Affiliations*, New York: Free Press, 1955.

—, *Sociology of Religion*, New York: Philosophical Library, 1959 (first published in 1905).

—, *The Sociology of Georg Simmel*, translated and edited by Kurt H. Wolff, Glencoe, Illinois: Free Press, 1964.

SLATER, Philip, *The Pursuit of Loneliness*, Boston: Beacon Press, 1971.

SMART, Ninian, *The Science of Religion and the Sociology of Knowledge*, Princeton: Princeton University Press, 1973.

SMITH, Huston, 'Do drugs have religious import?', in Solomon, David (ed.), *LSD, The Consciousness-Expanding Drug*, New York: Putnam, 1964, pp. 152–67.

SODDY, Kenneth (ed.), *Identity, Mental Health and Value Systems*, London: Tavistock, 1961.

SOLZHENITSYN, Aleksandr I., *The First Circle*, New York: Bantam, 1968.

SOROKIN, Pitirim A., *Social and Cultural Dynamics* (4 vols.), New York: American Book Company, 1937.

—, *The American Sex Revolution*, Boston: Sargent, 1956.

—, *Sociological Theories of Today*, New York, Harper, 1966.

SPENCER, Baldwin and Gillen, F. J., *The Native Tribes of Central Australia*, London: Macmillan, 1938.

SPENCER, Herbert, *First Principles*, New York: Appleton, 1896.

—, *The Principles of Sociology*, New York: Appleton, 1897.

—, *Reasons for dissenting from the philosophy of M. Comte and other essays*, Berkeley, California: Glendessary Press, 1968.

SPIER, J. M., *Christianity and Existentialism*, Philadelphia: Presbyterian and Reformed Publishing Company, 1953.

SPOERRI, Th., 'Zum Begriff der Ekstase', in Spoerri, Th. (ed.), *Beitrage zur Ekstase*, Basle: Karger, 1968, pp. 1–10.

STAFFORD, Peter, *Sexual Behaviour in the Communist World*, New York: Julian Press, 1967.

STARK, Rodney, 'Psychopathology and Religious Commitment', *Review of Religious Research*, Vol. 12, No. 3, Spring 1971.

STARK, Rodney and Glock, Charles Y., *American Piety: the Nature of Religious Commitment*, Berkeley: University of California Press, 1970.

STARK, Werner, *The Sociology of Religion*, Vol. II: *Sectarian Religion*, New York: Fordham University Press, 1967.

STEIN, Maurice R.; Vidich, Arthur J.; White, David Manning (eds.), *Identity and Anxiety*, Glencoe, Illinois: Free Press, 1960.

STEPHAN, Karen H. and Stephan, G. Edward, 'Religion and the Survival of Utopian Communities', *Journal for the Scientific Study of Religion*, Vol. 12, No. 1, March 1973, pp. 89–100.

STONEQUIST, Everett V., *The Marginal Man. A Study in Personality and Culture Conflict*, New York: Scribner, 1937.

STRAUSS, Anselm L., *Mirrors and Masks, the Search for identity*, Glencoe, Illinois: Free Press, 1959.

STROMMEN, Merton P.; Brekke, Milo L.; Underwager, Ralph C.; Johnson, Arthur L., *A Study of Generations*, Minneapolis: Augsburg Publishing House, 1972.

SUZUKI, Daisetz T., *The Essentials of Zen Buddhism*, New York: Dutton, 1962.

—, 'Lectures on Zen Buddhism', in Suzuki, D. T.; Fromm, Erich; De Martino, Richard, *Zen Buddhism and Psychoanalysis*, New York: Grove Press, 1963.

SWANSON, Guy E., *The Birth of the Gods*, Ann Arbor, Michigan: The University of Michigan Press, 1966 (first published in 1960).

SWEET, William W., *The Story of Religion in America*, New York: Harper and Brothers, 1950.

TAIMI, I. K., *Self-Culture* (The Problem of Self-discovery and Self-realization in the Light of Occultism), Adyar, India: Theosophical Publishing House, 1967.

TALMON, Yonina, 'Pursuit of the Millennium: The Relation between Religious and Social Change', in Lessa, William A. and Vogt, Evon Z., *Reader in Comparative Religion*, New York: Harper, 1965, pp. 522–37.

TAWNEY, R. H., *Religion and the Rise of Capitalism*, New York: Mentor, 1937 (first published in 1926).

TAYLOR, Wilfred, 'World of the Podospherist', *The Scotsman*, 31 May 1972, p. 8.

TEGGART, Frederick J., *Theory and Processes of History*, Berkeley: University of California Press, 1962 (first published in 1918 and 1925).

TEILHARD DE CHARDIN, Pierre, *The Phenomenon of Man*, London: Collins, 1959.

TEMPLE, Katharine C., *Ellul on Revolution*, Unpublished M.A. Thesis, McMaster University, Hamilton, 1972.

THAPAR, Romila, 'Asoka and Buddhism', in Birnbaum, Norman and Lenzer, Gertrud (eds.), *Sociology and Religion*, Englewood Cliffs, New Jersey: Prentice-Hall, 1969, pp. 303–9.

THORGAARD, Jørgen, 'Denmark', in Mol, Hetherton and Henty (eds.), *Western Religion*, The Hague: Mouton, 1972, pp. 135–41.

THRUPP, Sylvia (ed.), *Millennial Dreams in Action: Studies in Revolutionary Religious Movements*, New York: Schocken, 1970.

TILLICH, Paul, *The Protestant Era*, London: Nisbet, 1951.

—, *Dynamics of Faith*, New York: Harper, 1958.

—, *Theology of Culture*, London: Oxford University Press, 1959.

—, *Christianity and the Encounter of World Religions*, New York: Columbia University Press, 1961.

—, *Morality and Beyond*, London: Routledge and Kegan Paul, 1964.

—, 'The Religious Symbol', in Dillistone, F. W. (ed.), *Myth and Symbol*, London: S.P.C.K., 1966, pp. 15–34.

TIRYAKIAN, Edward A., *Sociologism and Existentialism*, Englewood Cliffs, New Jersey: Prentice-Hall, 1962.

TOCQUEVILLE, Alexis de, *Democracy in America*, Vols. I and II, New York: Vintage, 1955 (first published in Paris in 1835 and 1840).

TOFFLER, Alvin, *Future Shock*, New York: Bantam Books, 1970.

TOYNBEE, Arnold J., *A Study of History* (Abridgements of Vols. I–VI), New York: Oxford University Press, 1946.

—, *A Study of History* (Abridgements of Vols. VII–X), New York: Oxford University Press, 1957.

TREVOR-ROPER, *Religion, the Reformation and Social Change*, London: Macmillan, 1967.

TRIGG, Roger, *Reason and Commitment*, Cambridge: Cambridge University Press, 1973.

TROELTSCH, Ernst, *Protestantism and Progress*, New York: Putnam, 1912.

—, *The Social Teaching of the Christian Churches* (2 vols.), London: Allen and Unwin, 1931.

TUMIN, Melvin M., 'Some Principles of Stratification: A Critical Analysis', in Coser, Lewis A. and Rosenberg, Bernard (eds.), *Sociological Theory*, New York: Macmillan, 1957, pp. 420–32.

TURNER, Frederick Jackson, *The Frontier in American History*, New York: Holt, 1921.

TURNER, Ralph, *The Social Context of Ambition*, San Francisco: Chandler, 1964.

TURNER, Victor W., 'Three Symbols of Passage in Ndembu Circumcision Ritual', in Gluckman, Max (ed.), *Essays on the Ritual of Social Relations*, Manchester: Manchester University Press, 1962.

—, 'Myth and Symbol', in *International Encyclopaedia of the Social Sciences*, Vol. 10, New York: Macmillan, 1968, pp. 576–82.

—, *The Ritual Process*, London: Routledge and Kegan Paul, 1969.

—, 'Symbols in Ndembu Ritual', in Emmet, Dorothy and MacIntyre, Alasdair (eds.), *Sociological Theory and Philosophical Analysis*, London: Macmillan, 1970, pp. 150–82.

—, Metaphors of Anti-Structure in Religious Culture', in Eister, Allan W. (ed.), *Changing Perspectives in the Scientific Study of Religion*, New York: Wiley, 1974, pp. 63–84.

TYLOR, Edward B., *Primitive Culture*, London: Murray, 1871.

UNWIN, Joseph Daniel, *Sex and Culture*, London: Oxford University Press, 1934.

VIET, Jean, *Les Methodes Structuralistes dans les sciences sociales*, The Hague: Mouton, 1965.

VOGT, Edvard D., 'Norway', in Mol, Hetherton and Henty, *Western Religion*, The Hague: Mouton, 1972, pp. 381–401.

VRIES, Jan de, *The Study of Religion*, New York: Harcourt, Brace and World, 1967.

WAAL MALEFIJT, Annemarie de, *Religion and Culture*, New York: Macmillan, 1968.

WACH, Joachim, *Sociology of Religion*, Chicago: University of Chicago Press, 1944.

WAGAR, W. Warren, *Good Tidings* (*The Belief in Progress from Darwin to Marcuse*), Bloomington, Indiana: Indiana University Press, 1972.

WALKER, Benjamin, *The Hindu World* (2 vols.), New York: Praeger, 1968.

WALLACE, Anthony F. C., *Religion: an Anthropological View*, New York: Random, 1966.

WALLIS, Wilson D., *Religion in Primitive Society*, New York: Crofts, 1939.

WARD, Conor K., 'Ireland', in Mol, Hetherton and Henty, *Western Religion*, The Hague: Mouton, 1972, pp. 295-303.

WARNER, W. Lloyd and Srole, Leo, *The Social Systems of American Ethnic Groups*, New Haven, Connecticut: Yale University Press, 1945.

WARNER, W. Lloyd, *The Family of God*, New Haven: Yale University Press, 1961.

—, *American Life*, Chicago: University of Chicago Press, 1962.

WASHBURN, S. L. and De Vore, I., 'The Social Life of Baboons', *Scientific American*, Vol. 204, No. 6, 1961, pp. 62-71.

WATSON, Lyall, *Supernature*, Garden City, New York: Doubleday, 1973.

WATT, W. Montgomery, *Muhammed at Medina*, Oxford: Oxford University Press, 1956.

WATT, W. Montgomery, *Islam and the Integration of Society*, London: Routledge and Kegan Paul, 1961.

WATTS, Alan W., *The Two Hands of God*, New York: Braziller, 1963.

—, *Beyond Theology*, New York: Pantheon, 1964.

WEBER, Max, *From Max Weber, Essays in Sociology*, New York: Oxford University Press, 1946.

—, *The Methodology of the Social Sciences*, Glencoe, Illinois: Free Press, 1949.

—, *The Protestant Ethic and the Spirit of Capitalism*, New York: Scribner, 1952 (first published in 1904).

—, *Ancient Judaism*, Glencoe, Illinois: Free Press, 1952a (first published in 1917-19).

—, *The Religion of India*, Glencoe, Illinois: Free Press, 1958.

—, *The Sociology of Religion*, Boston: Beacon Press, 1964 (first published in Germany in 1922).

—, *The Theory of Social and Economic Organization*, Glencoe, Illinois: Free Press, 1964a.

—, *The Religion of China*, New York: Macmillan, 1964b (first published in 1920-1).

—, 'Church and Sect', in Birnbaum, Norman and Lenzer, Gertrud (eds.), *Sociology and Religion*, Englewood Cliffs, New Jersey: Prentice-Hall, 1969, pp. 318-22.

WEILER, A. G., 'De Kerk in de Middeleeuwen', in Weiler, A. G.;

Jong, O. J. de; Rogier, L. J.; Monnich, C. W. (eds.), *Geschiedenis van de Kerk in Nederland*, Utrecht: Aula, 1962, pp. 11-79.

WEISINGER, Herbert, 'An Examination of the Myth and Ritual Approach to Shakespeare', in Murray, Henry A. (ed.), *Myth and Mythmaking*, New York: Braziller, 1960, pp. 132-40.

WHEELIS, Allen, *The Quest for Identity*, New York: Norton, 1958.

WHITEHEAD, Alfred North, *Symbolism, its Meaning and Effect*, New York: Putnam, 1959 (first published in 1927).

WICKHAM, E. R., *Church and People in an Industrial City*, London: Lutterworth, 1957.

WIGGINS, David, *Identity and Spatio-Temporal Continuity*, Oxford: Blackwell, 1971.

WILHELM, Bernard, 'Germany: Democratic Republic', in Mol, Hans; Hetherton, Margaret; Henty, Margaret (eds.), *Western Religion*, The Hague: Mouton, 1972, pp. 213-28.

WILLEMS, Emilio, 'Protestantism and Culture Change in Brazil and Chile', in D'Antonio, William V. and Pike, Frederick B. (eds.), *Religion, Revolution and Reform*, New York: Praeger, 1964, pp. 91-108.

—, 'Religious Mass Movements and Social Change in Brazil', in Baklanoff, E. (ed.), *New Perspectives on Brazil*, Nashville: Vanderbilt University Press, 1966, pp. 205-32.

—, 'Validation of Authority in Pentecostal Sects of Chile and Brazil', *Journal for the Scientific Study of Religion*, Vol. VI, No. 2, Fall 1967, pp. 253-8.

WILLIAMS, Colin W., *Where in the World*, New York: National Council of Churches, 1963.

WILLIAMS, J. Paul, *What Americans Believe and How They Worship*, New York: Harper, 1962 (first edition in 1952).

WILSON, Bryan R., *Sects and Society*, London: Heinemann, 1961.

—, *Religion in Secular Society*, London: Watts, 1966.

—, 'An analysis of sect development', in Wilson, Bryan R. (ed.), *Patterns of Sectarianism*, London: Heinemann, 1967a, pp. 22-45.

—, 'The Exclusive Brethren', in Wilson, Bryan R. (ed.), *Patterns of Sectarianism*, London: Heinemann, 1967b, pp. 287-337.

—, (ed.), *Rationality*, New York: Harper, 1970.

—, *Magic and the Millennium*, London: Heinemann, 1973.

WILSON, John; Williams, Norman; Sugarman, Barry, *Introduction to Moral Education*, Harmondsworth; Penguin, 1967.

WILSON, Monica, *Religion and the Transformation of Society*, Cambridge: Cambridge University Press, 1971.

WINCH, Peter, 'Understanding a Primitive Society', in Wilson, Bryan R. (ed.), *Rationality*, New York: Harper, 1971, pp. 78-111.

WINICK, Charles, 'Physician Narcotic Addicts', in Becker, Howard S., *Outsiders*, Glencoe, Illinois: Free Press, 1963.

WINTER, Gibson, *The Suburban Captivity of the Churches*, Garden City, New York: Doubleday, 1961.

—, *The New Creation as Metropolis*, New York: Macmillan, 1963.

—, *Religious Identity* (The formal organization and informal power structure of the major faiths in the United States today), New York: Macmillan, 1968.

WITTGENSTEIN, Ludwig, *Philosophische Bemerkungen*, Frankfurt am Main: Suhrkamp, 1964.

—, *Lectures and Conversations on Aesthetics, Psychology and Religious Belief*, Oxford: Blackwell, 1967.

WOLF, Richard, '1900–1950 survey. Religious Trends in the United States', *Christianity Today*, 27 April 1959, pp. 3–6.

WORSLEY, Peter, *The Trumpet Shall Sound* (A Study of Cargo Cults in Melanesia), London: MacGibbon and Kee, 1957.

WUNDT, Wilhelm, 'Unterschied Zwischen Mythus und Dichtung', in Kerényi, Karl (ed.), *Die Eröffnung des Zugangs zum Mythos*, Darmstadt: Wissenschaftliche Buchgesellschaft, 1967, pp. 134–42 (first published in 1905).

YALMAN, Nur 'The Raw: The Cooked: Nature: Culture, Observations on Le Cru et le Cuit', in Leach, Edmund (ed.), *The Structural Study of Myth and Totemism*, London: Tavistock, 1969, pp. 71–89.

YANG, C. K., *Religion in Chinese Society*, Berkeley: University of California Press, 1970.

YINGER, J. Milton, *Sociology Looks at Religion*, New York: Macmillan, 1963.

—, *The Scientific Study of Religion*, New York: Macmillan, 1970.

YOUNGER, Paul, *Introduction to Indian Religious Thought*, Philadelphia: Westminster Press, 1972.

ZABLOCKI, Benjamin D., *The Joyful Community*, Baltimore: Penguin Books, 1971.

ZAEHNER, R. C., *Hinduism*, Oxford: Oxford University Press, 1969.

ZIJDERVELD, Anton C., *The Abstract Society*, Garden City, New York: Doubleday, 1971.

ZIMMER, Heinrich, *Myths and Symbols in Indian Art and Civilization*, Princeton: University Press, 1972 (1942 lectures).

Name Index

Subject Index